THE RESISTANCE TO CHURCH UNION

The
Resistance
to
Church Union
in
Canada
1904-1939

N. KEITH CLIFFORD

University of British Columbia Press
Vancouver
1985

The Resistance to Church Union in Canada, 1904-1939

©The University of British Columbia Press 1985
   All rights reserved

This book has been published with the help of a grant from
the Canadian Federation for the Humanities, using funds
provided by the Social Sciences and Humanities Research
Council of Canada.

Canadian Cataloguing in Publication Data

Clifford, N. Keith, 1930-
   The resistance to church union in Canada, 1904-1939

Includes index.
Bibliography: p. 261
ISBN 0-7748-0212-X

1. Presbyterian Church in Canada - History.
2. United Church of Canada - History. 3. Canada - Church history -
20th century. I. Title.
BX9001.C595 1985   285'.271   C84-091527-6

International Standard Book Number 0-7748-0212-X
Printed in Canada

For Sabine

All unities on earth have cutting edges that hurt some people. All holiness on earth retains some self-delusion. All churches betray some aspects of the Gospel.

Gregory Baum
The Ecumenist, 1974

Contents

List of Illustrations	ix
Preface	xi
Introduction	1
1. The Origins of the Church Union Controversy	13
2. The Beginnings of the Resistance	26
3. The Federation Alternative	43
4. The Preservation of Presbyterianism	60
5. The Second Vote	74
6. The Presbyterian Church Association	87
7. The Truce	101
8. The Resumption of Hostilities	116
9. The Road to Port Arthur	129
10. The Legislative Struggle	142
11. The Final Vote	165
12. The Parting of the Ways	185
13. The Continuing Battle	207
14. The Resolution of the Controversy	223
Conclusion	236
Notes	243
Bibliography	261
Index	269

Illustrations

Following p. 148

Cartoons from the *Toronto Globe* and *Montreal Daily Star*

Robert Campbell
Ephraim Scott
Duncan Macleod
John Penman
Thomas McMillan
William Hendrie
R.G. MacBeth
Frank Baird
A.J. MacGillivray
Thomas B. McQuesten
R.S. Cassels
G. Tower Ferguson
Wardlaw Taylor
J.W. MacNamara
Daniel Fraser
W.G. Brown
Eugene Lafleur
Thomas Eakin

Cartoon from the *Montreal Daily Star*

Preface

This book is a study of the resistance to church union which emerged within the Presbyterian Church in Canada during the early decades of the twentieth century. It examines the thought and action of those who wished to preserve the identity of the Presbyterian Church in Canada and opposed its incorporation into the United Church of Canada. By focusing on the Presbyterian opponents of church union, the object of the study is not only to throw some new light on a neglected aspect of the church union story, but also to examine some of the alternative responses to institutional change which existed in Canada during this period.

The decision to undertake the study was made in 1973 when the late Professor Allan L. Farris of Knox College, Toronto, informed me of his discovery of the papers of the Presbyterian Church Association which had been placed in a college vault at some point after 1925. By the time they were rediscovered, Professor Farris had suffered several heart attacks, and he was afraid he would not be spared the time to work on them. Therefore, he asked me, a United Churchman, to do a book on these papers.

Once the work began, it became apparent that the papers covered only the period between 1916 and 1925 and that they were the product of only one of three Resistance organizations. While of interest in themselves, it seemed that if the resistance to church union was to be properly understood it would be necessary to trace its development from the beginning, even though no papers existed for the earlier period. Moreover, once the outlines of the story began to take shape, it became clear that the controversy did not end in 1925 but continued for another fourteen years until the United Church of Canada Act was amended in 1939. Again, therefore, it was necessary to extend the study so that it would include the final resolution of the controversy. These decisions to trace the story from its origins in 1904 to its conclusion in 1939 delayed the completion of this study. My only regret concerning these delays is that Professor Farris did not live long enough to see the final outcome of a project in which he had taken such great interest and delight.

Telling the story of the resistance to church union in Canada has done more than simply fill in the gaps which existed in the literature. It has altered the dates which normally have been assigned to the story, and it has led to the inclusion of material not only on the opponents of union but also on many unionists who do not have a place in the earlier literature. Furthermore, the attempt to discover the social and intellectual context of the controversy has also involved the exploration of a number of areas that have not been sufficiently examined by Canadian historians. The range of relevant material at this level is, of course, so vast that only a tentative beginning has been made in suggesting some of the areas which need to be studied more fully. I hope this book will stimulate others to do further work so that ultimately the controversy can be seen not only as an isolated episode in Canadian ecclesiastical history but also as an event which sheds new light on many aspects of Canadian thought and action during this period.

In the course of ten years of research and writing I have greatly benefited from the help and encouragement of many individuals and institutions. The librarians and archivists at the Presbyterian Church Archives, the United Church Archives, the Ontario Archives, the Public Archives of Canada, the Douglas Library at Queen's University, the Redpath Library at McGill University, the National Library, the Toronto Public Library, the Hamilton Public Library, the Scottish Record Office and the William Patrick Memorial Library in Kirkintilloch, Scotland, have all been most generous in answering my many queries and in conducting searches for obscure materials, often with only partial or even inaccurate titles and descriptions. Without such assistance, the research for this volume would have been an immeasureably more difficult task.

In the early stages of writing, parts of the manuscript were read by John W. Grant and John S. Moir who made many helpful suggestions. Valuable criticism on the entire manuscript was also received from Gordon Harland, Ramsay Cook, Margaret Prang, Robert T. Handy and Martin E. Marty. I am extremely grateful for this assistance and for the invaluable editorial advice and guidance of Tirthankar Bose and Jane Fredeman, the managing editor of U.B.C. Press. In all cases they have made the process of revision and editing as painless as possible. For their help in preparing the photographs, I would like to thank Gordon Allison and Donald Rieger; I am also grateful to T.M. Bailey for his efforts on my behalf. The research for this volume has been generously supported by the Canada Council and the Social Sciences and Humanities Research Council.

Finally, I am particularly grateful to my research assistant Brian Fraser who, for many years after the research was completed, has acted as a sounding board and enthusiastic supporter of this project.

Introduction

When the Methodist, Presbyterian and Congregational Churches in Canada united on 10 June 1925 to form the United Church of Canada, one hundred and fifty thousand Presbyterians refused to join the new church. They chose instead to continue as the Presbyterian Church in Canada although the legislation creating the United Church stipulated that the church bearing this name had entered the union. These Presbyterians believed it was beyond the powers of the state to legislate their church out of existence. Therefore, they refused to accept any other name and continued to press their case until 1939 when the United Church of Canada Act was finally amended to recognize their continuity with the Presbyterian Church and their right to use the name.

There was also opposition to church union in both the Methodist and Congregational Churches. But it remained largely at the level of individual doubts and misgivings and never expressed itself in organized collective action against either the leadership of these churches or the legislation which created the United Church of Canada. Thus the opposition to union in the Methodist and Congregational Churches was neither very visible nor particularly threatening because at no point did it delay the proceedings or make a significant difference in the voting, the parliamentary debates, or the litigation before the courts. It was only in the Presbyterian Church where the opposition became organized that it was able to delay the consummation of union and eventually to have the church union legislation amended. This study, therefore, concentrates on the origins, development and significance of the organized resistance to church union among Canadian Presbyterians.

The extent and persistence of this opposition took many by surprise because during the nineteenth century Canadian Presbyterians had engaged without serious difficulty in three kinds of ecumenical activity: (i) the co-operation of individuals in non-denominational organizations such as the Bible Societies, the Y.M.C.A.'s, and the Evangelical Alliance; (ii) the participation of the Presbyterian Church in Canada in the World Alliance of

Reformed Churches; and (iii) a series of Presbyterian confessional unions which ultimately led in 1875 to the union of all the Presbyterian Churches in Canada. While there was some opposition to this union in 1875, the Presbyterian Church in Canada proved to be so successful that by the twentieth century few Canadian Presbyterians had any reservations about the value of confessional union. Indeed, it was the success of this union and the similar Methodist union of 1884 that led some Canadian churchmen to think about the possibilities of a transconfessional union in which churches from different denominational families would be organically united in a new kind of church.

But the fundamental problem with transconfessional union, as Stephen Neill has pointed out, is that "churches cannot unite [in this way] unless they are willing to die." The disappearance of great and honoured names like Methodist, Presbyterian, or Congregationalist, however, "is the very thing that many loyal churchmen are not prepared to face."[1] Canadian Presbyterians in the nineteenth century had not been required to confront this issue, but in the twentieth-century proposal to unite the Methodist, Presbyterian, and Congregational Churches, the prospect of the disappearance of Presbyterianism from Canada was raised in a way that many could not accept. Consequently, the elimination of the Presbyterian Church became the central issue around which the opposition to union crystallized.

At first glance this may seem like an oversimplification. But if this issue is taken as a starting point, then several distinctive features of this movement become visible. In the first place it becomes evident that this was not, as some have suggested, a reactionary movement which wanted "to recreate in the future some ideal that was assumed to have existed in the past."[2] It was a conservative movement which had no purpose other than the preservation of the Presbyterian Church in Canada from what was perceived to be an unwarranted attack upon its continued existence. It had no desire to turn the clock back, it had no great plans for the reconstruction of church or society and it was not opposed to change within the Presbyterian Church. All it opposed was any change which would involve the elimination of an historic institution. Consequently, its defence of the Presbyterian Church was simply a point by point rebuttal of all the unionists' arguments in favour of merging the Presbyterian Church into another institution.[3]

Once this becomes clear, the next feature which stands out is that unlike the church union movement, which was dominated and controlled by ministers, the resistance to union after 1912 was under the management and direction of laymen. These laymen were elders (that is, "overseers" of their congregations) who had taken a solemn vow to adhere faithfully to the Westminster Confession and to maintain and defend the Presbyterian Church in Canada.[4] They took this vow seriously, in fact so seriously that they felt betrayed when their ministers, who had taken a similar vow, seemed eager to abandon the Westminster Confession and to merge their church into another corporate body which would be Presbyterian neither in name nor practice. This sense of betrayal was so intense that when they reorganized their church after 10 June 1925, they would not, for several years, allow ministers to sit on the newly created Board of Administration of the Presbyterian Church in Canada. It would be overstating the case to suggest that the church union controversy was simply a revolt of the laity against their clergy because only 189 ministers lost their pulpits in this struggle. Yet it is clear that a very important dimension of this conflict was the refusal of those elders who directed and controlled the resistance movement to let ministers, theological professors, and ecclesiastical bureaucrats take their church away from them without a fight.

When its character as a conservative lay movement has been clarified, it is then possible to locate the sources of its support. Its major leaders and most of its money came from the older well-established Presbyterian congregations in the urban centres of eastern Canada. Its organizational centre was in Toronto, and most of its members were located in Ontario. With more than a third of all Presbyterians in Canada living in Ontario in 1921, it is not suprising that this was the area from which this movement drew its major support. Moreover, the primarily urban character of this movement was owing to the fact that the rural congregations of the Presbyterian Church, especially in eastern Canada, were suffering from a significant decline in membership resulting from the general shift of Canada's population from rural to urban centres that had been gradually taking place over the previous half century.

In 1913, John MacDougall described the effects of this population shift on the Presbyterian churches of rural Ontario in a book entitled *Rural Life in Canada*. He said:

> Rural churches are not and cannot be filled with worshippers as they once were. The Presbyterian Church in Spencerville, a village cathedral built in better days, never puts its spacious gallery to use. The most easterly church in the Presbytery of Glengarry, in Ontario and the most westerly one in the Presbytery of Montreal, in Quebec, are examples of churches whose auditoriums have been cut down in size since they were first built. Churches here and there are closed. Within six miles of Spencerville are two churches where congregations dwindled until they disappeared. [5]

Faced with declining memberships and in many cases losing their self-supporting status, the rural congregations of the Presbyterian Church were looking for solutions to their problems. Therefore, they were more ready to accept the radical changes which the church union proposal involved.

Church union, on the other hand, offered little to the large urban congregations. In most cases they were flourishing. They had memberships at least ten times larger than their rural counterparts, and they were able to raise large amounts of money which were well in excess of their own needs. Accordingly, they made the largest financial contributions to home and foreign missions and the various other schemes of the denomination. Hence they were the prestige congregations of the Presbyterian Church, and they were not accustomed to interference in their internal affairs. Moreover, because they provided the major funding for most of the denomination's projects, they expected their opinions to carry some weight in the courts of the church, and they did not take kindly to being completely ignored. Consequently, the ruling elders of these congregations were especially receptive to the accusation that those in control of the church's courts had acted in an improper and illegal manner on the question of union.

It is essential to keep these distinctive features of the resistance movement in mind before considering other dimensions of this controversy. For if this was a conservative lay movement, then it becomes evident that their way of dealing with the problem would not be primarily theological. Many, though not all, of the leaders of this movement were university trained men. But, unlike the leaders of the union movement, they had not been trained as theologians. Thus few of them had embraced philosophical idealism, biblical criticism, or the new theological liberalism, and they did not approach the question of church union from a perspective shaped by these new ways of thinking. As laymen, they approached the problem from a legal rather than a theological perspective.

They were, of course, aware of the fundamentalist-modernist controversy which was troubling the churches in the both Canada and the United States. In fact, some of those who were active in the resistance to union had fundamentalist sympathies. For the majority of these laymen, however, fundamentalism was not the central issue in their struggle to preserve and maintain the Presbyterian Church in Canada. Their purpose was to defend an institution rather than a particular theological position. Thus they did not bind their church to any theory of biblical inerrancy, premillenialism, or dispensationalism, and they did not insist that their church adopt an anti-ecumenical stance. Consequently, after 1925 the Presbyterian Church in Canada was completely free to follow Walter Bryden, their new young theologian at Knox College, beyond modernism and fundamentalism to neo-orthodoxy. Furthermore, it was also free after 1939 to enter the World Council of Churches and the Canadian Council of Churches because neither of these new forms of twentieth century ecumenism threatened the identity of the Presbyterian Church in Canada.

Although many features of this movement have not been adequately understood, its achievement in preserving the Presbyterian Church in Canada has been affirmed and celebrated by the membership of this church which over the past half century has established itself as Canada's fourth largest religious denomination. Today, therefore, it is clear that those Presbyterians who opposed church union made a significant decision which has withstood the test of time.

For historians, however, this conclusion creates problems because it is so contrary to the impression of the opponents of union which is contained in the literature on this subject. The question which arises is why the beliefs and actions of those who organized themselves to defend the Presbyterian Church in Canada have been cast in such a negative light? Among the reasons for this anomoly, there are two which go to the heart of the matter. The first is that in 1925 the Joint Committee on Church Union included in its final report an "Historical Statement," which presented the "official version" of the events leading up to the formation of the United Church of Canada. Such official statements are common enough, but when they arise out of contentious situations, it is usually recognized that they are remarkable less for what they say than for what they fail to mention. In this case, however, the Union Committee's "Historical Statement" has never been substantially revised because most of the authors who have written on this subject have been both unionists and participants in the controversy, who were more interested in presenting their own views than in writing critical historical accounts of the conflict. In addition, the standard work on this subject, C.E. Silcox's *Church Union in Canada*, was published six years before this controversy ended.[6] Consequently, it is not surprising that most of the literature on church union in Canada contains a negative impression of the opponents of union.

An even more important reason for this negative impression, however, is that all of this literature contains certain assumptions concerning the relationship between denominationalism and ecumenism which were rooted in the ecumenical theory that was dominant at the time of union. Before proceeding further it is essential to examine these assumptions and to indicate how ecumenical theory has changed over the past half century so that it is now possible to view the opposition to union from a perspective which contains different assumptions from those of the participants in the controversy.

The assumptions concerning the relationship between denominationalism and ecumenism that informed the unionists outlook in Canada were rooted in the ecumenical theory of theological liberalism which received its classic expression four years after the formation of the United Church of Canada in Richard Niebuhr's *The Social Sources of Denominationalism*.[7] In this theory denominationalism and ecumenism were seen as antithetical and antagonistic. So for Niebuhr, denominationalism was synonymous with "hypocrisy" and the "moral failure of Christianity" because it represented a fatal compromise with the world in which the churches accommodated themselves to the national, racial, and class divisions of men. Ecumenism, on the other hand, was God's will for the churches because its object was to transcend these man-made divisions and to adjust the churches "to the constitution of the unrealized kingdom of God." Though they never expressed it quite so precisely, this was exactly the way in which the Canadian unionists conceived of the relationship between denominationalism and ecumenism. Moreover, in North America this conception of the relationship of ecumenism and denominationalism was so pervasive that it took several decades before questions began to be raised about it.

The first aspect of this question to be examined was Niebuhr's extremely negative assessment of denominationalism. In 1954, Sidney Mead, focusing not on the social sources but rather on the historical origins of denominationalism, concluded that the denomination was a new and unique form of Christianity which emerged in the United States following the separation of church and state.[8] For Mead the significance of denominationalism was that it provided a guarantee of religious liberty because the competition which it fostered meant that no one group could ever achieve a monopoly over religious belief and practice. In this positive assessment of denominationalism, Mead has been followed by Winthrop Hudson, Timothy Smith, and others who have emphasized different aspects of denominationalism. But in all cases, Niebuhr's negative assessment of denominationalism has been reversed.[9]

Canadian church historians, however, have rejected this positive view of denominationalism. Following the lead of H.H. Walsh, they have argued that the Canadian attitude toward denominationalism is different from that of the American.[10] Thus they have not participated in the rediscovery of the significance of denominationalism for understanding many aspects of the role of religion in Canadian society. But more importantly from the perspective of this study, they have entirely disregarded the defence of the Canadian denominational system mounted by the Presbyterian opponents of union.

If Canadian scholars have dismissed the re-evaluation of denominationalism which has emerged in the United States over the past thirty years, it has been more difficult for them to ignore entirely the sociologists' re-appraisal of Niebuhr's positive attitude toward ecumenicity. In 1966, when Bryan Wilson's *Religion in Secular Society* appeared, the differences between the theological and sociological assessments of ecumenicity immediately became apparent.[11] Instead of seeing ecumenism as God's will for the churches, Wilson argued that ecumenism is not a revival of religion but rather "the turning in on itself of institutional religion." It involved a "surrender of distinctive beliefs and practice" and "an attenuation of positive and distinctive denominational commitment." Ecumenism by this account tends to be a priestly rather than a lay movement and one of its strongest motivations, has been "the wish of religious functionaries to maximize professional specialization." Closely related to this motive is the desire to provide a more rational use of resources for the greater convenience of administration. Ecumenism then, according to Wilson, is a policy not only induced by decline but also one encouraging decline, and, as a result, it is a product of weakness rather than strength.

At the other end of the spectrum, Wilson placed not denominationalism but sectarianism and especially those sects which tend not to become denominations. For Wilson these persistent sectarian movements have a heightened sense of commitment, a strong emphasis on doctrinal distinctiveness, and an unwillingness to compromise. Consequently, he concludes, that if any form of Christianity is likely to survive in our modern secularized society, it will be of the sectarian rather than the ecumenical variety.

Wilson is explicit in his attack on Niebuhr's conception of ecumenism and sectarianism, and in the case of ecumenism, it is clear that he is standing Niebuhr's antithesis on its head to the point where it now reads: ecumenism is bad and sectarianism is good. Unfortunately, from a theoretical point of view, this is not much of an advance because it has always been possible for those who opposed ecumenism to argue that it was bad for a variety of reasons. Yet Wilson's forceful presentation of this viewpoint has had a certain shock value which has forced many to re-examine their assumptions concerning ecumenism.

With the formation of the World Council of Churches in 1948, it became apparent that a new conception of the relationship between denominationalism and ecumenism was beginning to emerge, for increasingly these two phenomena were refered to as complementary rather than antithetical. It was not until 1963, however, that this conception was used by Peter Berger as the basis for a sociological explanation of "the paradoxical coexistence of ecumenicity and denominationalism."[12] The model which Berger constructed to explain this complementary relationship is one in which denominations are seen as economic units competing in a free market. Without government restraint, their competition tended to be extremely destructive. Eventually, however, this destructiveness gave way to a rationalization of competition through cartelization which reduced the number of competing units and divided the market between the larger units that remained. In explaining the complementary phenomenon of denominationalism, Berger argued that the rationalizing of competition also led to product standardization which made it increasingly difficult to distinguish between brand A and brand B. To distinguish these brands from one another, says Berger, it was necessary to introduce "marginal differentiation" (that is, "functionally irrelevant embellishments and packaging"). Denominationalism then, from Berger's perspective, is seen as a type of marginal differentiation which is necessary in a situation where one wants to remain competitive in spite of product standardization.

In this form the explanation of the complementary relation of denominationalism and ecumenism appeared to reduce both of these phenomena to a rather crude commercial analogy, which startled those who prefer to take their ecumenism with large doses of what Berger has referred to as "*ex post facto* theological legitimation." In a subsequent essay, however, Peter Berger and Thomas Luckmann placed this "market model for the analysis of ecumenicity" in a broader and more satisfactory context. Touching base with the work of American church historians, Berger and Luckmann argued that the separation of church and state produced both religious pluralism and secularization and that both denominationalism and ecumenism were complementary responses to the effects of religious pluralism and secularization. Thus, they concluded, that "the pluralistic situation has become not only the 'ecumenical era' but also the occasion for the rediscovery of 'confessional heritages.'"[13]

This explanation, as Brian Turner has pointed out, does not resolve all the problems in the sociology of ecumenism.[14] The resolution of these problems, however, is beyond the scope of this study. What is important for present purposes is Berger's view of the complementary relationship between ecumenism and denominationalism because when they are seen in this way it becomes possible not only to move beyond the assumptions of the unionists (Niebuhr) and the dissidents (Wilson), but also to remove the cloud of disapproval under which the opponents of church union have laboured and to look at them as important participants in the church union controversy in Canada. Furthermore, it makes it possible to see both denominationalism and ecumenism as different but complementary responses to the threats of pluralism and secularization.

While this change of assumptions is important, even more important for this study is the change of standpoint from which this controversy is viewed. Unlike previous accounts of church union in Canada, this study looks at the controversy from the perspective of the 1939 Amendment to the United Church of Canada Act rather than from the consummation of union in 1925. The question at stake here is, where does the story of church union in Canada end? The contention of this study is that the proper ending for the story is the 1939 amendment to the United Church of Canada Act because it resolves the controversy over church union.

The main effect of this change in viewpoint is to alter the image of the opponents of union in three significant ways. First, when the opponents of union are viewed from 1925, they are clearly the losers. They have been unable to prevent either the passage of the legislation or the consummation of union, and if they are left at this point their survival seems unlikely for, in effect, they have been legislated out of existence. Viewed from 1939, however, they have managed, against great odds, not only to survive but also to get an amendment to the United Church of Canada Act which gives them exactly what they wanted. Secondly, when the opponents of union are viewed from 1925, their arguments and actions seem to lack cogency, for they have been unable to persuade either their co-religionists in the Presbyterian Church or the members of Parliament and the provincial legislatures of the the validity of their case. Viewed from 1939, however, a major reversal in their fortunes has taken place, for the the Supreme Court of Canada has raised some serious doubts about the unionists claim that the Presbyterian Church in Canada has gone into union as a church, and the public's perception of the issue has changed to the point where the United Church's policy of denying them any claim to identity or continuity with the Presbyterian Church in Canada has become untenable. Thus a major compromise on the part of the United Church has become imperative. Thirdly, viewed from 1925 all of the unionists' actions appear to have been inspired by the highest and noblest of intentions, and the opponents of union are the spoilers who have sought to stand in the way of God's will for the churches. Viewed from 1939, however, it becomes clear that though the unionists were idealists, they were as capable as any of using the power of majorities for their own advantage and that the opponents of union had grounds for some legitimate complaints about the way the issue was handled in both the church courts and Parliament.

Using 1939, however, not only alters the image of both parties in the conflict, it also raises questions about where and when the story should begin. The first question which has to be faced is whether an introductory survey of Canadian ecumenical activity in the nineteenth century is necessary. In this study it has not been considered essential for several reasons. In the first place, this conception of the nineteenth-century background was developed as part of the unionists' propaganda during the controversy. Dr. W.T. Gunn, a prominent Congregational participant, for example, argued that the proposed United Church was not an isolated event but the result of a prevailing tendency within the Canadian churches. In a chart he showed that the Presbyterian Church in Canada was the result of nine unions which brought together nearly two dozen separate units and groups; likewise, the Methodist Church was the result of eight unions which brought together some sixteen bodies; and finally, the Congregational Church was the result of four different unions.[15] Later, C.E. Silcox, in his book on *Church Union in Canada*, picked up this idea and added to it an account of all the forms of Protestant co-operation in nineteenth-century Canada in order to show that the United Church was the result of an evolutionary process which was peculiarly Canadian.

Those Presbyterians who opposed transconfessional union, however, denied that this was the next logical step in a natural evolutionary process. They argued that the two types of union were quite distinct. They might also have noted, although it was ignored at the time, that ecumenism in nineteenth-century Canada was a more complex phenomenon than the evolutionary argument suggests. It was not the Methodists, the Presbyterians, or the Congregationalists who dominated Canadian ecumenical thinking in the nineteenth century, it was the Anglicans. Between 1874 and 1900 they published four major books on the subject.[16] It is true that some of these books emphasized a distinctively Anglican outlook which was unacceptable to the other denominations in Canada. But nevertheless, Canadian Anglicans were involved in all the various forms of nineteenth-century ecumenical activity, except confessional union, and they were the first to raise the question of transconfessional union at an interdenominational conference in Toronto in 1889.[17] Thus it appears that while some types of nineteenth-century ecumenical thinking and activity led to transconfessional union in the twentieth century others did not. Therefore, until it becomes clear why this is so, it has seemed best to lay aside the question of nineteenth-century ecumenism in Canada and to begin this study with William Patrick, who set a particular series of negotiations in motion by raising the question of transconfessional union at the 1902 meetings of the Methodist General Conference in Winnipeg.

The second problem concerning the beginning of this story is how and when the resistance to union began. R.G. MacBeth, one of the early opponents of union, claimed in his book, *The Burning Bush and Canada*, that the opposition to union began when the issue of corporate union was first raised in the General Assembly of 1904. He states that a group led by Dr. W.A.J. Martin of Brantford, Ontario, who was convenor of the powerful Foreign Missions Committee, "waited on the leading men in the Assembly" and urged great caution in pursuing union because the request for it had not originated with the people. They were told, according to MacBeth, that the appointment of a committee to discuss the question with the other churches was only "a matter of courtesy" and that there was no intention of pursuing union unless the people of the church favoured it. This understanding, MacBeth stresses, was subsequently incorporated into the first report of the Joint Committee on Church Union which stated that a "union of the churches to be real and lasting must carry the consent of the entire membership." Only with these assurances, MacBeth concludes, was the union proposal allowed to go forward in the General Assembly unobstructed.[18]

While this starting point makes it clear that there was opposition to union in the Presbyterian Church from the beginning and that the opponents of union believed they had a promise that union would not proceed without the consent of the church's "entire membership," the historian is left with the awkward problem that no substantiating evidence concerning such a meeting at the 1904 General Assembly appears to have survived. Moreover, MacBeth himself was not an eyewitness, and those who may have been present never referred to such a meeting or confirmed MacBeth's understanding of its significance. In this study, therefore, MacBeth's starting point has been abandoned and the origins of the resistance to union have been approached through Robert Campbell, the senior clerk of the General Assembly, whose thought and action on this question can be amply documented.

While starting with Campbell gives the origins of the opposition to union a firmer historical base, it undercuts the point which MacBeth was attempting to establish because Campbell was not interested in the "breach of faith" argument that MacBeth, Scott, and others continually reiterated throughout the controversy.[19] The essence of this argument was that the unionists had repudiated a solemn promise to the dissidents that the Presbyterian Church would not proceed with union without the consent of the church's "entire membership." The unionists never disputed the fact that this statement was contained in the 1905 report of the Union Committee, but they denied that it was "a pledge given to the church by the Assembly." In their view this statement was "simply an expression of opinion in the body of the report which contained no resolution and presented no recommendation to the Assembly for adoption."[20] Moreover, they argued that "whatever opinion any committee of the Assembly may have expressed in 1905, the Assembly of 1916, having received the consent of a large majority of Presbyteries, was both legally and morally free to consider the whole question in the light of the existing situation and to act in the way it considered would best conserve the interests of Christ's cause in Canada."[21] While the "breach of faith" argument was important for some of the opponents of union, from the perspective of 1939 it is irrelevant to the resolution of the controversy and therefore it has not been allowed, as was the case with MacBeth, to control the starting point.

Apart from these major changes at the beginning and end, this study follows the chronological framework established by other writers on this subject because it is firmly based on those critical points in the controversy where the major votes of 1911, 1915, and 1925 were taken. Part I of this study covers the events leading up to the formation of an organized opposition to church union just prior to the first vote and the General Assembly's decision in 1912 to postpone the consummation of union. Part II includes the opposition's preparations for the second vote, their reaction to the General Assembly's disregard of the increased opposition, and the 1917 decision to postpone once again the consummation of union until after the end of World War I. Part III deals with the opposition's attempts to forestall the introduction of the church union legislation, the passage of the United Church of Canada Act in 1924, and the final vote under this legislation that determined which congregations or minority groups would remain Presbyterian. Part IV contains an account of the final fourteen years of the conflict which resulted in the amendment of the United Church of Canada Act in 1939 and the ultimate resolution of the controversy. The utilization of this framework serves the purpose of emphasing that there is only one story of church union in Canada, not two. Viewing these events from the perspective of the opposition to union, however, indicates that there has been, and likely will continue to be, two quite distinct ways of understanding these events and the actions which were based on them.

1

The Origins of the
Church Union Controversy

The controversy over church union began as an argument over the way the issue was introduced, handled, and justified by Principal William Patrick of Manitoba College. The dissidents believed he had introduced the issue improperly, handled it illegally, and justified his action in terms which verged on blasphemy. Although there were other prominent Presbyterian leaders who supported the idea of union, the full force of the dissidents' attack was against Patrick, for they saw him as an outsider who had broken the rules and set the church on a course from which it could not retreat. In order to understand the resistance to church union, therefore, it is necessary to begin by taking a look at William Patrick and his proposal of organic union as a solution to the problems facing the Canadian churches.

When Patrick recommended organic union to the Methodist General Conference in 1902, he had only been in Canada for two and a half years. He knew very little about the Canadian West and even less about eastern Canada where 75 per cent of the church's membership resided. Outside of Winnipeg, he was almost unknown in the courts of the church, having first been introduced to the Presbyterian General Assembly in Toronto only three months prior to making his suggestion for union. In fact, he was so new to Canadian church circles that Albert Carman introduced him to the Methodist Conference as a "tenderfoot."[1] Yet, in spite of this, Patrick made his recommendation for union without being authorized to do so by the Presbyterian Church. To be commissioned by the General Assembly as a fraternal delegate did not authorize an individual to do or say anything which might come to mind. The limits of such a commission were clearly established by custom. All that was expected was a few well-chosen pleasantries, spiced with good humour and generously sweetened with compliments and good wishes for the future. The occasion was understood by all parties to be a formal courtesy call and nothing more. Fraternal delegates were never authorized to communicate major proposals from one denomination to another. Therefore to introduce an issue like organic union in this way violated both custom and the assembly's commission.

The Presbyterians had other well-established procedures for dealing with such proposals. If Patrick had observed these rules, he would have had to persuade Winnipeg Presbytery to request the General Assembly to invite the Methodists to discuss the question of union. In many ways this procedure was cumbersome. Yet it was designed to prevent individuals from taking action on their own authority which might embarrass the church. As a result of Patrick's independent action, the issue of church union did not come to the General Assembly through the usual channels as a well-considered proposal of the lower courts of the church but rather as an invitation from a sister denomination. Courtesy demanded a positive response regardless of what the Presbyterian Church might feel about the principle of union itself. This put the assembly in a difficult position which many resented. He also created another problem that was even more significant in terms of the total controversy. By going directly to the superior court of Canadian Methodism and prompting it to issue an invitation to the superior court of the Presbyterian Church, Patrick determined that from the beginning the church union issue would come down to the people from the assembly. Thus, the proper order of procedure, as Robert Campbell put it, was reversed.[2]

A way out of this dilemma would have been to present the principle of union to the people before any further action was taken. In 1907, Dr. James Barclay, a unionist from Montreal, proposed an amendment to this effect, saying that, "he wished to stand on the democratic constitution of the church and. . .the inalienable right of the people. . . .The voice of the people should be heard before steps were taken which might morally force a union." In supporting this amendment, C.W. Gordon, another unionist from Winnipeg, said that "the simple question of principle had not yet been submitted to the sessions and presbyteries." If this were not done early in the proceedings, he argued, it would "convey the impression that men were being led along in spite of themselves into a position from which it would not be possible for them to retreat."[3] As chairman of the union committee, Patrick fought this procedure and persuaded the assembly to handle the issue in a way which ensured that by the time the question of union finally reached the people, it would be what Ephraim Scott later characterized as a "loaded referendum."[4]

There were several steps in this process. After first making certain that the union issue would come to the General Assembly in terms of an invitation it could not refuse, Patrick then maintained that the acceptance of the Methodist invitation committed the Presbyterian Church to organic union and no other alternative. Secondly, he convinced the assembly that the issue of organic union should not be sent down to the people until the joint committee of the three negotiating churches had completed its work on the "Basis of Union." Finally, when the Basis of Union was completed, Patrick argued that the General Assembly should first approve it before sending it down to the presbyteries under the Barrier Act (a church law requiring the consent of a majority of the presbyteries before the introduction of any changes in doctrine, discipline, government, or worship). Only then was the question at last to be sent to the sessions and congregations. By this scheme the proposal would come to the people in a finalized form with the full weight of the authority of the church courts behind it.

Patrick's method of handling the issue was rooted in his conviction that the union movement was divinely inspired. From the beginning he claimed that "the movement had come upon them spontaneously; it was the result of no human effort. . . [and in it] the voice of God was being heard."[5] Writing about his part in inaugurating the movement, he admitted he had not discussed the issue with his brethren and had wondered at the time whether "it was prudent or becoming that a person simply commissioned to assure the conference of the good will of a sister church should venture to introduce a question of such moment?" Patrick claimed to be fully aware of the objections which could be raised about his course of action but, as he put it, "the more I deferred to them [that is, the objections], the more commanding became the voice which bade me to speak on this and no other topic."[6] In other words, Patrick was claiming to be motivated by the Holy Spirit; he admitted his action was not authorized by the Presbyterian Church, but he justified it by the higher authority of God Himself.

When Patrick first made this claim at the 1904 General Assembly in St. John, New Brunswick, Dr. William MacLaren of Knox College warned that "it was unsafe for Dr. Patrick and other advocates of union to take their own conclusions for the leadings of the Spirit." "Many things," he said, "had been accepted as leadings of the Spirit that Presbyterians could not accept."[7] While many heeded this warning and thereafter emphasized the practical aspects of the case such as the economies union would effect, Patrick continued to maintain the movement was God's will for the Canadian church.

For Presbyterians the test of divine guidance was Scripture; they believed the Holy Spirit would not contradict the Word of God. Consequently, throughout the controversy, the question of divine guidance revolved around the interpretation of John 17:21 where Jesus prayed that his followers might be one as he and the Father were one. Patrick and the unionists maintained this text was the Scriptural warrant for their belief that the movement was God's will. The dissidents, however, amassed so much critical evidence to prove there was no necessary connection between the unity for which Jesus was praying and the "organic unity" of the churches that some unionists found it difficult to justify the movement on this basis. Eventually, the Rev.

J.A. MacDonald, editor of the Toronto *Globe*, came to the rescue by standing this argument on its head. "I do not undertake to say just what the Saviour had in view in that prayer for unity," he said, "but I do know that the thing He did not pray for was the wasteful competition and petty denominational bickering and strife which are seen in many a Canadian town and village today."[8] Many of the most ardent unionists, however, continued to believe that John 17:21 was proof that the union movement was divinely inspired.

In opposing this interpretation, William MacLaren said that "men are insensibly lapsing into the Romish view of the church when they understand the Saviour's prayer literally."[9] The foundation of this argument had been laid by MacLaren in 1889 when he suggested that liberal Catholics and Tractarians were leading many Protestants astray by their view that John 17:21 and Matthew 16:18 referred to the unity of a visible ecclesiastical organization. There was nothing in these texts, MacLaren declared, to suggest "that all Christians should be embraced in one external organization." The oneness of the church from his perspective depended on "the presence of Christ by His Spirit in believers and their abiding in Christ by faith," not in external organization.[10] For Patrick, however, both Scripture and the whole of Christian history taught that "union is a duty unless conscience prevents."[11]

In 1909, Dr. Thomas Sedgwick, a former moderator of the Presbyterian church, became so frustrated by the unionists' arguments and the manner in which they were handling the issue that he paraphrased Galatians 3:1 and said to the assembly: "O foolish Presbyterians who hath bewitched you?"[12] Sedgwick could not understand what had happened. In five brief years, it seemed to him as if the assembly had taken leave of its senses. Who was responsible for this change in which all that had previously been considered sacred was now being treated as either non-essential or as an impediment to the furtherance of the church's work in Canada?

In answering this question, some pointed directly at William Patrick. His rapid rise to leadership in the Presbyterian Church in Canada seemed almost unnatural, and many accounted for it in various ways. Dr. G.B. Wilson, for example, thought "the removal by death of such great leaders as Caven, King, Grant, Warden, Robertson and MacVicar had. . . contributed to place him in a unique position in the General Assembly." Others like C.W. Gordon believed "his debating powers and his remarkable ability for clear statements gave him a foremost position." In fact, Gordon believed that as a master of logical expression, "he had no superior and few equals in the Presbyterian church."[13] More important than either of these factors, however, was Patrick's association with Scottish theological liberalism and the union movement between the United Presbyterian Church and the Free Church of Scotland prior to his arrival in Canada. Those with whom he was most closely associated in Scotland gave him a farewell dinner in Edinburgh before he left, and prominent among the guests were the leading liberal theologians and unionists of Scotland: Principal Robert Rainy, Lord Overtoun, Professor George Adam Smith, and Dr. Alexander Whyte.[14] All of these men were well known in Canadian Presbyterian circles, and Patrick was seen as a representative of a similar viewpoint.

By drawing distinctions between the essentials and non-essentials of Christianity, these liberals adopted an evolutionary concept of the development of Christian institutions and doctrine which saw both denominationalism and creedalism as non-essentials. Doctrinal confessions and forms of polity were seen as responses to particular environmental circumstances rather than as embodiments of essential Biblical truths which had binding power on the future. The essence of Christianity was above and beyond any particular historical manifestation of it in the past and therefore something which could be given entirely new shape in the future. Liberalism therefore tended to dissolve doctrinal particularity and to relativize the organizational principles of religious institutions.

Patrick's inaugural lecture at Manitoba College revealed that he shared this outlook. Speaking on "The Person of Christ," he said that "he saw Christ as the crown of the moral ideal; the goal of moral history; the starting point of a new evolution; the energy which conducts it and the goal to which it moves."[15] It was not until he published his first article on church union in 1904, however, that the implications of his liberalism became explicit. "The polity and administration of the church," said Patrick, "are matters of expediency to be determined in the light of reason and experience. The institutions of the church should be altered and improved like those of the state. . .the Word of God no more prescribes Episcopacy, Independency or Presbyterianism than it prescribes a monarchy or a republic." The same held true for doctrine. "We know that the substance is more than the form and we know also that some of the greatest truths can only be imperfectly expressed. The number of essential doctrines is small. It is idle to expect agreement in details of doctrine any more than in ethics or politics. . . .These truths felt rather than confessed have modified our attitudes towards statements of doctrine."[16] Similar attitudes were becoming widespread among the younger generation of Canadian Presbyterian leaders. Many of these men, such as Robert Falconer, Walter Murray, Alfred Gandier, Clarence MacKinnon, C.W. Gordon, and Robert Haddow, had received their graduate education in Scotland. They recognized Patrick as a powerful and articulate representative of Scottish liberalism, and he quickly became a leader of those who wished to reshape the religious and social life of Canada in accordance with these views.

The movement of this group of younger leaders into positions of power and influence manifested itself in the new set of priorities which gradually appeared on the agenda of the General Assembly. Concern for doctrine and polity was replaced by a zeal for social reform. The emphasis on individual salvation was replaced by an emphasis on social salvation. It was no longer adequate to snatch individual brands from the burning. If, as Patrick had put it, "Christ was the goal of moral history and the starting point of a new evolution," then the whole of society had to be shaped to conform with this moral ideal. It was this task which demanded a united Protestantism. In his brief statement of "Some Reasons for Church Union," Patrick placed this task even before the mission to the West. He said:

> Consider the moral influence of such a united church on the community. Take such questions as the observance of the Lord's Day, the promotion of temperance, the prevention of gambling, the charge of the poor, the sick and the criminal. With how much greater power would the voice of the Christian community be heard and to what more lasting results?[17]

Drawing on his experience in the temperance movement, Patrick argued that "the forces arrayed against that cause reckon confidently on hastily arranged and ill-matured common action on the part of the churches. . . .A united church would express the sentiments of Christian men more powerfully and secure their embodiment in legislation more easily than is possible at present." Patrick hailed the great benefits conferred on the Dominion by the Moral and Social Reform Council of Canada. But, he said, those who value these benefits "most highly are the first to perceive how much the cause of reform would gain in ease, directness and efficiency of the movement were the churches more united than they are."[18]

The shift from individual to social salvation in liberal theology was never simply confined to social reform. It also involved a vision of the nation as an instrument of God's design for the salvation of the world. Those who embraced this new outlook had little difficulty in endowing Canada, a new nation still taking shape, with a millennial role. One of the most "bewitching" qualities of Patrick's rhetoric on behalf of the union movement lay in his emphasis on the fact that Canada could be the first to show the Christian nations of the world the way to reunion. Why should Canada be the first of all Protestant lands to deal with this question? Because, Patrick answered, "Canada alone is in a position to deal with it. Canada is the only country in which Presbyterianism is one and Methodism is one."[19] Canada had already led the Christian world in the path of church union. Now a still greater opportunity offered itself. "The eyes of Christendom are upon Canada today," declared Patrick, "and the stand taken by the Canadian church will have a far reaching influence in other parts of the world."[20] For those desirous of making "this Dominion His Dominion," the possibilities of Canadians showing Christendom the way back to the original apostolic unity were irresistible.

The reformulation of Christian doctrine, social reform, and the reunion of the churches were all seen as phases of the evolutionary process in moral history. The capstone of this evolution was to be the creation of a new type of Christian character within the church. A united Protestant church, Patrick argued, would be more worthy of the Christian name than separate churches because "it would exhibit a richer and broader and more varied type of Christian character and achievement than is possible for any single church today."[21] It was Patrick's conviction that "a mixed church like a mixed race, would be a higher church."[22] Enlarging upon this theme, he said:

> The combined experience of the three churches in the united church
> will produce a nobler form of model of Christianity. The spiritual life
> of each section of the church will be enriched from the others. There
> will be new knowledge, new sympathies, new efforts. The horizons of
> the church's thought and aims will be widened; and the standard of
> spiritual attainment will rise.[23]

This fusion of the separate churches to produce a new type was necessary in Canada because the nation's rapid expansion demanded a new conception of the church's task. If the church's vision did not keep pace with the nation and provide it with adequate spiritual leadership, Patrick said, "the Christianity of the nation may become feebler, less energetic and less resourceful at the very time when its forces should be at their highest point."[24]

As Patrick and the advocates of the new evolution in moral history realized from the outset of the union negotiations, it was essential to establish that churches were living associations with personalities capable of change and development. If the new evolution was to achieve its purpose, it was necessary for the church to demonstrate it was not a creature of the state but an independent creation whose existence and freedom of development should be recognized. The problem which they faced, however, was that the common law refused to acknowledge the validity of such a conception of the church. The House of Lords had made this clear in the Free Church of Scotland Appeal Case when the justices refused to accept Lord Haldane's argument on behalf of the Scottish liberals and unionists that "the identity of the church is the identity of an individual human being. It is not the colour of his eyes, nor his opinions, nor his appearance because that changes from time to time; it is the continuity of his life that his identity lies in."[25] The Lord Chancellor, Lord Halsbury, countered this argument by defining the church as an "associated body of beneficiaries." The only thing it was necessary for the court to consider, therefore, was whether any article of the original trust had been violated.[26] Insofar as a church's doctrine was considered to be its articles of association and these had been changed, the House of Lords upheld the resistance of the "Wee Frees" and awarded all the property and assets of the Free Church of Scotland to those who had opposed the union.

The results of this decision were known in Canada before the joint committee on union held its first meeting in December 1904. Prior to this meeting, Alfred Gandier had published an attack on the decision, arguing that the Westminster Confession itself was "a charter of liberty, freeing the church from undue bondage to a dead past" and that the church was not a "trust corporation" but an association which "must always witness to such new light as God gives through His word and Spirit."[27] Patrick had left Scotland before the union was completed in 1900, and he did not publish a defence of the Free Church position. As soon as the inequities of the decision were rectified by legislation, however, he declared that in Canada legislation would be sought to avoid "the imbroglio of the Scottish church" and to make plain that "the church asserts its freedom to frame its own doctrines and to change its written creed from time to time."[28]

The need to use the legislative power of the state to declare the church's freedom to effect the changes a new environment and evolution demanded, however, would create more problems than Patrick seems to have recognized. For those who were convinced that the Westminster Confession was the clearest possible statement of Scriptural doctrine and that the Presbyterian polity was closest to that of the early church, the changes contemplated by the unionists appeared like an abandonment of those principles which every Presbyterian minister had taken a sacred vow to defend and promote. Moreover, the promised benefits of a united church appeared like a utopian fantasy, and any attempt to legislate them upon those who had no desire for them seemed like a denial of the historic liberties which generations of Presbyterians had fought to preserve. The shift to the new liberal outlook within the Presbyterian Church, however, was sufficiently far advanced by the turn of the century that many responded to Patrick's glowing rhetoric with such enthusiasm that ends became more important than means and the desire for union more compelling than the fear of disruption within the Presbyterian Church.

Of course, William Patrick was not responsible for the rise of liberalism within the Presbyterian Church in Canada. This change in the outlook of the church had been in the making for some time. Patrick happened to arrive in Canada, however, just as the new generation of young Presbyterian liberals was ready for a strong leader and an issue which would focus their energies. His appointment in 1900 as principal of the college which in Presbyterian eyes occupied a more important place in the "better life of the vast empire west of the Great Lakes than the Premier of the Province or the Governor of the Territories" made Patrick the first new liberal to be placed in a position of authority.[29] The other younger men who would eventually assume leadership of the union movement did not yet hold important offices in the church or community.

Robert Falconer, who would later become chairman of the Presbyterian union committee, did not become principal of Presbyterian College in Halifax until 1904 or president of the University of Toronto until 1908. Walter Murray did not become president of the University of Saskatchewan until 1908. Falconer's brother-in-law, Alfred Gandier, became principal of Knox College in Toronto in 1909, and a year later Clarence MacKinnon became principal of Presbyterian College in Halifax. Robert Haddow succeeded J.A. MacDonald as editor of the *Westminster* and the *Presbyterian* when MacDonald became editor of the *Globe* in 1902. C.W. Gordon had published five novels by 1902 and was well enough known by his pen-name "Ralph Connor" that Albert Carman could use it to introduce him to the Methodist General Conference in 1902. As the minister of a mission congregation in Winnipeg, however, he was not yet in a position of authority within the church.[30]

Many of these younger men who followed Patrick were already advocating union. For example, Alfred Gandier had written about church union prior to Patrick's arrival.[31] Several nineteenth-century leaders of Canadian Presbyterianism had also published articles favouring the idea of church union. Insofar as Canadian opinions about union appeared in obscure Canadian journals, however, it is unlikely that Patrick was aware of them. His own thinking was influenced by the ideas of the unionist leaders in the Free Church of Scotland. That he acted so quickly, without further exploring the Canadian situation, indicates he brought the idea of union with him rather than discovering it in Canada. What Patrick did discover in Canada was that the Presbyterian and Methodist churches were more advanced than the Scottish churches in confessional union. The various branches of Presbyterianism had been united since 1875 and those of Methodism since 1884. Any further union in Canada, therefore, would have to be across denominational boundaries. Before this major hurdle, the nineteenth-century Canadian leaders who supported union were hesitant. They were aware of the resistance to liberalism in many sections of the church, and they believed union across denominational lines should be approached slowly and carefully lest the quest for unity result in disunity. Since Patrick knew little about the Canadian church and was unaware of the anxieties of those who opposed the spread of liberal ideas, he was freer to act than his Canadian counterparts.

Had Patrick bothered to discuss the issue with other Canadian churchmen, he might have acted more cautiously. Those he did consult with were unlikely to put any constraints on him. It was reported, for example, that Patrick discussed the question with George Jackson, a Methodist preacher from Edinburgh, while Jackson was a guest of Professor Kilpatrick in Winnipeg during the summer of 1902. Jackson was a liberal who, when he later accepted an appointment in Canada, felt the sting of Albert Carman's accusation of heresy.[32] Therefore, he was hardly a person to raise any serious theological objections when Patrick told him that "the time was not merely coming, but had already come, when in the great North western provinces, Methodists and Presbyterians ought, without an hour's delay, to join their forces." Since Jackson knew nothing about Canada or the West, he found it "impossible to doubt the correctness of this view."[33]

Although Patrick's lack of roots in the Canadian church and his unfamiliarity with Presbyterianism in eastern Canada left him freer to act in initiating the union movement, these same factors were a liability once he became convenor of the Presbyterian union committee in 1906. Initially the church appears to have recognized this fact because the first two men appointed as convenors of the committee were old and trusted servants of the church: William Caven and R.H. Warden. Both men died, however, during the first two years of the committee's existence. Only then did the church turn to Patrick. In many ways it was a logical choice because since his appointment to the committee in 1904 Patrick had played a major role in the discussions and had filled in for Dr. Warden in presenting the committee's report to the 1905 General Assembly. He had risen in influence and gained the support of both the older and younger unionists. The church must have assumed these men would help Patrick overcome his difficulties as an outsider.

Yet none of them managed to keep Patrick from leading them into a procedural quagmire. There were several reasons for their failure to do so. Many unionists clearly misjudged their own strength and the extent of the opposition because they were not working pastors who were sensitive to the conservative feeling in many eastern congregations. As liberals who believed that church administration was a matter of expediency and who were out to create an entirely new set of procedures, they were less concerned with how things had been done in the past and more concerned with how they would be done in the future. Moreover, many unionist leaders did not have the background to assist Patrick in guiding the issue through the General Assembly.

The younger generation of Canadian Presbyterian liberals who followed Patrick had been born in the 1860's, and they were all either sons or grandsons of ministers. Since they had not been old enough to participate in the union of 1875, however, they were not familiar with the procedures used. Only one of their number, Robert Falconer, was a member of the original union committee. Among the older men born in the 1840's and 1850's who supported Patrick, many were also immigrants. Unionist leaders such as Dr. Samuel Lyle, Dr. F.B. DuVal, Dr. W.T. Herridge, Dr. G.M. Milligan, and Dr. M. MacGillivray had come from Ireland, the United States, England, and Scotland respectively. Thus they had also not participated in the union of 1875 and were equally unaware of Canadian Presbyterian practice.

The only ones in a position to advise Patrick were those Canadians who had been born in the 1840's, had participated in the union of 1875, and had received their education in Canada. Four of these men were prominent educators: Dr. John Forrest, the president of Dalhousie University, Dr. Daniel M. Gordon, the principal of Queen's University, Dr. George Bryce, the founder of Manitoba College and head of the Faculty of Science at the University of Manitoba, and Dr. John Scrimger, the principal of Presbyterian College, Montreal. Three others were church administrators: Dr. E.D. McLaren, who replaced James Robertson as superintendent of Home Missions, Dr. John Somerville, who replaced R.H. Warden as the church's financial agent and became junior clerk of the General Assembly and Dr. R.P. MacKay, the secretary of the Board of Foreign Missions. Only one was a pastor: Dr. W.D. Armstrong of St. Paul's Church in Ottawa. All of these men, except John Forrest and Daniel Gordon, had been ordained in the 1870's just prior to or immediately after the union of 1875, and as a result they too may have been unfamiliar with the procedures followed in that union. Since John Forrest and Daniel Gordon had both been ordained in 1866, however, they ought to have been able to advise Patrick. But Forrest supported Patrick uncritically on matters of procedure, and Daniel Gordon, who ultimately refused to enter the United Church, was involved in his own battle with Robert Campbell over the secularization of Queen's University. It was unlikely he would suggest that Patrick should listen to Campbell, even though Campbell was the most outstanding authority on procedure in the Presbyterian Church.

Consequently, the only major advice Patrick received on the matter of procedure came in the form of criticism from dissidents like William MacLaren, Thomas Sedgwick, Robert Campbell, the senior clerk of the General Assembly, and Sir Thomas W. Taylor, the former chief justice of Manitoba, who had drafted the legislation for the union of 1875 and had written the major reference work on the public statutes relating to the Presbyterian Church in Canada.[34] Patrick chose to ignore this criticism because he saw it as an attempt to disrupt what to him was a clear course of action. Moreover, even when the unionists passed criticism on to him, Patrick seemed to have been unaffected by it. In 1911, for example, Dr. R.P. MacKay, who was moderator at the time, pointed out to Patrick that many were deeply suspicious of his methods. He said:

I have heard it stated by those who are out of sympathy with the union proposals that the convenor of the union committee acts independently. As one person stated to me the other day, the report that came to the last Assembly, with its recommendations, was from the convenor's bat, without his committee.[35]

Patrick replied that his knowledge of mankind had prepared him for almost unlimited misrepresentation, but he believed that "persons in public life must be prepared to accept this lot."[36] Such aloofness could not conceal the fact that the mounting criticism would lead the 1911 Assembly to reject Patrick's procedure in a last minute attempt to give the congregations a free vote on the principle of organic union and the Basis of Union.

Eleven years earlier when the news of Patrick's appointment had leaked out, many had expressed doubts about the wisdom of appointing a man who was unfamiliar with conditions in the West and unacquainted with the Canadian church. J.A. MacDonald stated these reservations when he wrote:

> Experience has proved how unlikely it is that a man transplanted from Scotland to Canada after he has reached middle life will become thoroughly Canadianized or will enter with enthusiasm into new and strange work and become a real force in the life of the church. Not many imported ministers have been more than congregational in their success in Canada.[37]

Patrick was a forty-eight year old bachelor when he arrived in Canada, and even after a decade in Winnipeg he "was known only to a comparatively small circle of friends." C. W. Gordon, who was perhaps as close to him as anyone, attributed this isolation to "a serious physical disability" which prevented him "from mingling as freely in the social and intellectual life of the community as he would have liked" and meant that "he was unable to gain that extensive acquaintance with the church and country which would have added so greatly to his influence and usefulness."[38] Professor T. B. Kilpatrick in a eulogy for his friend and former colleague also mentioned that "there were few days when he did not suffer from physical uneasiness, which sometimes deepened to acute distress" and that "he was a very lonely man" who "no doubt in his solitary room had his hours of sadness."[39] Others who were not as close to Patrick perceived him in a different light. W.W. Buchanan of the Winnipeg Y.M.C.A., for example, suggested that "the mercilessness of his logic led some to regard him as severe."[40] Austin L. Budge, an opponent of union, said of Patrick that "in Scottish broadcloth of dustless lustre and neatness; Roman collar and bushy beard of a Puritan. . . he was easily one of the best dressed of clergymen and retained the clerical style of the Scottish church."[41] The picture which emerges is of a man with few close personal ties with the Canadian church in spite of his dominance as a leader. Both in his public and private life, therefore, Patrick apparently remained an outsider. As a leader, such isolation from the church and community was a serious drawback.

When Patrick died in Scotland on 28 September 1911, it was possible to question whether he had become "thoroughly Canadianized," but few could doubt he had been "a real force in the life of the church." Indeed, the Presbyterian Church in Canada would never again be the same. Nine months after his death, however, the resistance proved to be so large that the General Assembly of 1912 could not proceed with the consummation of union.

2

The Beginnings of the Resistance

The only major leader in the Presbyterian Church to oppose organic union with the Methodists and Congregationalists from the beginning was Robert Campbell, the senior clerk of the General Assembly.[1] There were indeed others who had doubts about union, but it was Campbell who defined the issues, exposed the irregularity of the unionists' procedure, and proposed the alternative around which the first resistance organization crystallized. Once the resistance became organized outside the structures of the church, however, Campbell's position as senior clerk of the assembly prevented him from assuming leadership of the movement, and he gradually slipped into the background. But the role which he played in the early years of the conflict was of paramount importance.

When the proposal of union first came before the General Assembly in 1904, Campbell opposed it because he thought there could never be a "coalesence between types so different as the Methodist and Presbyterian."[2] Still, he agreed to a meeting with the Methodists because he doubted that the churches would ever agree on questions of doctrine and polity. But when a compromise on these issues was found and the first draft of the "Basis of Union" was published in the Toronto *Globe* on 23 December 1905, Campbell realized that he had misjudged the situation and that union was an imminent possibility.[3] Therefore he decided it was time to take a stand by publicly attacking the union proposal in a sermon.[4]

Emphasizing that the representatives of the Presbyterian Church had not received a mandate from the church's membership warranting them to proceed to the lengths they had gone in the negotiations, he assured his congregation that no one was yet pledged to union. The recently published "Basis of Union," Campbell thought, was a document that ably set out "the main things in Christianity." Yet he failed to see anything that had been urged as a compelling reason for union. In fact, he had so many reservations that he was not prepared to be a party to the breaking up of the Presbyterian

Church to participate in it. These views, coming from the senior clerk of the General Assembly and a member of the union committee, were publicized in the press and the response prompted Campbell to develop his criticism further in a privately published pamphlet entitled, "Union or Co-operation — Which?"[5]

In this pamphlet Campbell attacked union, suggested that co-operation or federation was a more appropriate alternative, and charged that the union committee had failed to follow the assembly's instructions. When the committee had been appointed in 1904, it had been directed to confer not only with the Methodists and Congregationalists, but also with "any other churches" which might be interested.[6] When these terms of reference were mentioned by the Presbyterians at the first meeting of the joint committee, however, the Methodists claimed that their commission covered only the movement embracing the three denominations and only the Quadrennial Conference which appointed them could authorize negotiations for an extended union. The Methodists reasoned that it "seemed hopeless to expect the Anglicans to abate their claim to be the only properly constituted church amongst Protestants, or the Baptists to make any concessions as to the mode and subjects of baptism, and to ask them to join the negotiations would be only to lose time." To this Campbell replied that in a matter of such grave concern "men should not faint in the presence of even considerable obstacles."

Because Campbell's pamphlet was privately printed, not all Presbyterians had an opportunity to read it. Many were therefore surprised when William Patrick responded to Campbell's charge at the 1906 Assembly with a motion requesting the executive of the joint committee to invite the Anglican and Baptist churches to take part in the negotiations for union.[7] Some thought Patrick and the committee were making a tactical mistake in widening the scope. Robert Haddow, the editor of the *Presbyterian,* suggested that it would merely delay the consummation of union, since negotiations with these two groups were unlikely to go beyond the interchange of fraternal sentiments.[8] Haddow proved to be right. But Patrick could not afford to ignore Campbell, who was a master of the church's rules of procedure as well as a prominent leader.

In 1907 Campbell was elected moderator of the General Assembly. Elevation to the church's highest office, however, did not help him in promoting federation as an alternative to organic union. A few younger men, such as John Mackay, Wardlaw Taylor, R.G. MacBeth, Francis Baird and W.G. Brown supported Campbell's alternative because they saw it as a means of solving the problem of overlapping on the mission fields while still maintaining the identity of the Presbyterian Church. The Presbytery of Saugeen also sent an overture to the 1907 Assembly requesting that the union committee be instructed to consider seriously a federal union of the Protestant Churches in Canada.[9] But many others who had doubts about union would not support this alternative. William MacLaren, the principal of Knox College, explained why. Personally he was sympathetic to the idea, but he would not vote for it because he did not think it was either courteous or appropriate to change horses in mid-stream. He wanted the negotiations to run their course until the "Basis of Union" was completed. Then the church could express its mind on a concrete proposal and, if that proposal was defeated, federation could be considered at a later date.[10] Thus it was not until 1909, when the final draft of the "Basis of Union" came before the assembly, that most of the dissidents finally discovered the issue on which they could take their stand.

Subscription (a legally binding assent to a church's doctrine) was included in the first draft of the "Basis of Union," but Congregationalist objections resulted in its withdrawal before the final draft was submitted to the General Assembly in 1909. This change produced the first recorded dissent to the union proposal signed by twenty members of the Assembly. For Campbell, subscription was neither the basic issue nor the best point from which to launch an attack on the union movement. But by 1909 he was prepared to accept anything that would crystallize the resistance, so he joined the others in recording his dissent.

The following year, when the assembly met in Halifax, the unionists confined the debate to one hour on their controversial recommendation to send the "Basis of Union" to the Presbyteries under the Barrier Act. This procedure was vigorously attacked during the debate, but the unionists prevailed. The "gagging" of the assembly by confining the debate to only one hour, however, produced such resentment that there were five separate dissents (more than on any previous issue in the church's history) in which forty-eight commissioners recorded their opposition to the assembly's action.[11] Throughout this debate, Campbell remained silent in order to give others an opportunity to speak. A month after the assembly adjourned, however, he published another pamphlet entitled "Church Union" which threw the unionists into complete disarray.[12]

The object of Campbell's attack in his second pamphlet was the chairman of the union committee, William Patrick, and his "shadowy and far-fetched arguments" on three specific points. First, Campbell disagreed with Patrick's contention that union was a Christian duty. Second, he dismissed Patrick's claim that the Assembly had committed itself to organic union in 1904 when it accepted the Methodist invitation to discuss the question. Third, he challenged Patrick's referral of the issue to the presbyteries under the Barrier Act. This act, Campbell argued, was never intended to be used as the first step in determining the mind of the church. It was to be used only after the question had been sufficiently discussed in the lower courts to substantiate the belief that the matter was ripe for final decision. Sending the documents to the lower courts only for their information, as the unionists had done, was a different matter from allowing them to express their opinion on the issue. Campbell concluded that by failing to take these proper preliminary steps before using the Barrier Act, the church was being debarred from discussing the contents of the union committee's report, "except on the responsibility of killing the entire movement."

The unionists denied that this was true, but their defence began to fall apart when Dr. W.T. McMullen, the most senior of the union supporters and a former moderator of the General Assembly, agreed with Campbell. McMullen, who had taken part in the Presbyterian unions of 1861 and 1875, said the act had never been used until the documents were in their final shape.[13] McMullen's support of Campbell was so crucial that D.M. Ramsay, the minister of Knox Church in Ottawa and a prominent member of the union committee, asked him to reconsider his position.[14] Ramsay maintained that the Barrier Act was used because all legislation by the assembly involving any change in "doctrine, discipline, government, or worship" came under the act. McMullen agreed this was true before the legislation could be finally passed, but he denied its propriety while the legislation was taking final shape and remained open to amendments.[15] McMullen's support of Campbell proved to be the most damaging blow the unionists had yet received, and soon they were in serious trouble.

Under this pressure the unionists began counter-attacking and Dr. Ephraim Scott, the editor of the *Presbyterian Record*, became one of their main targets. Unlike other Presbyterian publications in Canada, the *Record* was the official voice of the General Assembly and its editor was appointed by the Assembly and directly responsible to it. Consequently, Scott became vulnerable to attack when he recorded his dissent from the assembly's action in 1910 and when he later charged that continuous promises made by all parties since the beginning of the church union negotiations had been violated because the matter had been sent to the presbyteries under the Barrier Act.[16]

Robert Haddow, the editor of the *Presbyterian*, an independent Toronto based publication was the first to suggest that if Scott could not accept the assembly's policy "he should tender his resignation."[17] Then, as the pressure against the use of the Barrier Act mounted, a group of unionists in Toronto decided to bring this matter to the attention of Dr. John Forrest, the president of Dalhousie University, who had been elected moderator at the 1910 assembly. Forrest was an ardent unionist and he readily complied with this request to bring the question of Scott's reporting before the assembly's committee on emergencies. Moreover, because it would be some time before a meeting of this committee could be arranged, he decided to write to Robert Campbell, the convenor of the assembly's committee on the *Record*, demanding that "nothing further of this kind be permitted until the matter can be dealt with by the emergency committee or the assembly itself."[18] This letter, dated 12 September 1910, did not reach Campbell in time, for he had left with his wife for an extended visit to Scotland on 1 September. When it became apparent that Campbell was not present to call a meeting of the *Record* committee, Forrest then asked the editor of the *Presbyterian* to publish his letter to Campbell together with a covering letter which referred to the utter absurdity of the charge made by a number of men who "are persistently endeavouring to create the impression that the assembly is ignoring the rights of the people."[19]

Scott immediately realized that in making public a private letter to Campbell which contained veiled threats of future serious action against Scott but no specific charges or evidence to back them up, Forrest had put himself in an awkward position. Therefore, he publicly challenged Forrest to point out a single statement in his reporting of the 1910 union debate which was contradicted by the assembly's minutes.[20] But by this time the attack on the assembly's procedure was becoming so severe that Forrest declined Scott's invitation. At the 1911 assembly, however, he defended his action and charged that the *Record* was not worthy of the church and needed shaking up. In this attack he was joined by another avid unionist, Dr. J.B. Fraser of Anin, Ontario, who moved an amendment to the motion for the adoption of the *Record* committee's report. Fraser's amendment was designed to force the editor to represent faithfully the assembly's policy on matters of controversy or at least to maintain strict neutrality. This amendment failed because it was attacked by both W.J. Clark, who would later succeed William Patrick as the chairman of the union committee, and George Pidgeon, who was not yet actively involved in the union movement. Clark objected to Forrest's speech because he felt Scott's reporting on the union issue was not sufficient cause to remove him as editor and Pidgeon opposed the amendment because he thought the church press should be free and its editor at liberty to express his own views.[21]

Part of the reason for the support of Scott by these unionists was that by June 1911 the results of the voting in the presbyteries was known, and it revealed that the church was more divided on the issue than the unionists had wished to acknowledge. This conclusion was confirmed in March 1912 when the votes from the sessions and congregations were tabulated. Consequently in April, the union committee concluded that "organic union is not possible at present."[22] Campbell was at the 1912 General Assembly in Edmonton when this finding was accepted, but he made no comment about it since he was writing a major book on the subject which appeared in 1913 under the title, *The Relations of the Christian Churches*.[23] This volume was a defence of the denominational pattern of Canadian religious life and the Presbyterian church, and it was one of the most important statements of the dissidents' case against union.

In view of the importance of the *Relations* it seems strange that it has been overlooked by historians of the union question. Their disregard of this major work and Campbell's other contributions to the controversy has weakened much of the force and significance of the argument over union. To bring that argument back into focus, therefore, it is necessary to take at least a brief look at Campbell's book.

Underlying the church union scheme, as Campbell saw it, there was a radical demand for change which involved a revolutionary attack on denominationalism in general and Presbyterianism in particular, not because they had failed or were inadequate, but because neither conformed to the unionists' theoretical ideal of a united church. In responding to this attack, Campbell made two things clear at the outset: first, he was not opposed to change, but he believed that the burden of proof lay with those who were demanding change and not with those who had doubts about the proposal; second, while he did not adopt the position that "whatever is, is best," he was convinced that "whatever is, as a result of men's eager search after truth, is not a thing to be ignored or denounced."[24] From these premises he set out to formulate a defence against the unionists' attacks on denominationalism and Presbyterianism.

Campbell did not believe that denominationalism was a sin. On the contrary, he thought its emphasis on persuasion and voluntary support had led to healthy competition and mutual respect between the various religious groups in Canada. It was not a system that should be hastily rejected. For Campbell there were good historical reasons for the separate existence of the churches, and insofar as each was still making a unique contribution to the spiritual life of Christendom, the abandonment of denominational diversity in favour of a monolithic uniformity was unjustified. To emphasize the historical reasons for the separate existence of the churches, Campbell devoted five chapters of the *Relations* to tracing the origins and development of the six most important Canadian denominations: the Roman Catholic Church, the Church of England, the Methodists, Congregationalists, Baptists, and Presbyterians. In focusing especially on the origins of these denominations, Campbell's unique perspective on denominationalism came into view.

Denominations, he believed, were the products of the culture and historical experience of particular nations and peoples. Thus, the Anglicans, Baptists, Congregationalists and Methodists were products of the English soil and a people who were different in their genius and temperament from the people of Scotland and Northern Ireland. Presbyterianism, on the other hand, was the unique cultural creation of the Scots and Scots-Irish who for centuries had proven resistant to Anglican, Baptist, Congregational and Methodist attempts to evangelize them. Therefore, he contended, if the Congregationalists and Methodists felt the need for union, they should merge with the Anglicans from whom they had initially separated and not with the Presbyterians.

Today this argument has a modern ring, for it is similar to the outlook of those who see denominations as ways of organizing ethnic groups and preserving ethnic identities. But when Campbell presented these views during the union debate, he was dismissed as a "religious snob" by those who felt constricted by the racial and cultural identities to which he was pointing in his defence of denominationalism.[25]

Moreover, in some of Campbell's less formal presentations of his views, he expressed himself in ways which many found offensive. For example, in a letter to the editor of the *Presbyterian* in January 1907, he claimed that "the religious atmosphere of Presbyterianism was further removed from that of the Methodist church. . .than. . .from any other of the evangelical denominations." The reason for this disinclination of Presbyterians toward Methodism, he believed, "was easy enough to account for." In the Presbyterian Church, laymen had always had a prominent place in church government, and the people did their own thinking. The Methodist Church, on the other hand, was "a church of preachers" in which "their people have had their thinking done for them to order." Although the Methodists had recently flattered Presbyterians by introducing "the lay element into their conferences," Campbell did not believe it was possible to undo in a day the damage done by this "spoon feeding." Therefore, he concluded, amalgamation with the Methodists would "dilute" and "emasculate" the best features of Presbyterianism and especially the strong type of character which it produced.[26]

Dr. F.B. DuVal of Knox Church, Winnipeg, one of the prominent westerners on the Presbyterian union committee, took exception to Campbell's comparison of Methodism and Presbyterianism. He thought Campbell's remarks were not only a serious breach of politeness, but also contrary to the spirit of Christianity and especially "the spirit of that virile Presbyterianism that is ready to enter any forum and contest the truth in any nation." "The Presbyterian church," he continued, "can neither thank nor sympathize with Dr. Campbell in his unfortunate expressions. And it can only hope that the Methodist body will have grace enough to think of them as the incidental effusion of a single mind."[27]

As far as Campbell was concerned he was simply stating the obvious as he had often done before, and he refused to retract one word. Instead he shot back at DuVal, asking, "Has it come to this that a Presbyterian minister is to blame for believing in the superiority of our church, for wanting to preserve it in its integrity, for reminding our people of the privilege they enjoy in belonging to it, and for justifying their wish for its continuance?" "I pledged myself," he continued, "to this high estimate of our church when I entered the ministry. So did DuVal. Has he ceased to hold it? If so, I humbly submit he should at once resign the pastorate of Knox Church, Winnipeg."[28]

It was these sorts of exchanges in the religious press which attracted public attention and left the impression that the argument seldom rose above the level of guttersniping. There was, however, one unionist who understood what Campbell was talking about and who chose to meet him on his own ground. A.S. Morton, one of the most capable church historians in the Presbyterian Church, challenged Campbell's contention that Scotland had proven resistant to Methodism. In a well documented article published in the *University Magazine,* Morton explored the impact of Whitefield and Wesley on Scotland and the influence of Scottish piety on Methodism in order to show that the case was not quite as open and shut as Campbell had suggested.[29] It was an impressive piece of research, but insofar as it admitted in effect that Wesley had not swept Scotland off its feet, it tended to confirm Campbell's argument.

In developing his defence of denominationalism and Presbyterianism, however, Campbell was not content with simply pointing out the historical and cultural differences between Presbyterianism and Methodism. In the *Relations* he went further and rooted this argument in a more fundamental challenge of the unionists' environmentalist assumptions. His unique perspective on denominationalism had been formulated as early as 1871 in his prize winning essay "On The Union of Presbyterianism in Canada."[30] His hereditarian attack on the unionists' environmentalism, however, was a much later development which stemmed from his work as an amateur botanist, his association with the Natural History Society of Montreal and his editing of the society's journal, *The Canadian Record of Science.*[31]

Basic to the activities of social reformers at the turn of the century was the belief that changing an individual's environment would change the individual. They directed their efforts, therefore, toward the removal of bad housing, poor sanitation, child labour, sweat shops, saloons and cheap entertainments. Advocates of the social gospel shared this assumption and declared that the church must be concerned not only with saving individual souls but also with transforming the social environment in which people lived. Pointing to this new understanding, J.A. MacDonald, speaking at Canada's Missionary Congress in 1909, said: "Christianity has to do, not merely with individuals and with salvation into an afterworld, but also with the social fabric, with the organized society of individuals and with the institutions of civilized life under which we live."[32]

There were, however, other dimensions to this environmentalist outlook, for if it was possible to change an individual by changing his environment, it also followed that changes in the environment would lead to institutional change. Environmentalism was, therefore, not only a philosophy of social reform but also a way of viewing change in human history. The first person to see the significance of this environmentalist conception of history for the church union movement was Arthur S. Morton who published a book in

1912 entitled *The Way To Union,* which showed how environmental forces had been operative in shaping the history of the Christian church since its beginnings and why church union in Canada was inevitable.[33]

Surveying Christianity from New Testament times to the present, Morton concluded that there were two forces at work in its history. The first was that changes in the structure of secular society "inevitably" produced ecclesiastical changes. Secondly, recurring revivals of religion reshaped the old machinery and invented new institutions to solve the problems of the age. "These two factors, one secular and the other religious," argued Morton, "have been able to build and rebuild the Church even when its constitution has been the most rigid and when it has been fortified by the belief that it was divine and unchangeable." Together they constituted "a law of life" and there was no reason why Canada should be exempt. Pointing to Confederation and the emergence of the Dominion, he concluded that this was "the great secular fact dominating the development of the church in Canada." The religious factor, Morton suggested, "is a quickened religious life which has made us all in Canada work together for a Christian Canadian people." The "needs and spirit of the land" demanded a remodelling of the church if it were to accomplish its mission.

Morton had studied with Adolph Harnack in Berlin and the basic theme of his book can be traced to Harnack's discussion of "The Relation between Ecclesiastical and General History."[34] In arguing that the history of the church is part of universal history and cannot be understood apart from it, Harnack stated that "the church has at all times shown a tendency to copy within itself the constitution of the state in which it lived." Morton elaborated on this theme in order to show that the union of the churches was necessary in Canada. Following the death of his wife in March 1912, Campbell decided he had to answer Morton and dedicate the fruit of his labour to the memory of his "beloved wife Margaret Macdonnell who was loyally attached to the church of her fathers."

The Relations of the Christian Churches was, thus, a clear response to a conceptual challenge. In it Campbell argued that the issue was not one of environment but heredity. Using Mendel's recently rediscovered work, he contended that heredity was so persistent that accidental variations were powerless to compete with the typical characteristics of a species. Assuming, as most scientists did in the first two decades of the twentieth century, that Mendel's work disproved Darwin's theory of natural selection, Campbell further stressed that there was "a constant return to type when type and variety are mated and therefore it is impossible that any one of the existing species has been evolved out of the one lower in the scale."[35] That is why, Campbell concluded, nature abhors miscegenation. "In the realm of nature," he continued, "it is found that like begets its like; but that there is a bar to the mating of things that are unlike." From this perspective, he suggested that "crosses between varieties of a species are always weaker than parent stocks, and in competition with the originals always go to the wall, as is illustrated in Mendel's law." And finally, "an amalgam does not retain the outstanding qualities of parent metals, nor when chemical substances act on each other, do they exhibit the qualities which belonged to them in the separate state."

It was Campbell's intention to prove by this argument that organic union was against the clear plan of both God and nature and to show that the workings of divine providence from the perspective of environmentalism was false. But in his eagerness to show that the evolutionary argument could not be applied to the realm of faith and morals, Campbell weakened his case by suggesting that Henry Drummond, the Scots' reconciler of evangelism and evolution, had failed "to draw a clear line of demarcation between the realm of physics and metaphysics." Similar failures, of course, were all too apparent in Campbell's own thinking. Nevertheless, the main thrust of his case against union, was, to his way of thinking, devastatingly clear. If the cross-breeding of horses and donkeys produced mules which were sterile, the uniting of Congregationalists, Methodists and Presbyterians would produce a hybrid offspring equally anomolous and sterile.

In adding what he thought was valid scientific support to his historical and cultural arguments, Campbell was not only attempting to strengthen his defence of denominationalism and Presbyterianism, but also linking the opposition to union with one of the most important aspects of conservative social thought in Canada during the early decades of the century. When the issues of immigration, pauperism, crime, prostitution, illegitimacy, insanity, alcoholism, venereal disease, public health and child welfare were discussed by groups such as the Canadian Medical Association, the Canadian National Committee for Mental Hygiene, the Canadian Conference on Charities and Correction, and the National Council of Women, Canadians' fears about the transformation of their society surfaced in the doctrines of hereditarianism. From this perspective Canadian society was threatened with degeneration because of the massive influx of misfits and inferior racial types. These fears were fanned by studies which focused on the problem of "feeble-mindedness" in Canada, claiming that the majority of criminals, prostitutes and illegitimate mothers were either feeble-minded or insane and that it was costing Canadians millions of dollars a year to look after them.

Statistics of this sort made it easy to conclude that the environmentalists' proposals were not only superficial but also would undermine the very foundations of Canadian society. Dr. William D. Tait, Professor of Psychology at McGill and a member of the Montreal branch of the Presbyterian Church Association, later made this clear in an article on "Democracy and Mental Hygiene."[36] He argued that the "flabby maternalism" of social reformers would lead to social degeneration by protecting the unfit. Pampering legislation and mistaken welfare schemes allowed the "drones and wastrels" of society to flourish. This violation of the law of natural selection meant that soon those who were fit to lead would find their task impossible because the Canadian people would lack all intelligence and moral stamina. It was an irony, Tait thought, that this misdirected reform was being done in the name of Christian virtue. Canada's soft-minded reformers were forgetting the sterner aspect of Christianity as revealed in the injunction: "To him that hath shall be given and from him that hath not shall be taken away even that which he hath" (Matt. 13:12, 25:29 and Luke 8:18, 19:26). "We must rid ourselves of the weak," concluded Tait, "else we perish with him; we must save the race, not the individual, and we can only save the race by cultivating the superior type."

Far from being the opinion of isolated cranks, such views were reinforced by many prominent scientific authorities in Canada, England and the United States.[37] Because of this, hereditarianism not only nurtured a distinctive conception of Canadian society and its problems but also gained intellectual respectability. The fact that Campbell invoked this concept in support of the opposition to union revealed how deeply the roots of opposition lay in the conservative social thought of the period.

When Campbell's book appeared, James A. Sedgwick said he intended to place it "next the Bible and Confession" amongst his earthly and heavenly possessions.[38] Thomas T. Smellie of Port Arthur even went so far as to suggest that it be "regarded as one of the Subordinate Standards of the Presbyterian Church."[39] It never achieved that status, however, because its theological implications were unacceptable to many conservatives. Morton's theological liberalism, which dissolved transcendence into immanence, made it easy for him to see God acting in history through natural laws and the forces of the environment. Campbell attacked this immanent doctrine of providence with a biological doctrine of predestination. This type of scientific Calvinism was an effective weapon with which to meet Morton on his own ground, but it also translated the doctrine of predestination into immanent terms and this was much too liberal for many dissidents.

Consequently, although its hereditarianism clearly reflected the social conservatism of the resistance to church union, the book did not continue to play a major role in the later stages of the controversy. In retrospect, such theological restraint against a full-blown hereditarianism seems extremely significant because it prevented the dissidents from identifying their case too closely with the excesses of racist doctrine to which hereditarianism and the eugenics movement ultimately led. But the failure of the majority of the dissidents to respond favourably to this book points to one of the basic difficulties they experienced in mobilizing an effective opposition to union during the early years of the controversy.

Sharing a common theological outlook, broad commitments to social reform, and a willingness to overlook past differences, the unionists were a more homogeneous group than the dissidents. There was no single alternative to the new liberal theology upon which the dissidents could agree. Some were attracted to the type of fundamentalism that Henry M. Parsons of Knox church and Samuel H. Kellog of St. James Square had represented in Toronto.[40] But others rejected its premillennialism. More were attracted to the biblical literalism of the Princeton theology.[41] But not all Canadian conservatives were as opposed to biblical criticism as their American counterparts. The same was true of social reform. Some were opposed to prohibition, others were not. Many rejected moral extremism and the legislation of righteousness but eugenics was not an essential aspect of their conservative social outlook. The dissidents saw church union as a threat but they could not agree on why it was so. Initially, therefore, they had difficulty finding a basis upon which they could unite. They all agreed with Campbell that the unionists' procedure was illegal, but very few accepted his alternative of federation and fewer still accepted his view that the union proposal represented a revolutionary attack on established institutions. Consequently, in spite of every effort, Campbell was unable to rally the opposition to union during the first phase of the controversy.

Part of the reason for this difficulty can be traced to Campbell's background. He was forty when the union of all the Presbyterian groups in Canada took place in 1875. He was one of the prominent young leaders of the "Auld Kirk" minority who entered the new church and afterwards, in a pamphlet entitled "The Pretensions Exposed of Messers Lang, Burnet and Co.," he led the attack against those "Auld Kirk" ministers who remained out of that union.[42] But in spite of his commitments to confessional union and the new Presbyterian Church in Canada, his outlook had been shaped by the "Auld Kirk" and he retained the marks of this background for the rest of his life.

Born on a farm near Perth, Ontario in 1835, Campbell took his training at Queen's University, which was an "Auld Kirk" institution, and for a number of years prior to his ordination in 1861 he was headmaster of the Queen's Preparatory School in Kingston. Unlike his brother-in-law, Daniel J. Macdonnell, Campbell did not go to Scotland for postgraduate training. Consequently, he did not encounter at an early stage in his career the new philosophical idealism and theological liberalism which was beginning to transform the outlook of Scottish churchmen. At Queen's in the 1850's he was trained by James George in the older philosophical tradition of Scottish Common Sense Realism and he retained this outlook throughout his life. Indeed, it was this aspect of his background that attracted him to Sir William Dawson, the principal of McGill University in Montreal, who in turn introduced Campbell to the study of science, especially to botany. Consequently, during the last two decades of the nineteenth century, Campbell found himself much more at home with the anti-Darwinism of Dawson than with the philosophical idealism which George M. Grant and John Watson were promoting at Queen's.[43] In many ways this separated Campbell from other "Auld Kirk" men in the Presbyterian church, for their contact with idealism and liberal theology had made them more sympathetic to church union than Campbell. But in other respects he retained enough of his "Auld Kirk" background to distinguish him clearly from the "Free Kirk" majority within the Presbyterian Church in Canada.

Many of the issues he was involved in during the early years of the controversy served to emphasize these differences in outlook. One of these issues was the secularization of Queen's University. Campbell and his brother-in-law, George Miles Macdonnell, who was chairman of the Board of Trustees opposed secularization. This opposition placed them at odds with Daniel Gordon and the Queen's faculty. It also won him no support from the "Free Kirk" majority because they believed that the state should be responsible for higher education and the church should provide funds only for theological education. Yet, the issue was so important to Campbell that he was not above using histrionics to achieve his purpose. He told the assembly meeting at Vancouver in 1903 that they would break an old man's heart if they insisted on pursuing the question. A reporter for the Vancouver *Daily World* noted that a sudden hush came over the Assembly and they quickly moved on to other business.[44] But while this appeal for sympathy served Campbell's immediate purpose, it did little for his reputation.

Another issue that emphasized the differences between Campbell and the "Free Kirk" conservatives was biblical criticism. At the 1907 Assembly in Montreal where Campbell was elected moderator, a major conflict developed over the appointment of Dr. Alexander R. Gordon to the chair of Old Testament at Presbyterian College, Montreal. This appointment was opposed by Dr. Thomas Sedgwick, who had read Gordon's article on "The Religious Value of the Narratives in Genesis" in which he had written:

> He who finds in the Old Testament a revelation from the living God must face the questions: Can the spirit of God stoop to such "beggarly elements" as myth and legend?   And. . .a still graver question. . .if all these results are produced by the "religious genius" of Israel where does the action of the Spirit appear at all?[45]

In Sedgwick's view, anyone who could raise such questions was not fit to occupy the chair of Old Testament in any Canadian Presbyterian College. William Patrick, who had known Gordon in Scotland where they had served neighbouring parishes in Dundee, assured Sedgwick that Gordon's position was that of a "believing conservative criticism" similar to his own and to that taught in all the Canadian Presbyterian colleges except one. This assurance, however, did not placate Sedgwick and as the intensity of the debate increased, Principal Scrimger of Presbyterian College Montreal referred to Dr. Sedgwick as "ignorant." This remark created an uproar as Sedgwick charged up to the platform demanding an apology. With some difficulty Campbell managed to restore order and to have Scrimger withdraw his remark in a manner acceptable to Sedgwick.

This whole episode, however, put Campbell in an awkward position, for Sedgwick was one of those who had nominated him for moderator. Yet, Campbell did not share Sedgwick's views on biblical criticism and as a trustee of Presbyterian College, he had approved of Gordon's appointment. Their differences on biblical criticism were also apparent in their views on union, for while both opposed it, they opposed it for different reasons. Consequently, on the church union question, the "Free Kirk" conservatives did not look to Campbell for leadership. The man they looked to was William MacLaren, a former moderator and Caven's successor as the principal of Knox College.

MacLaren was perhaps the best systematic theologian that Canada ever produced until very recent times. His ability was recognized by the Princeton conservatives when they invited him to be a member of the board of directors of the Bible League of North America, whose journal, the *Bible Student and Teacher*, was one of the most important conservative Presbyterian publications in North America.[46] MacLaren was also a vice-president of the Toronto branch of the Bible League of North America which included such Canadian conservatives as Albert Carman, Elmore Harris, Principal T.R. O'Meara of Wycliffe College, S.H. Blake, and C.S. Gzowski.[47] He was well-known to Campbell, for both were anti-Darwinists and both shared a philosophical outlook grounded in Scottish Common Sense Realism. Furthermore, MacLaren had played a prominent part in the 1876 heresy trial of Campbell's brother-in-law, Daniel J. Macdonnell.[48]

Campbell was also aware of his negative views on church union, because MacLaren had opposed organic union at the 1889 Conference on Unity sponsored by the Anglicans, and following the conference he had engaged in a lengthy newspaper debate with the Rev. John Langtry of St. Luke's Anglican Church in Toronto, which was later published as a pamphlet entitled "The Unity of the Church and Church Unions."[49] Indeed, it was because of MacLaren's theological conservatism and anti-unionist stance that Campbell was convinced that the proposal to unite the Methodist, Presbyterian and Congregational churches would never get off the ground. But because of their entirely different religious backgrounds, Campbell misjudged MacLaren.

In the Committee on Doctrine in 1905, when the discussions seemed about to collapse as a result of an impasse over the Westminster Confession, Dr. R.P. MacKay pulled out of his pocket a copy of Henry Van Dyke's "Brief

Statement of the Reformed Faith" and laid it on the table. MacKay had been one of MacLaren's pupils at Knox College, and he was aware of MacLaren's Princeton sympathies. Therefore, though Van Dyke was one of the more liberal figures at Princeton, MacKay believed that MacLaren might accept this revision of the confession as a basis of discussion. MacKay was right, and as soon as MacLaren and Chancellor Burwash of Victoria University indicated they could accept Van Dyke's statement, church union became a practical possibility.[50]

The unionists were delighted by this breakthrough and claimed that MacLaren had come over to their side, but he publicly denied that he was a supporter of union.[51] However, having adopted a wait and see attitude, MacLaren refused to accept the alternative of federation until the work on the "Basis of Union" was completed. It was not until "subscription" was removed that MacLaren withdrew his support. Referring to this matter in a letter to Dr. William Farquharson, MacLaren said:

> The Doctrinal Statement is on the whole pretty good, but subscription is abolished. An examination by men who themselves may need to be examined is substituted for it. The constituent elements go into the united church, not by a personal acceptance of the doctrinal articles, but by a vote, and a man may vote for union notwithstanding that the doctrinal articles are to him unsatisfactory. What will an examination by such men amount to? This is a point which needs some attention.[52]

The explanation the dissidents later gave for taking their stand on this issue was based on historical experience. Wherever Presbyterians had abandoned subscription, as in seventeenth-century England, they argued, Calvinism had dissolved into Unitarianism. The same fate had overtaken the Congregationalists in New England because they did not subscribe to a creed. As a result, New England had become fertile soil for "Universalism, Christian Science, Esoteric Buddhism, New Thought and other kindred errors." To build Canada's religious future on a creedless system to which no one was pledged would be to take a long step downwards and backward and to expose Canada to the same influences which had done so much "to blight the religious life of England Old and New."[53]

For Campbell subscription was too narrow an issue upon which to base the defence of Presbyterianism and he only devoted one paragraph to it in *The Relations of the Christian Churches*. But in 1909 when the dissidents recorded their dissent on this matter, he joined them, thereby ensuring that the opposition to union would not follow the old lines of division between the "Auld Kirk" and the "Free Kirk," but would be a new alliance of conservatives. Even this action, however, did not establish Campbell as the major leader of the resistance.

The problem in this instance was not Campbell's background but his position as senior clerk. He had been appointed to this permanent position in 1892, more than a decade before the church union question appeared on the assembly's agenda. Consequently, he saw himself as a leader of the whole church and not just a part of it. When the dissidents organized in 1910, therefore, he would not accept a leadership position, even though the purpose of the group was to support his alternative of federation. Thus, when the resistance movement began to take on a life of its own, shaped by those who assumed leadership, Campbell gradually faded into the background of the controversy to the point where later opponents of union failed to appreciate that except for his efforts the unionists might very well have accomplished their purpose in 1912.

Furthermore, after 1912, no one who was opposed to union was elected moderator or appointed to any major committee responsibility in the church. As a result, from 1913 until his death in March 1921, Campbell served an assembly dominated by unionists. His role tended to deflect attention even further from his importance as an early opponent of union. The ironic twist in all this was that the unionists recognized the significance of Campbell's refusal to accept an office in any of the resistance organizations, and when he died, they were the only ones who publicly eulogized him for his service to the church during his twenty-nine years as clerk of the General Assembly.

Of these eulogies, three in particular make it clear why the unionists respected him. "Some of us," said Professor Andrew Baird of Manitoba College, "differed with him in opinion on church union and occasionally on the adaptation of the legislation of a historic church to new conditions: yet we never ceased to admire the lucidity of his argument, his confidence that he was right, and the courtesy with which he treated an opponent." Dr. John Neil of Toronto, who was moderator in 1917, added that Campbell was "a man of intense energy and strong convictions, always ready to enter the lists in defence of what he believed to be the truth. He was a keen debater and could give and receive hard blows, but he never harboured ill will. He was without bitterness and never allowed public differences to interfere with private friendships." But it was Professor James Ballantyne of Knox College who spoke for all those elected to the office of moderator when he said: "To the moderator especially he was an unfailing source of guidance and support. He had an unequalled knowledge of Presbyterian law and practice, and he was willing to put this at the disposal of the occupant of the chair without making the latter feel his inferiority."[54]

The high esteem in which they held him is obvious from these statements. Yet by emphasizing his service to the church and ignoring his opposition to union, they were blinding themselves not only to Campbell's contribution to the rise of the resistance but also to the basic questions he had raised concerning the union proposal. This is unfortunate, for Campbell not only established the irregularity of their procedure but also pointed to the fact that the givens of belief, sympathy, loyalty, and piety are neither expendable nor easily transferable to new and more comprehensive organizations which lack deep roots in a particular culture.

3

The Federation Alternative

When the opponents of union formed the Church Federation Association in Halifax during the 1910 General Assembly meetings, John Mackay, the principal of Westminster Hall in Vancouver, was elected president. There were several reasons why he was chosen. Since 1906, he had led the fight in the General Assembly for considering federation as an alternative to organic union. More important from the dissidents' point of view, however, was the fact that Mackay was a college principal. Throughout the debate the unionists had implied that only old reactionaries were opposed to union and that anyone with a degree of commonsense could see that organic union was the obvious solution. The election of Mackay, a college principal who was neither old nor reactionary, was an effective reply to this charge. Equally important was the fact that Mackay was located in Vancouver, for again this served to counter the unionists' claim that the West was solidly in favour of union.

Mackay's election, however, created more problems than it solved, both for Mackay and for the new organization. While at first glance it seemed appropriate to have a westerner and a college principal as the leader of the opposition to union, Vancouver was not the best place from which to organize a resistance movement, especially when two-thirds of the members of the Presbyterian Church lived east of the Great Lakes. Thus, as soon as the organization was formed, it found itself with a president in Vancouver and the majority of its members three thousand miles away in the cities and towns of Ontario and Quebec. In retrospect it seems remarkable that no one thought of this at the time, but it must be remembered that the formation of such an organization was totally unprecedented. This was the first time a formal organization had been created outside the structures of the church to oppose the action of the General Assembly publicly. Consequently, it is not surprising that the organizers made mistakes.

Both Mackay and the dissidents, however, learned a lot from their experience with the Church Federation Association. By 1912 Mackay had come to the conclusion that he did not want anything more to do with the controversy.

The dissidents, on the other hand, had decided that never again would they focus their energies around the question of federation.

Mackay's doubts about union first began in Scotland where he had an opportunity to observe the union between the United Presbyterian Church and the Free Church of Scotland in 1900. In 1899, following graduation from the University of Toronto with first class honours and the Governor General's Medal, Mackay had gone to Scotland to study theology at the United Free Church College in Glasgow. As he later indicated, he was an ardent and unquestioning supporter of that union, but the problems which later arose out of it shook his conviction and forced him to reassess his views on the question of church union.[1]

Shortly after Mackay returned to Canada in 1902 to become the minister of Crescent Street Presbyterian Church in Montreal, the American Presbyterian Church North and the Cumberland Presbyterian Church were united in 1906.[2] Here again, as in the Scottish case, a significant number opposed this union and bitter strife ensued over the allocation of property. These two unions between Presbyterian churches in Scotland and the United States caused such difficulties that Mackay was led to the conclusion that the "re-adjustment of denominations is not a great and sacred duty laid upon us by the nature of the church and the mind of the Master, but a pure matter of expediency."[3]

Mackay was too young to be included on the Presbyterian union committee in 1904, but when the issue came before the General Assembly in 1906 neither his youth nor his lack of experience prevented him from expressing his opinion. When the first draft of the "Basis of Union" was presented to the assembly, Mackay immediately challenged the union committee's conclusions and suggested that it would not be "in the best interest of the Presbyterian Church in particular or of Christian life and work in Canada in general" to pursue organic union along these lines. Therefore he proposed in an amendment that "any further negotiation. . .be in the line of federal or co-operative union."[4]

William Patrick was so stunned by this attack that he poured ridicule on Mackay. Before submitting the amendment, he said, any sensible man would have asked himself, "Is this proposal for federation one that is possible now, or that would be considered for a moment by the negotiating churches?" Adding insult to injury, Patrick suggested that Mackay had not advanced one argument against the statement of doctrine and polity and that his speech breathed "the spirit of separation."[5] In the face of this outburst by the chairman of the union committee, Mackay's amendment was defeated by a vote of 179 to 22. But it was not the last time the assembly would hear of this alternative nor of John Mackay.

In 1906 few appreciated the significance of the Federation proposal. In 1908, however, the founding of the Federal Council of Churches in the United States provided a model for co-operation which could be achieved without dissolving denominational identities. As a result, many opponents of union gradually began to see federation as a viable alternative. Moreover, Mackay's appointment in 1908 as the first principal of Westminster Hall, the new Presbyterian college in Vancouver, dramatically enhanced his status and prestige and established him as the leader of those who supported the federation alternative. By the fall of 1909 Mackay's leadership of this group was further strengthened by the publication of six articles on "The Case against Union." [6] These articles constituted the most extensive and well-reasoned argument against organic union since Robert Campbell's 1906 pamphlet, and they appeared at a crucial point just a few months after the dissidents resolved their differences at the 1909 Assembly. Being published in the *Presbyterian,* they secured a much wider audience than Campbell's privately published pamphlet and thus posed a more serious threat to union.

Mackay began his discussion by drawing a distinction between the Protestant and Catholic views of the church. The Roman Catholic view was that the church should be one organization, directed from one legislative centre. The Protestant view, on the other hand, was that the unity of the church could be secured by a variety of organizations, held together, not by an legislative tie, but by a common devotion to Christ. From the papal point of view, Mackay argued, "the existing denominations are a misfortune or a sin, and ought to be got rid of wherever and whenever possible." But there was no scriptural warrant for this idea, and history had proved it subversive of the best life of the church. Mackay argued that instead of being a sin or a calamity, denominationalism was necessary for religious freedom and true spirituality. It preserved the church from the deadening pall of uniformity and the dangers of ecclesiastical tyranny which result when it is forced to follow the mandate of an earthly headquarters.

Mackay admitted that organic union might be warranted if it could be proved that the church would do its work more efficiently by the abolition of separate denominations. But he had serious doubts about such a proposition. In foreign missions there was no reason for union because through comity each church had its own territory to work. At home the task of ministering to English-speaking communities provided no warrant for "such a radical movement as organic union." The situation became serious only when the large foreign population which was massing at different points in the country was considered. Mackay, however, believed this problem could be solved along the lines of the Ruthenian experiment.[7] In this experiment the Presbyterian church had taken under its wing a group which had refused to accept the discipline and worship restrictions placed upon them by the French-Canadian Catholic hierarchy in the West. For a number of years, the Presbyterian

Church supported them financially and helped to educate their leadership until they adjusted to Canadian life. "We may not be making them Presbyterians," said Mackay, "but these foreign peoples will become good Canadians not by forgetting or loving less the lands that gave them little, but by loving Canada more." If the Ruthenian experiment taught anything, Mackay argued, "it is that we ought to look forward to a number of such churches organized from within and federated with some of the stronger denominations, instead of trying to impose the same deadening uniformity upon all peoples." Only those who wished to force all immigrants into conformity with Anglo-Saxon Protestant culture could suggest uniformity of church organization as a solution. "To get the best out of the human material every nation under the sun is pouring into our great Canadian heritage," Mackay concluded, "we must allow the utmost freedom of organization for the expression of every type of religious life, without the dead hand of an omnipotent ecclesiasticism to repress its most sacred promptings."

Mackay then turned to an examination of the doctrinal statement in the "Basis of Union." He said:

> The best that can be said for the new document is that no one disbelieves its articles very seriously, and the worst that can be said against it is that no one believes them any more seriously. It lacks the lofty nobility of language, and clear consistency of thought of the older creeds as much as it lacks the vitality and realism of the age that is dawning. . . .It is a compromise at best and a compromise can never be the inspiration of a living church. . . .These articles show nothing more, nothing less than that a large number of the ablest men of the three churches can produce a document sufficiently ambiguous to be accepted as a Methodist document by some Methodists, a Presbyterian by some Presbyterians, and a Congregational by some Congregationalists. But not their wildest admirer will dare aver that they are the clear, real vital statement of the living common faith of the three churches.

These comments, Mackay said, were not made "in any spirit of unkindly criticism of the articles of union." He believed the committee had done its best under impossible conditions during a period of great perplexity in theological thinking. But he felt that "no creed has ever come out of such a time as this."

In concluding his case against union, Mackay disclaimed "any ill-natured intention to try to frustrate the will of the church," but he made it clear that he was upset by those who assumed their opinions were the dictates of the Holy Spirit. "It has been exceedingly painful," he said, "to some of us, who are anxious to do right above all else, and who, after the most careful consideration, have felt impelled to take one side of this question, to be confidently told that the Holy Spirit is on the other side and we must justify our opposition at the bar of conscience. . . .All that we ask for is that both sides of this question in all its bearings be fully and frankly given to the people."

When Mackay's articles appeared, W.J. Clark, the minister of St. Andrew's Church, Westmount, and one of the youngest members of the union committee, challenged them in a series of letters to the editor of the *Presbyterian.* Clark took particular exception to the fact that Makay had begun his argument against union with an "academic discussion" of the doctrine of the church. Such theological discussions, he said, are "a cloud form so distant, so vague, so indistinct, that we need not waste time or strength over it."[8] In a second letter, Clark suggested that Principal Mackay should not allow the nightmare of a church controlled by ecclesiastics to haunt his slumbers. Mackay, he thought, had been so deaf to favourable expressions about the proposed union, especially from laymen, that he had miscalculated the strong favourable vote which Clark believed laymen would give to organic union.[9]

In his third and final letter, Clark defended the doctrinal statement in the "Basis of Union." He was persuaded that this "much scorned creed is a great deal nearer the thought and belief of the best people today than the Westminster standards." Conceding nothing, he argued that the rigidity of creedal subscription in the Presbyterian church was not to its credit. "The freedom that is proposed," he continued, "in regard to the subscription of ministers is one of the most wholesome things in the union document. There is a very small proportion of the ministers of our church today who accept the Westminster standards in anything near the sense in which they were accepted by those who framed them, and the sooner we get away from this disingenuous condition of things the better for our spiritual health."[10]

Clark left little doubt that the unionists believed they were on the Lord's side and that for them there was only one side of the question worth considering. But this confidence led them to make one of the most serious tactical errors in the entire controversy. Confident by 1910 that union could not be denied, they proposed that the presbyteries vote on the union question under the terms of the Barrier Act. Mackay warned the assembly against this course of action. It was, he said, an irrevocable step which implied the annihilation of the church. He pleaded with the assembly to let the people have a chance to express their opinion without having laid upon them the weight of the assembly's decision. To this effect he proposed the following amendment:

That the proposed basis of union be sent down simpliciter without further delay to Presbyteries, Sessions and Congregations for the fullest discussion and for the expression of their opinion thereon, their decision to be reported to the Clerks of the Assembly not later than the first day of May, 1911, in time to be considered by the General Assembly of 1911, thus placing that Assembly in a position to decide what steps should, under the circumstances, be taken and that the Presbyteries, Sessions and Congregations be invited to consider at the same time the feasibility of some scheme of co-operation or federation between all Protestant Churches in the Dominion of Canada.[11]

Had the Assembly listened it might have averted the disaster into which Patrick was leading them but Mackay's amendment failed and the union committee's motion was carried by a vote of 180 to 73.

No one apparently foresaw that the immediate effect of this decision would be to deny the dissidents any reasonable hope of having their complaints heard within the courts of the church. As far as they could see, their expectations of reaching a compromise within the General Assembly were destroyed. Consequently, their sense of desperation drove them to organize a resistance movement outside the structures of the church for the purpose of publicly opposing the actions of the General Assembly. Once this happened, the point of no return was reached, for it suddenly transformed the controversy from a debate within the assembly into an organized fight within the church as a whole over the right of the General Assembly to legislate the church out of existence. By pressing the dissidents too hard, the unionists thus lost whatever chance they had of exercising institutional control over them.

Until a pamphlet entitled "The Church Union Question" appeared, few seem to have been aware that an organizational meeting of the Church Federation Association had taken place at the 1910 General Assembly. Its first paragraph stated:

The blotting out of the Presbyterian Church in Canada, by merging it in a new denomination is being seriously proposed to our people by the union committee. An organization of ministers, elders, laymen and women from all parts of Canada has been formed within the Presbyterian church, to oppose this suicidal policy, and to suggest what seems to us to be an infinitely better programme in the interest of the Kingdom of our Lord and Master.[12]

When this pamphlet arrived on W.J. Clark's desk, he immediately sensed the presence of a new and dangerous factor in the union negotiations. Previously, the opponents of union had been isolated individuals or congregations who had never reached the point of organized resistance. Now, however, a "nameless" organization had been formed to oppose the policy not only of the union committee but also of the General Assembly. Clark wanted to know who had initiated this "extraordinary and deplorable course of action."

He asked them, therefore, to publish a list of their names so that all Presbyterians could weigh their wisdom and influence.[13]

Clark ignored the contents of the pamphlet, but there was a new twist in it that should have been taken seriously. It voiced suspicions of a conspiracy against the Presbyterian Church in Canada and thus formulated for the first time a conspiracy theory which would prove to be one of the dissidents' most effective weapons in mobilizing their movement. The plot that the pamphlet claimed to uncover was said to be a unionist scheme to rob Presbyterians of their priceless heritage by turning the church's courts and established procedures against them. The slippery path along which they were supposedly being led was traced in careful detail. Every year the assembly had been asked to allow the negotiations to proceed so that it would be possible to find out what sort of plan could be worked out with the other churches. But now the assembly was informed that in allowing negotiations to proceed, the church was approving of union. Every year the assembly was promised that no binding steps would be taken until the church's membership had been given a chance to express their opinion. But now, instead of sending the question to the people, it had been sent to the presbyteries under the Barrier Act. This meant that if a majority of them approved of union, the next General Assembly could legislate the Presbyterian Church out of existence without ever consulting the people. Every year scores of "unsuspecting men" had allowed themselves to be led forward by abstaining from voting or voting in favour of the committee's report on the ground that it was of little significance since the people would pass on it. But now, the people will be told, "Six Assemblies have passed in favour of union (which is not exactly true), and that a certain number of Presbyteries have also passed favourably on the matter. They will then be asked, at least by implication, 'Do you feel so strongly on this matter as to desire to reverse the action of the courts of the church?'"

Later, other elements would be added to the charge of conspiracy. But this was the first time it appeared as the official view of an organized opposition. It was also the first time anyone had suggested it was the "duty" of Presbyterians to resist ecclesiastical tyranny and to demonstrate that they were not ready to submit to the dictates of those who were out to destroy their church.

Most of the unionists did not share Clark's anxieties about this new organization, and they dismissed its charges of conspiracy as nonsense. Confident that organic union was the only acceptable course for the Canadian churches, they heaped scorn on every aspect of the federation proposal. Robert Haddow, for example, attacked the English Free Church Council which the federationists cited as an illustration of what they had in mind. Claiming that this council was powerless to resist the arrogance of the established church in education and other matters, he suggested that there was even less to be expected from it in Canada and that it was unlikely that Canadians would bother themselves with such a futile scheme.[14] From the perspective of the rural Ontario churches, Hugh Matheson of Caledon East charged that federation would involve urban interference in rural affairs. Completely misreading the pamphlet, he thought it was saying that while organic union was fine for the country, federation was all that was necessary for the large city churches. He disagreed and demanded that there must be either organic union for all or none.[15]

These criticisms, however, failed to come close to the real weakness in the federationist case. In view of the past failures of the churches to implement either comity or federation, the federationists needed to show how such reluctance could be overcome, how federation could be implemented, and how it would solve the problems on the mission fields. The English and American experiments to which Campbell, Mackay, and the pamphlet on "The Church Union Question" referred were not enough to dispel the suspicion that they would not work in Canada. To turn the edge of Patrick's criticism that "the history of the Canadian church was strewn with abortive attempts at federation," the federationists needed an indigenous example of a workable plan. The man who came up with it was W.G. Brown, the minister of Knox Church in Red Deer, Alberta.[16]

Early in 1911, Brown published a report on the Alberta Plan for Cooperation in the Home Mission Fields. The object of this plan was to solve the problem of overlapping, which was defined as: "a condition in a rural or village community where either or both churches are receiving support from the missionary funds, and where in the opinion of a District Committee, one of the churches can adequately supply the need."[17] The district committees in this plan were appointed by a provincial committee of the Methodist and Presbyterian churches in Alberta, and they consisted of two ministers and two laymen from each church. These district committees were to meet every six months with the superintendents of home missions to determine whether there were any communities in their district where one of the denominations should withdraw or the work of the two denominations should be amalgamated. In reaching their decisions, the district committees were to be guided by four considerations: (1) priority of occupation; (2) strength of the cause; (3) value of the investment; and (4) the preference of the people. In new areas the district committee would decide beforehand which denomination should enter the field, and if one of them withdrew or allowed the other to occupy the area, it was agreed that they would remain out until the district committee agreed there was room for another church in the area. It was also clearly understood that wherever any changes were contemplated in a community, the people directly affected by the change had a right to present their case to the district committee and if anyone did not desire to unite with an amalgamated church, he had a right to transfer his membership to a church of his choice in an adjacent area.

Here for the first time was a workable plan of comity and co-operation which had the full support of both the Methodist and Presbyterian churches in Alberta. It was no longer necessary for the federationists to point to non-Canadian experiments. Brown made it clear that he was proposing this plan as an alternative to organic union.[18] The way in which the negotiations for church union had been handled in the Presbyterian church, he was convinced, would split the church. But this new plan would solve the problems of the mission fields while preserving the existing strengths of the churches as well as their distinctive identities. The unionists, however, could not accept Brown's proposal and immediately began to criticize it.

In the face of these attacks, the federationists decided that another meeting was necessary. When John Mackay came east to visit his ailing mother in late February 1911, they met at St. Andrew's Church, Toronto. At this meeting reporters were present, and a statement was issued to the press concerning the association's aims and purposes.[19] There was little that was new in this statement, but what caught everyone's eye was the list of prominent ministers who were present. It included Dr. D.D. McLeod of Barrie, who presided, Principal John Mackay of Vancouver, Dr. C.H. Smith of St. Catharines, Rev. R.G. MacBeth of Paris, Rev. H. Logan Geggie, Rev. T. Crawford Brown, Dr. Andrew Robertson, Rev. Daniel Strachan, Rev. J.W. Stephen, Rev. D.T.L. McKerroll, all of Toronto, and Rev. A.H. MacGillivray of Weston, who acted as secretary.[20] For those like W.J. Clark who wanted to know who was backing federation, the names of Mackay, MacBeth, Geggie, and McLeod brought no surprise because they had recorded their dissent from the assembly's action in 1910. But the other seven were new, and no one could help noticing that six of them were ministers of important Presbyterian churches in Toronto.[21] This, of course, was not enough to silence the unionists' criticism of their proposal, but most of the critics began their attacks from now on by noting that "a movement of this kind entered into by a number of the most prominent ministers and elders of our church, including the Principal of one of our Theological Colleges and the senior clerk of the General Assembly of our church, can scarcely be allowed to pass without comment."[22]

In response to the second statement of the Church Federation Association, the unionists put forth three major objections which reflected a more serious attempt to analyse the weaknesses of the federation alternative. First, it was untimely to propose federation while voting on the question of organic union was in progress. Second, federation was a poor substitute for organic union because it would provide neither as complete an economy of resources nor allow for a mingling of type and an interchange of spiritual graces necessary for the full perfection of the church as the Body of Christ. Third, the term federalism was applicable only to states or provinces with well-defined geographical boundaries, and since such geographical separation was not possible, except on foreign mission fields, federation in this form would not work in Canada. The only appropriate type of federalism was that envisioned in the "Basis of Union" which gave localities control of their local affairs and a federal authority control of relations common to all.

While there was a certain logic to the first of these criticisms, it totally ignored the fact that attempts had been made to get the church to consider federation since 1906. Moreover, it also overlooked the dissidents' warning that even if organic union were approved by a majority, it would split the church. The federationists believed, therefore, that rather than being untimely, their proposal was being advanced just in time to prevent the inevitable disruption of the church. The second argument was a refutation of Robert Campbell's charge that a mingling of types was neither necessary nor desirable and John Mackay's contention that diversity rather than uniformity was essential for the health and vigour of the Body of Christ. But insofar as neither Campbell nor Mackay were mentioned and no attempt was made to elaborate on the biblical and theological basis of this conception of the full perfection of the Body of Christ, this criticism failed as a serious challenge to the concept of federation or to the dissidents' defence of denominationalism. Finally, in view of the success of the Federal Council of Churches in the United States and the Alberta Plan for Co-operation in the Home Mission Fields, the third criticism was clearly a "red-herring," which even appeals to "governmental science" could not conceal. It was true that an element of federalism had been incorporated into the "Basis of Union," but the price of this type of federalism was the complete loss of identity of those entering the merger. For the federationists this was too high a price to pay for a scheme that was without precedent, especially when there were proven alternatives. Consequently, though these were relatively serious criticisms, they did not succeed in cutting the ground out from under the federationists, and they tended to confirm the suspicion that the unionists were unwilling to consider any other alternative.

Rigid as the unionists were in their stand, they nevertheless did seem to have popular support. As the early returns of the presbytery voting began to come in, the question no longer appeared to be "Is church union possible?" but rather "Can church union be denied?"[23] Out of the church's seventy presbyteries, fifty approved of union and only twelve disapproved. Three presbyteries did not vote and eight under the terms of the Barrier Act were declared to be opposed. The final tally therefore was forty-seven for union and twenty-three against. The individual votes in the Presbyteries confirmed these figures with 739 voting in favour and 476 opposed.[24] With such a clear majority in favour of union, the 1911 Assembly would be free to consummate the proposed union. Thus, if union could not be denied, the next question was "What would be the minorities' reaction?" Would they say: "We decline to believe there has been divine guidance in this matter; we hold by our opinion; we refuse to go with you; we will disrupt the church?"[25] Robert Haddow, speaking for the unionists, could not believe that the minority would adopt this position. But R.G. MacBeth, the secretary of the Church Federation Association, assured him they would. Moreover, John Mackay maintained that it would not be the minority who disrupted the church, for "when the majority proposes to vote the church out of existence, the minority has a perfect right to say, 'you may vote yourselves into the new organization if you wish, we refuse to go with you.'"[26] Consequently, the call for a conference and a compromise was voiced by those who feared the immediate disruption of the Presbyterian Church.

John Gibson Inkster of London, Ontario, who had not yet entered the controversy, recommended a conference. He noted that industrial leaders advocated this method of resolving disputes, and the clergy often urged people to confer in order to avoid industrial strife. Now was the time for Christians to practise what they preached and he called upon the church's leadership to find a remedy for the discord which had broken out.[27] James Rollins of Peterborough echoed Inkster's call for a conference, and he suggested a series of compromises which included sending the church union question to the sessions and congregations "simpliciter" (that is, without comment concerning either the assembly's or the presbyteries' prior approval of the issue); the preparation of a uniform ballot and the simultaneous recording of the vote taken in the negotiating churches; and working at federation without organization until that vote had been taken.[28] This suggestion was picked up by Robert Haddow, who had suddenly changed his mind about the seriousness of the situation, and he presented it as a three point conciliation programme. If some such procedure was followed, he asked, "would it be too much to ask our brethren of the other side that they preserve an open mind and refrain from committing themselves to a policy of separation and litigation until the present negotiations are complete?"[29]

Haddow's sudden change of mind is interesting, especially as it was clear that the unionists had won a majority of the presbyteries and there was apparently nothing that could stop them. MacBeth's and Mackay's warning that the dissidents would not enter the united church was not enough to daunt Haddow. He had been more concerned about Robert Campbell's pamphlet on "Church Union," which had accused the unionists of illegal procedure, and he was among those who were genuinely alarmed by McMullen's support of Campbell. But again, the large majorities that the unionists had received seemed to confirm that they had the support of the church. Therefore, even the combined attacks of Campbell and the Church Federation Association did not provide a sufficient explanation of why the unionists suddenly felt on the defensive. A new element was responsible for creating this change, and that was the opposition that came from James Ballantyne, professor of church history at Knox College, Toronto.

Had it only been Inkster and Rollins who were calling for a compromise, their suggestions could have been ignored. But when Ballantyne joined them and asserted that nothing short of disaster could come from any attempt to regard the vote as the final answer of the presbyteries, the whole balance of power suddenly shifted. Ballantyne was a moderate unionist who had opposed the sending of the union question to the presbyteries under the Barrier Act. When he warned that if the unionists forced the issue, many moderates like himself would be driven into a more extreme position, the unionists' grand design suddenly collapsed.[30]

Ballantyne had been Caven's and MacLaren's choice as the successor to William Gregg at Knox. He was appointed to this position by the assembly in 1896 after a brilliant academic career at the University of Toronto, graduate study at the universities of Leipzig, Edinburgh, and Princeton, and pastorates in London, Ontario, and Ottawa. In 1907 the Board of Knox College unanimously recommended Ballantyne as MacLaren's successor in the principalship. He declined this position because of indifferent health, but everyone at Knox knew that it was Ballantyne and not Gandier who was the true successor to Caven and MacLaren. Like Caven, Ballantyne's major role in both the college and the church was that of counsellor, mediator, and peacemaker, and everyone trusted the soundness of his judgment and his ability to see both sides of a question. Consequently, when it became apparent that he was willing to lead those moderates who feared the immediate disruption of the church, the response was immediate and overwhelming.[31]

How large a group were the moderates? It is difficult to say, for they were never an organized party. But some measure of their strength can be gained by taking a second look at the voting on the union question in the assembly. From 1906 to 1910, the unionists managed to defeat the dissidents with votes of approximately 180 to various figures ranging from 25 to 75. These appeared as decisive victories but when one takes into consideration that every assembly averaged about 500 to 550 commissioners, it becomes apparent that a great number of them were not voting on the union question. Campbell and the dissidents knew this, and it was one of the reasons why they felt encouraged to keep fighting against what appeared to be impossible odds. The unionists knew it too, of course. Consequently, when Ballantyne came out against them, they realized that in spite of their impressive majorities in the assembly and the presbyteries, the situation had suddenly become very serious. They were prepared to fight Campbell, Mackay, and the Church Federation Association, but if McMullen and Ballantyne were to swing the moderates into the dissidents' camp, they knew the game was lost. Therefore, during the month of May 1911, they reached the point at which they were prepared to accept any compromise that Ballantyne might suggest.

When the General Assembly gathered in Knox Church, Ottawa, on 7 June 1911, Robert Campbell sensed that the time was right to recommend that the union question be referred to a special committee under the chairmanship of Professor James Ballantyne.[32] Consequently, a new committee on Church Union Documents was formed. It recommended that the church union issue be sent to the sessions and congregations in the form of four questions:

(1) Are you in favor of organic union with the Methodists and Congregational churches? (2) Do you approve of the proposed Basis of Union? (3) Have you any suggestions or alternatives to offer? (4) If not in favor of the proposed union, are you in favor of the Federation of Churches?

The first three questions were agreed to without comment, but the fourth provoked debate. Ballantyne said he was not prepared to take responsibility for this question because it was added at the last meeting of the committee when only a few were present and it was only carried by a small majority.[33] In order to secure full discussion, W.L. Clay of Victoria and Dr. D.D. McLeod of Barrie moved that the fourth question be approved. During the debate which followed, several suggested that the intent of question 3 was similar. Moreover, when W.D. Reid pointed out that federation was already in operation in Western Canada and there was no reason for submitting it to the people, Clay agreed, with McLeod's consent, to withdraw the motion. This compromise appeared satisfactory to everyone, and the debate on church union called forth no recorded dissents in 1911. But before the vote in the congregations was taken, this compromise was shattered.

Although the assembly had instructed that three questions be placed on the ballots, the committee in charge of arranging the vote put on only the first two. The third question, asking for "suggestions or alternatives" was handled by an instruction that answers to this question could be sent in on a separate sheet. This change alarmed the dissidents, and R.G. MacBeth accused the unionists of deliberately eliminating the question so that those who preferred federation could not vote for it.[34] This charge required an immediate reply, and Dr. John Somerville replied on behalf of the committee. The assembly's instructions were clear, he argued, concerning the documents which were to be sent to the sessions and congregations, but no instructions had been given regarding the manner in which the third question was to be answered or reported. He admitted that "the committee possibly went beyond its instructions" when it relegated to a footnote on the ballot the proposal that suggestions or alternatives be sent up through the session to the clerk of presbytery along with the record of the vote. He denied, however, that the committee had failed to carry out the instructions of the assembly. For the unionists this was an adequate explanation of an "unfortunate misunderstanding," and they refused the dissidents' request that the ballot be withdrawn so that another could be issued which conformed to the assembly's instructions.[35] For the dissidents, however, the elimination of question 3 from the ballot was a deliberate attempt on the part of the unionists to leave the impression that the issue was organic union or nothing. Furthermore, Somerville's reply totally ignored the fact that question 4, as proposed by W.L. Clay and D.D. McLeod, was a specific question which could have been answered by a simple "yes" or "no." Consequently, this bungling of the ballot confirmed the dissidents' impression that the unionists would stop at nothing to get their way.

Ballantyne did not share the dissidents' suspicions, but as a member of the Presbytery of Toronto, which had voted against union, he was well aware of the confusion and resentment created by the ballot. Therefore, in yet another attempt to save the situation, he strongly supported Somerville's explanation of the problem and suggested that the only way for the assembly "to secure the fullest possible expression of the mind of the church" was for everyone to send in their suggestions. He also urged ministers to explain the "Basis of Union" to their congregations so that everyone would understand the issues and the assembly could be confident that the vote represented the intelligent judgment of the church's entire membership.[36] Ballantyne thought that in presenting the issues to their congregations ministers should act not as an advocate for one side or the other but as judges clearly setting forth the main points in the charge to the jury. While this was undoubtedly high-minded advice, it tended to overlook some rather obvious difficulties.

For example, Ephraim Scott, the editor of the *Presbyterian Record,* followed Ballantyne's advice to the letter. He skilfully presented every argument for and against union. But by placing the pros and cons side by side, Scott not only made them cancel each other out but also revealed his own bias. Every argument against union was presented by him in such a way that it was clearly meant to be an answer to those arguments in favour of union.[37] It was this sort of seemingly judicious presentation of arguments for and against union in the official paper of the General Assembly that exasperated the unionists, driving them to ask W.J. Clark to write a response from the unionists' point of view. Scott immediately accepted the proposed article and asked Clark to "make it good and strong." When he published it, however, he noted that the publication of a statement on one side of the question required one on the other side. So together with Clark's article he published another statement of his own which had been previously printed in leaflet form, and he announced that copies of this leaflet were available at a rate of fifty cents a hundred, which would be sent postpaid in parcels of any size to any address.[38] To advertise his own anti-union literature in this way was certainly improper, but it was also typical of Scott's insistence on having the last word.

Clark's article set out to dispel the "bogies" of the anti-unionists, and he managed in a forceful and hard-hitting way to score a number of points. One was that there had been a federal election in September 1911, and as in all elections, one party had been victorious and the other defeated. No one from the defeated party, however, said that they were going to leave the country or start a rebellion because they could not get their way. "Would members of the church prove less rational than those of the body politic?" asked Clark. "Would reasonable men allow themselves to be terrified by such bogies?" Scott did not think the analogy was appropriate and countered with another case in which the majority had wanted to unite with the United States and a minority had wanted to remain Canadian. While this analogy was probably more accurate, Clark's point was one of the best shots at the dissidents' continued threat of schism and disruption. He also scored in replying to the charge that unionist ministers were playing fast and loose with their ordination vows. The assumption behind this "bogey," he pointed out, was that the Presbyterian Church in Canada was a perfect human organization which should remain forever unchanged. To adopt such a position, said Clark, was "Ecclesiasticism run mad." If John Knox were to return, asked Clark, would he find no differences from what he had been used to and would he not be grievously disappointed if his church had not made any progress? Again Scott countered that the dissidents were not arguing against progress in the Presbyterian Church but against its obliteration.

What effect these debates in the religious press had on the voting or whether they were what Ballantyne had in mind when he recommended that every effort be made to assure an intelligent vote in the congregations is difficult to determine, for details of the voting in individual churches were not recorded. What is apparent about this first vote, however, is that there was so little organization on both sides that very little effort was made to bring out the vote or to influence congregations from the outside. This first vote was therefore the least politicized of the three votes held in the Presbyterian Church during the controversy.

By 25 March 1912, most of the results were in, and on 3 April the union committee gathered in Toronto to study them. The following summary was prepared for the committee by Dr. E.D. McLaren:

Question I

Elders	Yea	6,245;	Nay	2,473
Members	Yea	106,755;	Nay	48,278
Adherents	Yea	37,175;	Nay	14,174
Total	Yea	150,175;	Nay	64,925

Question II

| Elders | Yea | 5,105; | Nay | 2,192 |
| Members | Yea | 77,993; | Nay | 37,197 |

The figures showed an almost two-thirds majority in favour of organic union, with slightly less support for the "Basis of Union."[39] But what they did not show was that 45 per cent of the church's membership had not bothered to vote. With 35 per cent of those voting clearly opposed and 45 per cent failing to indicate their preference, the committee decided that "the strong minority in opposition shows that organic union is not feasible at present." Some members of the union committee wished to go even further. They recommended that the negotiations for organic union be dropped entirely. But the majority, in view of the positive response to the proposal, did not think it could be completely abandoned. So they recommended that the negotiations be continued "in the belief that organic union may yet be consummated."[40]

The task of guiding this resolution through the General Assembly at its Edmonton meetings in June 1912 fell to Principal Daniel Gordon of Queen's University, who, as vice-chairman of the union committee, had had to take over following Patrick's death.[41] Gordon was one of the few men in the church who commanded the respect of both parties, and his attempt to steer a course between the extremists on both sides won the support of all. The resolution which he presented to the assembly clearly stated that while organic union was not "immediately feasible," it was nevertheless "the end to be aimed at and striven for," and in the meantime arrangements should be made for co-operation in the church colleges and on the Home Mission fields, for the modification of the "Basis of Union," and for the addition of many well-known opponents of union to the committee so that it would be more representative of opinions within the church. These recommendations were referred to a special committee, and after careful consideration they received the unanimous approval of the Assembly.[42]

Neither Gordon's eloquence nor his skills as a mediator could, however, hide the problems created by the indecisiveness of the first vote. With 45 per cent of the church's membership expressing no opinion, it was an open question whether they should be considered as "passively opposed" or "acquiescent." Both sides saw the uncommitted as a challenge and an opportunity to increase their support. Consequently, the results of the first vote simply set the stage for the second phase of the controversy. Never again, however, would the dissidents advocate federation. From 1906 to

1912 they had tried to place this alternative before the church, but few would listen. Their object in proposing federation was to provide for cooperation with other denominations without loss of identity. But when this alternative failed to gain a hearing and was mishandled in the courts of the church, the dissidents decided to shift their emphasis to the preservation and continuation of the Presbyterian Church in Canada, no matter what the cost.

In March 1913 Mackay's wife died, leaving him with a five-year-old son to raise. But even before his wife's death, Mackay had arrived at the conclusion that if the dissidents wished to continue the fight, they would have to do so without him. He had not changed his mind about union, for until his dying day he was convinced that large institutional mergers were detrimental to the spiritual life of the church. But he had had enough of ecclesiastical politics, and after 1912 he turned his attention to the development of the Corpus Christi Movement in Canada, which concentrated on the spiritual renewal of the church through small groups.[43]

4

The Preservation of Presbyterianism

Following the decision to halt the union proceedings temporarily, the unionists hoped an accord could be reached. Walter C. Murray, president of the University of Saskatchewan, felt that the 1912 agreement had brought about better understanding and cordial relations which would make it possible for the entire Presbyterian Church to enter union.[1] Similarly, Dr. W.J. Clark, who became chairman of the union committee in 1912, saw the inclusion of dissenters on the committee as a sign of hope that all would be brought into harmony.[2] Ernest Thomas, a Methodist writing under the pen name of Edward Trelawney, also predicted that the deference being paid to the opposition would effectively disarm it.[3] These optimistic assessments of the situation, however, were to prove unwarranted.

In order to achieve unanimity, the unionists were prepared to make several minor concessions. The least important of these was a variety of amendments to the "Basis of Union." In addition, they recommended that a national survey of church conditions be made to establish the need for union. Finally, they agreed to the extension of co-operative arrangements in the Home Mission fields and the theological colleges. These efforts would, of course, require time. The other denominations had to be reassured that such a delay was essential to win over the Presbyterian opposition, and, consequently, it was essential that the Presbyterian Church reaffirm its intention to unite as soon as possible. But the dissidents refused to accept this basic condition because they were determined to preserve the Presbyterian Church. Therefore, the unionists found themselves caught between conflicting pressures from the dissidents in their own church and their counterparts in the other churches. In this predicament, they reacted either by vacillating or by attempting to bludgeon the opposition into conformity. Both postures only served to stiffen the resistance.

It is no wonder then that although the Presbyterian union committee was expanded after 1912 to include dissident members, its negotiations did not produce harmony. The opposing parties were not willing to retreat from any of their basic positions and were entrenched in mutual distrust. Neither side would contemplate any real compromise. W.G. Brown, who attended these meetings, recalled some twenty years later the pervasive atmosphere of tension. Many stalemates ended in angry encounters. After one acrimonious meeting at which the dissidents demanded that their case be heard in a session of the joint committee, Dr. Clark heatedly vowed that as long as he was chairman "no man opposed to union will be appointed to meet the Methodists." On another occasion, Dr. Lyle of Hamilton rushed at Brown, shaking his fist, and demanded "would you dare to resist the will of God?" "No," answered Brown, "but I would dare to resist your interpretation of it."[4]

The unwillingness to compromise was already evident at the first meeting of the committee in December of 1912. Dr. E.D. McLaren, the secretary, compiled a classified list of suggested amendments to the "Basis of Union" for consideration at the meeting. Of one hundred and twenty-eight amendments, only ten were approved to be sent to the joint committee. Admittedly, some of the suggestions, such as requests to include articles on the person of Satan and the position of the Protestant church with reference to the Roman Catholic church and the Second Advent, were by their nature inadmissible. But others that more adequately reflected the dissidents' concerns might have been forwarded to the joint committee if the unionists had been ready to make fundamental alterations in the "Basis of Union." As it was, their concessions were confined mainly to wording rather than to principles.[5]

The dissidents' report of 1913 revealed that they too were not prepared to compromise on the question of organic union. They wanted the matter to remain in abeyance while information was obtained regarding the organization and working of the Federal Council of Churches of Christ in America, so that a wider plan of co-operation or federation could be presented to the next Assembly.[6] Consequently, the unionists were unable to achieve a unanimous report before discussing the issue further with representatives of the Methodist and Congregational churches.

In an effort to build a better case and to prove that conditions existing in Canada were such that a united Protestantism was sorely needed, Alfred Gandier advocated a survey of church conditions throughout the Dominion at a committee meeting in December 1913.[7] When the committee accepted this idea, Gandier indicated to the Methodists that the Presbyterians wanted the information to be presented to the assembly in June 1914. As a result, the survey had to be carried out in less than six months. With such a deadline there was little time to hire professional consultants to design the survey or to consider carefully the nature of the questionnaires which were to be sent out. It was quickly put together by denominational representatives from the joint committee under the convenorship of Principal Gandier. The thirteen questions which they formulated sought information in four general areas: (1) immigration statistics which would reveal the races represented and the special work, in which the churches were engaged, among the different classes of foreigners; (2) areas of excessive concentration of churches and overlapping; (3) the number of Union churches and Union Sabbath schools which were in existence and the problems they presented; (4) the number of new men required each year in the theological colleges and the measure of co-operation existing there.

The idea of a national survey of church conditions was predicated on the complete and immediate co-operation of all concerned. As might have been expected, in those areas where there was considerable opposition to union, this co-operation was not forthcoming. In the Synod of Montreal and Ottawa, for example, only 94 replies were received out of the 200 questionnaires sent out. Furthermore, 59 of these replies either expressed no opinion or indicated that no rearrangement of church work was necessary.[8] The lack of co-operation was even more apparent in the Synod of Toronto and Kingston which received answers from only 141 out of a possible 535 Presbyterian, Methodist, and Congregational churches[9] Two presbyteries, Lanark and Renfrew and Whitby refused to take part in the survey, and no communication was received from the presbyteries of Barrie, Saugeen, London, Dauphin, Swift Current, Vermillion, Red Deer, Castor, and High River.[10]

Those who participated in the survey, therefore, were obviously unionists whose responses revealed their attitudes toward the various problems facing the church. As members of a middle class movement, they perceived threats to their standards and values coming both from below and above, from the working classes and immigrants, on the one hand, and the well-to-do classes, on the other. For example, in Toronto the survey report indicated that a "certain element" was constantly trying to secularize Sunday: "The foreigners would like to act as they did in their own land. Some of our wealthier people through foreign travels are led to have less respect for the habit of church attendance. The larger the city the more apparent is the tendency sometimes called 'Americanizing.'" Suburban Toronto provided few problems, but if there were proper buildings and a large enough staff of trained workers in the congested districts, "the foreign sections would not then be such a menace to what we hold most sacred in our national life." Similar complaints came in from Winnipeg, which reported "a growing tendency among the well-to-do classes to attend only one service." This laxity, it was felt, was at least partly owing to the attraction of automobiles. Furthermore, old country people were inclined to neglect church attendance on coming to Canada and the working classes also tended to lose interest in church matters in favour of unions and trade associations.[11] Though it was not mentioned in this survey, temperance was another issue on which middle class Presbyterians were being challenged from both above and below. These challenges were seen as a menace to the things that they held most sacred.

In its general conclusion to the survey, the joint committee singled out a quotation from the Manitoba report which accurately described what they felt was "the new attitude and changed conditions that are more and more prevailing in many parts of this Dominion and which must be reckoned with by the Christian Church." The report said:

It is to be recognized that the growing diversity of population in newer districts is breaking up the old simple denominational unit, such as Presbyterians, Methodists, Anglicans, etc., so that in few districts are there a sufficient number of any denomination to form a congregation. Any church under such conditions must be composite. Generally speaking, in the West, so far as Protestants are concerned, the denominational spirit is secondary to community interest. It is impossible to exaggerate the importance to the church of such an alliance with the community spirit as is only possible in a union church. Just as Luther made use of the national spirit in his religious revolt, so, in our judgement, the Church in western Canada should seek to ally with herself the vigorous and almost universal community spirit so dominant in our rapidly expanding towns and cities.[12]

For the committee this was the "new ferment in the religious and social life of this Dominion," and it concluded that "the new wine demands a new bottle if it is to be preserved."

Working as it did with limited co-operation and participation, the committee was aware that the survey only partially revealed the need for the readjustment of Canadian Protestant forces in order to achieve economy and effectiveness. But they were confident that the Canadian churches could not afford to ignore the facts the survey had brought to light. Among the dissidents, however, the findings of the survey carried little weight. Ephraim Scott characterized it as a "misleading document" and pointed out that "it was prepared in the interests of organic union."[13] The minority had no representation on the survey committee and no voice in forming its questions. Thus, he asserted, it was no wonder it produced results which supported the unionist cause.

More important than the amendments to the "Basis of Union" or the survey was the development of co-operative efforts in the Home Mission fields in the Canadian West. In September 1912, A. Ritchie Robson of Indian Head, Saskatchewan, pointed out that many in the West were not prepared to wait while the church authorities resolved the difficulties over union in the Presbyterian Church. Instead of waiting for the "slow-going machinery of the churches," many in western communities had realized they could have union "by holding a few preliminary meetings and then going ahead. . . .There were now five union congregations in Saskatchewan organized by the people themselves," he said, and "a number of other settlements are working toward the same goal."[14] Such local action was all very well, but it threatened chaos, for these churches owed no allegience to any denomination. They were, in fact, congregational churches and having no machinery for dealing with the settlement of ministers, church property, and missionary funds, they would in time become a separate denomination. Consequently, in April 1913 a conference was held in Regina between representatives of the various union congregations in the West and official representatives of the Methodist, Presbyterian, and Congregational churches which formulated a tentative policy for union congregations.[15]

By 27 October 1914 when the union churches of Manitoba, Saskatchewan and Alberta held their second major conference in Regina, a denominational advisory council had been established with Dr. Chown representing the Methodists, President Murray of the University of Saskatchewan representing the Presbyterians, Rev. W.T. Gunn representing the Congregationalists, and Rev. T.A. Munroe representing the union churches. Before any new union church was formed, this conference recommended that a petition signed by residents of the community and containing all the relevant information in the case should be directed to this advisory council. The council would then attempt within sixty days to assist the community in the solution of problems concerning church property and in suggesting the proper procedures to be followed in the formation of a union church. The advisory council also assumed responsibility for the disposition of funds raised in the union churches for missionary and educational purposes.[16]

Rev. Robert Garside of Alameda, Saskatchewan, was the only dissident at this point to react against the formation of these union churches. He accused the union congregation at Frobisher, Saskatchewan, of being so vindictive towards Presbyterians that they had driven several families out of the community. He also accused the union church of ostracizing Presbyterian young people from social gatherings, boycotting businessmen, persecuting church members, threatening adherents, scoffing at the minister, and appropriating the funds of the Women's Missionary Society.[17]

Mrs. Louise McKnight of Oxbow, Saskatchewan, who was treasurer of the Women's Missionary Society, replied that Garside's charge was "pure libel," and she gave a detailed accounting of how the funds of the society had been disposed of before the union church came into existence. Rev. T.A. Munroe, the minister at Frobisher, also replied, indicating that most of the Presbyterians in the district had joined the union church. As a result, the Presbyterian Church of which Garside had been minister had ceased to hold services in Frobisher.[18] It was evident that Garside had a rather special axe to grind, and this tended to take some of the edge off his more general criticism of the union churches. In any case, Garside's problems in Frobisher seemed rather far removed from the concerns of those Presbyterian dissidents in Ontario who were determined to organize another group to oppose union. At this point, therefore, they ignored the union churches in the West and devoted their attention to the formation of the Organization for the Preservation and Continuance of the Presbyterian Church in Canada.

The event which brought this organization into being was the General Assembly of 1913. A minority on the union committee contended that since the previous assembly nothing had emerged to change the situation substantially, and they therefore recommended that the matter of organic union remain in abeyance. The majority, on the other hand, believed that the church "was on trial before the whole of Canada and the Christian world."[19] Dazzled by the prospect of the Canadian churches showing the whole of Christendom the way back to apostolic unity, the assembly once again expressed the hope that union might be consummated with no unnecessary delay. The minority, which had brought the negotiations to a standstill in 1912, were alarmed and realized they must organize once again.

In a letter published shortly after the 1913 Assembly, R.G. MacBeth announced that a new national organization was being formed to preserve the Presbyterian Church. Federalism was no longer the issue. The purpose now was to "abide in the church of their fathers." He declared, "Some may secede from it, to enter a new and very unpresbyterian denomination, but the Presbyterian Church in Canada will continue its work and hold its property."[20]

Although the first organizational meetings were held in Toronto in June 1913, news of the group and its plans was not revealed until September, when its committees met again to prepare a statement for publication in the press.[21] But even when the organization was ready, a month later, to present its views to the public, publication proved difficult. The editor of the *Presbyterian,* Robert Haddow, refused to publish their statement on the ground that it contained nothing new.[22] This arbitrary curtailment of access to the media produced an angry reaction because it implied the refusal of unionists to recognize the new organization. As D.D. McLeod observed, the editor's decision was a mistake because it would only confirm the dissidents in their determination to resist change.[23] That their determination should harden was not surprising in view of the non-conciliatory attitude of the unionists. When the *Record* published the dissidents' statement, W.J. Clark asked for a list of names of this "self-constituted committee."[24] Insofar as they had not been appointed by the assembly, this designation was undoubtedly correct, but Ephraim Scott took exception to it as a further rebuff. His protest signified that at least for some the *imprimatur* of appointment by the assembly meant very little at this stage in the controversy.

When the union committee met in December 1913, R.G. MacBeth, in response to Clark's request, presented a list of one hundred and fifty lay supporters of the organization.[25] The list contained fifty-six names from the Maritimes, thirty-four of which were from Nova Scotia; fifty-eight names from Ontario, and twenty-four from Quebec. The rest came from the West, with only two from British Columbia and none from Saskatchewan. A preface stated it was a partial list in the process of being completed. The representation from the various regions, however, showed that lay support was located in the East, especially in Ontario, and was basically urban rather than rural. It consisted of professional men, with a high proportion of lawyers and businessmen who were founders of their own companies rather than executives in the new corporate structures. All of the laymen who had previously recorded their dissent in the assembly appeared on this list. Three men whose names appeared for the first time, however, became the backbone of the organization: John Penman, C.S. McDonald, and H.E. Irwin. Penman was president of the General Committee, and McDonald and Irwin were joint conveners of the Finance Committee.

John Penman was recruited by R.G. MacBeth, his minister in Paris, Ontario. Although he was born in New York City, Penman had lived in Paris since 1868 and there had developed the Penman Manufacturing Company into the largest manufacturer of knitted goods in Canada. In 1907, he sold the company to David Morrice of Montreal, and, though the firm retained his name, he had no financial interest in it. From 1907 to 1915 Penman lived in semi-retirement in Paris and during this period he became active in the resistance movement. As one of the founders of the Canadian textile industry, he was a wealthy man whose generosity on many occasions kept both MacBeth and the organization financially afloat.[26] He was, however, neither a "front man" nor simply an "angel" for MacBeth's organization. As president he assumed complete control. No major decision was made by anyone before it was cleared by Penman.

The joint financial conveners of the organization were C.S. McDonald and H.E. Irwin. McDonald was born in Bayfield, Ontario. He began his commercial career with the firm of Aikenhead and Crombie, Toronto hardware merchants. Later he went into partnership with C.H. Willison in a firm known as McDonald and Willison Lighting Studios Ltd., where he continued until his retirement in 1915. McDonald was the movement's first real administrator. To produce a list of names of prominent men prepared to identify themselves as supporters of the movement was one thing. To discover who was prepared to finance such an organization was quite a different task, and it was McDonald who patiently and systematically canvassed the constituency with endless appeals for support.

H.E. Irwin never became involved in the day-to-day administration of the movement. His role as the co-convener of the finance committee was more that of a "bagman" amongst the major contributors. As a lawyer, he acted as legal counsel to the organization's executive and it was through him that lawyers who worked for the committee from 1913 to 1916 were contacted. Irwin was born in Tecumseh Township, Simcoe County, Ontario, in 1862, and after graduation from the Newmarket High School he entered the University of Toronto, receiving his B.A. in 1885. He became a barrister in 1888, and in the following year became the clerk of the peace for York County. While maintaining this position, he practised law in Toronto with the firm of Mills, Raney, Lucas, and Hales and was legal counsel to numerous companies. He was an elder of the Presbyterian Church and a strong advocate of temperance measures. Irwin's business contacts in Toronto were extremely helpful to the committee based there. In all cases of financial difficulties, his efforts with the major donors managed to keep the organization solvent.

The crusader for the cause was MacBeth. He would speak anywhere and spend endless time writing rebuttals to every unionist argument. He was, however, an administrator's nightmare, seldom bothering to date a letter and spending money on travel and publication without keeping any receipts. When he ran out of money, he simply wrote a bank draft on the personal accounts of McDonald or Penman. Penman always honoured these drafts, but McDonald was not a wealthy man, nor did he approve of MacBeth's methods. On several occasions, after consultation with Penman, he honoured the drafts but warned MacBeth that in future he must produce vouchers for his expenditures. When MacBeth failed to heed his warning, McDonald finally cut him off. When this happened, it cost MacBeth two hundred and fifty dollars at a time when he could ill afford it. He was not a man to hold grudges on such matters, nor did he appear to learn very much from the encounter. It ought to have been clear to him, however, that by placing a businessman in charge of finances and administration of the movement, he had radically altered its structure and had introduced a new element of control on his crusading zeal. From 1906 to 1912 the resistance movement had been in the hands of preachers. After 1913, it was controlled by laymen.

Lay control, however, was not apparent to outsiders for two reasons. First, compiling a mailing list of supporters and contributors was essentially a backroom task. The list of one hundred and fifty laymen which MacBeth presented to the union committee in December 1913 was a start, but there were some 314,832 members in the church as of 31 December 1913, and according to the 1911 census there were 1,121,394 Canadians who identified themselves as Presbyterians.[27] How many of these were against union, who were they, where were they, and which of them were prepared to make financial contributions to the preservation of the Presbyterian Church? As Penman, McDonald, and Irwin knew, it was impossible to answer these questions without identifying their constituencies, and it was to this task that they devoted their immediate attention in a quiet but systematic fashion. They made no speeches and issued no statements: they simply sent out hundreds of letters and carefully filed the names and addresses of those who gave them a positive response. Vital as these tasks were, they had none of the visibility that speeches and articles had, and consequently, few people knew what laymen such as Penman, Irwin, or McDonald were up to or how important they were to the organization.

Moreover, much more in the public eye were the three laymen and six ministers who had been added to the Presbyterian union committee in 1912 to represent the dissidents. James Rodger of Montreal and T.C. James of Charlottetown had both signed the 1910 dissent against the assembly's action. Although Walter Paul of Montreal was present at the 1909 Assembly, he did not record his dissent. By 1913, however, all three of these prominent elders were prepared to sign the minority report of the union committee.[28] The six ministers who signed this report were all well-known opponents of union by 1913. Dr. Sedgwick had initiated the 1909 dissent, and R.G. MacBeth, Ephraim Scott, and W.G. Brown had signed the 1910 dissent. Dr. A.T. Love of St. Andrew's Church in Quebec City and Frank Baird of Woodstock, New Brunswick, were the only ministers who had not previously recorded their dissent. But Love was known to be a close friend of Robert Campbell, and Frank Baird's views became forcefully apparent in his extremely negative review of A.S. Morton's *The Way To Union*.[29]

It was this group that attracted everyone's attention because they were responsible for frustrating the Presbyterian union committee's attempt to achieve harmony. Their refusal to accept the goal of union as a legitimate one for the Presbyterian Church turned W.J. Clark's term as chairman of the union committee into a nightmare and made it impossible for him to present a united Presbyterian front in the discussions with the Methodists and Congregationalists. But while it was important to remind everyone that the resistance to union was not dead, in the long run it was more important to define, as Penman and his colleagues were doing, the nature and extent of the constituencies of those who were opposed. Consequently, the dissidents on the union committee soon discovered that the time for independent unco-ordinated action was past, and in future they would take their marching orders from John Penman and no one else.

Not knowing these inner dynamics of the organization, the unionists had no way of understanding the changing nature of the opposition. All they knew was that their various concessions had not brought about the harmony and unity they desired. Unable to placate the opposition within their own ranks, the unionists decided to alleviate the pressure from their allies in the other denominations by recommending to the assembly that another vote be taken.

Pursuing this strategy, the union committee made three recommendations to the 1914 Assembly: first, the Methodist and Congregational churches should be invited to consider the amendments to the "Basis of Union;" second, if agreement could be reached with the other denominations, the amended Basis ought to be submitted to the Assembly of 1915; third, if this new document was approved by the assembly, then another vote should be taken in the presbyteries, sessions, and congregations.[30] But instead of winning general approval, this plan of action was vigorously opposed by the dissidents. Overtures from the Presbytery of Montreal, from the Presbytery of Lanark, and from Sir Thomas W. Taylor, representing eighty-three other individuals, were presented, suggesting that the union negotiations be either delayed or dropped. But these overtures, as well as the minority report and the various motions of the dissidents, were either ignored or defeated on the floor of the assembly. In advocating a new vote, Clark declared that union should be consummated even if it brought disruption. "I am prepared to pay the price of union," he said "even if it should be that great price."[31] The fifty-three commissioners who recorded their dissent were determined the cost of disruption would be even higher than Clark anticipated.[32]

The prospect of a new vote on the amended Basis led both sides to accelerate their campaigns. The dissidents, having failed to gain a hearing in the assembly, decided to present their case to the Methodists. When the Methodist General Conference met in Ottawa in October 1914, they circulated among its members a pamphlet containing the text of Ephraim Scott's address to the 1914 Assembly and a statement by the organization's executive.[33] Scott reviewed the union negotiations from 1902 until 1914 and suggested there were two ways out. One was to continue negotiations and press towards another vote, even though the fact that "the opposition to change is growing steadily stronger, and a part of the church has decided to remain Presbyterian" was proof that in two years thence there would be "no prospect of being any nearer to organic union." The other was "to step out of the whole matter into immediate peace and undistracted work." In opposing the latter course the unionists had argued that "if the Assembly were to drop the matter now. . .the world would sneer; the Methodists would think that we had been only trifling with them and would resent it. . .and we ourselves would forever lose all pride in the Presbyterian Church, whose glory has always been that of a true democracy where majorities rule and minorities obey."

Scott answered each of these charges, but what he had to say about the Methodists was especially significant. He said that if the Presbyterians asked the Methodists to continue negotiations, they would naturally ask two questions: (1) Had there been any change to warrant the reappointment of the union committee? and (2) Was there any prospect of greater unanimity within the Presbyterian Church two years later? Scott answered both these questions in the negative because the only changes involved were a few verbal amendments in the "Basis of Union," and there was no prospect of being nearer union in two year's time. He advocated therefore "the straight and square and manly and Christian course" of action which was to say to the Methodists:

> Gentlemen, twelve years ago, you invited us to conference on Organic Union. We accepted your invitation. We laboured with you to perfect a Basis. We have laid it before our people, but many of them are not prepared to give up their tried and well-beloved Church for a something new and strange. They think that, for the present, our two Churches will do more by working in harmony and co-operation, adjusting our fields where this can be done, than by attempting organic union. We wish you God-speed in your great work. Let our only rivalry be to emulate the Master, in his self-devotion in seeking the lost, and in the beauty of His blameless life.[34]

Scott believed that such a course would command the respect and win the esteem of all men of whatever name who honour fairness and truth. The executive of the new organization agreed with him, and it was this message they wished to present to the members of the Methodist General Conference.

When W.J. Clark learned that this proposal had been presented to the Methodists without the approval of the Presbyterian Union Committee, he was furious and issued a rebuttal. The union movement, he said, had not lost its importance to Presbyterians and would be brought to a successful conclusion by the 1916 Assembly.[35] Clark commended his fellow unionists for abiding by church procedure and not acting independently of the union committee as the dissidents had done. But his commendation was premature, for in view of the impending vote several members of the union committee decided that further organization was necessary. Calling themselves the "Presbyterian Friends of Union," this group, without consulting Clark, met independently following the December 1914 meetings of the union committee to plan their strategy. A month later they circulated a confidential letter to unionist ministers conveying their intention to compile literature for distribution at the next assembly. Recipients of the letter were asked to solicit contributions to finance this campaign. The letter also requested unionists "to be quietly on the watch" in their presbyteries against any attempts to deprive them of a fair share of representation at the coming assembly, so that "the church at large be not puzzled or misled by an abnormally large opposition."[36]

Insofar as the unionists controlled most of the presbyteries where the commissioners to the General Assembly were elected, the dissidents could scarcely have considered such a strategy feasible. Consequently, when the letter was made public, they claimed it was an obvious attempt to deny them fair representation. In defence, the author of the letter, D.M. Ramsay, questioned the "sweet innocence" of the minority and repeated his suspicions that attempts had been made to pack both the 1914 and 1915 Assemblies.[37] But when the opposition in the 1915 Assembly proved to be less than before, the letter was used extensively by the dissidents as a further example of the unionists' "dirty tricks."

The charge that the assembly might be packed revealed how politicized the situation was becoming. In preparation for the crucial vote of the 1915 Assembly, both parties attempted to extend their power base. The unionists sought subscribers for their organization, and the dissidents continued to add names to their lists of adherents. Yet at the assembly these political manoeuvres were overshadowed in the debate by a major new concern—the war. While party tactics tended to narrow the fight down to wrangles about procedure, the world situation seemed to demand that such petty quarrels be set aside in the interest of a higher call to duty.

Far from providing a broader perspective for reaching agreement, however, the war became an occasion for both sides to vindicate their positions. The 1915 Assembly was deeply moved by the war, and almost every speech was coloured by it.[38] The unionists argued it had brought about a "changed judgement of values," "a weakening of class distinctions," and "a new spirit of self sacrifice," all of which emphasized the need for union. The war also revealed "the world's financial exhaustion," which would require the utmost possible economy of resources and "the greatest concentration of moral and religious forces" both for the present and for the expected increase in the volume of future immigration to Canada following the war.[39] The impact of the war on the unionists' thinking was especially evident in Sir Robert Falconer's address in support of the majority report of the union committee. He was so obsessed by it that he suggested the war had been providential and that it was a mercy the statesmen had led Canadians into it; the war had endowed Canadians with a new spirit and had created a new Canada. In this new Canada, he said, "it will be necessary for us to learn from our foes the lesson of heightened efficiency. The principle of conservation must be applied. We must stop the waste of our moral and spiritual resources." Therefore this was not the time for a truce, which would only check and keep back the movement towards unification.[40]

Dr. D.D. McLeod of Barrie, Ontario was the first to demonstrate how the war could be used to argue the opposite case. Attacking Falconer's suggestion that something might be learned about efficiency from the Germans, McLeod said he "did not think it was a very good time to learn anything from the Germans and he did not think great men should go about the country speaking so kindly of the Germans." In further rebuttal of Falconer, McLeod argued that traditions were not to be despised and that he believed that "we should give up neither the traditions of our country nor of our church." As one reporter on this debate put it, "In short the bombs President Falconer brought down from Toronto were of the kind that don't explode and frightened Dr. McLeod and his party not a whit."[41]

In the midst of the debate a cablegram from Dr. John Pringle, chaplain with the Canadian forces in England, was read: "Christ and Canada needs, demands, union. I daily pray for it."[42] Then, as D.D. Millar was drawing an analogy between the nations coming together for the overthrow of Kaiserism and the churches coming together for the overthrow of Satan, Dr. Herridge, the immediate past moderator of the assembly, entered the court khaki-clad in his uniform as a chaplain. When it was his turn to speak, he argued against a truce because "such a truce would be equivalent to a retreat." It might have been mere coincidence, but it must have appeared that the whole thing had been stagemanaged. The dissidents, however, refused to be intimidated, and both Ephraim Scott and Judge Farrell of Moosomin, Saskatchewan, argued that throughout the Empire in both church and state contentious matters ought to be laid aside till the war ended. Dr. Heine of Montreal managed to get in the final shot by suggesting that "the whole of the Presbyterian Church in Canada is not in Canada now. There are members of our church with the army abroad and the vote should not be taken in their absence."[43]

The 1915 minority report, signed by fourteen members of the union committee, pointed out that the large opposition recorded in the previous vote was now organized and resolved to continue the Presbyterian Church. It therefore recommended that no further steps be taken towards organic union because the church was not ready for union on the proposed Basis.[44] The majority report, on the other hand, recommended approval of the revised "Basis of Union" and the sending of this amended document down to the presbyteries, sessions, and congregations for another vote. The unionist motion was carried by a vote of 368 to 74. Telling as these figures seem to be, neither the number of those who voted against the motion nor that of those who recorded their protests may actually be taken as an accurate index of the amount of dissent in the 1915 Assembly, for many who were opposed to union were not opposed to another vote designed to ensure that the will of the church be once again heard. Moreover, the vote itself was less significant than the fact that during 1915 not only dissidents but also the unionists had organized for a fight.

The three years between the Assemblies of 1912 and 1915 had not brought the peace and harmony that the unionists had anticipated. The dissidents had argued that no changes had occurred which justified a second vote. In fact, the only change that had taken place militated against the unionists' cause. This change, as the unionists were to discover, was the forming of a new resistance organization which was more extensively mobilized and more determined than ever to preserve the Presbyterian Church in Canada. During the 1915 Assembly debate, Rev. F.B. Wilson of Trochu, Alberta, "brandished before the Assembly a list of over 700 ministers and laymen who had pledged themselves to hold together the Presbyterian church."[45] This list, which was subsequently published in the first issue of the *Presbyterian Advocate,* indicated that, since December 1913 when MacBeth had presented a list of one hundred and fifty laymen who supported the Organization for the Preservation and Continuance of the Presbyterian Church in Canada, Penman and McDonald had done important groundwork and they were ready to demonstrate what this new lay-dominated organization could do. Thus, the vote in the assembly was simply a preliminary skirmish in the battle which would take place over the second vote on the church union issue within the Presbyterian Church in Canada.

5

The Second Vote

Even in the face of mounting opposition, the unionists failed to gauge its strength. On the contrary, they pressed for a second vote as recommended in the 1915 majority report of the union committee and persuaded the assembly to authorize it in spite of the dissidents' objections. Their hopes, however, did not materialize, and when the returns showed a dramatic increase in the opposition, they suddenly reversed their position. Since the vote was not up to their expectation, they chose to ignore its results. Plebiscites, they argued, were unnecessary in Presbyterian practice since the courts of the church alone were empowered to make these decisions. This sleight of hand was taken by the dissidents as proof that the unionists were determined to have union at any price.

Initially the dissidents objected to the second vote because they claimed nothing had changed between 1912 and 1915.[1] Yet they sensed that the tide was turning in their favour, and they were determined to capitalize on this new mood. The prospect of a second vote, therefore, actually strengthened their determination, and in spite of unionist jibes that they were trying to "pickle" rather than "preserve" the Presbyterian Church, the dissidents campaigned vigorously to convince as many Presbyterians as possible that they should not abandon their church for an untried experiment.

In the months prior to the second vote the dissidents campaigned better than they had ever done before because now they were better organized. In comparison, the unionists were virtually unprepared for a public controversy. W.J. Clark, the chairman of the union committee, was against the unionists organizing outside of the committee and when the Presbyterian Friends of Union discredited themselves by circulating a letter asking unionists to be on the lookout for attempts to pack the assembly with opponents of union, no further effort was made to set up a unionist campaign organization. Consequently, the dissidents had the field of public relations largely to themselves, and they did a much better job of using the press, producing pamphlets, and holding public meetings.

Probably the most important medium for this debate was the religious and public press. The letters-to-the-editor columns of the newspapers provided a free arena to anyone who held strong views on church union. Anyone could write a letter with fair expectation of drawing public attention to his side of the controversy. Both dissidents and unionists used this opportunity freely, the dissidents more actively than their opponents. The only limitation was the amount of space which any particular editor was prepared to devote to the subject. Sometimes what the editor would publish was influenced by his own or his publisher's stance on the issue, and on occasion this led to complaints from both sides that they were not receiving fair treatment. The religious press was also especially important in this controversy, and editors like Robert Haddow and Ephraim Scott became central figures in the debate.

Realizing how important the press would be, John Penman hired Dr. William Farquharson of Agincourt, Ontario, to monitor and answer all unionist press releases.[2] Up until this point in the controversy answering press releases had been a hit and miss affair. With the hiring of Farquharson, however, it became systematized, and in many cases Penman specifically asked Farquharson to answer specific items such as Robert Haddow's editorial urging Presbyterians to make the vote in favour of union unanimous.[3] Referring to those who had pledged themselves to continue the Presbyterian Church, Haddow said that he hoped they would change their minds because the reasons they had given for voting against union had all been countered by "men who are more expert upon the points at issue." Farquharson, who disliked the elitism of the unionists' arguments, responded by saying that never was there more need of commonsense to correct the bias and narrowness of the expert. Even if they were experts from heaven, he concluded, "any attempt to encourage people to accept their opinions ready-made would only be injurious."[4] By this type of systematic monitoring, the dissidents did an effective job of counteracting the unionists' arguments in the press.

To ensure that the people were given an alternative point of view on the issue, however, the dissidents relied more on pamphlet literature. And here again they managed to do a more effective job through centralized planning. Earlier in the controversy individuals like Campbell and MacBeth had written, published, and circulated pamphlets at their own expense. For this reason the number published and the audience to which they were directed had been necessarily limited. The first of the pamphlets widely circulated by the Organization for the Preservation and Continuance of the Presbyterian Church was initially published in this way. D.D. McLeod's "The Present Duty to Preserve the Presbyterian Church"[5] was a point by point rebuttal of the unionist pamphlet entitled "Church Union: An Opportunity and a Duty."[6] McLeod originally published it at his own expense and circulated it among friends and acquaintances within the church. Penman and several other members of the dissidents' organization, however, considered it so effective that they reprinted it in large quantities and sent bundles all across the country for distribution by local organizations.

McLeod was a particularly effective combatant because he did not believe that a bad argument became a good one when used by a principal, professor, or university president. Like Farquharson, he despised the unionists' elitism and their continuous attempt to suggest that in the opinion of the church's most outstanding experts organic union was the only possible solution to the problems facing the church in Canada. In his pamphlet McLeod tackled Professor T.B. Kilpatrick of Knox College,[7] who had said that refusal to work for union and for the removal of every barrier to Christian fellowship was a sin. Professors, McLeod suggested, ought to be very cautious about making new sins. Would any rational man, he asked, believe it was a sin not to agree with Professor Kilpatrick and the union committee? There was no obligation lying on any Christian to leave his church in order to make a new and different denomination, and Kilpatrick had no authority to force any man's conscience by telling him it was a sin to remain a Presbyterian.[8]

McLeod systematically worked through all the unionists' arguments, revealing their false premises and unfounded conclusions. His object was to show why the dissidents believed they "should not give up a system tried through hundreds of years and which we believe is in harmony with apostolic teaching, for a new, untried system." The unionists might believe the Holy Spirit was with them, but McLeod was equally certain that "the plea for union is not a divine call. . .but a very human one."

McLeod's pamphlet was among the best pieces of writing produced by the dissidents in the whole controversy and the committee were pleased with it. But they were not at all satisfied with the first issue of the *Presbyterian Advocate,* which was supposed to be their first official piece of campaign literature. Although a national editorial committee consisting of such prominent opponents of union as W.L. Clay, D.G. McQueen, and Frank Baird were supposed to be in charge of its publication, the first issue of the *Presbyterian Advocate* was entirely the work of Ephraim Scott.[9]

Some members of the dissident's executive committee in Toronto felt that Scott had taken an inordinate amount of time to put together an inadequate publication. Others complained that he would not allow any interference with the publication. Aside from Scott's personal criticism of union, the only notable feature in the *Advocate's* first issue was a list of seven hundred supporters of the Organization for the Preservation and Continuance of the Presbyterian Church. It did not give a cross-section of dissident opinion, which was its intended purpose. The executive committee members wanted to have some control over the *Advocate's* content, especially since they were responsible for raising the money for its printing and publication. They had sent out almost a thousand letters soliciting contributions, but received little response. If the publication was to be financially viable, any further editions would have to gain more support. With these considerations in mind, the Toronto committee decided to send A.H. MacGillivray of St. John's Presbyterian Church, Hamilton, to Montreal to convey their wishes regarding the second issue of the *Advocate.*

Upon arriving at Scott's office, MacGillivray discovered that Scott had not consulted the publication committee about the first issue of the *Advocate* and did not seem to think it was necessary to call upon their advice at all. After some discussion he prevailed upon Scott to call the Montreal members of the committee together that same day. At the meeting it became apparent Scott had decided that the best policy would be "to push the circulation of the first number of the *Advocate* and print no more editions." His stated reason for not wanting a second number was "that the letters he received would not make as good a paper as the first number." When MacGillivray went through these letters, however, he discovered "splendid material, just the very thing we want."[10] With the help of Robert Campbell, who attended the meeting, MacGillivray was able to put together what he had been seeking: a second number of the *Advocate* with nothing at all written by Scott. It would consist of selections from a series of "telling letters" and would be ready in about ten days.[11]

When the second issue of the *Presbyterian Advocate* appeared, it contained excerpts from letters by thirty-four Presbyterian ministers and laymen from coast to coast.[12] What it lacked in consistency and organization was more than made up for by the clear indication it gave of the number of reasons which individuals had for opposing the merger. The dominant opinion was expressed in a letter from the local continuation committee in Sydney, Nova Scotia, which said: "They ask us to give up one of the smoothest working organizations in the world, and in lieu thereof they have given us the skeleton of an immoral spineless compromise, the working of which no one can conjecture."[13]

The *Advocate* was sent to the local committees of the national organization for distribution. Where there was an active local committee, this procedure worked well, but in many cases those to whom the bundles were sent for distribution failed to circulate the paper. This, however, was not too great a setback since there were other methods of making the dissidents' message public, such as press reports and public meetings. MacBeth, who had left Paris in 1914 to become an itinerant evangelist on the west coast, reported that the British Columbia committee of the Organization for the Continuance of the Presbyterian Church had decided to use the press as the major vehicle for their propaganda. Frank Baird, who was asked by the committee in Halifax to assume campaign responsibility for New Brunswick, reported that he planned to hold a mass meeting in the St. John Opera House on 14 September 1915. He also planned to hold such meetings throughout the mission fields of New Brunswick and then to proceed to Nova Scotia, Cape Breton, and Prince Edward Island. In the conclusion of his report, Baird clearly identified the major source of the dissident's difficulties in the Maritimes: "I mean to deal with MacKinnon's activity soon. The whole weight of the college [Presbyterian College, Halifax] is against us. It is an outrage and the College is being ruined. $16,000.00 in debt and teaching German heresies boldly. We mean to speak strongly and show everything up."[14]

MacBeth anticipated that the West would "give a good account of itself" in the coming vote. He realized, however, that in spite of the organizational effort in both the Maritimes and the West, the issue would be settled in Ontario "because two-thirds [sic] of the Church's membership are there." He therefore hoped that McDonald and the Toronto committee were organized well enough to cover the province.[15]

In approving a second vote the General Assembly of 1915 had instructed that "the vote be taken in Mission fields before October 1st, 1915, and in Pastoral Charges before December 1, 1915."[16] It had also ruled that the vote was not to be taken in the presbyteries before 1 January 1916 and not later than 1 March. By 16 September 1915, therefore, the *Presbyterian* announced that "the documents connected with Church Union are now being sent out." Robert Haddow also added in his editorial that in his "humble judgement the answer ought to be in the affirmative and the vote ought to be unanimous." He recognized that some might think this was a futile plea since certain members had pledged themselves to continue the Presbyterian Church regardless of what the vote might reveal. Yet he hoped these brethren would change their minds because he could not regard the reasons the minority had given for voting against union as convincing, and "we shall be surprised," he said, "if they have much weight with the thoughtful members of our Church."[17]

One of the major problems with the previous vote and one of the reasons why it had been considered indecisive was the fact that only 55 per cent of the membership had bothered to vote. A.J.N. Beckstedt pointed out "in a municipal or other civil election, persons who fail to vote do not as a rule, count one way or the other; but in the present case delinquents constitute a problem. Opponents of union have declared that non-voting members and adherents should be regarded as virtually opposed. On the other hand, advocates of union have been inclined to take the view that 'silence gives consent.'" Everyone was aware of this problem. Consequently, there were few dissenters from Beckstedt's suggestion that every effort ought to be made to secure as large a vote as possible.[18] Robert Haddow echoed this sentiment two weeks later and added that "the issue which is being decided will affect the interests of the Kingdom of God in this Dominion and throughout the world for years to come."[19]

On 23 December 1915, the *Presbyterian* published the unofficial results of the returns counted up to that point. From the unionist point of view, the results were staggering. The total number of members voting for union was 123,821, but the opposition had risen to 83,491. The congregational figures were slightly more favourable to union, with 1,060 congregations voting for union and 434 voting against.[20] Commenting on these figures Robert Haddow noted that about two-fifths of those who voted were not in favor of organic union with the Methodist and Congregational Churches upon the proposed basis. A considerable proportion of this minority had declared they would not enter into union if it should be consummated because they believed it was in the best interests of religion that Presbyterianism be perpetuated as a separate organization. If union was attempted, Haddow warned, this group could be counted upon to foster disruption in as many congregations as possible and to oppose the transference of property to the United Church by litigation and parliamentary obstruction. "The way to union would thus be rough and stormy, if not impossible," he concluded.[21] Yet in view of the majority support for union, Haddow appealed to the minority to attempt something more constructive than a policy of "simple obstruction."

The extent to which the minority could hinder the union movement depended largely upon the presbytery vote to be taken in the new year. In the 1911 vote there had been considerable debate about the presbyteries voting under the Barrier Act prior to the voting of the sessions and congregations. That procedure had been revised in the second vote, but the revision had not prevented confusion. This time the question arose whether the presbyteries should take the results of the congregational vote into consideration when they voted. The question was critical because if a majority of the presbyteries rejected union, the General Assembly, under the terms of the Barrier Act, would have to drop the whole issue.

The problem had arisen because the assembly's instructions for the vote were confusing. They called for a presbytery vote on the merits of the "Basis of Union" but gave directions indicating that the presbytery was expected to vote on the advisability of union in view of the congregational returns.[22] Letters poured in to the *Presbyterian* arguing the case from both sides. Throughout January 1916 Robert Haddow tried to make the issue clear in a series of editorials. He pointed out that the presbyteries were not to consider the question, "Shall we proceed to consummate this union?" That was a question for the General Assembly. The presbyteries were simply asked to give their judgment on the "Basis of Union" by answering yes or no to the question, "Are you in favour of union with the Methodist and Congregational Churches of Canada on the 'Basis of Union' approved by the General Assembly of 1915?" If a majority of the presbyteries answered no, said Haddow, "for all time to come, and throughout the whole Christian world, that vote of the Presbyteries would be pointed to as the mature judgement of the Canadian Church on the question of union — whereas it would not represent the judgement of the Church at all." It was true the opposition at the congregational level had increased, but in fact the majority of congregations had voted for the union. Therefore, his advice was that the presbyteries must vote for the Basis of Union and leave the assembly free to deal with the situation.[23] His constant argument was that the presbyteries should not foreclose discussion in the assembly as would be done if a majority of them voted no upon the remit. "Such a calamity," he said, "must, by all means, be averted."[24]

While the church awaited the final vote of the presbyteries, many began to speculate about what the General Assembly should do. Some unionists agreed that nothing would be gained by trying to coerce the minority and that the 1916 Assembly could not, therefore, proceed to complete the union. But the question remained: What should be done? Among the possible answers was an amicable separation of the two parties. This solution, it was thought, would be preferable to having either a union limited to one or more of the Western Synods or a crop of union churches in the West which would be bound to spring up.[25]

William Farquharson replied that such a solution would never pass the assembly and would impoverish the church by limiting it to people of one class or one opinion. "The final test of character," he said, "is our power to learn from those who oppose and thwart us. One proof of our capacity for union will be the way we act one towards another in the present crisis." His solution to the union problem was to "frankly acknowledge that in the meantime we cannot carry out the scheme proposed and thus let the agitation rest."[26]

Such a stalemate, however, was not acceptable to the unionists. The majority would not abandon their efforts towards organic union.[27] Farquharson tried to clarify his position by suggesting that the proper course of action was "not to persuade one or the other to surrender their principles, but with time and patience to seek to learn the fulness of the divine message as it comes to us through parties, who, though united in heart, are on the present issue divided in opinion. Our present mission is not to separate, but to resolve the discord in a fuller harmony."[28] As the official spokesmen of the dissidents' executive committee, Farquharson made it clear that at this point the committee's objective was not separation but the removal of the organic union issue from the church's agenda. They were shortly to discover, however, that separation, amicable or otherwise, was inevitable.

On 12 April 1916 the Presbyterian union committee met in St. James Square Church, Toronto. After two days of discussion, Principal Gandier of Knox College and Dr. Bryce of Manitoba College managed to convince the majority to adopt a motion calling upon the General Assembly to commit the Presbyterian Church to union at a date to be fixed sometime later. As matters stood, the committee's recommendation seemed rash. Not only had the vote revealed increased opposition to union, but the unionist majority within the union committee was a narrow nineteen to twelve.[29] In their report, the committee's minority emphasized that the results of the vote did not warrant the motion to continue with union. Between 1911 and 1915 the membership of the Presbyterian Church in Canada had increased by nearly 40,000 from 298,916 to 338,322. In 1911, 113,000 had voted for the principle of organic union and 50,733 had voted against it. By 1915, the vote in favour of union had increased by only 557 whereas the vote against union had increased by over 32,000. The total vote, which four years earlier was in a proportion of approximately 69 to 31 per cent, was now approximately 60 per cent to 40 per cent. As far as the dissidents were concerned, this was anything but a clear mandate to proceed further.

Closer examination of the returns, the report continued, revealed that the four synods east of the Great Lakes (that is, east of the Presbytery of Superior which included Fort William, Port Arthur, and Fort Francis) had a communicant membership of 258,750, or more than three-quarters of the church's entire membership. In these synods, 80,962 voted for and 64,618 voted against union. The proportion, therefore, was not far from an equal division, with 55 per cent in favour and 45 per cent opposed. As for the four synods west of the Great Lakes, the membership there was 79,572, or slightly less than one-quarter of the membership. In these western synods 32,534 voted for and 9,214 against union. At first glance this result might appear as an overwhelming majority for union. The minority report pointed out, however, that a large percentage of the 720 congregations voting in the four western synods were mission fields dependent upon the churches in the east for support. Their vote, therefore, should not be given the same weight as that of the much larger congregations which were supporting them. A union based on their vote could lead, in fact, to greater financial difficulties for the western churches by causing the wealthy eastern Presbyterian churches to withdraw their support. Thus, any claim that either the vote or the needs of the West made union necessary would be dubious.

The ambiguity of the vote also forecast the legal problems that would come with a disputed union. Before the 1916 Assembly met, William Farquharson suggested that instead of the church pledging itself to union and seeking legislation later, as the union committee proposed, the process ought to be reversed. Since the request for legislation would not be supported by the unanimous voice of the church, he believed that the legislation could not be the same as that required for a formal transfer of property to the same party under a new name. There would be rival claimants, and the processes of the law would have to settle the dispute. If any legislation that foreclosed a legal claim were granted, depriving the claimants of further legal rights, then surely such legislation would have to secure for each party the maximum to which a successful process at law would entitle it. Therefore, said Farquharson, it might be wise to ascertain the extent of such obligations before pledging anything. Although the union committee talked of "equitable provision" for the minority, Farquharson claimed that they had tried to make the amount of such claims appear as small as possible. They proposed that only the claims of those congregations which voted against union in 1915 should be considered on the condition that these congregations give notice, within a year of the end of the war, of their desire to remain outside the United Church. This proposal, however, was technically inapplicable. The vote in 1915 was merely a statement of opinion of individuals in congregations and not the expression of a congregation's judgment on the matter through a meeting called for that purpose. To make the vote decisive, therefore, was "to make it determine a question that was never submitted and of which no previous notice was given." No legislature, Farquharson declared, would for a moment confirm any such limitation of congregational rights.

Not only was the committee's provision for congregational claims inadequate, continued Farquharson, its report did not even consider the probable claims of the abiding Presbyterian Church. For example, he asked, "Is this church to be allowed the right to retain its original name and to have its legal identity with the Presbyterian Church as now constituted established?" And again, "What about its natural claim to the official records and all the rights and privileges of the church of which it is the continuation?" Although he did not know whether these claims would be made or whether they could be sustained, Farquharson thought it would be wise to settle all such difficulties before entering a binding obligation to consummate the union.[30] However, as the unionists were quick to point out, it was impossible to seek legislation at this point. No legislature would enact legislation to validate a union that had not been decided on or to incorporate a united church which the separate churches had not yet agreed to form.

In spite of all the dissidents' arguments urging that the union proceedings be stopped, the unionists saw the vote as a mandate to continue. Even while they argued that plebiscites were not necessary, they knew the value of winning one and were anxious to consolidate the marginal gains the vote had given them. The returns of the presbytery vote were still to be counted at the coming Assembly. In order to maintain their position, the unionists depended on this vote to bring about a result in favour of union. The General Assembly of 1916, scheduled to meet in Winnipeg, therefore promised to be a critical one for the future of church union.

Many unionists were determined that in Winnipeg, where the union movement began fourteen years earlier, action should be taken to consummate union without further delay. They were aware that to commit the church to union at this point would split it, but they were certain that men of faith would be vindicated. Principal Gandier of Knox College expressed their feelings when he said: "Some good and honest hearts will be sore, a few congregations may refuse to enter, but twenty-five years from now all will be included in the United Church of Canada, and all will thank God for the faith which enabled the Presbyterian Church, at the turning-point in the nation's history, to go forward in the face of grave difficulties and make possible a new era in Canadian life."[31]

Behind Gandier's rhetoric lay several significant assumptions. First of all, there was the myth of 1875 which plagued unionist thinking about the issue throughout the controversy. Their environmentalism led them to believe that union was inevitable and that those who opposed it would find themselves as part of the backwash of history. The few who had opposed the union of 1875 had found themselves in that position, and the same would happen to those who opposed the new union. The failure to recognize or admit the differences between the union of 1875 and the one they were proposing, however, created a blind spot in the unionists' thinking. The union of 1875 was a confessional union which united various groups of Presbyterians. The proposed union involved the merging of three separate denominational families. To oversimplify these differences was to mythologize the past. Secondly, when this mythologized past was projected into the future and it was claimed that within twenty-five years all sections of the church would be within the United Church of Canada, this involved a type of prophecy which contained all the essential features of millennial thinking. Thirdly, reducing the issue to a dualistic equation in which denominationalism is evil and unity is good added the final and most disruptive assumption. This dualism transformed the issue into a cosmic struggle between the forces of good and evil for the control of the spirit, in which the dissidents were clearly not in desirable company! Furthermore, in such a struggle there can be no compromise or synthesis of conflicting forces. The only way such a dualism can be finally resolved is by the absolute triumph of one over the other. Consequently, the unionists could not accept the unfavourable implications of the 1915 vote, which clearly indicated an increased opposition.

Many thoughtful Presbyterians, however, refused to accept this kind of thinking. For example, Professor W.G. Jordan of Queen's University, describing himself as one "who until recently quietly voted with the majority," publicly declared his dissent from the policy of the union committee before the Assembly met. "I know," he said, "that I am expressing the opinion of many who are not connected with what is technically and strictly called 'the minority' in saying that ruthless haste and coercion at this stage would not be the kind of statesmanship that we need."[32] The majority of commissioners who gathered in Winnipeg, however, did not share such doubts. Convinced that "the interests of the kingdom of God demand that the Evangelical Churches in Canada should no longer halt between two opinions," they were determined to carry through organic union as soon as practicable.

Westminster Church, where the assembly was meeting, was crowded when the fight began. The preliminary bout featured Robert Campbell's report on the presbytery vote. In tabulating the votes, Campbell ruled that of the church's seventy-six presbyteries only thirty-two made returns in due form. After eliminating the returns of forty presbyteries on the grounds of various technicalities, Campbell contended that the remit had failed to gain the thirty-nine votes necessary to carry it.[33] Understandably, the unionists were furious. Dr. Duval of Knox Church, Winnipeg, expressed their sentiments when he said, "the Barrier Act was never intended to be the skinflint of a critic." After heated debate, the matter was referred to a special committee which, paying little attention to technicalities, reported that "fifty-three Presbyteries might be recorded as voting for union." Campbell made an official protest against the committee's findings, arguing that they "did not understand the practice of the church" and that their report was not, in his estimation, "a fair reading of the law." He was overruled, however, by a vote of 384 to 47.[34]

The main event began later when Dr. W.J. Clark presented the majority report of the union committee and Dr. Ephraim Scott presented the minority report. Both reports had been published previously, so attention focused mainly on the supporting presentations. Both Clark and Dr. Murdoch MacKinnon of Regina, who seconded the adoption of the majority report, launched extensive attacks on the organized opposition to union. Clark stated that "if the minority report should carry it would mean that any group in the church could set aside that policy by organizing to oppose it." Discussing possible disruption, Dr. MacKinnon said, "the onus of any disruption would rest upon the minority since the church as such by a majority proposes to go into union."[35] Dr. Scott and Dr. W. Leslie Clay of Victoria, who seconded the motion to adopt the minority report, argued that the present division within the church made it impossible for the church to proceed with union. Dr. Clay emphasized that the "Assembly had no warrant from the people to consummate union at this time," and he warned that the adoption of the majority report "was a noose to be put around the neck of the Church today and to be tightened tomorrow."[36]

In the debate which followed, President Falconer of the University of Toronto "characterized Dr. Scott as being essentially a defender of the 'Wee Free' Church of Scotland attitude," and the Hon. W.R. Motherwell scorned Scott for his "fear of trying the untried." On the other side, R.G. Stewart of Edmonton charged corruption in the taking of the vote. Several counselled delay, and a series of amendments were offered. On at least two occasions Forrest and Campbell had altercations which even the moderator could not settle. The uproar they created was described as "a pandemonium of noise." When the debate was over, it was agreed that the most effective speaker had been President Murray of the University of Saskatchewan. Even his closest friends had never heard him speak with such force against further delay in the matter of union.

On the request of W.G. Brown and others, the names of those voting "Aye" and "Nay" were recorded for the minutes, a procedure which took nearly two hours. When the final result was announced there were 404 votes in favour of union and 89 against. "Men threw their hats in the air and cheered. You would think it was an election under Tammany Hall, New York," wrote Brown describing the event many years later.[37]

There were many attempts to explain what had happened at the 1916 Assembly in Winnipeg. From the dissidents perspective, C.S. McDonald believed that "the members [of the assembly] were in the grip of psychologic forces." Elaborating what he meant by this, he said:

> To begin with they were convened just at the time of the loss of Kitchener—there was also the indefinite character of the reports from the North Sea—then there came the terrible battle of Zilleke and the messages to some of the commissioners regarding the fate of their own boys. The heart of the Assembly was tense with the highest kind of emotion—it was outside the range of the possible things that they could give to any matter, much less the highly contentious question of union, that calm and rational consideration which it ought to receive. . . .Then on the back of that Murray of Saskatoon got up—with all his emotions stirred—and in "the speech of his life" swept the Assembly from its bearings. Those who were there tell me that you could not get the house to listen to anything when Murray sat down. I hear that he, himself, admits he was carried away by the pulses of the moment—but whether that be so or not the whole church is swept out into contention by the sudden work of that one moment. It is nothing less than tragic—the finding of the Winnipeg Assembly is tragedy and nothing less.[38]

Whether it was "psychologic forces" or the influence of the "Holy Spirit" as the unionists would later claim, some extraordinary explanation seemed necessary to account for the assembly's decision in 1916 to proceed with union in view of the significant increase in the opposition.

For the minority, the result meant the beginning of a new struggle. They drifted down to the basement where they had been holding meetings as a group. "Never shall I forget that little meeting after the vote" said Brown. "They were mostly old men. The few old elders were weeping. With great spirit they rose and said to us ministers—If you ministers will stand by the Church we'll stand by you till the day of your death."[39] With that assurance, the little group, led by Robert Campbell, returned to the evening session to present their formal dissent and protest which declared that "all those who have gone on record as voting for the adoption of this new constitution, by that act have ceased to be the Presbyterian Church in Canada."[40]

6

The Presbyterian Church Association

In 1911, the Honourable John C. Brown of New Westminster declared that "the powers of the General Assembly do not include hari-kari."[1] Vehement as it was, this summing up showed how fundamental an issue of identity church union had become for the dissidents. Their understanding of the limits of the assembly's power and authority, therefore, presaged further contentions. Robert Campbell's dissent at the 1916 Assembly stated that those who voted for union had "ceased to be the Presbyterian Church in Canada." But who then were the true Presbyterians, and how was that to be determined? Furthermore, what were those who voted against union going to do? How could they resist the assembly's decision and still maintain the continuity they wished to preserve? If they could not recognize the authority of this assembly and withdrew their financial support or set up a competing assembly, would it not be they rather than the unionists who would be withdrawing from the church to set up a new denomination? Again, who was disrupting the church? Who were the schismatics? If, as the dissidents charged, the church's leaders and its established courts were abandoning the church's doctrinal standards and counselling a radical revision of its policy, was there anything that could be done to defend the faith and integrity of the church? Having invested their elected representatives with power and authority, did the congregations have any recourse if those representatives proved irresponsible? Was it responsible to resist established authority, and if so, how? In their desire to limit the assembly's powers would the dissidents not subvert what was so precious to them, the structure of the church itself?

All of these issues had been implicit in the resistance to church union from the beginning. Following the decisions of the 1916 Assembly, however, they became explicit and demanded careful answers. Ironically, after collective deliberation on these issues at the 1916 convocation, the dissidents discovered that in attempting to limit or deny the assembly's power to vote itself out of existence, severe limits had to be placed on their own action lest they destroyed what they were trying to preserve.

Shortly after the commissioners returned home from Winnipeg, the dissidents announced they would take action against the General Assembly's union vote.[2] On 29 June 1916, some three hundred Presbyterians, meeting in the St. Andrew's Institute in Toronto, demonstrated their determination to resist the assembly's decision by covenanting to preserve the Presbyterian Church in Canada. The meeting heard a report on the Winnipeg Assembly from Dr. T. Wardlaw Taylor and a number of other speakers who urged that a more efficient organization be set up for the preservation of the Presbyterian Church.[3]

Steps in this direction had already been taken by the central committee in Toronto. They had to find someone to replace John Penman whose new and growing interest in the Mercury Knitting Mills of Hamilton severely limited his time. Therefore, Dr. Andrew Robertson of St. James Square Presbyterian Church in Toronto was appointed chairman of the central committee. During the early years of the resistance, Robertson had been the minister of St. Andrew's Church in St. John's, Newfoundland. In 1909 he succeeded Alfred Gandier as minister of St. James Square, but for the first six years of his ministry there he was not prominently associated with the dissidents. Not until after the Winnipeg Assembly did he become active in the resistance movement and one of its ablest leaders.

Following the meeting in St. Andrews, the committee began to lay plans for a national convocation to be held in October 1916. To carry out their plans they hired the Rev. J.W. MacNamara of Drayton, Ontario, as secretary of the organization.[4] Born in Liverpool of Irish parentage in 1864, MacNamara came to Canada at the age of fifteen and received business training in Angus Munn's store in Ripley, Ontario. MacNamara had been raised as an Anglican, but during his years at Ripley he became a Presbyterian. In 1893 he attended a student convention in Detroit and returned with his mind made up to enter the ministry. He graduated from Knox College in 1900 and in 1901 was ordained at St. Paul's Church in Nelson, Ontario, where he served for several years prior to accepting a call to Drayton. MacNamara's early business training gave him the necessary qualifications for the job of convention organizer, and his congregation in Drayton, which had voted almost unanimously against union, were prepared to release him for several months. Initially the committee did not realize how fortunate they had been in choosing him. It was not until several months later, when they found themselves caught up in a whirlwind of activity generated almost singlehandedly by MacNamara, that they began to fully appreciate his organizational ability.

The convocation was designed to be a show of strength on the part of the minority and a visible reminder that in spite of the previous assembly's action, the dissidents were determined to preserve and continue the Presbyterian Church in Canada. As McDonald said in a letter to MacBeth, "it is impossible to exaggerate the importance of that gathering. We will be judged by it. It is on it we must rely to make ourselves and our cause visible to the eye of the 'man in the street.'" [5]

No one was more aware of the immensity of the task lying ahead than C.S. McDonald, who as treasurer of the organization for the past three years, knew how difficult it would be to raise money when everyone was being bombarded with appeals for the war effort. In the summer of 1916, machine guns and airplanes were a higher priority than contributions to the preservation of the Presbyterian Church. The rhetoric of resistance flowed easily, but when it came to paying the bills, McDonald knew that but for a very few men like John Penman the organization would have been bankrupt long ago. In the year and a half prior to 31 July 1916, McDonald reported, the committee had spent $3,135.37, almost entirely in printing the *Presbyterian Advocate* and other literature. All the committee's work up to this point had been done entirely by volunteers, except for stenographers. Now that it had hired MacNamara and rented an office in Toronto, these expenses, together with the expense of holding a convocation, would be undoubtedly higher. Although McDonald received a few sizable contributions, the majority ranged from one to five dollars, with the usual apologies and promises of more sometime in the future. Consequently, McDonald was not too enthusiastic about some of the ambitious schemes suggested by his fellow dissidents, such as the establishment of a newspaper to counteract the effects of the *Presbyterian*. In stating his views to Penman he said, "We will require to have a good deal of financial backing for our campaign itself apart from the launching of a newspaper and I am interested to learn how well our wealthy laymen are prepared to support the movement. We have not yet had much evidence of it." [6]

As efforts were made to draw up a programme for the convocation, more and more voices were heard concerning how it should be handled, what should be emphasized, and who should be featured as speakers. MacBeth suggested that the committee should press into service former president Francis L. Patton of Princeton as a speaker for the occasion. [7] Searching for other influential personalities, Penman spotted J. Kier Fraser's letter to the *Outlook* of New York criticizing their reporting of the church union question in Canada. Penman thanked him for the letter and asked if he had any suggestions for the convocation. [8] Fraser had only returned to Canada nine months before, after thirteen years as minister of the Second Church in Charleston, South Carolina, to accept a call to Knox Church, Galt, Ontario in November 1915. Consequently, Penman must have been surprised when Fraser in reply said "the less Dr. Campbell and Dr. Scott have to say on the question the better for us. I find that men all over the church resent their attitude. We ought to consult with them but it will be better for them to keep in the background." [9] Many agreed that new voices ought to be heard from on this important occasion, but others recommended that the old stalwarts, such as Campbell, MacBeth, and McLeod should be featured. In the attempt to find ways of popularizing the convocation, one enthusiast went so far as to suggest that everyone should be given a button with the Burning Bush and the legend "not yet consumed" on it. "Enlisting and badges are features of the day," he said, "so why not in this struggle also."[10]

The man who gradually brought order out of this confusion was MacNamara. He corresponded with everyone who was even remotely interested in the question and spurred local committees in many major cities to hold preliminary meetings. He arranged special train rates for the delegates and financial assistance for those coming from the West in order to ensure that this region would be well represented. Thanks to his organizing genius, Presbyterians from all across the country were present at the convocation.

The key to the representative character of the convocation was a series of preliminary meetings which were held across the country to elect delegates. The meeting in Victoria was typical. W.L. Clay presided and MacBeth, as special speaker, reviewed the situation leading up to the present "crisis." There was little that was new in MacBeth's arguments. What was new was the determination of the gathering, which was reflected in the unanimous vote on a resolution saying: "We respectfully but firmly declare our intention and purpose to remain in the Presbyterian Church and engage by all lawful means to maintain and defend our church with all its rights and privileges."[11]

In a letter to MacNamara, Robert Campbell reported that they had held a rousing meeting in Montreal and had appointed twenty-four delegates. The only fly in the ointment, he said, was the appearance of W.J. Clark.[12] Apparently, Clark attempted to interrupt the meeting several times. The audience made it clear his interruption was unwelcome and would not let him speak. He had refused to read an announcement of the meeting from his pulpit, and since he had denied his congregation the right to attend, it was suggested he also ought to have stayed away. When Clark again attempted to be heard, he was told in no uncertain terms to go home, and finally he angrily left the meeting.[13]

Not all the preliminary meetings were quite as rousing, but Clark's attempted interference was an indication of the unionists' growing alarm. Another indication of the extent to which the conflict was escalating was the refusal of Ephraim Scott and the *Record* committee to publish the official "Message to Sessions" issued by the new union committee under the chairmanship of Sir Robert Falconer. The *Record* committee, according to the "exact minute" which Ephraim Scott forwarded to Falconer, considered this item a "controversial matter" which would damage the *Record's* circulation.[14] In reply, Falconer pointed out that "union is now the definite policy of the church" and therefore an official announcement of the assembly's union committee could not be considered controversial.[15] The "Message to Sessions," however, was never published in the *Record*.

The dissidents' actions revealed clearly that they would not accept the assembly's decision to continue with union. They were not only questioning the wisdom of the decision, but also challenging the competence of the assembly in making it. At the convocation it would be decided where that questioning would lead them.

While the convocation was in session, Robert Haddow wrote an editorial in the *Presbyterian* asking "Who are the Presbyterians?" He argued that those represented in the convocation were wrong in assuming that they were the true Presbyterians and that their organization would be the true Presbyterian Church. Since the Presbyterian Church in Canada was going into union, those who went with it were "the real Presbyterians." The dissidents were untrue to the principles of Presbyterianism, he concluded, and thereby "forfeited their right to the historic name."[16]

The dissidents' answer to this question was stated most clearly by Robert Campbell. He defined the Presbyterian Church in Canada as a voluntary religious association composed of those who had agreed to accept the Westminster Standards as setting forth their understanding of Scriptural teaching regarding the Christian faith and the duty embraced therein, which the association had bound itself to teach and uphold. This definition of the church as a "voluntary society" was similar to that developed by the Princeton conservatives in their resistance to the inclusive tendencies emerging in American Presbyterianism.[17] Although members of a voluntary association acting together could change their attitude towards those standards and resolve to accept a different statement of doctrine and polity, Campbell continued, nothing in the terms of agreement, stated or implied, allowed them to impose a similar change of mind on other members of the association who desired to remain on the original terms. As far as Campbell was concerned, the church courts were required to confine themselves "to carrying into effect the terms of association," and only those who desired "still to associate themselves together on the original terms are to be connected as the Presbyterian Church in Canada."[18]

For the unionists this definition was both intolerable and unpresbyterian. Dr. Duval challenged it on two key points. First, he claimed that the church had a right to adapt itself to the needs of its age. To claim that individuals must stick to the old positions eternally or leave the church forbade all institutional reform. "It is not only opposed to the genius of Protestantism," he said, "it is a stupid opposition to the constitutional course of God in the works of 'creation and providence.'" Secondly, he argued that the Baptist and Congregational churches were democracies but that the Presbyterian church had a representative government. In Presbyterianism every judicial and legislative function was performed by representative assemblies, governed by majorities acting in a constitutional manner. To suggest that majorities in these courts could not rule was disruptive of orderly government. Duval concluded that "if a majority, proceeding in a constitutional way, is not to rule, then a single recalcitrant crank, or even an idiot, might hold up legislation of vital importance, which is an absurdity."[19]

None of the dissidents would have questioned Duval's first point. Nor would they have challenged his contention that Presbyterianism was a representative system quite distinct from Congregationalism. They did argue, however, that the assembly had no right to legislate the Presbyterian Church out of existence. The logic of their position was not based upon grass roots democracy, although at times their argument tended in that direction. What they were groping for, although they never found it, was the doctrine of "residual powers" which lay deep within the Catholic heritage of the church. It was true that the people in the Presbyterian Church had delegated authority to their representatives and church courts. Nevertheless, if their leadership proved unfaithful, the people had the right to revolt in defence of the faith and the integrity of the church. This argument, essentially an early Catholic view, was a powerful one, but their anti-Catholicism was so great that this resource was closed to them, and all they could muster by way of a defence was an intuitive reaction against "ecclesiastical tyranny" and "popery." On these grounds the unionists could outargue them without, however, diminishing their intuitive resistance. When the convocation met, therefore, its delegates believed they were merely claiming their rights as church members in taking action against the 1916 Assembly's decision on union.

The convocation took three major steps. First, the delegates signed a "solemn league and covenant," pledging themselves to maintain and continue the Presbyterian Church in Canada. Secondly, a new organization was created to continue the fight against union. The name for this new body was "The Presbyterian Church Association." Rev. Daniel J. Fraser, Principal of Presbyterian College, Montreal, was elected president, and Andrew Robertson was elected first vice-president. A vice-president was also elected for each province, with the understanding that regional organizations of the association would be formed in every province. C.S. McDonald remained treasurer of the central executive, with James Turnbull of Toronto and James Rodger of Montreal acting respectively as its chairman and deputy chairman. Thirdly, the convocation decided to establish a weekly paper to set forth the views of those opposed to union. John Penman suggested that this venture be funded through the sale of stock issued in shares of twenty-five dollars each, to which Robert Campbell's enthusiastic response was "as the oldest man here and possibly the poorest I will take four of those shares."[20]

A unionist onlooker at the convocation reported that the most ardent unionist could heartily agree with most of what was said. The speakers were courteous and showed respect for the convictions of others—with the notable exception of Ephraim Scott. His address on "The Present Crisis" was filled with bitter and biting remarks. He accused the unionist leaders of committing "a breach of trust" and "usurping the power of the people," in order to create a united church, which was "an ecclesiastical combine" and "a church trust." The union committee was charged with being indifferent to the pain and sorrow caused by the war because it had chosen to continue with union.

The unionist reporter especially enjoyed a "clever and racy production" by F.W. Monteith, a layman from Edmonton, on "The Future Policy of the Church" which advocated a return to the older, more literal view of the Bible and its inspiration that, so the speaker contended, had been destroyed by modern teaching in the colleges. In a speech under the same title, Robert Campbell claimed that the unionists were not prepared to make sacrifices for their cause and that if the people asserted themselves, their ministers would submit to their wishes. He also expressed the hope that the other parties to the union would think twice about joining a mutilated Presbyterian Church. "They may say," suggested Campbell, "as did the young woman, in Hood's ballad, to her lover, who came home with a wooden leg, 'you know you stand upon another footing now.'"[21]

The speech which sparked the most discussion, both inside and outside the convocation, was that of W.G. Brown on "Our Financial Relations to the Schemes of the Church." In private correspondence the suggestion had already been made that the most effective way to deal with the unionists would be for the dissidents to withdraw their financial support from the church, but Brown's impassioned speech was the first public espousal of this option. He recommended that the Presbyterian Church Association should create a sustentation fund for the support of ministers and church officials, to which those opposed to union could send their contributions for carrying on the church's work in the event that its unionist members seceded to join the United Church of Canada after 1916.

A special committee was set up to consider these proposals. It advised that although Brown's recommendations were of great potential value, the time to implement them had not yet come. The committee felt that the convocation's "defensive purpose" did not involve, at this point, reorganization of the church. As members of the existing Presbyterian Church, delegates were bound to abide by its recognized administration as long as its Presbyterian character remained unchanged. Any recommendation to withdraw financial support from the church could be interpreted to mean that the convocation was arrogating to itself powers belonging to the church's government. Realizing that such a charge would damage their cause, the committee reasoned that the convocation had to adhere to the legitimate structures of the church and therefore ruled against further discussion of Brown's proposal.[22]

For the time being, the dissidents confined themselves to carrying out the other plans made at the convocation. Their immediate concern was to keep the unionists on the defensive. The Presbyterian Church Association retained the firms of Messrs. Blake, Lash, Anglin, and Cassels of Toronto and Messrs. Lafleur, MacDougall, and Macfarlane of Montreal as legal advisers to deal with the situation as it developed. The association made it clear that they were prepared to "prosecute quietly but firmly, with fixed and unalterable purpose" the duties laid upon it by the convocation. Within two months they had established a strong central committee, a head office in Toronto, and local organizations in every province.

The association also pursued the convocation's recommendation that a weekly paper be established. Although it was decided at a meeting of the General Committee on 5 and 6 December 1916 to "proceed immediately with the incorporation of a Company with an authorized capital of $100,000 for the purpose of publishing a high class national weekly," this project never managed to get off the ground. Instead, a monthly called *The Message* was established "to expound in a systematic manner, the cause of the Presbyterian Church." The first issue appeared in December 1916, and four more issues appeared at regular intervals between February and May of 1917. During that time it grew from four to twelve pages before financial difficulties led to its demise. Though it was superior to anything that had been produced before by the resistance movement on a continuing basis, the fact that it was distributed free and was entirely dependent upon voluntary contributions doomed it as a financially viable venture. It served a purpose, however, especially at a time when the *Presbyterian* had closed its columns to any expression of opinion against organic union and when the *Record* had to appear neutral.

The convocation had been designed as a show of strength and determination to resist the action of the 1916 Assembly. Unionist ridicule could not hide the fact that the Presbyterian Church was faced with disruption if the issue was pursued. Yet there was a major constraint on the dissidents' action following the convocation. Their goal was not simply to rid themselves of leaders who were trying to demolish their church. Given the roots they had in the Protestant tradition, rebelling against institutional leaders would have been simple enough. All they had to do was leave or refuse to support financially those who they believed were wrecking the church. But because they were a minority who wished to preserve their church, these usual approaches were not open to them. To refuse financial support or to walk out entirely would destroy the essential element of continuity which they were trying to preserve.

The objective set by the convocation was to preserve the Presbyterian Church in the face of any further attempts at organic union. To achieve this goal it had been decided to challenge by all possible means the previous assembly's decision on union without appropriating the Assembly's powers or withdrawing financial support. But this decision left the dissidents in a dilemma. Their actions following the convocation were hindered by the means they allowed themselves; these self-imposed limits also put their objective out of their reach. Had the convocation decided to withdraw support of the church, as Brown suggested, they might have succeeded in having the issue of organic union removed altogether from the church's agenda. Having decided against this option, they simply did not have enough leverage to make the unionists abandon the issue.

Given the strategy adopted by the convocation, the association's efforts could at best only force the unionists to re-evaluate their position and reconsider negotiating. They could buy some time. At worst, their efforts would draw angry reprisals. It was in the likelihood of rejection that the dissidents faced the great irony of their situation: it would better serve their objective if the unionists chose either to retaliate or to dismiss their case out of hand. Further negotiations and probable compromises would weaken the case the dissidents had built up for preserving the identity of the Presbyterian Church. Their hopes could only fructify through the institutional breach they were trying to avoid. Strategically, their case would gain strength only if the unionists proved their unfaithfulness to the church by going ahead with union and by unjustly silencing all dissent. Any further request for negotiation would put the dissidents in an awkward position. They could not accept a simple delay and remain true to their objective of removing the union question from the church's agenda. Yet by refusing to negotiate, they would endanger their credibility.

One of the first questions to come under dispute between the association and the unionists was church finances. Although the convocation had not discussed the withdrawal of financial support, an argument arose over the money spent in the unionist cause. In a letter to the editor of the Toronto *Globe* on 21 October 1916, John Somerville protested that the public press had circulated misleading statements that $40,000 of the church's mission funds had been improperly spent by the union committee on union propaganda. The exact figure was $17,519.43, he said, and it had been spent, as directed by the General Assembly, on the travelling expenses of the committee's sixty members and the printing of materials in connection with the two votes on union taken in the church.[23] Andrew Robertson, answering Somerville on behalf of the Presbyterian Church Association, denied that such allegations had been made at the convocation, but he pointed out how easy it was to have come to such a conclusion.[24] The union committee had never given any statement of its income and expenditure. Somerville's figure was the first specific accounting of the amount spent between 1904 and 1916. Although the facts had been published each year in the treasurer's report, the peculiar procedure of charging the committee's expenses proportionally against the various schemes of the church made it impossible for anyone but an accountant to determine the yearly expenses of the union committee. Consequently, when the minutes of the 1916 General Assembly recorded a four-thousand-dollar expenditure, many assumed an equal amount had been spent in each of the twelve years of agitation from 1904 to 1916 and concluded the church had spent upwards of thirty or forty thousand dollars on union.[25] To avoid similar problems in the future, Robertson suggested, the union committee should make clear just what their expenditures were and should give their authority for such actions as in the case of the publication of the "Message to the Sessions."[26] Accepting this suggestion, the committee did so henceforth. It was a minor victory, but it proved that the association, although limited in power, could challenge the union committee successfully.

Another challenge to the unionists was the proposal to circulate in the church the covenant drawn up at the convocation. In response, Robert Haddow suggested it was "not a document which thoughtful and loyal Presbyterians ought to sign." After pouring ridicule on all of its clauses, he said, "upon the whole one cannot but feel that it is a 'Covenant' not worthy of the good men who formed and signed it. The great covenants of the past were not based upon figures and mathematical calculations, but upon strong principles of faith and life."[27] In spite of his objections, however, Haddow realized that the convenanters' convictions were strong enough to make them resist the action of the 1916 Assembly. Therefore, a week later he appealed to Daniel J. Fraser and Andrew Robertson to use their powerful influence to induce the other members of the association to withdraw their opposition, so as to avert disruption.[28]

Robertson replied that he would gladly help repair the breach which had been made, if the unionists could reasonably explain why the assembly had taken the step which divided the church.[29] Although this request received a number of replies, including the suggestion that the assembly delegates had voted for union because of a "divine compulsion" which informed them that "they would be sinning against the Holy Spirit not to vote as they did," none of the explanations seemed any more reasonable to the dissidents than those offered previously.[30] The unionists still contended that the assembly had simply been fulfilling its function as the court of the church in deciding by a majority vote to pursue union. That explanation could not alter the dissidents' conviction that the assembly, led by a number of men who wanted their "cherished scheme" of union fulfilled immediately for fear of the growing opposition, had acted blindly and rashly.[31] In fact, Robertson probably did not expect an acceptable answer. His purpose in asking the question, like that of the association he represented, was to put the unionists on the defensive.

The moderates, however, were prepared to make yet another attempt to avoid disruption. At a meeting of the Presbytery of Toronto in November 1916, James Ballantyne introduced a motion suggesting that the assembly should take steps to avert the schism in the church that would follow the carrying out of the assembly's last resolution.[32] Although this motion was not actually dealt with in the Presbytery of Toronto until February 1917, it was widely discussed both in the press and amongst those Presbyterians who shared Ballantyne's fear of disruption.

Shortly before Christmas 1916, Robertson received a letter from Daniel M. Gordon of Queen's University, asking if the association would accept the kind of motion suggested by Ballantyne if it was approved by the next assembly.[33] This request, coming from one of the few elder statesmen of Canadian Presbyterianism who still retained the confidence of both sides in the dispute, put the dissidents in an awkward position. They were bound to the commitments made by the convocation, but they could not reject the moderates' attempts at mediation without the danger of losing their advantage. To Daniel Fraser, Robertson admitted that it would be "difficult and delicate. . . to carry ourselves in the face of this new movement." [34] In his reply to Principal Gordon, however, Robertson explained why the association would not abandon its current objectives to pursue another compromise. Two similar motions previously had been rejected by the assembly. Since the vote in Winnipeg, the unionists had said repeatedly that the question was closed and had emphasized their position by forming a new union committee which excluded all those who had any leanings away from the findings of the court. This action had forced the minority to the wall and had given rise to the convocation and a new association. Since the convocation had decided by a unanimous resolution that "our present duty is to remain with the Presbyterian Church," there could be no qualification of that decision until the association itself made a change in it. Whether the association would do so, Robertson concluded, "it is impossible for me or anyone else to anticipate."[35]

Not all responses to Ballantyne's motion were so tactful. MacBeth called it a "trap" because it committed the church to organic union on the "Basis of Union" in spite of the proposed postponement. "Let the unionists vote on that if they will," he said, "our business is to go on with our Association and our Church." [36] Robertson agreed the association was committed to pursuing the resolution made at the convocation without "let or hindrance" and advised its members in Toronto Presbytery to let the debate and vote remain in the hands of the majority. "The day for parley between this man on that side and that man on the other is at an end," he wrote to MacBeth, "we should hold no conference except with the union committee itself." [37]

Many unionists, believing disruption to be inevitable, also argued against any proposal to postpone union. Robert Haddow pressed this view forcefully. "No church union of importance," he said, "has ever been effected without a measure of loss, and in the present instance the step proposed is so radical and involves such a break with tradition that the loss must be naturally greater." All organized society, he continued, was divided into progressive and conservative elements, and no movement involving a departure from use and wont was ever launched without opposition. The opposition to the union movement, he said, was twofold. Some opposed union on principle and others on the grounds of expediency. There was no hope of conciliating by delay those who opposed union on principle. Those who opposed the union on the grounds of expediency believed that the imminent schism in the Presbyterian Church was too great a price to pay. However, if schism in the Presbyterian Church was an evil, Haddow argued, what of the enormous and manifold schism existing in the Church of Christ? "There lies before us in Canada," he concluded, "the opportunity of being the first to lay a healing hand upon these wounds in the body of Christ. Shall we reject that opportunity?[38]

Those unionists who had accepted the fact that a breach was inevitable were prepared for a showdown. But those for whom the prospect of disruption was painful tried to avert what they perceived as disaster. In the first few months of 1917, these moderates began to make themselves heard and to exert pressure on the union committee to reconsider the stand which had been taken at the previous Assembly. A number of overtures to the General Assembly were also being debated in various presbyteries, requesting the assembly to take measures to prevent a disruption of the church. By February, the *Message* could report that there were "many evidences which show an increasing distrust of the hasty and illconsidered action of the last Assembly."[39]

Though the unionists found themselves on the defensive early in the year, they were nonetheless able to exert pressure where it would hurt most. The first indication of their direct action against the Presbyterian Church Association was a brief announcement of the resignation of Dr. Andrew Robertson from his pulpit at St. James' Square Church in Toronto.[40] According to the *Globe*, his resignation was precipitated by the receipt of letters from members of the congregation criticizing his opposition to church union.[41] Both Principal Gandier, the congregation's former minister, and President Falconer, chairman of the new union committee, together with other prominent unionists, were members of St. James Square. In the face of such opposition, it would have been difficult for any man to survive, and after the convocation Robertson was so prominently associated with the dissidents that it was impossible for him to continue his ministry. As it turned out, there was ultimately no Presbyterian church in Canada open to him, and he was forced to accept a call to the Broadway Presbyterian Church in Nashville, Tennessee.

The removal of Robertson gave the dissidents grounds for the charge of intimidation. There were many ministers, they argued, who refrained from taking a stand because they feared the consequences which might ensue "at the hands of some of our 'noble progressives.'" The unionist tactics were compared to the Inquisition and the ecclesiastical bastinado, with their power to mark men for "execution." The intolerance of some unionist leaders seemed to indicate that anyone who opposed the disruption of the Presbyterian Church "should be pilloried as recusants, deserving of condemnation or a punishment more condign." It was even rumoured that if the unionists had known Daniel Fraser was a dissident, his appointment as principal of the Presbyterian College, Montreal, would never have been made. The rumour was unfounded because Fraser had made his views known in an article published in the *Harvard Theological Review* a year prior to his appointment.[42] But the dissidents used it to argue that if prejudice would ignore a man of conspicuous ability who could meet the needs of an important institution, it was no wonder that "men in less influential positions, and less able to defend themselves, should yield to intimidation."[43]

Another attempt by the unionists to counteract the moderates' effort at compromise was the formation of a Unionist Publicity Committee in Montreal, composed of W.M. Birks, B.K. Sandwell, J.M. Gibbon, and the Rev. R. Bruce Taylor. This committee published a number of articles on union by leaders of the Presbyterian Church, including a public appeal to the people of Canada, signed by well-known laymen selected from all parts of the country. Like the forced resignation of Robertson, this project backfired badly. The main problem was that fourteen of the forty-eight who signed the appeal, including W.M. Birks, were not members of the Presbyterian Church in Canada, but belonged to the American Presbyterian Church, which was associated with the Presbytery of New York. Dr. Bruce Taylor, secretary of the committee and minister of St. Paul's Presbyterian Church in Montreal also had been in Canada only a few years. Thus, men who were not even members of the Presbyterian Church in Canada, or who had only recently joined it, were calling for its obliteration. Moreover, the elitism of their appeal offended the dissidents. Ephraim Scott scorned them for trying to make an impression by publishing a list of prominent laymen who supported union and by attaching the author's photograph to their articles. "Presbyterians usually do their own thinking," he said. "They do not suppose that a little prominence in finance, politics or law specially qualifies for deciding questions of faith and conscience for others." The committee did publish some effective articles, but under the continuous criticism of Scott and the *Message,* their project finally collapsed.

One of the marks of organizational effectiveness is the ability to make a threat stick. By that standard, the measures taken by the dissidents were certainly effective. The dissidents described the General Assembly of 1916 as a "Western Stampede" which threw the church into disruption. They argued that the decision of that assembly should be reconsidered and gave point to their suggestion through the convocation and the formation of the Presbyterian Church Association. Within three weeks of that event, Ballantyne gave notice of his motion to postpone the consummation of union. By the time the assembly met in June 1917, it was faced with eleven formal overtures from presbyteries and synods all across the church urging in one form or another that some way be found to avoid schism and disruption. Following the Winnipeg Assembly, the unionists had said, "Union is an accomplished fact." Within one year, however, the dissidents had, largely with the help of moderates, forced them to retreat. The radical unionists were prepared to pay the price of disruption and schism, but the moderates, under Ballantyne's leadership, believed that such a price was unacceptable. Consequently, by the time the General Assembly met at Montreal, the radical unionists again found themselves unable to use the assembly's decision of 1916 for the immediate consummation of union.

7

The Truce

Throughout the spring of 1917, the Presbyterian Church Association kept up their devastating pressure of propaganda against the unionists. As they did so, the unionists tried harder than ever to convince everyone that the issue had been settled by the previous assembly. The Winnipeg Assembly, they suggested, had seen a vision, "a vision of our nation's need and the world's need of the life giving Gospel: a vision also of how that need could be met, promptly and efficiently, by the well organized effort of a United Christian Church." The great question was whether the commissioners to the 1917 Assembly would reaffirm this vision. The unionists readily admitted that this vision was shot with the "dread" that union with others could only be achieved by parting company with "some of our own household." Therefore, every effort was made to remind the commissioners to the 1917 Assembly that "pain is the price of progress" and that "great causes come to their own, not by smooth and easy ways, but by conflict and tribulation."[1]

Faced with the implacable opposition of the Presbyterian Church Association, the unionists suggested that the necessary legislation for union should be sought immediately instead of waiting until after the close of the war. If the activities of the Presbyterian Church Association were not immediately countered, "the Presbyterian element in the United Church will be weaker than it ought to be," and waiting would create a state of civil war within the Presbyterian Church.[2] W.R. Motherwell of Regina strongly underlined the absurdity of leaving the date for the consummation of the union up to the Kaiser. "Like extracting a refractory tooth," he said, "let us have it out and be over with it, even though it does cause some pain at the time."[3]

Both sides were fighting so hard that no one asked what would happen if the 1917 Assembly reached a new understanding to end hostilities. The unionists thought any delay would mean victory for the dissidents. Apparently, they did not realize that resistance organizations thrive when there is something to resist but collapse without a cause to champion. Even the resistance movement did not seem to understand this fact until they discovered themselves deeply in debt and unable to drum up any enthusiasm for paying the bills after the fight was over. As in other conflicts, victory and defeat turned out to be ambivalent for the combatants. The Presbyterian Church Association emerged out of the ashes of defeat in 1916 with what seemed substantial gains, only to discover that the fruits of victory are more often bitter than sweet.

Following his resignation from St. James Square in Toronto, Andrew Robertson became the executive secretary of the Presbyterian Church Association and devoted his full time to its national organization. Working on the assumption that the parting of the ways was inevitable, the association's object was to sign up as many members as possible. The strategy they planned was to offer resistance by applying to the courts to prevent the transfer of the Presbyterian Church's property and funds to the proposed United Church, by opposing any application for enabling legislation, and by preparing to assume the administration of the church against the contingency of ultimate disruption. If these goals were to be realized, it was imperative that every Presbyterian in sympathy with them should be enrolled as a member of the association, "in order that weight of numbers may be added to the weight of reason and justice in the cause."[4] All communicants and adherents of the Presbyterian Church over fifteen years of age were eligible for membership.[5]

The association was certain they could establish their legitimate claim to the trusts and interests of the Presbyterian Church. The difficulty, they believed, would arise when the legislatures asked whether they were able to administer the trusts and properties. The key to meeting this crucial test in an incontrovertible way would lie in their membership lists. Each name added to the list would help to win the association's cause. Those who failed to sign would "by that much assist to defeat the interests of the Presbyterian Church."[6] The subscription campaign was conducted by representatives of the Presbyterian Church Association making a house to house canvass of the Presbyterians in their area. All members and adherents of the church over fifteen years of age were invited to sign cards for membership in the association. The effort was not confined to congregations that voted against union, but extended into unionist domains. This did not pass without comment. "The wedge of division," said Robert Haddow, "is being thrust into every congregation in the land."[7]

The membership drive was supplemented by equally effective pamphlet literature. The *Message*, edited by Thomas Eakin and Andrew Robertson, was distributed nationally by the organization. This official publication was supplemented by a number of pamphlets, the most effective of which was a series of twenty-one "Letters to an Inquirer" by Ephraim Scott, which

appeared in May 1917.[8] Although Scott's arguments suffered from incon-
sistencies, their scope was impressive. One of his letters in particular made a
damaging case against the unionists by answering the question: "If we
oppose this change is it not possible we are fighting against God?" Scott
suggested that Christ Himself had given a simple unerring test in such cases:
"By their fruits ye shall know them" (Matt 7:16). The unionists had belittled
those who did not think union the wisest course, had attempted to suppress
the dissidents' viewpoint by refusing their literature and speakers access to
many congregations, and had used coercion to force the issue through the
church courts regardless of increased opposition. On these grounds Scott
concluded that "the fruits of this movement from first to last show it is not of
God." In the name of Christian unity, the union movement was destroying
the unity of the Presbyterian Church. Instead of healing divisions, it had led
to greater division.

The most telling tactic of the Presbyterian Church Association was to
hold a second convocation in Montreal on 5 and 6 June 1917, just before the
General Assembly. This very proximity made the crisis in the church apparent.
As a report in the *Montreal Star* aptly observed, "The man in the street will
ask in what relation do they stand to each other?" The unionists saw it as
rebellion, whereas the dissidents held that the General Assembly was no
longer "true to her commission."[9]

The object of the dissidents' convocation was to reaffirm the Toronto
convocation's covenant to preserve and maintain the Presbyterian Church
and to remind the commissioners that if they did not take immediate action
disruption and schism would result. Approximately two hundred and fifty
persons were present at the meeting, which was chaired by Principal Fraser.
The majority of speakers reported on the growth of anti-union sentiment
across the country, but otherwise offered little that was new. Frank Baird of
Woodstock, N.B., assured the delegates that "the loyalist province of New
Brunswick would be loyal—when the unionists attempted to disturb the
church." Dr. Ephraim Scott observed that the "centre of controversy had
shifted from the earlier question as to whether the church approved union to
the later question of whether it would submit to be driven into surrendering
its existence for a proposed new one. But loyal Presbyterians would not
accept by coercion that which they would not accept from conviction."[10] A
different note was struck by the Hon. R.M. MacGregor of New Glasgow,
N.S., who was the only speaker to advocate further efforts at conciliation. In
terms of subsequent events, however, his speech proved to be the most
significant of all. Believing that the seriousness of the crisis demanded
conciliation rather than recriminations, he deprecated the convocation's
talk of "the parting of the ways." Personally, he was prepared "to go a long
way to meet his unionist friends and have the matter shelved for the time

being." If such a truce was not possible, he hoped there would be some way of getting together and avoiding "the scandal of going into all the civil courts and legislatures to get the difficulties settled."[11]

The convocation concluded by sending an open letter to the moderator and commissioners of the General Assembly. The letter stated that "We have no right to forget that the church has by more than one of its leaders given expression to its faith on this question." It then went on to quote statements made by Principal Patrick to the effect that "from first to last the question must be a people's question," by President Falconer to the effect that "it would be utter madness to go forward to a union that did not carry the whole Church with it," and by Professor T.B. Kilpatrick to the effect that "it is agreed on all hands that union must not be engineered, must not be a paper union accomplished in committees, but must be an organic union accomplished in the hearts of the members of the churches concerned." The letter concluded that "this is the faith of the church on the matter. It is in reliance upon the good faith of these utterances that the movement has reached even the stage to which it has come. This is the faith by which it must guide itself until the end. If the confidence of the church is not to be utterly wrecked, then this faith 'agreed on all hands,' as Professor Kilpatrick declares, must be kept without fail."[12]

The membership drive, the pamphlet literature, and the convocation were important factors in keeping the pressure on the unionists. It was neither the unionists nor the dissidents, however, who would have their way in the 1917 Assembly. It was the moderates responding to the numerous overtures on union which the presbyteries and synods had sent forward to the assembly who really determined the issue in 1917.

The assembly opened on the last day of the convocation, but the report of the union committee was not presented by Sir Robert Falconer until three days later. He was not in a conciliatory mood and began by launching an attack on Ephraim Scott and the *Record* committee for refusing to publish "A Message to Sessions." Falconer said that he protested against this action on the ground that the union committee was simply carrying out the policy of the assembly, which was not a "controversial matter." In Falconer's view the assembly's policy on union was no longer debateable. "It is finally fixed," he said, "and was so announced to the other negotiating churches." Therefore, he asserted "the question of policy ought not to be again discussed."

There was one qualification here, however, and that was the large number of overtures on the question of union which the assembly had received. Falconer recommended that the moderator appoint to the union committee ten additional men representing various opinions for the purpose of considering the overtures.[13] A motion to this effect was presented by Dr. Alex MacGillivray and Mr. John Fleming. Dr. R.W. Dickie of Montreal thought it would be wise to submit the overtures to a more representative committee consisting of thirty-five men, of which fifteen could represent the union committee, fifteen could represent the opposition, and ten could represent neutral opinion. Dickie's arithmetic was faulty because this would have resulted in a committee of forty, but in any case his amendment was defeated by a vote of 139 to 120. Consequently, the committee to consider the overtures consisted of the union committee plus ten men named by the moderator. Only four of these represented the opposition: Leslie Clay, Judge Farrell, Frank Baird, and William O. Mulligan.[14] It was agreed that there would be no debate of the union committee's report until this committee made its report.

Predictably, it issued two reports. The majority recommended that the assembly reaffirm its duty to keep faith with the other negotiating churches, that no further action be taken until the second assembly after the close of the war, and that debate and organized propagandism on either side be discontinued in the meantime. The minority recommended that the assembly recognize the widespread anxiety which existed over the disruption of the church, that it agree to refer the whole question of organic union to the people once again after the war, and that in the meantime all agitation on the question should cease. The minority report was presented as an amendment, and the situation was further complicated by an amendment to the amendment offered by R.W. Dickie and Professor W.G. Jordan of Queen's, which suggested that the date for further action be extended to 1922, that the union committee confine itself in the meantime to co-operating with the negotiating churches, and that all parties refrain from propaganda and controversy during this period.[15]

In the debate that followed, the implicit issues became clear. In speaking to the minority's amendment, Leslie Clay recommended that the assembly's union committee be disbanded because its very existence, especially in its revised form since 1916, was "itself a propaganda." Judge Farrell was even more specific. He objected to the majority report because it affirmed the principle of union which was "the very bone of contention" and continued the union committee while asking the other side to call a halt. This was not, in his opinion, "a square deal." Dr. Dickie said that he represented those who had not taken a prominent part in the discussion up to this point and who regarded the promotion of union in the Presbyterian Church as the paramount issue. Although he had voted for union at six assemblies, he called a halt when the impending disruption of the church became evident. The reason for his amendment to the amendment was that he felt the minority were asking too much when they wanted the union committee disbanded and the matter referred to the people for a third vote. On the other hand, he did not like the main motion "because it probated the honor of the church which is unnecessary."

On the morning of 12 June as the debate continued, Dr. Thurlow Fraser and G.M. Macdonnell suggested that "the movers and seconders of the various motions be instructed to retire and try to bring in a common deliverance." Before the voting on this motion took place, Daniel Fraser spoke and warned that if Robert Falconer's motion went through there would be greater indignation than ever amongst the constituency which the Presbyterian Church Association represented. "The resolutions had a fine literary style," he said, "but they showed an almost cynical indifference to the sentiments represented in the Presbyterian Association."[16] When Principal Fraser was finished, Fraser and Macdonnell's motion was carried unanimously and the movers and seconders of the respective motions retired for consultation.

That same evening Falconer and Clay returned to the assembly with a compromise motion which became the basis for the truce. It asked the assembly to recognize the desire expressed in many of the overtures that disunion within the Presbyterian Church be avoided, to urge all parties that they cease their controversy on the matter of organic union, and to confine the work of the union committee to the superintendence of such practical forms of co-operation as had already been authorized. As soon as the motion had been moved and seconded, Principal Fraser rose and moved that it be adopted without debate. When this was agreed to by a unanimous standing vote, the assembly spontaneously broke into singing: "Praise God from whom all blessings flow."

In keeping with the spirit of the occasion, President Falconer asked on behalf of the union committee that before its report was presented for adoption, permission be granted to delete all references in it to the *Record*. This was agreed to and the union committee's report was adopted. The next afternoon Dr. D.R. Drummond moved that the matter of the union committee's personnel be referred to the same committee which had worked out the truce, and they added Daniel Fraser, Andrew Robertson, C.S. McDonald, Leslie Clay, T.F. Fullerton, G.M. Macdonnell, and James Rodger to the committee.

In his report on the assembly, even Ephraim Scott enthusiastically praised the solution which had been found. The assembly, he said, had opened in cloud, cold and rain which reflected the uncertainty, anxiety, and foreboding of many concerning the impending crisis. It closed on "as lovely a June day as seen in any clime," which reflected the universal thanksgiving of the church that the long impending strain and shadow of this cloud were so simply and quickly gone. "Strong men are wont to veil their emotions," concluded Scott, "but it is safe to say that there were more full hearts and moist eyes that night than ever before in an Assembly of our church."[17] After this exercise in brinksmanship, the relief was so great that it took some time before both sides started to face the realities of the new situation.

The executive of the Presbyterian Church Association met on 26 June 1917, and the Finance Committee was instructed to take measures to raise $12,000 to cover present liabilities and provide sufficient funds for carrying the expenses of the office until the next year. Up to this point the association had made no serious effort at fund raising. Following the 1916 convocation they had tried to sell shares in a company to produce a newspaper but—as C.S. McDonald had predicted—this campaign came nowhere near raising the projected $100,000. They had, however, published five issues of the *Message* and hired Andrew Robertson as executive secretary. There were expenses in running an office, maintaining a stenographer and paying for Fraser's and Robertson's trip out West in the spring of 1917. They had also footed the bill for the Montreal Convocation in June.

Their method of financing all of this activity was to establish a $25,000 line of credit with the Imperial Bank on the strength of a series of guarantee bonds which were sent to the different provincial associations for signatures. The only persons to respond, however, were a few friends in the Maritimes, who guaranteed some $2,750 worth of these bonds, and John Penman, who signed a guarantee for $2,000. These guarantees were sent to the bank without any effort being made to secure a larger body of guarantors. Consequently, for almost a year the association was trading on their guarantee alone.[18]

By 26 June 1917 everyone recognized that this was a very improper and risky way to finance the movement, especially when their existing liabilities were in the neighborhood of $7,000. As a way out of the predicament, the association launched a serious drive for funds. By 6 September 1917 they had received only $3,500 of the projected $12,000. The summer months were not the best time for fund raising, but what was most startling was the picture that emerged when the contributions were broken down from the different provinces as follows:

Prince Edward Island	2.00
Nova Scotia	82.25
New Brunswick	7.00
Quebec	1,226.25
Ontario	2,005.00
Manitoba	113.00
Saskatchewan	18.50
Alberta	40.50
British Columbia	3.00

On 6 September 1917, therefore, the Finance Committee sent out a confidential letter to all the provincial associations, suggesting the minimum amounts that would be a fair distribution of the $12,000 which had to be raised in order to meet present liabilities and keep the office open until the end of the year. These were as follows:

Prince Edward Island	250.00
Nova Scotia	1,500.00
New Brunswick	750.00
Quebec	2,000.00
Ontario	4,000.00
Manitoba	1,000.00
Saskatchewan	1,000.00
Alberta	1,000.00
British Columbia	500.00

The letter concluded by asking for an acknowledgement by 5 October 1917 and suggesting that in view of the importance of the work, the assigned amounts were not really very large.[19]

The response to this letter, however, was negligible. Consequently, the executive issued a further circular indicating first of all, that the association was still maintaining an office, was still in existence, and was urgently in need of funds. Secondly, it pointed out that while it had ceased all operations, there was still a role for it in policing the truce. To underline this fact, the circular pointed out that there were several loopholes in the 1917 truce agreement which needed to be understood by all.

Under the terms of the truce the Union Committee was confined "to the superintendence of such practical forms of co-operation as have already been authorized." At first glance these instructions appeared unambiguous, but as Andrew Robertson pointed out, further scrutiny revealed that these instructions could be variously construed. Prior to 1916, co-operation was an end in itself, but following the decision of the Winnipeg Assembly to enter the union, co-operation could now be seen as a forerunner of the proposed new church. On behalf of the dissidents, Robertson denied that co-operation with a view to organic union was legitimate. The unionists, however, believed that efforts should still be made to eliminate overlapping and competition among the negotiating churches. Moreover, they contended that if such co-operative unions were a success and produced a demand for a larger union, then this would clearly indicate the path of duty which the church should follow. In this way, as Robert Haddow put it, "The co-operative movement might 'further' the decision of the Winnipeg Assembly, but no one would be to blame."[20]

Haddow's peculiar phrasing of the matter in terms of "blame" concealed a unionist arrangement which Andrew Robertson suspected but could not document. The arrangement involved two simple steps. Sir Robert Falconer never called a meeting of the expanded union committee of 1917, and therefore the responsibility for superintending the practical forms of co-operation passed to the board of Home Missions under the chairmanship of George Pidgeon. Many years later, Pidgeon wrote in his "memorabilia" on church union:

> When Dr. Ballantyne asked me to sign a petition to the Assembly for a truce, I explained that I could not honestly do so. I said: I am head of the Board that will do more to bring union into effect than any other agency the moment that local unions are allowed, and I should be charged justly with double-dealing, if I signed a petition for a truce and then led such a movement.[21]

By the time the truce was over and George Pidgeon became chairman of the union committee in 1921, 1,260 mission charges had united. This meant, as Pidgeon pointed out, that "over 3,000 worshipping units had already united on the basis of their church's decision to enter the union in 1916."[22] Not signing a petition might have saved Pidgeon from pangs of conscience, but whether, in retrospect, it frees the unionists from the charge of double-dealing is another question. As the dissidents understood the terms, they could not engage in any organized activity against union. The unionists, on the other hand, entered the truce with the mental reservation of the casuist and refused to abide by the truce in terms which would preclude activity in furthering the interests of church union.

The realization that this would be the new strategy of the union committee could not have come at a more awkward time for the Presbyterian Church Association. They were deeply in debt, they were restrained by their understanding of the truce from launching a public campaign to expose these violations, and consequently there was no way to gain public support for their financial campaign. In order to economize, they closed their office in the Kent Building and opened a new one in the Confederation Life Building next door to the *Presbyterian* offices on the sixth floor. In their new quarters, which they managed to rent for $18.00 a month (one-quarter of the rent for their previous accommodation), they had little else besides a rented desk and telephone. They could not afford a stenographer, and Andrew Robertson found himself doing alone almost everything that had to be done.

By 1 March 1918 the situation had not improved. In a desperate letter to Principal Fraser, Andrew Robertson detailed the dismal response which they had received in their financial drive. "As you know," he wrote, "we have been trying since the month of September last to arouse the conscience of the Association in connection with the financial support which the Association needs and deserves at the hands of all those who would preserve the church in its integrity in this Dominion." Outside of Ontario and Quebec, however, the response had been minimal. "Look at the figures," he said:

Manitoba	113.00
Nova Scotia	86.00
Alberta	65.00
Saskatchewan	18.00
New Brunswick	7.00
British Columbia	4.00
Prince Edward Island	2.00

He acknowledged that Fraser was not expected to take any responsibility for fund raising, but he pointed out that the financial situation was threatening the very existence of the association. "It is not in reason to expect," he said, "that an Association like ours should drift along to bankruptcy and to shame." Therefore, he requested a meeting of the General Committee at the earliest possible date.[23]

Under this financial pressure real differences had emerged between the Toronto and Montreal members of the association. Montreal had agreed that Professor D.A. Murray and Robert Campbell's son, George A. Campbell, would undertake to raise the $2,000 which the committee had agreed was Quebec's share of the expenses. However, when the members of the Toronto Finance Committee suggested that further guarantees should be placed in the bank so that they could secure the funds to meet pressing liabilities, the Montreal executive initially refused to solicit further guarantors on bonds of $100.00 each to cover their $7,000 liability with the bank and provide a further $8,000 working capital.

Robertson finally managed to persuade them to produce their share of guarantors when he pointed out that the friends in the Maritime provinces who had been amongst the original guarantors refused to release any of the funds they had collected until this inequity was cleared up. Further, he reminded them that the Finance Committee was not asking the Montreal members to do anything that the Toronto men had not already done. To make his point, Robertson gave a list of the Ontario men who had each signed bonds for $100.00 a piece together with the amount they had donated for current expenses. The list was as follows:

Mr. C.S. McDonald	$500.00 and bond
Mr. Joseph Henderson	$300.00
Mr. John MacKay	$250.00
Mr. John Michie	$125.00

Mr. Angus Sinclair	$250.00
Mr. James Scott	$400.00
Mr. James Turnbull	$400.00
Mr. W.D. Ross	$250.00
Mr. George Hope	$50.00
Mr. William Hendrie	$100.00

Mr. John Penman (since the beginning of the year) $1,450.00 and 4 bonds.

Apparently this list was all that was necessary, for Professor D.A. Murray was the first to respond with his guarantee and others soon followed.[24] James Rodger sent his guarantee for $1,000.00, but confided to C.S. McDonald that, to begin with, he had had some reluctance. He had already put out between $400 and $500 and he said, "I feel pretty confident in my own mind that the guarantors will each be called upon to pay the greater part of the amount of their guarantee, as I do not see from what other source the money is likely to come. It is a matter like many another one, which has to be financed by a comparatively small number, even though the benefit which it is expected will accrue will be for the benefit of a very large number."[25]

While Robertson was sorting out these problems, typing his own letters with frequent mistakes and never, as he admitted, mastering the duplicating machine so that copies of the minutes could be circulated, he was acutely aware of two things. First, it was impossible to raise money since the truce, because "our constituency have persuaded themselves that there is no further need for aid."[26] He believed this was a mistake of the worst kind because while everything looked calm on the surface, the unionists were trying to hustle the church into union. Under "the camouflage of innocent seeming co-operation they are making dispositions of districts and congregations which will change the complexion of the vote, if another should be taken after the war."[27] With this going on and the association apparently on the verge of bankruptcy, Robertson was soul-sick because he felt it would be "practically impossible to recreate the Association if it goes out of business—this is the danger and it is on this that the other side are counting."[28]

The second matter on Robertson's mind was the fact that as general secretary he was the biggest single continuing drain on finances. Consequently, through the early months of 1918 he was looking for a position elsewhere. As he confided to C.S. McDonald, "there is not much chance of my getting another settlement in Canada, at least for some time to come. As you know I am anxious to relieve the Association of its obligations to me at the earliest possible moment. It is just possible that the visit I am going on now [to Pittsburgh] may open up the way for a permanency in the States, or at least give me an opportunity of getting myself known."[29] Nothing immediately happened as a result of his visit to Pittsburgh, but Robertson handed in his resignation as executive secretary, effective June 1918. As he wrote to A.H. MacGillivray, "this leaves the Association free from all further obligation to me, and in a very large degree simplifies the financial situation."[30] Within a month he preached his farewell sermon in Toronto and was off to the U.S.A.

While the truce brought an end to the controversy within the Presbyterian Church, it did not bring an end to all discussion. The Methodists, for example, were not a party to the truce, and they were free to discuss the matter wherever they wished. The public at large was equally free to raise the issue in the international Protestant journals. During the truce, therefore, interest in the prospects of church union in Canada was sustained, and so absorbing was that interest that it eclipsed the conflict within the Presbyterian Church in Canada.

Discussion of the proposed Canadian experiment began in 1913 in the international Protestant journals when Sir Robert Falconer mentioned it in an article on "The Present Position of the Churches in Canada."[31] In discussing the problems facing the Canadian churches, such as urbanization, the depletion of the countryside, and the magnitude of immigration to Canada, Falconer indicated that efforts to cope with these problems had impressed upon the churches the need for co-operation and had raised the question of organic union, especially among the nonepiscopal Protestant churches. Emphasizing the practical character of this proposed venture and its parallels with political experimentation in Canada, Falconer said, "Confederation arose out of the pressures of provincial necessities: religious union if it comes will be the result not of theory but of practical urgency."

Two years later, Daniel J. Fraser focused attention on the Presbyterian opposition to union in the *Harvard Theological Review*.[32] Fraser favoured co-operation rather than organic union as he made clear in his discussion of the theological colleges affiliated with McGill University and the organization of the Church Union League. However, unlike many of the Presbyterians who opposed union, Fraser was not a theological conservative. He was a liberal who thought that the Doctrinal Statement in the "Basis of Union" was not an improvement on the Westminster Confession. "Its prescientific account of the origin of sin, its pathological view of human nature, and its crude statement of human solidarity," he said, "represent a distinct victory for the traditionalists." Moreover, as a modern statement of faith, it failed to be "a working theory of life today" for those "brought up in the atmosphere of evolutionary thought." This was especially true in the light of attacks on Dr. George Jackson and Dr. George C. Workman by some militant leaders of the Methodist Church which "left an impression of dogmatic intolerance of scientific investigation, scribal literalism, a lack of human kindness and a certain almost cynical indifference to causing public scandal." By 1915 Canadian unionists were used to attacks from theological conservatives, but this attack from a fellow liberal seemed to leave them confused, for no one attempted to answer Fraser. Such liberal criticism, however, could not continue to be ignored because other critics raised similar questions.

Among these was Father Herbert H. Kelly, the founder of the Society of the Sacred Mission, an Anglican monastic order, and one of the few Anglo-Catholic theologians to take an early interest in the ecumenical movement. He became aware of the Canadian church union movement when he visited Canada and the United States in March and April 1912. In a 1917 article in the *Constructive Quarterly,* Kelly attempted to examine the Doctrinal Statement in the "Basis of Union" from a "Catholic" point of view.[33] His intention was "not to criticize but to be quite sure of the meaning" and he hoped that if there were a number of points which seemed ambiguous or different from the "Catholic" view, "some competent person on behalf of the U.C.C. will explain to us what is meant and how far the difference is intentional." The person who rose to this challenge was Dr. T.B. Kilpatrick, Professor of systematic theology at Knox College, Toronto, who was later described by George Pidgeon as "one of Scotland's greatest gifts to Canada."[34]

Kelly's first question focused on the statement that the Scriptures contain "the only infallible rule of faith and life and a faithful record of God's gracious revelations." Kelly suggested that "at the present day these are rather strong assertions" and the wording seemed to be a definite repudiation of the modern critical view. In his reply, Kilpatrick unequivocally defended the statement. He said:

I venture to think that 'infallible' is an epithet which may justly be used in reference to the rule of faith and life contained in Scripture; and I am sure that the authors of the document did mean that God's gracious revelations to His chosen servants, and through them to mankind, throughout the Old Testament and the New Testament are matters of historic fact. If the modern critical view reduces the history to fable or parable, so much the worse for the modern critical view!

Pursuing the matter further, Kelly suggested that the articles on the Trinity, the Virgin Birth and the Atonement were from a "Catholic" point of view "a little ultra orthodox." He asked, therefore, whether a candidate for ordination would be accepted if he held "modern critical views" and could not accept the "homoousian," the Virgin Birth, and the phrase "satisfied Divine justice" with reference to the Atonement. In his reply, Kilpatrick drew a distinction between the Virgin Birth and technical theological terms such as "ousia" and "satisfactio." On the former, Kilpatrick declared:

> The Virgin Birth is a fact of history....The man who denies it has no right to use the Apostle's Creed, or any other creed which contains it, as his personal confession of faith....As long as the Virgin Birth holds its place in the Creed, no man should be ordained who denies it.

This was a statement designed to make many pro-union liberals wince. However, Kilpatrick's suggestion that the "ousia" and "satisfactio" were technical theological terms, which did not necessarily give adequate expression to the divinity of Christ or the significance of His atoning work as declared by the New Testament, must have reassured them that not all liberals would be tried for heresy in the new church.

When the discussion moved on to questions about the church, the ministry, and the sacraments, the differences between the "Catholic" and "Protestant" perspectives of Kelly and Kilpatrick became much clearer. On these subjects Kilpatrick's theological outlook did not produce formulations which would offend liberals. Indeed, his answers to Kelly's questions seemed to reflect what most pro-unionists believed to be the essential theological differences between their position and that of the Anglo-Catholics in this period. This exchange between Kelly and Kilpatrick was an important examination of doctrinal issues which would have gained in depth if Kilpatrick had additionally addressed himself to Kelly's *The Church and Religious Unity*, which contained a sustained treatment of the issues Kelly had raised in his article.[35]

In 1919 Ernest Thomas, who was to become one of the most outstanding journalists to serve the United Church of Canada, brought American audiences up to date on the subject of church union with an article in the *American Journal of Theology*.[36] As a Methodist, Thomas was firmly committed to union because he saw the movement as a reversal of the Protestant revolution with its tendency towards religious separatism. In his excellent review of the background of the movement, the "Basis of Union," and the problems which had arisen within the Presbyterian Church, he revealed that he was aware of the "social differences" between Methodists and Presbyterians which were rarely referred to in public discussion, but were nevertheless "no insignificant part of the more private discussion of the matter." He also emphasized that "there is no ambiguity" concerning the status of the declaration of faith in the "Basis of Union." Unlike Kilpatrick, Thomas was certain that it would be impossible for any court of the church in the future to find itself obliged "to condemn as heretical a minister whose character and teaching it approved, solely on the ground that the written standards of the church so define the faith as to prevent them from maintaining fellowship with such a minister."

In referring to the position of the Anglicans regarding church union in Canada, Thomas believed that they were not susceptible to that same pressure of national conditions which had compelled the other communions to enter upon negotiations. The following year, however, the Right Rev.

Edward J. Bidwell, bishop of the Diocese of Ontario, in an article on "The Church of England in Canada and Reunion," raised some serious questions about this assumption.[37] His purpose was to explain to an English audience at the time of the Lambeth Conference the conditions in Canada which were raising the question of reunion in ways that were quite unique within the larger Anglican communion.

Among the pressures which Bidwell mentioned was the fact that the Anglicans in Canada had none of the prestige of a national church, since they were simply one communion among others which had to justify their existence by their message and efficiency. Secondly, with the trifling endowments they had, it was almost impossible to meet the demands of the expanding West. Most important of all was the ever-present danger that "sheer stark materialism may triumph over all spiritual ideals." Therefore, Bidwell's conclusion was that the only chance the "spiritual forces in Canada have of triumphing over the foe of sheer materialism which threatens to destroy them is by uniting those forces in one common task." "We are engaged," Bidwell continued, "in endeavouring, in the face of great difficulties to build up a nation on the only sure and lasting basis—that of righteousness. And the feeling is shared by most religious leaders of all communions in Canada that, while by a strong united effort we might grapple with the task with some hope of success, it appears to be almost beyond our powers in our present divided condition."

Bidwell's appeal seems to have struck a responsive chord in the Church of England, for the Lambeth Conference in July 1920 issued its famous "Appeal to All Christian People," which urged Anglican churches throughout the world to initiate discussion concerning church union. In response to this appeal, the Most Reverend S.P. Matheson, the primate of the Church of England in Canada, appointed a committee in 1921 to meet official representatives of other denominations. An active correspondence developed between the primate and the Rev. George Pidgeon, the recently appointed convenor of the Presbyterian union committee. However, with the Presbyterians deeply split, it was decided not to complicate the issue and to leave further discussions with the Anglicans until after union had been achieved with the three negotiating denominations.[38]

The significance of this wider discussion of the Canadian experiment was that it kept the prospect alive both at home and abroad without violating the truce. With the dissidents' organization moribund, they were not in a position to monitor this activity or the even more serious proliferation of union congregations. Consequently, during the truce the unionists gained the initiative, and when it was over they were in a much stronger position than when it began. The dissidents, on the other hand, found it very difficult to revive their organization when church union once again became a major issue on the General Assembly's agenda.

8

The Resumption of Hostilities

The second assembly after the war met at Chalmers Church, Ottawa, in June 1920. One of the principal items on the agenda was a letter from Sir Robert Falconer which expressed grave doubts about the existence of the union committee which had not met since it was appointed in 1917. Sharing Falconer's concern, the assembly referred his letter to a committee especially constituted to consider the matter. The convener, Principal W.H. Smith of Westminster Hall, Vancouver, recommended that the 1917 committee on union be reappointed to deal with several overtures that had been received on the subject. Robert Campbell, in what was to be his final official act with reference to church union before he died, seconded this recommendation.[1]

The reactivation of the union committee marked the beginning of the final stage of the union debate. It was not apparent until 1921 that this act would involve the resumption of hostilities, and it was not until after the 1922 Assembly, which again met in Winnipeg, that a level of hostility and bitterness would be reached similar to that following the Winnipeg Assembly of 1916. But, since this stage of the union question involved the seeking of legislation to establish the United Church of Canada, there was little prospect that conflict could be avoided. The only question was when and how it would break out.

The truce between 1917 and 1921 had been uneasy; the union issue had not been resolved but merely shelved, and the battle lines remained drawn the way they had been in 1916. As World War I came to an end and the nation began to return to normalcy, the Presbyterian Church began to find more time to discuss the union issue, especially during the year prior to the 1921 Assembly. Four presbyteries forwarded overtures on the subject to the assembly that year. In addition, the Presbyteries of Brandon, Manitoba, and MacLeod, Alberta, specifically urged the assembly to act on the question. Both referred to the large number of union congregations which had come into existence during the truce. There were now approximately four hundred united congregations on one hundred and sixty charges in the Synods of Manitoba, Saskatchewan, and Alberta. This figure represented 43 per cent of the self-sustaining charges in these synods, excluding the cities. These congregations, together with those in Northern Ontario, as the overture from the Presbytery of Timiskaming pointed out, were growing restless and "weary of waiting for the highest court of our church to take action." Co-operation had been successful in many areas, but now there were problems arising from unused, deteriorating church property and from the action of many congregations which were entering into negotiations for union churches free from denominational ties. Only the overture from the Presbytery of Pictou, N.S., requested that the assembly make every effort to maintain the peace and unity of the church and postpone final action on the question "until the matter has again been submitted to the people for their verdict."[2] It was this overture drafted by the Rev. D.M. Matheson, of Stellarton, N.S., and the Rev. R. Johnston of New Glasgow, N.S., which foreshadowed the position the dissidents would take in the future debate.

The action of the dissidents following the 1916 Assembly showed that they continued to resist the decision to proceed with organic union. In view of the increased opposition revealed in the 1915 vote, they believed that the assembly's decision had been unwarranted, and to prove their point they wanted another vote. The unionists, on the other hand, believed that the issue had been finally settled in 1916. Consequently, they had no intention of once again referring the question to the people. During the truce they had gained the initiative by encouraging the formation of three thousand union congregations. These unions were founded on the understanding that the Presbyterian Church would enter the union. To reconsider the decision of 1916 and refer the question back to the people would have been to run the risk of losing these congregations to a new and separate denomination. The unionists, therefore, could not afford to look backwards. Their next logical step was to move forward as quickly as possible to draft legislation to effect union. The only question, for them, was how to achieve that purpose with as little friction as possible.

The differences between the unionists and dissidents were irreconcilable, but after the peace and calm of the truce both sides wished to avoid hostilities. As the debate on the issue resumed in the 1921 Assembly, therefore, an effort was made to approach the question cautiously. To gauge the mind of the assembly, the union committee decided to present a motion by Dr. W.J. Clark and an amendment by Principal D.J. Fraser. Clark's motion recommended that steps be taken to consummate union "as expeditiously as possible." Fraser's amendment asked that the assembly "at no time seek the consummation of organic union without a clear and unmistakable mandate from the people."[3] Put to a vote, the amendment was defeated, with 414 commissioners voting for the motion and 107 for the amendment. In the subsequent debate Dr. Clark moved that his motion become the finding of the assembly. Though the vote had been decisive, the dissidents refused to accept this defeat. Countering the unionists, Dr. Banks Nelson and the Hon. R.M. MacGregor moved an amendment which stated that in view of the fact that it had been six years since a vote had been taken on the issue, steps should be taken as soon as possible to take a further vote.[4] The moderator, C.W. Gordon, ruled this amendment out of order. Nelson, however, re-introduced his amendment regarding a third vote in reference to clause nine of the motion which referred to "the spirit of peace and harmony" manifest in the Presbyterian Church during the past four years and looked forward to the continuance of these blessings. Nelson's amendment to this clause, as reported by the *Presbyterian Witness*, read as follows: "And that for the continued peace and harmony of our church we *refer* our action to the membership of our church, *to be guided by them* as to the steps and the expedition with which organic union shall be consummated."[5] This amendment, however, never came before the assembly for a vote. It was simply referred to the union committee for consideration. But when this amendment appeared in the assembly minutes it had been edited to the point where it said something quite different from Nelson's intended meaning. It now read: "And that for the continued peace and harmony of our church, we report our action on organic union to the membership of our church, as to the steps and the expedition with which organic union shall be consummated."[6] This rephrasing was a subversion not only of Nelson's purpose but also of the deliberative machinery of the Presbyterian Church itself, for it showed an unprecedented and indefensible intervention in the assembly's proceedings by a partisan official. The 1921 minutes were the first for which Robert Campbell was not directly responsible since the union issue had been raised. R.B. Cochrane was the staunch young unionist who had succeeded him in the post of assembly clerk. Such an alteration in the wording of the amendment could not have been unintentional, and it reveals the extent to which some unionists were prepared to go in keeping the question of a third vote off the assembly's agenda. It is surprising that Nelson and his fellow dissidents slipped up on this issue, because they could have challenged the revised wording of the minutes, which would have been presented the next day to the Assembly. However, they already had other urgent concerns. Following the referral of Nelson's amendment to the union committee, attention quickly shifted from a third vote to the dissents presented by Wardlaw Taylor and Ephraim Scott against the assembly's action, and the dissidents had to bend their energies along this new line.

Taylor's dissent was a fresh attack upon the "Basis of Union." He pointed out that the assembly's adoption in 1916 of the "Basis of Union" under the terms of the Barrier Act made the Basis a law of the church. For this reason, he charged, the action of the assembly as interpreted on the floor of the house "affords no relief to those Ministers and Members of the Church who experience conscientious difficulties in accepting the said Basis."[7] Scott's dissent, in which thirty-four commissioners joined, was a more conventional statement which reiterated the assembly's actions since 1905 on the church union issue. He pointed out that pledges and promises had been made to the membership of the Presbyterian Church that were being violated by the present assembly's action.[8] Although the committee appointed to prepare an answer to this dissent was chaired by Principal John Mackay, a former leader of the dissidents, their reply differed in no way from the previous ones. It reiterated the unionists' contention that every constitutional step had been taken and that there had been no unlawful usurpation by the assembly of the people's rights.

The final act of the 1921 Assembly on the church union issue was to appoint a new committee on church union which was much less representative of all shades of opinion than the 1917 committee and to appoint a new chairman, Dr. George C. Pidgeon.[9] Pidgeon was in many ways the logical man to appoint. In 1917 he had been appointed chairman of the Home Missions and Social Service Committee. Throughout the period of the truce, he had supervised all the local unions which had taken place, thereby assuming the function of the 1917 union committee. Pidgeon's appointment as chairman of the new union committee therefore simply recognized and formalized the role he had been playing for the past four years.

The new union committee dismissed all requests for another vote. Banks Nelson's amendment to clause nine was rejected on a motion of President Murray and W.J. Clark.[10] A communication from the Presbyterian Church Association for the Maritime provinces asking that no further steps be taken without "a clear and unmistakable mandate expressed by a vote of the membership of the whole church" and an overture from the Presbytery of Red Deer also asking for another vote were read but ignored in their deliberations.[11] The main concern of the union committee at its meetings in October 1921 and January 1922 was to set up an inquiry concerning the legislation necessary to consummate organic union with the negotiating churches "as expeditiously as possible." W.N. Tilley, K.C. and Richard S. Cassels, K.C., were retained as legal counsel. At the April 1922 meetings of the committee, Principal Fraser asked that a minute be recorded giving his interpretation of this action. Fraser wanted it understood that the committee was engaging legal counsel "to make an impartial survey of the legal situation." Not having been present at the meeting when this action was taken he wanted to make sure the information from this survey would be available to the whole church and not exclusively to the section of it committed to consummating the union.

When the union committee met again during the 1922 General Assembly at Winnipeg, it received an extremely detailed memorandum from counsel as to the legal status of the Presbyterian Church and the federal and provincial legislation relevant to its property and funds. The committee was sufficiently satisfied with the report to recommend that counsel be instructed to prepare drafts of the legislation which would be necessary both to consummate the union and to conserve the rights and interests of all parties involved. The union committee incorporated this recommendation in its report to the General Assembly.

When the church union committee presented its report to the 1922 Assembly, Pidgeon claimed that it was simply a progress report which asked leave to let the union committee complete the necessary enabling legislation. He therefore tabled a motion seeking the assembly's assent to his view. An amendment presented by Ephraim Scott proposed that the whole matter of church union should be dropped or referred once more to the people. During the debate which followed, Dr. W.T. Herridge of Ottawa suggested that the issue being debated was not church union but rather the authorizing of legal counsel to continue with its work in drafting proposed enabling legislation. Scott replied that if he received a written declaration to that effect, he would withdraw his amendment. Pidgeon then prepared a statement which was read to the assembly, and Scott withdrew his amendment. Principal Murray, however, objected to the statement being recorded in the minutes or added to the union committee's report. The moderator, C.W. Gordon, sustained his objection.[12] This action alerted the dissidents and immediately John Lennox and Banks Nelson submitted another amendment proposing that the union committee discontinue all proceedings for five years.[13] But the amendment received no support, and the report of the union committee was carried.

Up to this point both sides were careful to keep the lid on hostilities. Both in the union committee and in the Assemblies of 1921 and 1922, there was obvious restraint. It might have continued longer if Dr. Chown, the superintendent of the Methodist Church, had not provoked Ephraim Scott by publishing a pastoral letter to the Methodist Church on the question of church union in which he made a number of unguarded remarks about Presbyterians.[14] Scott replied sharply to five statements by Chown in an extensive letter.[15]

Chown claimed that the Presbyterians had initiated the union movement, to which Scott retorted that it was Patrick, speaking with no authority whatsoever from the Presbyterian Church, who had raised the issue. In the past many dissidents, including Scott, had made a point of the fact that the Methodists had surprised the Presbyterians by taking Patrick at his word and appointing a committee to discuss the matter with them. Chown's second point to which Scott took exception was that there were "limits of propriety" which the opposition in the Presbyterian Church should observe. "From our point of view," Chown said, "it seems that they have a right to withdraw from any arrangement made to carry out the will of the General Assembly, but not to block the consummation of its declared purpose." Scott suggested that Chown himself had overstepped the "limits of propriety" by commenting on what Presbyterians could do in their own church. The Methodist Church was a legally incorporated church so that if the General Conference decided to transfer the church with its civil rights and possessions to the control of another body, the only alternative for those who opposed this action was to withdraw. This was not the case with Presbyterians, however, because their church was not incorporated as a legal entity. The church was the people. The assembly had no power to transfer their civil rights and possessions to another jurisdiction. Therefore, Presbyterians who did not wish to be transferred did not have to withdraw; they could simply continue their church.

Chown believed that the negotiating churches had placed themselves under an ethical obligation to consummate the union, and therefore he placed his confidence in the "good faith" of all concerned that the union would in fact take place. Scott believed the implications of this statement to be offensive, especially if they referred to those in the Presbyterian Church who had consistently opposed the merger of the churches as a backward step. He took particular exception to Chown's statement that, "if the major churches of Protestantism cannot unite, the battle which is going on for the purpose of religious control of our country will be lost in the next few years." In clarifying what he meant by this statement, Chown said, "I refer not to the school question only, but to the whole Movement within Canada in the religio-political realm." Scott thanked Chown for being so frank about the purpose of the proposed United Church. He believed it would give Presbyterians an added imperative to continue their own church because their purpose was simply to win men and women to Christ, not to be a power in the "religio-political realm."

Chown's final point on which Scott commented was that a divided church could not speak with good effect to a future united world. Scott pointed out that the future united world that statesmen were working towards was not a world under one control. That ideal was what Germany had vainly attempted to achieve. What statesmen were attempting to achieve was a world in which self-determining nations, large and small, would live in amity and peace. Scott believed that Evangelical Christendom had already achieved this kind of unity through the Bible Societies, the World Missionary Conferences and the Evangelical Alliance in which self-determining churches were living and working together.

In his reply Chown dismissed Scott's letter as propaganda, saying "it would be a reflection on the intelligence of your readers to suppose that Dr. Scott's letter made it necessary for me" to reply to his charges. He complained that Scott had construed his address "in such a way as to foist upon me opinions I never thought of entertaining—especially in regard to the United Church being a 'religio-political machine.'"[16] Dr. J.B. Fraser thought it was unfortunate that Scott should have arrogated to himself the right to speak for the Presbyterian Church. He also thought it was a pity that Scott had not been able to rid himself of the obsession that "there is a sinister design of 'effecting a great organization under central control' like the proposed 'O.B.U.'"[17] Scott then asked Chown to "play fair" and to condescend "for a moment to those of us whose intelligence may be less discerning." He specifically wanted answers to three questions. First, was his letter any more "propaganda" than Chown's previously repeated and widely published statements? Secondly, if Scott had misinterpreted Chown's statement on "good faith," could Chown tell him what Chown had meant? And thirdly, if Chown had never thought of the new United Church as a "a religio-political machine," what was the phrase doing in his statement?[18] Chown declined to reply, which was unfortunate because his unexplained statement about the "religio-political realm" was much used in the subsequent propaganda campaign.

The reactivation of the Presbyterian Church Association, however, took place independently of Scott's attack on Chown. Throughout the summer of 1922 a number of meetings had been held in Toronto and Hamilton. These meetings were called together by prominent laymen who were becoming restless under the continued efforts to carry out the plan of organic union regardless of the cost or consequences.[19] This was the first indication that the Presbyterian Church Association, which had remained dormant since June 1918, was reorganizing itself for action. Like the main thrust of Scott's attack on Chown's statement, the reactivated association would raise serious questions about the legitimacy of the church union legislation.

The initiative in reactivating the Presbyterian Church Association was taken by the local committee in Hamilton. As a first step they hoped to hold a large meeting in Toronto prior to the 1922 Assembly, and they asked J.W. MacNamara, now minister at Port Colborne, Ontario, to organize it because they believed he could "do it better than anyone we know." The meeting never materialized, but MacNamara was persuaded to take on the job to plan for a meeting later in the year, and arrangements were made to set up an office for him at the St. Andrew's Institute on Simcoe Street.[20] By August a local committee to assist MacNamara had been organized which consisted of James Turnbull, James Scott, T. McMillan, C.S. McDonald, Rev. James Wilson, Rev. J.G. Inkster, Rev. J.H. Borland and Rev. A.J. MacGillivray.[21] One thousand dollars had been raised from Toronto and Hamilton to cover initial expenses. By mid-August John Penman was pressing MacNamara hard for a statement on the situation. "I feel," he said, "that it is important that the church at large should know that this Presbyterian Association has been revived and is now at work."[22]

In a very revealing statement Penman asked MacNamara to let Ephraim Scott know what was going on. Then he said, almost as an afterthought, "communicate also with Principal Fraser, he ought to know as head of this organization, what we are doing."[23] Nothing could have made clearer who was really in charge. As chairman of the Ontario Branch of the Presbyterian Church Association, Penman once again took control of the organization. Through his unrelenting efforts and those of his old friends, C.S. McDonald and J.W. MacNamara, the Presbyterian Church Association began to put itself back in fighting trim.

The dissidents scheduled a convocation to meet in October 1922. That September both the joint committee on union and the Methodist General Conference were to meet in Toronto. The draft bills of the federal and provincial legislation had not been ready when the General Assembly met in June. Dr. Chown announced, however, that they would be ready for consideration by the Joint Committee and the Methodist General Conference.[24] This meant that by the time the Presbyterian Church Association met in October they would know both the contents of the legislation and the position taken by the Methodist Church.

The Presbyterian union committee met in the board room of Knox College on Thursday, 21 September 1922. The chairman of the subcommittee on legal matters, Angus MacMurchy, K.C., presented copies of the draft bills to be presented to the federal and provincial legislatures and spent the morning expounding them. Several of the dissidents objected that copies of the proposed legislation should have been in their hands thirty days in advance of the meeting in order for them to have had time to study it. But even without this opportunity, it was soon apparent that there were three serious problems. First of all, the proposed bill did not call upon the new church to assume responsibility for the present financial obligations of each of the contracting parties. Secondly, the commission which was to assume responsibility for dividing and allotting funds and properties between the new church and the dissidents would be composed not of Presbyterians but of representatives of all three churches. Some were especially alarmed by the fact that the decision of this commission was to be final with no right of appeal and no legal revision. Thirdly, if a congregation decided, even by a majority of one, to be a union church, the minority would have no rights to any of the funds or property. These three items, although ultimately revised, indicated the hard line taken in the proposed legislation drafted by the committee on law and legislation under the chairmanship of N.W. Rowell of the Methodist Church.[25]

Meanwhile the executive of the Presbyterian Church Association was meeting concurrently in Toronto at St. Andrew's Institute. They prepared a document which was sent to each of the negotiating committees stating that no endorsement of the bills seeking enabling legislation could be undertaken by the Presbyterian union committee, nor should the bills be sent to the joint committee until such time as the bills and the report of the Presbyterian legal committee had been presented to the Presbyterian General Assembly in 1923.[26] In an interview Principal Fraser, who was both president of the Presbyterian Church Association and a member of the union committee, indicated that the major problem in the proposed legislation was that those churches wishing to stay out would have to vote themselves out of the United Church. This consideration plus the fact that sufficient provision had not been made for the dissenting minorities rendered the proposed legislation unacceptable. Fraser also pointed out that the Presbyterian committee had been instructed only to explore the legal situation. It was unfortunate, he said, that they had not done this independently but had, instead, collaborated with the joint committees. Fraser's statements made it clear that the draft legislation was unacceptable to the dissidents and that they were prepared to resist it. Moved by the determination to do so, the Presbyterian Church Association handed the draft legislation over to its legal counsel, who predicted a lengthy legal fight.[27]

A totally different interpretation of the proposed legislation was given by George Pidgeon in his statement to the press. He characterized the bill as being admirably drawn and well-fitted to give effect to the basis of union. It had never been for a moment "tacitly agreed," he emphasized, that those who remain out of the proposed union, would remain in the Presbyterian Church, as a press report had stated. Pidgeon said that those staying out of the union would not remain in the Presbyterian Church, but would have to go out of it and form a new one.[28] The ground for this statement was the recent decision of the British Parliament in authorizing the Church of Scotland to unite with the United Free Presbyterian Church. In that legislation it was ruled that a church entering union did not thereby lose its own identity but entered the new relationship as a unit.

In an already volatile situation, Pidgeon's remarks proved explosive. When asked if it was true that congregations remaining out of the union could not be known as the Presbyterian Church in Canada, Fraser replied grimly, "Yes, if Dr. Pidgeon is right and if the legal counsel of the union committee are right, that's what it means." He did not believe, however, that the majority in the General Assembly would press for any such action. "I think," he said, "they would be too generous for that."[29] If Pidgeon was right and he was wrong, however, he predicted a "formidable controversy on this technicality."

At the Methodist General Conference which followed the union committee meetings, there were indications that the dissidents in Montreal had not been idle and that the exchange between Dr. Chown and Ephraim Scott had not gone unnoticed. When the church union issue came up for discussion Principal James Smyth of Wesleyan Theological College, Montreal, spoke against a precipitate union with the Presbyterians. "I do not want union with any mere fragment or section of the Presbyterian Church," he said. "I would rather see the whole thing voted on again than see any church dragged in by the nape of the neck." When he had consulted with a leading Presbyterian on the union committee, he had been told, "union is not going through in its present form." His impression was that the 1922 General Assembly had given union a death blow when instead of giving a clear yes or no, it had simply instructed its committee to make legal inquiries to discover if there were any insuperable obstacles. Even the general superintendent, Smyth, declared, had intimated that this action was tantamount to a breach of faith. When Dr. Chown interrupted to deny making such a statement, Smyth accepted the correction but said that someone must have made it, because it was that which had drawn Ephraim Scott's rejoinder that there had been no breach of faith on the part of those Presbyterians who had been opposed to union from the beginning. All this, said Smyth, gave reason for uncertainty as regards union. "If others are willing," he said, "to march with us for the Kingdom of God the Methodists are ready to advance." But if their allies could not carry their people with them, then the Methodist Church should march alone.

Salem Bland joined Smyth. The Methodists, he said, ought not to give the impression that they were pressuring the Presbyterians, but should leave them absolutely free. If, however, the Presbyterians could not make up their minds, then the Methodists should wash their hands of the whole arrangement. As this type of attack began to increase there were calls of "Rowell, Rowell, Rowell" after each speaker, since many members hoped N.W. Rowell would intervene. Rowell waited, however, until the debate had been adjourned and recommenced after the dinner hour. Then he let loose a torrent of fiery eloquence which completely obliterated the opposition.

"The Methodist Church is not making negotiations with either the majority or the minority of the Presbyterian Church," Rowell said, "but with the Presbyterian Church as a whole." The Methodists could not issue an ultimatum to the Presbyterians, for they had no right to interfere with the action of any other church. He believed that the General Conference was assembled to move along the lines designated and all they could do was to approve the legislation and trust in the good judgment of the Presbyterian Church to do its duty. When Rowell finished, reporters noted that there were a few who did not rise in favour but none who had the courage to stand in opposition. Consequently, the Methodist Church accepted without dissent the legislation which had been drafted on church union.[30]

The members of the press who were covering both the Methodist General Conference in Metropolitan Church and the Presbyterian Church Association Convocation in St. Andrew's Church could not help noting the contrasting scenes. The Methodist Conference unanimously affirmed union, whereas the seven hundred delegates to the Presbyterian Church Association Convocation committed themselves to preserve the Presbyterian Church in Canada in a resolution which read:

> We, the members of the Presbyterian Church Association of Ontario, whilst affirming our belief in the spiritual unity of all believers, our cordiality towards our brethren of other communions and our willingness for all feasible co-operation with them, in the interests of the Kingdom of God, express our conviction that the time has not arrived for the discontinuance of the Presbyterian Church in Canada.

J.W. MacNamara said to the press just prior to the opening of the convocation, "We do not like the name Anti-Unionists. We have not a negative but a positive programme, a definite policy of co-operation with the other churches along every practical line and we feel this can be secured without destroying the identity of the churches."[31] Most of the speakers at the convocation were careful to observe this distinction, but the reporters, like the unionists, failed to appreciate its significance.

The chairman of the convocation, C.S. McDonald, opened the proceedings with a candid and belligerent speech against the draft legislation which had been endorsed by the joint committee on union and the Methodists. McDonald characterized the legislation as "an iniquitous piece of coercion and spoilation" which threatened the Presbyterian Church with absolute discontinuance. Unless a determined stand was taken against the legislation, Presbyterians would see their property confiscated and handed over to another organization. "If union takes place," McDonald concluded, "we will receive only the consideration which we can compel by our opposition and it is our duty to prevent such a state of affairs from becoming possible."[32]

Thomas McMillan told the gathering that the unionists' purpose was "to take us into union and turn us out afterward," but he defied them to do it. In a carefully prepared speech lasting three-quarters of an hour, he deplored the temerity of W.J. Clark, moderator of the assembly, who had, in a speech the night before, belittled the standards he was entrusted to defend. Many unionists, McMillan said, supported union because they believed they could teach and preach whatever they liked in the new church. Another new voice at the convocation was that of J.H. Sinclair, the M.P. for Pictou, N.S., who said his constituency was the cradle of Presbyterianism in the Dominion of Canada and urged those who opposed union to defeat the bill in Parliament. Surgeon-General J.T. Fotheringham indicated that he had formerly voted for union but had changed his mind on deeper reflection because he believed what was at stake was loyalty to the nation's forefathers. Both Banks Nelson and R.G. MacBeth berated N.W. Rowell as the culprit behind the legislation designed to deprive the Presbyterian minority of their property.

At the meetings next day Daniel Fraser startled everyone by declaring that if another vote showed the majority in favour of organic union, he would abide by the decision and cease his opposition. T. Crawford Brown said that if the church went into union, he would become an Anglican and he believed that hundreds of people had already decided to do that. Dr. Murray MacLaren, M.P. for Saint John, N.B., advocated a vigorous publicity campaign and Mr. George F. Macdonnell, K.C., son of the late Rev. D.J. Macdonnell, said that "the best way to avoid disruption" was "to arrange to have one." The private bills committee of Parliament, he was certain, would not hand all the property of the Presbyterian Church to the one-third that had voted for union.

Judge James Craig, formerly of the Yukon, focused on the need for great vigilance and vigour at Ottawa. As an old politician he could see, he said, that this was a lobby matter and that those who could show the greatest strength would get the greatest results. No house would dare to defy a vast Presbyterian minority. Although a variety of reporters indicated that Craig was advocating a large lobby, he later denied that he had done so. "Personally," he said, "I disapprove of lobbies because I think they are always unfair. I prefer open fighting, foot to foot and steel to steel." But he anticipated a lobby because the tactics of the unionists had been "from the very inception of this contest always unfair and domineering." "If the unionists," he concluded, "are so convinced that the name Presbyterian is vile, why didn't they make their iniquitous bill complete by imposing fines and imprisonment on anyone daring to use the name?"[33]

To make certain that some of these suggestions were put into effect, the convocation passed a number of resolutions unanimously. The most important of these read:

> Recognizing that a section of the Church is determined upon union, resolved that we, the Ontario Branch recommend to the Presbyterian Church Association of Canada that a committee be appointed to take the necessary steps for the protection of property rights, funds and assets of the Presbyterian Church in Canada, with authority to deal with all matters in the interests of maintaining the Presbyterian Church in Canada, and to take such other action as is necessary in the premises.[34]

Banks Nelson sponsored another resolution, which was accepted unanimously, protesting against the use of funds for the payment of lawyers to frame bills that sought to disrupt the Presbyterian Church. These funds had been given to the Presbyterian Church for home and foreign missions, for the Aged and Infirm Minister's Fund, and for the furtherance of the preaching of the Gospel. A final resolution also was adopted which declared "that in the judgement of the Ontario Branch of the Presbyterian Church Association, the bills now prepared providing for organic union are manifestly and grossly unfair and unjust, and we recommend that these bills be now referred to our own counsel, with instructions to take such steps as they may deem necessary."[35]

In order to make certain that the resolutions and proposals of the convocation were carried out, a new executive committee was chosen. John Penman was elected honourary president with Thomas McMillan as president, Dr. A.J. MacGillivray, vice-president, J.W. MacNamara, secretary, and C.S. McDonald as treasurer. The coerciveness of the draft legislation reactivated the opposition and strengthened their determination and commitment to oppose it at any cost. In a letter criticizing George Pidgeon's statement on the proposed legislation, Daniel Fraser accused him of failing to carry out the instructions of the assembly in drafting legislation. It was framed "in anticipation of a factious opposition on the part of a number of diehards" rather than with a view towards an amicable settlement. "If in 1916 Presbyterians all over Canada rose in indignation against a policy of coercion," he warned, "how much greater will be their indignation when the suspicion spreads among them that they are being trapped."[36]

9

The Road to Port Arthur

The proposed legislation for the new United Church of Canada was ready in September 1922. The joint committee on union and the Methodist General Conference accepted it, but the question was, would the General Assembly, scheduled to meet in Port Arthur in June 1923, accept it? The Presbyterian Church Association, reactivated in October of 1922, had to make every possible effort to ensure that the assembly did not do so. The dissidents had eight months in which to accomplish this task. Their organization, however, had lain dormant for five years, and as Andrew Robertson had predicted, reorganization was difficult. Moreover, in view of past experience, it was necessary to assume that the assembly in Port Arthur would pass the legislation. In the few months at their disposal, therefore, the dissidents had to lay plans to oppose the legislation not only at the assembly, but also in Ottawa and the provincial legislatures. As first steps toward such action they had to reactivate their organization in local centres across the country and organize a new publicity campaign to place their case once again before the church's membership. All of these plans required money. But having let their organization lapse, the dissidents had little time to mobilize sufficient resources to challenge the unionists effectively at the 1923 Assembly.

It was clear to the dissidents that if they were going to make any impression on the 1923 Assembly and were to be ready to carry the fight to Parliament, their national organization had to be put back into shape. In October 1922, the convocation sponsored by the Ontario branch of the P.C.A. had elected new officers for the provincial branch. The reactivation of the Ontario branch, however, was but a first step. If a national organization was to be mobilized, the association also needed financial resources and a central administration. In enlisting the necessary support, it was the Ontario executive committee, spurred by John Penman, which took the initiative.

The first major need was money. The Ontario executive planned to raise $25,000 by subscription as soon as possible. John Penman was anxious to get this subscription plan off the ground and immediately pledged $1,000. As he explained to MacNamara, "we do not want to be in a position we were placed in at the last campaign, spending money before we had collected it. This time we must collect the money in advance of spending it. Every effort must be made now to secure this amount." Penman had already contributed more than any other individual to the preservation of the Presbyterian Church in Canada. Although there is no indication that he ever regretted any of the money spent in this cause, he did reflect on the dilemma in which the dissidents found themselves. "It does seem strange," he wrote to MacNamara, "that we are asked for $25,000 to help retain the Presbyterian Church in Canada, while those who are seeking to merge our church with other churches can use the general fund of the church, our contributions as well as others, but I presume nothing can be done in this matter."[1]

The second need was for a permanent secretary to establish a permanent office from which a national campaign could be directed. There was never any question in the minds of the Ontario executive who this man must be. There was great rejoicing in the committee when MacNamara accepted the position.[2]

The reactivation of the federal executive of the Presbyterian Church Association proved to be a greater problem. As D.A. Murray, treasurer of the Montreal executive committee, reported to MacNamara, there were initially some difficulties in arranging such a meeting. When the Montreal branch met in November 1922, Principal Fraser, who had been made president of the federal executive in 1916, expressed his concern that "a great deal of the work must be carried on by and under the direction of local committees."[3] Since the executive of the Ontario Branch was pressing for a centrally directed national campaign, Fraser's emphasis on local committees thwarted their intention. It took several months therefore before a meeting of the federal executive in Montreal in January 1923 could be arranged.

This tension between the Ontario and Montreal Branches of the Association hindered the formation of a national organization at a time when the dissidents could ill afford any delay. Whereas the Ontario Branch organized on a provincial basis, the Montreal Branch insisted on organizing on a synodical basis. Moreover, Montreal was part of the Synod of Ottawa and Montreal, but Quebec City was in a separate synod. This organizational confusion led to a variety of clashes between the Toronto and Montreal executive committees, especially over financial questions and the question of who was responsible for planning meetings in districts where the two jurisdictions overlapped. Meanwhile, those in Quebec City and eastern Quebec province were left on their own.

At the January meetings of the federal executive, however, representatives from both the Montreal and Ontario branches, as well as from the Maritimes, did reach agreement on the strategy to be followed in the months leading up to the assembly. In their statement to the press, the executive attacked the proposal to legislate Presbyterians into the United Church against their will and to deprive them of the name of the church to which they wished to remain loyal. This threatened coercion of conscience, they said, had only strengthened the determination of many to continue the church of their fathers with its historic traditions and missionary spirit. The Presbyterian Church Association intended to use every legitimate means to protect its constituency against the proposed confiscation of property and other rights, and it called on all who shared its purpose to stand firm in their convictions.[4]

Although the executive's statement made a strong call for resistance, it did not repeat the dissidents' demand for another vote. To promote this issue it was agreed that MacNamara should send to a member of the association in each presbytery a copy of a resolution, which had been adopted unanimously in Hamilton Presbytery, suggesting that "the General Assembly should not proceed to the consummation of Church union until an authoritative mandate has been given by a vote of the present membership of the church."[5] In letters to the *Presbyterian Witness*, J. Keir Fraser had pointed out that 100,000 new members had been added to the Presbyterian Church since the last vote had been taken.[6] W.F. McConnell wrote in a similar vein that in 1915 when the second vote was taken 150,000 Canadians were under arms and about 100,000 were overseas. "It would be a fair estimate," he said, "that 50,000 of these were Presbyterians," and these members had not had an opportunity to express their choice in the vote.[7] In sending out copies of the resolution from Hamilton Presbytery as a model for action in the presbyteries across the country, the object was to build up pressure through a series of overtures to the assembly for a third vote. The federal executive, however, refrained from making any specific reference to a third vote in their official statement. That matter was left in the hands of the minority on the union committee to deal with as they saw fit.

The major policy decision of the federal executive was to hire a dominion organizer for the Presbyterian Church Association. While they wanted MacNamara to set up a permanent office in Toronto, they believed that it was also necessary to have a man who would devote his full time to travelling across the country to assist local branches in organizing against the proposed legislation. Many individuals were approached for this position, including W.G. Brown and R.G. MacBeth. Both declined because they felt they could do more for the cause by remaining in the West. After several others were considered and either declined or were rejected, the job was finally offered to Dr. A.J. MacGillivray, who, after much hesitation, agreed to undertake the work from March through May of 1923.[8] Although in many ways an ideal man for the job, MacGillivray was uncertain that he wished, at age fifty-six, to take it on for longer than three months.

In the reactivation of the Presbyterian Church Association MacGillivray had played an important role. As vice-president of the Ontario Branch he had been at the centre of all its major decisions. Another of his qualifications was that he was familiar with the church in the West. He was born and raised near Port Elgin, Ontario, but upon graduation from high school he had gone to Winnipeg where he had worked for a time with the Department of Education of the Province of Manitoba. After deciding to train for the ministry, he entered the University of Manitoba from which he received his Bachelor of Arts. Then, like many who had come under the spell of James Robertson, he had proceeded to Princeton for his M.A. and his theological training. Upon graduation in 1894, he spent three years in mission work in Oklahoma before returning in 1897 to New St. James Church in London, Ontario. In 1906 he accepted a call to St. John's Church, Vancouver, where he remained for five years prior to going to Scotland for postgraduate studies. Returning to Canada in 1912, he became supply minister of Knox Church, Guelph, Ontario, during the illness of Rev. Arnold. After the latter's death, he became minister of the congregation and remained there until he died in 1938.[9]

During this three months as dominion organizer, MacGillivray spent most of his time reactivating the resistance movement in the East, although he did make one trip to the West. Part of his task was to set up a series of meetings for W.G. Brown, who had been released by his congregation in Red Deer, Alberta, for a six week speaking tour of Eastern Canada. The plan worked out by MacGillivray and MacNamara was to have Brown spend a week in the Maritimes, a week in the Montreal area, and the rest of the time in Ontario. While these meetings were going on, MacGillivray was also speaking on every possible occasion. He found the work very tiring, and when his brother wrote asking him to supply for a month in Somerville, Massachusetts, he replied, "I'm afraid I will feel so tired out by this running about from place to place until next June, that I will feel like crawling into some quiet place nearer home."[10]

During the meetings of the federal executive, another meeting held in Montreal was the first meeting of the Ladies Auxiliary of the Presbyterian Church Association. Several of the men present at the federal executive addressed this women's meeting which passed the following resolution:

We the members of the Presbyterian Women's League, meeting at Montreal on January 17th, strongly protest against the proposed action of the General Assembly regarding Church Union. We regard this action as tending to deprive the Presbyterian Church of its name and status among the great churches of the world. We affirm our determination to uphold in every way in our power the action of the Presbyterian Church Association for the preservation of their church.[11]

Though few church leaders at the time appear to have been aware of it, behind this rather innocuous resolution lay a major source of discontent in the Presbyterian church.

Because Presbyterian women were not eligible for ordination either as ministers or elders, they could not be members of the church's courts, such as the presbytery and the General Assembly. They had no voice, therefore, in the formulation of the church's policy. Although great progress had been made by 1922 in giving women the vote, the church had not kept pace with these changes in Canadian society. For years, however, Presbyterian women had been making a significant contribution to the church's missionary effort.[12] Since 1876 when the first Women's Missionary Societies were formed in the Presbyterian Church, they had grown rapidly. They were independently organized and administered by women and were not controlled by the church's Mission Board. In running these societies women had proven that they were capable not only of raising large sums of money to support women missionaries at home and abroad, but also of efficiently administering their property and funds. Yet when the church union legislation appeared in 1922, the women discovered that, without their being consulted, all of their funds and property would pass into the United Church of Canada. As a result, many Presbyterian women decided to put their organizational abilities to work for the resistance movement.

It was John Penman's idea that the women of the Presbyterian Church should be separately organized in the defence of the church. Since Penman's major interest in the church was missions, he was well aware of the effective work being done by the Women's Missionary Societies. He was confident that the women would prove to be a great asset to the resistance movement, and in many of his letters he pressed for their organization. Not everyone, however, shared his enthusiasm. When it was proposed that there should be an organizer for the various women's auxiliaries across the country, T.B. McQuesten of Hamilton declared this would be a major mistake because to have a woman organizing women would lead to all sorts of petty jealousies. The best results in organizing women, as all political organizers knew, would be obtained with a male organizer.[13] MacNamara noted McQuesten's objections and indicated they would be passed on to the executive committee. Diplomatically, however, he pointed out that Mrs. J.J. McCaskill had done splendid work in Montreal and in view of the excellent leadership she and other women were displaying it might be difficult for McQuesten to sustain his objections.[14]

Frances McCaskill, the wife of the Rev. J.J. McCaskill of Maisonneuve Presbyterian Church in Montreal, was elected corresponding secretary of the Presbyterian Women's League at its first meeting in January 1923.[15] Two months later she became the organizer for the Presbyterian Women's Leagues throughout Ontario and Quebec. Not being used to such work, she soon found that her throat gave out from so many speaking engagements. "It is only by will power that I keep going just now," she reported. "My choice would be to crawl into a dug-out and stay there for six months rest."[16] Her will power prevailed, however, and she kept going. During a visit to Peterborough, she discovered a Mrs. E.H. Howson who was willing to help organize the women there. "Mrs. Howson," she wrote, "is young and a hustler and a true 'Scot'. I think she would like the fun of the thing."[17] On arriving in Kingston, she found that Miss Minnie Gordon, the daughter of Principal Daniel Gordon of Queen's, was the key organizer. Miss Gordon apparently did not wish to take a position on the executive of the Kingston branch of the Women's League because of her father's position, but as the report concluded, "she is the power behind the throne."[18]

By June 1923 Frances McCaskill announced a minor organizational miracle. In less than six months the Presbyterian Women's League had enrolled, 173 members in Eastern Canada, and she told J.W. MacNamara that "this is just the beginning." Equally startling was the fact that they had raised $4,750 and turned over $3,000 to the Presbyterian Church Association.[19] By providing much needed financial support and paying for all their own organizational expenses the Presbyterian Women's Leagues became the most important new factor in the resistance movement and certainly the most successful element in the association's reorganization prior to the 1923 General Assembly.

The problems of reorganizing the Presbyterian Church Association almost from scratch tended to focus most of the executive committee's energies on mobilization. This necessity left little time to concentrate on publicity. Most of the older men like Campbell and McLeod who previously had played such an effective role as propagandists were dead. Only Ephraim Scott remained of this older group, and he immediately began to turn out brief pamphlets. However, it was necessary to put together a new publication committee and to search out carefully a new group of writers who could effectively present the dissidents' case. It was not until after the 1923 Assembly when the Presbyterian Church Association published the *Presbyterian Standard* that they managed to put together an effective bulletin equal to the *Message* or even the *Presbyterian Advocate*.

Prior to the 1923 Assembly the most effective propaganda published by the dissident leaders was a series of articles on "The Church Union Situation" which appeared in the *Presbyterian Witness*. George Pidgeon, as convenor of the union committee, published a long series of articles on the legislation in which he discussed the union situation as he saw it. The purpose of the dissidents' articles, as Daniel Fraser noted in his introductory article, was "to offset the influence of Dr. Pidgeon's copious contributions."[20]

In analysing the situation, Fraser repeated his earlier charge that the 1922 Assembly had asked only for an exhaustive exploration of the legal issues involved in union for the information of the General Assembly and people of the Presbyterian Church. It had not instructed the legal counsel of the Presbyterian union committee to collaborate with the legal counsel of the joint committee in preparing enabling legislation for the proposed united church. Fraser contended that the Presbyterian committee should have retained independent counsel to examine the legislative situation from the point of view of their own church. As a result of the precipitate action of the Presbyterian union committee, the 1923 Assembly would be presented with drafts of legislation framed by lawyers who were neither engaged by the assembly nor instructed by the assembly as to what type of legislation should be prepared. In fact, they were being faced with legislation prepared for and accepted by the Methodist General Conference. Thus the 1923 Assembly would not really be free to study the legislation on its merits.

Fraser then asked whether the union committee would present this legislation to the assembly as legislation that was "necessary" for consummating union, in the sense of being the only legislation possible under the circumstances, when in fact it simply reflected the unionists' self-interest. There was no reason, he argued, that the assembly had to accept legislation that would coerce a minority into a new denomination. Instead, the assembly could instruct the legal counsel to draft new legislation leaving those who wished to go into the new denomination free to do so and the rest with their present status and rights. The unionists did not want this type of legislation, Fraser maintained, because they were determined that the Presbyterian Church should go into union as an entity and that those who chose to remain out would be denied identity as Presbyterians.

There were many, Fraser concluded, who were appealing for an amicable settlement. As he saw it, however, this would be a problem as long as the leaders of the union movement persisted in their uncompromising attitude towards the minority. So long as they insisted on the present form of legislation, any effort at conciliation was impossible.

Professor Cyrus Macmillan of McGill University underlined Fraser's conclusion in his contribution to this series entitled "The Medievalism of Church Union."[21] The theme of Macmillan's article was that since the unionists' raving had failed to convince the church of their scheme, they were now intending to drive the church into it, coercion taking the place of persuasion. This was "ecclesiastical tyranny" as far as Macmillan was concerned, and he asserted that it would not work. "When men," Macmillan said, "state their conviction in a way that repels, when they act like star chamber officials and when they attempt to stifle freedom by coercion, their schemes are doomed to failure. That such a form of religious conversion should even be contemplated in the 20th century says little for the conception of Christianity held by the men who advocated it." Although Macmillan hesitated to predict what Parliament would do with the proposed legislation, he was confident that Parliament would recognize "that a chain-gang doing a lock-step does not mean the communion of saints, and that a million people doing the goose step to the orders of either a Prussian or an ecclesiastical jack-boot cannot bring in the Kingdom of God in Canada." Managing to get all of his pet peeves out at the same time, Macmillan concluded that "Parliament has always looked with suspicion on collective bargaining at the expense of the individual, and has never sympathized with a Soviet control of conscience either by a Ku Klux Klan, a Labor Union or a Church Court."

Macmillan had given the substance of this article in an address to a meeting of the Women's League of the Presbyterian Church Association in Montreal on 22 March 1923. When John Penman's wife showed him a newspaper report of the address, he was shocked and wrote to MacNamara deploring such bitter language and indicating that this sort of a defence of their cause was completely uncalled for.[22] Apparently, however, the letter arrived too late for MacNamara to stop publication of Macmillan's article in the *Presbyterian Witness* on 5 April.

The third article in the series by Banks Nelson and T.B. McQuesten of Hamilton was a two part attack on Pidgeon's plea for "an indigenous church."[23] Nelson took exception to Pidgeon's claim that the early Christian churches "were indigenous to the soil, and in them the national spirit expressed itself religiously." Nelson expressed surprise that an educated Presbyterian minister could make such a statement. "Aaron's golden calf," he said, "was 'the national spirit expressing itself religiously,'" and he made it clear that Presbyterians, who were at home anywhere in the world, would not bow down to such an idol. McQuesten went even further in rejecting the whole idea of an indigenous church as "pure bosh" and he pointed out that "a Canadian type of Christian" was so obscure that Pidgeon himself was unable to describe it. All this "blather about Canadianism," he continued, revealed "what has been described as 'the immodesty of provincialism'." Then taking another tack, reminiscent of Robert Campbell, he said:

> For many years in the United States the current theory was that a finer race was produced by a mixture of all races. No one believes this theory now. All modern writers on the subject declare that the mixture of an inferior race produces nothing but degeneration. Of all things in our national life this should be the most discouraged.

McQuesten concluded that "for the religious Protestant people of this country to cut themselves off from their racial and religious traditions and model themselves on a spurious Canadianism" was not the way to discourage degeneration.

By this point, of course, the battle lines had been so firmly drawn that it is doubtful whether these articles changed anyone's mind. They are interesting, however, because they reveal a consistency of outlook on the issue which bound together both the earliest opponents of union and those who joined the ranks of the resistance at a much later date. Also they disclose a similarity of response in their continued reliance on a point by point rebuttal of the unionists' arguments for change. On the other hand, Cyrus Macmillan's identification of church union with everything that was wrong with the world seems at first glance to be uncharacteristic of the movement as a whole. It is essential to recall, however, that when the Presbyterian Women's League of Montreal invited Macmillan to address them, they had no desire to hear another technical dissertation on the evils of the union legislation. They were angry, and they wanted something that would stir them up. If Macmillan's address represented a new element in the resistance, therefore, it was as much a reflection of the women's newly acquired militancy as it was of Macmillan's ability to include medievalism, Bolshevism, Junkerism, and the Ku Klux Klan in the same sentence with church union.

As tension rose prior to the meeting of the Presbyterian union committee and the forthcoming General Assembly, the moderates responded with another effort to avert disaster. The conciliatory movement was led this time by Dr. D.R. Drummond of Hamilton. Drummond had been a moderate unionist until he saw the legislation and faced the prospect that it would inevitably disrupt the church. Convinced that disruption would be "a horror too unspeakable," he revived in a pamphlet entitled "Is There Not A Way Out?" the alternative of federation which had been vigorously discussed over a decade before.[24]

Drummond believed there was much that was new in his plan, but neither the staunch unionists nor the dissidents could see it. Nonetheless, the plan did appeal to a number of moderate unionists who did not want union at any price. An organization chaired by Rev. D.T.L. McKerroll of Toronto, with Rev. A.L. Budge of Hamilton as secretary, was formed to promote the federalist plan. This group, meeting in Toronto on 1 April 1923, passed a resolution advocating federation as the way out of "the calamitous schism that at present seems impending" and recommending its consideration by the union committee and the forthcoming General Assembly.[25] Dr. Clarence MacKinnon of Pine Hill Divinity Hall in Halifax and a group of professors and ministers in that city also endorsed the plan and suggested to Dr. Drummond that he attempt to find out what the Presbyterian Church Association thought of the idea.[26]

The most stunning support, however, came from Dr. Daniel M. Gordon, former principal of Queen's University, and Dr. E.D. McLaren, who had served for many years as the secretary of the union committee. McLaren's statement in response to Drummond's suggestion must have given many staunch unionists cause to reconsider their stand seriously. He wrote:

The consummation of Union under existing conditions would mean a setting aside of the pledge that the representatives of the three negotiating churches gave to one another at the first meeting of the Joint Union Committee, and a departure from the understanding—based on that pledge—on the part of the people of all the churches, that the only union that could possibly be considered was one that would be a genuine healing of our ecclesiastical divisions.[27]

The newcomers to the union movement, including George Pidgeon, Alfred Gandier, Walter Murray, Robert Falconer, and C.W. Gordon, had been arguing for years that the church had never bound itself to any such pledge. Here, however, was the statement of the first secretary of the original joint committee on union saying that the pledge had been given. Daniel Gordon, who was also a member of the original union committee, confirmed McLaren's statement when he said he could not imagine that the present union committee would approve of the proposed legislation because it was "so out of harmony with the history, traditions and requirements of the Presbyterian Church."[28]

Thus, if Drummond's pamphlet did nothing else, it broke the silence of many moderate unionists, who like McLaren had "deliberately refrained from giving utterance to my views and feelings, because I was unwilling to encourage the opposition." As McLaren was later to state, "the distressing consideration is, that insofar as our original objective in this union movement is concerned, namely the healing of our ecclesiastical divisions, all this painful experience will have been comparatively fruitless; we will have sacrificed almost everything and gained almost nothing."[29]

Pidgeon and Gandier wasted no time in rejecting Drummond's plan. Pidgeon claimed that the suggested way out was "nothing more than co-operation with a more elaborate machine and a new name." The issue which had to be faced, he argued, was that if union were blocked, the churches in the West would go into union anyway. The schism which this would cause would be greater because when the union was consummated few would leave "much fewer proportionally than in 1875." For Pidgeon, therefore, Drummond's proposal was "simply a desperate effort to evade an issue."[30] Gandier agreed that "the scheme has value only as a means of side-tracking church union." To negate union now would give new life to denominationalism for twenty years to come and brand the Presbyterian Church as a sect by deliberate choice. Such a thing was unthinkable, Gandier said, and he concluded that those who believed in union should have the courage of their convictions.[31]

With this response, it became clear that the leading unionists would have nothing to do with Drummond's suggestion. On previous occasions the moderates had played a significant role in preventing total polarization. In

1923, however, their response came too late for them either to organize as an effective force or even to get a fair hearing. Consequently, they were not in a position to mediate. At Port Arthur the moderates would have to choose to stand on one side or the other.

The union committee held two meetings prior to the debate on church union at the assembly. In these meetings a few minor amendments to the draft legislation were considered, the motion which the committee would present to the assembly was drafted, and the minorities' dissents and protests were recorded in the committee minutes without comment. It also became apparent at these meetings that the moderates who wished to avoid schism had nowhere to stand except in opposition to the action of the majority in the committee. Thus, merely by counselling moderation they found themselves drawn to the side of the dissidents. But as they did not wish to opt specifically for the role of dissent, they had no action left whatever and no further role to play in the conflict. The schism they feared so much had already come into existence.

At the 24 April meeting of the union committee held in Knox College, communications were received from branches of the Women's Leagues of the Presbyterian Church Association in Toronto, Ottawa, Cornwall, Montreal, New Glasgow, and the Maritime Synod. These communications pointed out that although women had no voice in the union committee or General Assembly, the actions of both would affect women's work in the church, and if the present legislation went through, they would be forced into the new denomination against their will. They therefore recommended that the union committee seriously consider "a better way to preserve the unity and peace of the church." These resolutions were noted in the minutes without comment and appear not to have been taken very seriously.

Careful consideration, however, was given to the recommendations which the committee would present to the assembly. C.W. Gordon and Judge Swanson presented the motion of the majority in the committee asking the assembly to approve and adopt the draft legislation "as necessary" to give effect to the union. On behalf of the moderates Dr. Drummond and Dr. Dickie presented an amendment which noted the increasing opposition to the draft legislation in the Presbyterian Church Association, the formation of the Women's Leagues, and the alarming proportions of the deficit in the budget. The amendment proposed, therefore, that the assembly recognize that the consummation of organic union would be fraught with such financial and legal difficulty "as to make inadvisable further effort to that end." This amendment was lost and the original motion carried by a vote of 20 to 11.

At the union committee's second meeting in Port Arthur on 6 June, just prior to the assembly debate, the report of the minority was presented by Thomas McMillan, who intimated that the report would be presented to the assembly. It recommended that the assembly "proceed no further in the matter of organic union" until the practical unanimity agreed upon by all parties in 1905 was attained. Twelve members of the committee signed the report, with Adam W. Ballantyne asking for a third vote. Drummond did not sign, however, because he wished to be free to promote his own motion.

Through a series of defeats over the past twenty years the unionists had learned a number of lessons from the dissidents about organizing. As the union committee's report on overtures from the synods and presbyteries revealed, they had made sure they would not be outflanked on the floor of the assembly by a flood of overtures recommending further delay. Of the forty-five overtures received on the question of union from the presbyteries, forty-one urged the consummation of union without delay. Of these forty-one, four suggested that steps should be taken to protect minority rights. Four synods overtured the assembly asking for the speedy consummation of union. Clearly, the unionists had moved wisely and thoroughly to have gained the support of so many. By contrast, only three presbyteries (Hamilton, Red Deer, and Barrie) opposed union, and one supported Dr. Drummond's plan. Four overtures from individuals which opposed further action on union were forwarded by the presbyteries. Percy Blanchard of Ellerhouse, Nova Scotia, presented his own scheme of federation described as "The Ten Points of Federal Union." In the past the dissidents and moderates had been able to muster many more overtures recommending moderation.

When the assembly debate on union began on the afternoon of 7 June, Ephraim Scott stirred up a minor skirmish by moving that the vote be by ballot. The moderator ruled his notice of motion out of order, but Scott and a few others persisted in pursuing the matter during the following discussion. The inner circle of the dissidents from Ontario, however, knew there was no point in this type of manoeuvring.

After Scott's unsuccessful motion, George Pidgeon presented the union committee's report. The draft legislation had already been printed, so it was not necessary for Pidgeon to read it. He simply presented a series of resolutions to commit the church to union upon the terms in the draft legislation, to create a new union committee, to provide for the appointment of 150 members to represent the Presbyterian Church at the first General Council of the United Church, and to require the presbyteries to furnish lists and descriptions of all congregational property. When he moved the reception of this report and the consideration of its recommendations seriatim, D.J. Fraser presented the report of the minority on the church union committee and then proceeded to speak to Dr. Pidgeon's motion.

When Fraser was finished, Drummond submitted an amendment which, although mentioning the idea of federation in passing, did not specifically recommend the plan he had outlined previously. Instead, the amendment called for a conference between the advocates and opponents of organic union to seek "some way by which the peace of the church could be preserved and the threatened division averted."[32]

The debate which followed contained few surprises, and not many speakers distinguished themselves. W.J. Clark of Montreal, who had the ability to sense the significance of new factors in the situation but lacked the commonsense necessary to keep from putting his foot in his mouth, ridiculed the work of the Women's League. In his address he said:

> There was a lady of the Presbyterian League who called up another lady and said, 'Won't you give us your name to put on this petition we are getting up?' 'Oh, I am in favour of church union,' the woman replied. 'But cannot we put your name on?' 'Oh, well, if you want to put my name on, all right.' That is the sort of propaganda that is being carried on.[33]

By trying to make the women look like fools, Clark simply stoked the fires of the women's resistance.

When the vote was finally taken, 427 voted for the union motion and 129 against. Steps were then taken to form a new union committee which would consist solely of unionists and to appoint the 150 members who would represent the Presbyterian Church at the first General Council of the United Church of Canada. As the assembly went through these motions, they suddenly received their first taste of what the division and disruption would mean.

James Rodger, who had been at the core of the dissidents' movement from the beginning, submitted his resignation as chairman of the Church and Manse Board and as the representative of that board on the General Board of the Church. Rodger had been a familiar figure in the General Assembly for twenty years, and he was greatly respected. His resignation moved Dr. Laird to deliver a tribute to his great service to the church, following which President Walter Murray jumped to his feet and, joined by Dr. W.J. Clark, moved that Rodger be asked to reconsider his resignation. The assembly unanimously accepted the motion, but it was too late.[34] The decision which would destroy lifelong friendships and turn brother against brother had already been taken.

10

The Legislative Struggle

In 1923, the controversy reached a crucial turning point when the churches decided to proceed with the consummation of union. Now Parliament and the provincial legislatures, rather than the churches, would become the forum for debate. Clerics would have to take a back seat to lawyers and legislators, and the union proposal would be subjected to a different set of pressures and priorities. The dissidents hoped that with this change of venue their case would receive a better hearing and the coercive aspects of the legislation would be eliminated. Few, however, foresaw how this new setting would alter the character of the conflict.

The imperatives of organizing a mass protest movement from coast to coast, for example, brought to the forefront of the dissidents' ranks a type of individual different from the leading spirits of the resistance movement earlier in the controversy. The veterans still remained in control of the organization, but those who attracted the greatest amount of public attention were relative newcomers, and their presence altered the movement's public image. The lawyers who prepared the dissidents' case also viewed the struggle from a new perspective, which tended to distort the dissidents' theological position and expose them to ridicule. In Parliament and the provincial legislatures, moreover, there were many elected representatives who were not Presbyterians, Methodists, or Congregationalists. Here Roman Catholics, Anglicans, Baptists, and some with no religion at all were called upon to consider this issue and to weigh its significance. Inevitably, this meant they would view it in terms of their own political interests and its potential for disturbing delicate balances of power in their constituencies. As the pace quickened, the impact of these new forces on the nature of the conflict became quickly apparent.

The dissidents' strategy was to make their appeal directly to the membership of the church against the action of the church courts. To do this it was necessary to set up an effective network of provincial organizations which could present their case to every congregation. Consequently, the first step the dissidents took in their preparation for the legislative struggle was to appoint the Rev. William F. McConnell of Leamington, Ontario, as dominion organizer of the Presbyterian Church Association.

McConnell was a thirty-nine year old Ulster Irishman from County Down who had come to Canada in 1905 and taken his training for the ministry at McGill University and Presbyterian College, Montreal. When he graduated in 1915, he was ordained as a chaplain in the Canadian Army, and he was immediately sent overseas. After returning to Canada in the spring of 1919 with a distinguished service record and the rank of major, McConnell spent several months organizing four counties for the Ontario Referendum Committee and organizing a religious survey of the city of Montreal for the Forward Movement, prior to accepting a call to the Presbyterian Church in Leamington in April 1920. It was this organizing experience and his military record which convinced C.S. McDonald and Thomas McMillan that he would be the right man for the job.[1]

McConnell's task was to create organizations in every synod, presbytery and congregation and to supervise the publicity campaign of the Presbyterian Church Association across the country. He was to report his activities to the association's secretary, J.W. MacNamara, and in turn he was to receive his instructions from a special committee on organization chaired by the Rev. A.J. MacGillivray of Guelph, Ontario. Within a few months it became apparent that one person could not be expected to cover the whole country. As a result, a number of provincial organizers were appointed to assist McConnell, and in Ontario, special organizers were appointed in almost every synod and presbytery.[2] With each area responsible for its own finances, it was difficult to support a full-time organizer in provinces such as Manitoba and Saskatchewan, where great difficulty was experienced in raising money. Consequently, in these areas McConnell had to do most of the work.

In this organizational work, McConnell was invaluable. As organizer he estimated that he travelled 53,000 miles back and forth across the country, and in the process he became one of the most visible and familiar figures in the resistance movement in every major centre in Canada. McConnell's Irish brogue, however, gave the impression that those opposing union were recent immigrants and that the resistance to church union was somehow non-Canadian. This impression was further confirmed by the extensive use which the dissidents made of ministers such as Banks Nelson of Hamilton and Stuart Parker of St. Andrew's Church, Toronto. Like McConnell, Nelson was Irish, and Stuart Parker was a Scot who had arrived in Canada only in May 1923. Both were extremely effective speakers who were prepared to travel extensively, but their defence of Presbyterianism seemed more characteristic of the old country than of the new loyalties to which the unionists were calling Canadians.[3]

The second step in the dissidents' preparation for the legislative struggle was to provide literature which would make their position clear to church members across the country. The first pamphlet prepared by the executive in June 1923 was "A Statement of the Case of the Presbyterian Church Association," which reviewed the origins of the association, the history of the opposition to union, the dissidents' reasons for opposing union, and the duties of those who agreed with them.[4] It was an able statement of the case, and it was soon followed by *The Presbyterian Standard,* a publication much like its predecessors, *The Presbyterian Advocate* (1915) and *The Message* (1916-1917). The first issue appeared in July 1923.[5] However, in his trips across the country, McConnell discovered that bundles of *The Presbyterian Standard* often remained unopened in church vestibules unless individuals took responsibility for distributing them. It was for this reason that McConnell turned to newspaper advertising and hired H.R. Cockfield, the head of the Montreal-based General Advertising Service, to assist the association with a national advertising campaign.[6]

The only exception to this new policy was the executives' decision in 1923 to purchase five hundred copies of E. Lloyd Morrow's book, *Church Union in Canada* and to send a copy to every member of the Senate, the House of Commons, and all the provincial legislatures in Canada.[7] The book, which earned its author a Ph.D. degree from the University of Chicago, was a review of the pros and cons of the union controversy. It concluded that the organic union of the three negotiating churches was "unnecessary, unwise and impossible." From the dissidents' point of view, the publication of a book which dismissed the idea of church union as "a cheap and man-made panacea" could not have been better timed. But in spite of initially favourable reviews, the book had some serious shortcomings.[8] These became apparent when John T. McNeill, another Chicago graduate, who was professor of church history at Knox College, Toronto, published a pamphlet which ripped the book to shreds.[9]

McNeill's general assessment was that "as a record of church union in Canada the book is grossly uninformed and grossly unfair." He then proceeded to examine the "freaks of historical research" which it contained. First, there was a problem of proportion. The "motives against union" received fifty-three pages while those for union received only twenty. It was no wonder, said McNeill, that the arguments against union far outweighed those in support. Secondly, Morrow's account of origins was questionable. Morrow made "his readers gasp at the sudden and 'fortuitous' origins of the union negotiations in 1902!" This was possible, argued McNeill, because "there is a range of facts quite outside our author's purview." The "range of facts" was the history of the church union movement in Canada during the 1880's and 1890's which McNeill carefully sketched. Thirdly, there was the "red herring" of federation. Morrow claimed that federation had never been adequately discussed. McNeill, however, believed it had been "fairly discussed" and "fairly rejected." It was rejected as "unsatisfactory and immoral," because "it recognizes on the one hand, while denies on the other, the principle of union."

Morrow was extremely upset by this "rotten review," and he wrote to MacNamara suggesting that Stuart Parker and Banks Nelson be asked to reply to McNeill's attack on his book.[10] By this time, however, the demands of the controversy had so far outstripped scholarly discussion that no one had the time to rescue Morrow. The legislation had already been introduced in Manitoba, Saskatchewan, and Alberta, and the fight was just about to begin in Ontario. The time, therefore, had come for action rather than academic debate.

The third step in the dissidents' preparation for the legislative struggle was the formulation of their legal case. Following the 1916 General Assembly when the decision was made to proceed with union, the dissidents had retained the services of one of Canada's most eminent lawyers, Eugene Lafleur.[11] The contact with Lafleur was made through Robert Campbell's son, George, who was a Montreal corporation lawyer. When the Presbyterian Church Association was reconstituted in 1922, therefore, it was natural for them to turn once again to Campbell and Lafleur for advice in the presentation of their case at the 1923 Assembly. When the assembly voted to consummate union, however, the advice of Campbell and Lafleur began to be questioned by a number of newcomers in the resistance movement.

The executive became aware of these rumblings of discontent through Robert Campbell's nephew, George F. Macdonnell, who was practising law in Ottawa. Macdonnell felt that if some dramatic action were not taken to show that the decision of the assembly was not conclusive or binding on the dissidents, the opposition to union would dissolve in despair. He was supported in this opinion by another prominent Ottawa lawyer, F.H. Chrysler, who had recently joined the Ottawa branch of the Presbyterian Church Association. Although Macdonnell had great professional respect for Campbell and Lafleur, he thought there were reasons why they were hesitant about initiating immediate legal proceedings to test the validity of the assembly's action. First of all, he thought they were approaching the issue from a strictly juridical point of view and were not alive to the need to arouse public opinion and maintaining interest in the matter. Secondly, because they both practised law in Quebec, they were unfamiliar with the Ontario procedure of obtaining a declaratory judgment on the legality of the assembly's action. Macdonnell, therefore, recommended that the executive and its legal committee consult with Chrysler, who was the senior elder at St. Andrew's Church, Ottawa and a lawyer whose opinion was highly respected in Ontario legal circles.[12]

Macdonnell's misgivings were echoed by J.G. Pelton, a Montreal insurance agent who had recently become a member of the Montreal executive of the association. Pelton complained that Lafleur was always out of the country arguing cases before the Privy Council and suggested that "Mr. Campbell is entirely lost in an action of this sort" because his practice was exclusively in commercial law. In view of these opinions the executive decided they would have to hear Mr. Chrysler's suggestions.[13] In September 1923, therefore, the executive and legal committee met in Toronto. At this meeting Chrysler recommended a course of action which many dissidents later agreed was perhaps one of their most serious blunders in the whole controversy.

Chrysler had extensive experience as government counsel on contracts and legislation for the national transcontinental railway system. He had argued many cases before the Railway Commission and the Supreme Court of Canada, and by the 1920's his reputation was well established.[14] Thus, the executive committee had to listen when he suggested that there was a possibility of obtaining an injunction against the officers of the assembly restraining them from acting as the authorized representatives of the Presbyterian Church in Canada and from taking any further steps toward effecting organic union by petitioning Parliament to pass legislation for the purpose of incorporating the United Church of Canada. The attractiveness of the proposal was that even if it failed, it would stall the proceedings because it was unlikely that Parliament would act on a unionist petition for legislation if the authority and competence of unionist officials to make such a request was being examined by the courts.

Neither Campbell nor Lafleur believed that the union movement could be stopped or that it was possible for the unionists and dissidents to continue to live together in the same church for much longer. "My personal view of the matter," said Campbell, "is that the 'disruption' is here and permanent—I would be inclined, therefore, to recognize separation as a permanent [sic] and proceed, if possible, by consent to work out the details of a reasonable settlement."[15] Campbell's basic principle was that "a bad settlement is better than a good law suit," and he was convinced that every effort should be made to reach a settlement immediately, rather than engaging in years of conflict in court or in Parliament. It was for this reason that when a letter arrived from George Pidgeon seeking such a settlement, both Campbell and Lafleur advised that this alternative should be considered.[16]

Chrysler, however, was opposed to carrying on any correspondence or discussions with the unionists. His position was that the whole matter of union was illegal and beyond the powers of the General Assembly. From this position he argued:

> If so, is it not equally beyond the powers of any officers or members of
> the Presbyterian Church Association, on the one side, or of representatives

of the General Assembly, on the other, to make a treaty of any kind of the nature indicated in their correspondence? Is it not simply an offer on the part of the union committee to hold out the hope of some satisfactory settlement in order to induce the Association to refrain from taking such proceedings as they deem proper to oppose it?[17]

Chrysler found many sympathizers among the dissidents. By 1923 many of them were fearful that if there were backroom discussions of a settlement, there might be a sellout. So they supported Chrysler's suggestion that they get an injunction against the officers of the General Assembly.

After many delays the writ was issued in the Supreme Court of Ontario on 25 January 1924.[18] Among other things it argued that it was not within the power of the courts of the Presbyterian Church to alter or vary the trusts upon which the property was held or to alter the purposes for which it was founded and established. In trying to establish that the articles of association of the trusts would be radically altered by union, the writ went into a detailed comparison of the doctrinal changes which were involved in the "Basis of Union." Pointing out the differences between Calvinism and Arminianism, the writ noted in detail how such Calvinistic doctrines as total depravity, double predestination, and a limited atonement had been abandoned in the "Basis of Union." For those who might not be able to tell the difference between these theological systems, explanatory comments on specific points were provided, as, for example, "The Arminian theory is that man initiates the work of salvation asking and receiving of God; whereas Calvinism teaches that God initiates the work, giving so that man cannot resist the gift."

Once the writ became public, two problems arose immediately. First, the unionists turned it into an object of ridicule. Besides giving wide circulation to it, they published a pamphlet entitled "The Gospel of Anti-Unionism," which lampooned the doctrine of double predestination.[19] "Do you see anything objectionable or unchristian in the statement that 'God in the Gospel freely offers His all-sufficient salvation to all men'?" it asked. "Do you prefer the anti-union statement that 'Christ died only for the elect' and 'passes by' the rest of mankind? Do you prefer to believe that God foreordained men to everlasting death?" Those who did not believe this, it concluded, could have no part of anti-union Presbyterianism. Their place was with their "mother church which is going into union." J.R.P. Sclater, the minister of Old St. Andrew's Church, Toronto, explained to his congregation that since he was such a new arrival from Scotland, he had kept his own counsel on this Canadian question. When he saw the doctrinal position of the dissidents as set out in the writ, however, he immediately made up his mind to join the unionist cause. Illustrating how the writ could be used homiletically in support of the unionists, he said, "'Reprobate, non-elect infants' 'The others

God passed by!' Think of it, mothers with children—think of it, you on whose heart is graven the name of your friend. It may be, according to that, that from eternity to eternity, he has been an outlaw from the love of God. . . is this the God in whom you trusted?"[20]

Such reactions might not have been too serious if the writ had stalled the legislation. But because no application for an interlocutory injunction was made, it failed to achieve this end. Chrysler wanted to proceed in this direction immediately, but D.L.McCarthy and C.C.Robinson, the executive's legal counsel in Toronto, advised against it. "Our experience," said McCarthy, "is that judges in this province are very timid about interfering with matters of state, and we are afraid that no matter how clear the case might be they will hesitate to apply the legal remedy where the matter is to be dealt with in parliament, and our feeling is that on an interlocutory motion there are few, if any, judges who would in their discretion make an order at the present time."[21] If there had been a clear right of appeal to the Privy Council, McCarthy said, he would have looked more favourably on the proposal. But the right of appeal was limited. Leave for such an appeal had to come from another judge, and if this failed, the motion itself would fail. Then the courts would have to make a mandatory order that the defendants withdraw the petition. In this event, C.C. Robinson pointed out, the unionists could say to Parliament that the courts had refused to interfere.[22] The only possible advantage Robinson could see in making the application for an interim injunction would be to show "that we were really in earnest about the action." But a more effective way of accomplishing the same end, he suggested, would be to press the litigation as actively as possible, so as to get the pleadings closed and the case on the non-jury list without delay. Then a day could be fixed for the hearing and Parliament could be informed that a hearing was forthcoming.

The failure to proceed with the interim injunction, however, destroyed the effectiveness of the action and exposed the dissidents to the charge that they were not serious. Arthur Meighen saw even more sinister intentions behind this action. "Why," he asked during the debate on the issue in the House of Commons, "after initiating the action in January 1924 had no application been made by 26 June 1924 for an interlocutory injunction which would have been the only way to take practical action to get the restraint?" The reason, he suggested, was that the dissidents were trying "to hold the sword of litigation over this parliament." Furthermore, they were setting a trap. If Parliament agreed that the legislation should not come into effect until the courts had determined whether the General Assembly had the power to enter union, the dissidents could defeat the legislation "by simply dropping the action" and thereby making sure that the courts would never have to make a judgment one way or the other.[23] There is no indication the dissidents had thought their strategy through to this conclusion, although it

Editorial cartoons from the *Toronto Globe*, 16 June 1913 (top)
and the *Montreal Daily Star*, Thursday, 8 May 1924.

Robert Campbell

Ephraim Scott

Duncan Macleod

R.G. MacBeth

Frank Baird

A.J. MacGillivray

Wardlaw Taylor

J.W. MacNamara

Daniel Fraser

John Penman

Thomas McMillan

William Hendrie

Thomas B. McQuesten

R.S. Cassels

G. Tower Ferguson

W.G. Brown

Eugene Lafleur

Thomas Eakin

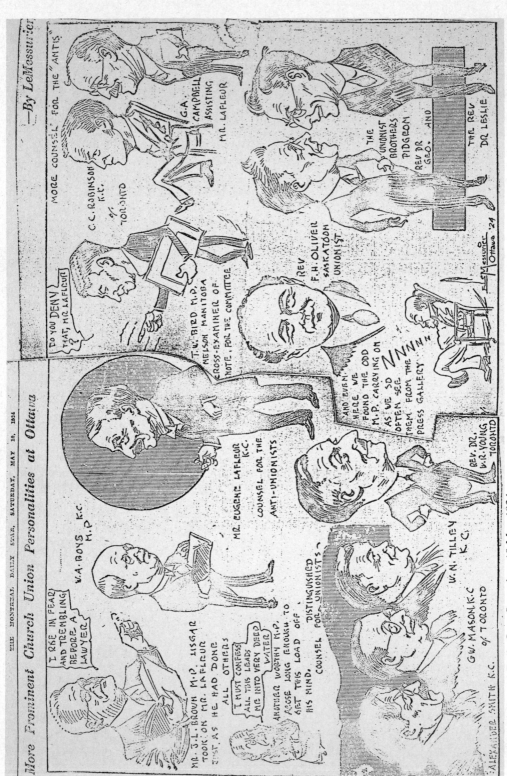

From the *Montreal Daily Star*, Saturday, 10 May 1924.

is clear from the McCarthy and Robinson correspondence that they were not averse to holding the sword of litigation over Parliament's head. Deciding on how to do so was, however, a gamble and in attempting to take the safest course, they found that the action proved much more costly than anything they gained from it. Consequently, yet another element of the dissidents' preparation for the legislative struggle went awry. Fortunately for them, the actual legislative struggle went better than their preliminary preparations.

There were no dissidents on the Presbyterian union committee following the 1923 General Assembly. Consequently, they had no way of knowing when or where the unionists would introduce the legislation. It was obvious that the unionists would require both federal and provincial legislation, but which they would seek first was a matter of speculation and all that could be done was to be on the alert for their first move. The unionists, on the other hand, could not be certain what the legislators would do. Therefore, they decided to test parliamentary reaction by introducing the legislation in the West where they were most confident it would receive little opposition. They went to Manitoba first.

Judge H.A. Robson of Winnipeg, the local leader of the dissidents, had suspected that the unionists would choose Manitoba as a testing ground. On 27 December 1923, Robson wrote to Thomas McMillan saying, "I am afraid our opponents will select Manitoba as their first field because they think they will have less opposition here." He thought they would begin with Manitoba in order "to get the tactical advantage of being able to say in the other legislatures that they already got so much accomplished, and therefore, might as well be allowed the same treatment as here."[24] Robson recommended that those in the East move quickly to issue the writ "so as to take the attention there instead of here."

When the bill was introduced, the reason for Robson's apprehension became apparent, for only three members spoke against it: John Queen, the leader of Manitoba's Labour Party, J.K. Downes, an independent, who was the leader of Manitoba's Moderation League, and N.V. Bachynsky, the member for Fisher, Manitoba. Opposing them were the attorney general, R.W. Craig, a member of C.W. Gordon's congregation, F.M. Black, the provincial treasurer and a personal friend of George Pidgeon, and two members of the Labour Party, William Ivens, a former Methodist minister and founder of Winnipeg's Labour Church, and W.D. Bayley, a graduate of Manitoba College and a prominent exponent of the Social Gospel. Premier Bracken, who was a former Methodist married to a Presbyterian, was in favour of church union and was responsible for treating the bill as a government measure rather than as a private member's bill. Faced with this opposition, the dissidents had little hope of stopping the legislation in Manitoba, but John Queen made certain that the bill did not go through unchallenged.

When it was introduced by A.M. McGregor of Gladstone, Queen attacked the form in which the bill was presented, arguing that Alfred Gandier had no right to sign the petition on behalf of the Presbyterian Church. As moderator, his only function was that of chairman of the General Assembly while it was in session. He was not an executive officer of the church who was authorized to perform any legal functions. Moreover, because the church was not an incorporated body, it was improper for Gandier to use its seal in such a petition. The bill, Queen emphasized, affected the property rights of Presbyterians in Manitoba, but not one Presbyterian from Manitoba had requested the Manitoba legislature to consider this bill.[25] He suggested, therefore, that the bill be withdrawn until the Ontario courts had dealt with the question of whether Gandier and other members of the union committee had any right to represent the General Assembly or the Presbyterian Church. Speaking on behalf of the government, J.T. Haig countered Queen's argument by maintaining that the writ issued in Ontario was irrelevant to the Manitoba legislature and by pointing out that the identity of the Presbyterian Church had been previously recognized in Manitoba. Though his arguments really did not deal with the points raised by John Queen, they were greeted with loud applause from the government benches, and the motion to introduce the bill was passed with only Queen dissenting.

During the debate on second reading, J.K. Downes joined the opposition and described the bill "as an attempt by a group of ministerial autocrats to bring about the downfall of the church of their fathers by an act of tyranny."[26] But with only two opponents speaking against it, the bill easily passed and was referred to the law amendments committee. Here again John Queen revealed that he had been well briefed. Reminding Gandier that 100,000 Presbyterians had not voted on church union in 1915 but had been counted as being in favour of union, he asked, "Don't you know that is an illegal procedure?" Gandier replied that many church members believed that ministers and elders were in a better position to judge what was for the good of the church and were prepared to follow their decision. "That was held to be illegal on the part of the trade unions," Queen observed. The government, however, chose to ignore the relevance of Queen's questioning.[27] They also ignored the advice of a delegation of Presbyterian laymen headed by A. McLeod, James H. Black, and George A. Young, who said they represented a large body of unionist and anti-unionist opinion that believed there was "too much coercion in the bill." They suggested that people should not be compelled to enter the United Church if they did not wish to become a part of it and that the legislation should be amended to allow members to withdraw before the bill came into effect.[28] None of these appeals, however, had much effect, and the bill left the committee on law amendments largely unaltered and passed its third reading in the legislature on Thursday, 13 March 1921 without division.

Queen's opposition might have been more effective if he had been a Presbyterian speaking on behalf of the dissidents. But he made it clear that personally he did not have anything to do with the churches and that he thought all of them were a menace to society. Describing them as "docile servants of a dominant class in the system," he said that he was opposing the legislation out of a sense of public duty, for he saw the church union movement as "an attempt to get a further strangle-hold on the people."[29] This perspective made his opposition more of an embarassment than an asset. He raised the points the dissidents felt should be raised against the legislation but from a viewpoint that none of them could accept.[30]

When the legislative battle reached Saskatchewan, the dissidents' prospects appeared bleak. Dr. E.H. Oliver of St. Andrew's College, Saskatoon, had produced a series of maps which purported to show that most of the Presbyterian churches in Saskatchewan were already union churches and that the passage of the legislation would simply confirm what already existed. But whereas Manitoba had only one Presbyterian minister openly opposed to union, there were several in Saskatchewan, and they were supported by a much stronger lay organization led by Judge A.G. Farrell. Moreover, with a Liberal government in power which refused to make the legislation a government issue, the struggle in the Saskatchewan legislature proved to be less one-sided.

Determined to prevent a repetition of the Manitoba experience, the dissidents in Saskatchewan set out to muster as much political clout as possible, and their major coup was to enlist the support of Justice W.M. Martin, the former premier, in their cause. Martin appeared before the select committee on private bills and argued that some of the provisions were unfair to any minority and that others were of "a very vicious character." While Martin had not been active in the resistance movement, he was the son of a Presbyterian minister sympathetic to the dissidents' cause.[31] With his extensive legal and legislative experience, he was able to subject the legislation to a critical scrutiny that few others could have equalled, and as a Presbyterian his defence of the dissidents' position carried much more weight than had John Queen's in Manitoba.

Among the points Martin raised in his attack on the provincial legislation was its anticipatory character. He argued that because the act of incorporation had to be passed by Parliament some time in the future, the members of the Saskatchewan Assembly were "being asked to legislate in the dark." No one knew what the Parliament of Canada would do, and because Parliament was not authorized to deal with property or civil rights in the provinces, the unionists would have to come back after Ottawa had dealt with the legislation to ask for a commission to deal with them. Furthermore, he was opposed to the legislation because he was convinced it was designed to put the minority out of business. Principal Oliver objected to this charge, arguing that no attempt would be made to deprive those who wanted to remain out of union of the right of using the name "Presbyterian." Martin, however, was not convinced that this was the case on the basis of the legislation.[32] The unexpected appearance of Martin, together with W.F. McConnell, J.J. Galoway of Regina, W.G. Ross of Moose Jaw, and Judge Farrell of Regina, speaking on behalf of the dissidents, made a dramatic impression on the committee; and the chairman, sensing that it was impossible to proceed, asked both sides to try to resolve their differences before the committee reconvened.

A conference between the unionists and dissidents was held on Monday, 10 March 1924, but it ended in failure. When the proceedings of the select committee opened on 12 March, the dissidents showed a disposition to make concessions, but the unionists stood adamant on all the contentious clauses of the bill. Therefore, the Hon. A.P. McNab, who was chairman of the committee, said that in view of the inability of the parties to agree, it was useless for the committee to listen to them any further and he suggested that both sides submit their amendments and leave the committee to make up its own mind.[33]

Premier C.A. Dunning supported this idea and recommended that several clauses be referred to the legislative counsel, R.W. Shannon, to condense and redraft. Dunning further indicated that he wanted questions of faith and doctrine left out of the bill and made it clear that the unionists, in asking for anticipatory legislation, left the legislature with the right to pass retroactive legislation later. With this understanding safeguarding their action, the committee completed its work, introducing no changes which conflicted with the basic principle of the bill, but making specific regulations regarding the holding of congregational meetings to vote for or against union.[34] This recognition of the coercive character of the legislation and the government's reservation of the right to deal with it retroactively was hardly a great victory for the dissidents, but it was a step in the right direction and certainly an improvement over the treatment they had received in Manitoba.

According to the 1921 census, there were seventeen thousand fewer Presbyterians in Alberta than in either of the other two prairie provinces, but several of the most prominent ministers in the resistance movement were from Alberta. In Manitoba and Saskatchewan it had been laymen who had led the opposition to the church union legislation, but in Alberta it was Dr. D.G. McQueen of Edmonton, a former moderator of the General Assembly, W.G. Brown of Red Deer, J.S. Shortt of Olds and F.D. Roxburgh of Edmonton who were the spokesmen for the dissidents. However, in Alberta as in Manitoba, the Progressive Party was in power, and as a result the dissidents fared little better than they had in Manitoba.

The only difference was that Premier H.H. Greenfield announced that his government would not take sides on the issue and that the legislation would be introduced as a private member's bill. "There are only two points," Greenfield declared, "on which the legislature will have any right to act in regard to this church union situation. . . . The first is as to whether or not the regular rules or methods of the churches have been observed in the preliminary procedure leading up to the present stage and the second is whether or not the rights of the minority have been protected as far as they can be protected by law."[35] But when the leader of the Opposition, the Hon. J.R. Boyle, suggested that full protection was not offered in the bill for minorities and recommended that the Alberta legislature should wait until the Ontario courts had dealt with legality of the procedures followed in the General Assembly, O.L. McPherson, the Speaker, ruled that the legislature could take action nevertheless.[36]

When the unionists presented their case to the private bills committee on 6 March 1924, J.R. Boyle, Donald Cameron, and M.C. McKeen, a farmer from Lac Ste. Anne, thought the union would be unfair to the minority, and Boyle thought there should be another vote. Both remained unconvinced by Leslie Pidgeon's reply.[37] The following day the committee heard from the dissidents. McQueen argued that the legislation was coercive and confiscatory and would lead to the disruption of the Presbyterian Church. The opponents of union, he said, saw the case as a matter of conscience. Presbyterian ministers and elders had taken vows to maintain the church's peace and unity, and he felt he could not be true to these vows and support the union bill.

F.D. Roxburgh argued that the resistance to union in Alberta was steadily growing and that its strength had been underestimated. The vote in the Synod of Alberta at its meetings in the fall of 1923, he said, had been thirty-two to twenty-eight and in Edmonton, "out of a Presbyterian membership of 3,500 some 1,300 signatures had been secured to a petition against the bill." W.G. Brown took particular exception to Leslie Pidgeon's claim that the General Assembly had a right to force the Presbyterian Church into a merger. The General Assembly, he asserted, was the servant of the church, not its master. In typical fighting fashion, one he had followed from the beginning of the controversy, Brown concluded with a prophecy: "It has been said we are in rebellion against official authority in our own church and so we are, but I tell you that if this bill goes through you will see that the rebellion has only started." J.S. Shortt took a less threatening approach when he indicated that the opponents of the bill did not object to the principle of the majority having its way but to the way in which the majority was seeking to drag others with them. His plea was that the Presbyterians who wished to remain out of the union should be left undisturbed and that the coercive clauses of the bill be eliminated.[38]

All in all the presentation made by these Alberta ministers with no outside help from McConnell or the P.C.A. executive was impressive. It failed, however, to influence the Progressive Party members in the Alberta legislature, who seemed much more impressed by R.B. Bennett of Calgary, legal counsel for the unionists. Consequently, the church union bill emerged from the private bills committee virtually unaltered and passed its third reading on 12 April 1924.[39]

The defeat of the dissidents in the three prairie legislatures was a blow, but it was not unanticipated. Throughout the struggle the dissidents had experienced the greatest difficulty in organizing this region of the country and had found the least amount of financial support. Only in Alberta did the dissidents have significant ministerial leadership, but even there they remained a minority. Consequently, it was not surprising that the governments granted the wishes of the majority and passed the enabling legislation.

The 51,614 members of the Presbyterian Church in the Maritimes represented only about one-seventh of the church's total membership. But the roots of Presbyterianism in many communities there went extremely deep, and therefore the dissidents had more support than on the Prairies. Nevertheless, the best they could do was to win some amendments that would protect their rights. In New Brunswick the legislation was passed with no major alterations. In Nova Scotia, however, where the provincial secretary, D.A. Cameron, supported the dissidents' cause, the conflict was extremely tense. Cameron submitted an amendment which would provide the dissidents with the opportunity to vote themselves out of the United Church of Canada before it came into existence rather than after. This amendment was defeated in the lower house, but when the bill reached the executive council or upper house, several further amendments were made, including the right of dissident congregations to vote themselves out of union and exempting the Presbyterian College at Halifax from the terms of the union. These amendments produced a deadlock between the two chambers which was finally resolved by accepting the amendment on voting and by dropping the others.[40]

In Prince Edward Island the bill passed in the legislature with a substantial majority, but Lieutenant-Governor McKinnon prorogued the legislature immediately after the passage of the bill and refused assent. This action produced a minor constitutional crisis, for the unionists appealed to Ottawa. On 27 June 1924 the minister of justice, Ernest Lapointe, tabled a report in the House of Commons which considered it regrettable that the lieutenant-governor had in effect vetoed the bill and rejected the advice of the Legislative Assembly of Prince Edward Island. If he questioned the legislation, he should have reserved the matter for the governor general. But insofar as the bill could only be sanctioned by the lieutenant governor on the advice of the provincial legislature, it was necessary to pass the bill again in a later session.[41] While these manoeuvres helped to delay the legislation, it was apparent that nothing could be done to stop it. All that was possible was to remove the coercive aspects which would have forced all Presbyterians into the United Church whether they wished to be part of it or not. The dissidents had to be content with this single victory in the Maritimes.

One more crucial provincial struggle, however, remained before the debate on the legislation began in Ottawa and that was in Ontario. Two-thirds of Canada's Presbyterians lived there and many of the largest Presbyterian congregations had already voted and given a clear indication that they had no intention of entering the United Church. It was in this province, therefore, that the dissidents planned to stage their most intense fight and the outcome was to be the most crucial, for the province of Quebec had already indicated that it was not going to consider the matter until it saw what Ontario planned to do with the bill.

The bill was introduced into the Ontario legislature on 26 February 1924 and arrangements were made for its presentation to the Private Bills committee on 26 March 1924. This committee was chaired by the Attorney General, W.F. Nickle, who was an opponent of union and a son-in-law of Daniel Gordon, the ex-principal of Queen's. The committee consisted of sixty-two members, a majority of whom were opposed to the bill as it was presented. This became apparent when after hearing testimony from representatives of both the unionists and dissidents, the debate in the committee focused on a number of amendments. Among these was an attempt to defer consideration of the bill until it had been dealt with by the dominion Parliament, another to defer passage of the bill until a fresh vote was taken in the Presbyterian Church, and yet another to recommend a procedure for dividing the assets of Presbyterian congregations which were split over the issue. The most important of these amendments, however, was one that instructed the law clerk of the committee to add clauses to the bill "providing for the preservation of the Presbyterian Church in Canada, the Methodist Church or the Congregational Church as separate entities and for giving to any congregation the right by vote of its members to remain in its mother church and to keep therein any property owned by it." When this amendment passed by a vote of thirty-six to twenty-six, the unionists decided to withdraw the bill.[42]

In accepting the withdrawal, W.F. Nickle, the chairman of the committee, made a lengthy statement on both the procedure of withdrawal and the conduct of the parties involved. He indicated that though the committee had been subjected to a great deal of outside pressure, it had been his intention to see that the committee "should so conduct itself that when the proceedings were over, no one could say a mighty problem had been hurt, either by strenuous objection or boisterous interruption." He also pointed out that the General Assembly of 1923 had empowered the union committee "to use its best effort by amendment of the proposed legislation or otherwise — to maintain the unity of the church or if that be not possible, then to reach a satisfactory agreement with the minority in reference to the name and status of the non-concurring congregations and division of denominational property."

It was "a matter of deep regret," Nickle said, "that both parties had not used the amended bill as a 'via media' for the establishment of religious peace." He hoped that before the legislature met again the parties would get together and by mutual concessions "reach a conclusion that will make possible the attainment of a great ideal and at the same time recognize a conviction of many that stirs them to their very depths."[43]

In writing to his brother Leslie, George Pidgeon claimed that the combination that really defeated them was "one of anti-union Presbyterians, Anglicans... and wets. In fact," he continued, "a hatred of the O.T.A. [the Ontario Temperance Act] seemed to be the chief motive for smashing union and so indirectly hitting the Methodist church." In the face of this opposition, the only course open to the unionists was to withdraw for "the fight was only increasing the antagonism in a legislature that we have to face again next year and raising far more difficulties at Ottawa than the withdrawal could possibly do."[44]

Withdrawal of the legislation, however, came at an extremely awkward time for the unionists, because the date of 30 April had already been set for the Private Bills Committee to begin hearings in Ottawa on the federal legislation.

When the committee met, its first task was to hear several days of testimony from a host of ministers, laymen, and lawyers representing both sides of the union question. However, despite the outstanding array of talent presenting the cases, most of the arguments were old ones. When all the repetition is eliminated, the case for and against the legislation boils down to a few simple propositions.

The unionists argued that the reason they were seeking legislation was to avoid the type of difficulties which had arisen in Scotland following the decision handed down by the House of Lords in the Scottish Free Church Case. They suggested that instead of looking at the Scottish case for precedents, Parliament ought to look at the action of the Imperial Parliament in rectifying the problems created by the decision. This was a powerful argument, since the committee knew that if it denied the legislation, it would be forcing the churches into costly litigation. The committee also knew that even if the courts decided the churches did not have the power to change their doctrine or to unite with other denominations, the churches would return to Parliament to seek that power as they had in Scotland. Moreover, as E.H. Oliver reminded the committee, there were already 1,245 union congregations in existence, and the legislation had been passed in five provinces. Consequently, refusal to consider the legislation would create endless confusion.

The problem with the unionists' argument was that they also claimed they were legally justified in insisting that the church's identity and continuity went with the majority and that the minority had no right to the use of the name nor any claim to continuity with the Presbyterian Church in Canada. For the minority this was an arrogant and arbitrary position because the majority was denying them their heritage and identity. To assume, as the proposed legislation did, that only those who went into union were Presbyterians was unjust. No property or financial settlement, however generous, could compensate them for this loss, and no court or parliament could ever make them accept this fundamental injustice.

Sensitive to this difficulty, J.S. Woodsworth attempted to give the unionists a way out by asking if it was not possible that one entity or identity could be divided into two. Fifteen years later this line of thought provided a solution to the controversy, but at this point Leslie Pidgeon insisted that one of the two must be dissenting from the body. From his perspective the Presbyterian Church in Canada would go into union as an entity and take its name with it, for its name was the only distinctive mark of its identity. Furthermore, he contended that the church would enter the union with its traditions and spiritual gains and its entire heritage from the past.

Sensing that this was the weakest point in the unionists' argument, the dissidents trained their strongest guns on it. How far, they asked, could an "entity" be transformed without loss of "identity?" If the Presbyterian Church was fused into a new church with a different name, a different creed, and different formularies, then surely the Presbyterian Church had ceased to exist. The effect of the legislation, therefore, was to destroy an historic church which the dissidents wished to preserve so that they might continue to worship in it as their forefathers had done before them.

Emphasizing the unreasonableness of this attempt to destroy an historic church, Eugene Lafleur said:

> As to their church, it has been taken from them, and as to its name, they never get it back . . . . Not only that, but they are taking the name and are not using the name. They are going to put a fence around that name so that we, who want to carry on the old church cannot keep the name. Now can you imagine anything more arrogant and unjust, and may I say, unChristian, than that?

Being fully aware of the strong argument for passage of the legislation, the dissidents suggested that if Parliament passed the bill in its present form in order to avoid the debacle created by the Scottish Free Church Case, it would be incorporating and merging together people who did not want to be incorporated, people who were already incorporated under provincial statutes, and people who had never requested incorporation in a dominion corporation. It was beyond the powers of Parliament to bring within a corporation entities—whether persons or corporations — that were unwilling. Secondly, it would be vesting the property of congregations held under provincial laws in a church that was to be a creation of the dominion Parliament. Again this was beyond the powers of any dominion act. Thirdly, it would be diverting trust funds in a manner that was both unjust and dishonest. The new church would be different in doctrine, in formularies, and in church discipline and management. Therefore, a deflection of trust funds to this new entity would be a clear violation of the original trusts. In short, to pass such nugatory legislation was to invite litigation. Logically forceful as this line of reasoning was, it proved strategically unsound. The basic weakness of the argument lay in the fact that it is pretentious to tell Parliament what it can or cannot do and that it is even more dangerous to hold the sword of litigation over its head.[45] For the moment, however, the dissidents seemed to have secured a strong position.

After hearing the arguments, the committee adjourned for several weeks. By the time it met again on 28 May, the unionists' counsel had introduced a crucial amendment allowing those congregations which did not wish to enter the United Church to vote themselves out prior to the act coming into force on 10 June 1925. This amendment was accepted by the committee, but when the chairman asked if the committee wished to adopt the preamble of the bill, William Duff, the Liberal member from Lunenberg, Nova Scotia, and Gus Porter, the Conservative member from Hastings West, Ontario, moved an amendment which would prevent the union taking place until the Supreme Court of Canada had ruled on the power of the Presbyterian General Assembly to form any union with other churches and on the power of Parliament to enact such legislation either in whole or in part. Although T.W. Bird protested that this amendment denied the principle of the preamble, the amendment was ruled in order, and a committee was struck to consult with the unionists and dissidents concerning the legal effects of the amendment.

When the committee convened the next day, the amendment was presented in a reworded form, and when the vote was taken it was passed by a division of twenty-seven to twenty-three. In spite of several attempts to remove or reconsider the amendment, it remained the committee's finding when the bill was finally reported to the House on 14 June 1924. The fact that the amendment was passed when fifteen members of the committee were not present was seen by some unionists as a devious maneouvre on the part of the dissidents. The committee members, however, had received a day's notice of the amendment and could presumably have been present if they thought it would pass. The rumour was also circulated that the prime minister favoured the amendment and that this was the reason it had passed. Mackenzie King later declared that the rumour was totally false and that his failure to support the amendment was one of the reasons it failed to gain the support of the House.

The negative reaction to this amendment among the unionists was immediate. Newton Rowell wired King that the amendment would "kill the bill. . .and block the great movement for Christian unity."[46] He claimed the Methodists would have no part in a bill which involved directly or indirectly litigation on the capacity of a sister church to determine its own policy. The unionists also published a pamphlet on why the amendment was unacceptable and sent a copy to every member of Parliament. In addition, the General Assembly meeting at Owen Sound on 9 June 1924, opposed the amendment by a vote of 426 to 96 and declared that:

> This church has the right and power, subject to no civil authority, to legislate and to adjudicate finally in all matters of doctrine, worship, government and discipline in the church, to frame, adopt, and modify its subordinate standards of faith, and the right to unite with any other Christian church without loss of its identity on terms which it finds to be consistent with its own principles, doctrine and religious standards.[47]

It was this very claim, however, which the amendment proposed to test in the courts.

External agitation was one thing, but on 30 May 1924, the Honourable W.R. Motherwell, minister of agriculture, addressed a letter to all the Liberal members of the House of Commons. He indicated that if the amendment referring the whole matter to the courts was passed, two million Canadians who stood firmly behind the bill would, even though it was a private bill, hold the Liberal Party responsible for not allowing it to go through as introduced. In 1921, he pointed out, the Church of Scotland had asked the Imperial Parliament of Great Britain for authority to unite with the United Free Church, and this had been granted. In view of this precedent, it would be unthinkable for the Canadian Parliament to refuse such authority and to encourage the Canadian churches to seek redress in the courts. Therefore, he suggested, the amendment to the preamble should be removed and the bill passed without rider or reservation.[48]

William Duff, the author of the amendment, was also a Liberal, and he accused Motherwell of butting into the discussion "like a billy goat at a billboard." He believed it was dangerous for Motherwell to turn this private bill into a political and party issue, especially when all the parties were deeply divided. Duff assured the House that his amendment was a compromise. It was much less than the dissidents wanted, and he had not discussed the matter with them when he drafted his amendment. He also assured the House that he did not wish to deny incorporation to the new church but that he did not believe Parliament had any right to destroy an historic church, and if the bill was passed as introduced, the Presbyterian Church in Canada in which the minority wished to remain, would be destroyed. From Duff's perspective this would be "religious coercion." "It would mean," he continued, "the denial of religious liberty and civil rights to a great body of Canadian people on the demand of some other people. . . .It would mean that this new incorporated combine, born of coercion and confiscation and claiming the right to coerce and confiscate, would in future be a menace to the freedom of statesmen and parliaments in their efforts for the wellbeing of our country."[49]

In the face of this split in the Liberal ranks, everyone looked to the prime minister. Mackenzie King, however, gave very conflicting signals. He indicated his disagreement with the Duff amendment, but then he voted against the motion to remove it. This confusion created a great deal of merriment among those who were convinced that he was always talking out of both sides of his mouth. However, it seems clear, in spite of this mixup, that King wanted a quick reference to the Supreme Court and not the lengthy litigation to which he thought the Duff amendment would lead. It is also clear that King felt the doubt surrounding the assembly's power should be removed before the union was effected. Still, the distinction between the reference to the court which he wanted and that recommended by the Duff amendment did seem muddled. The initiative in the debate, therefore, fell to the leader of the Conservative Opposition, Arthur Meighen.

Meighen came out unequivocally for deletion of the Duff amendment and against any reference of the legislation to the courts. He made it plain that whatever the outcome of the litigation, the result would be the same. If the courts decided that the General Assembly did not have the power, the unionists would return to Parliament. So Parliament might as well act now. This was an oversimplification, but at least it was clear, and for most members of the House it settled the issue. As a result the amendment was deleted, and the bill was passed without reservation.

When the bill reached the Senate, those who were opposed to it ran into difficulties. The case for the legislation presented by Gideon Robertson assumed that so much time had already been spent on the bill in the House of Commons that everyone in the Senate was familiar with the issues. Yet when J.D. Reid attempted to refer to the debate in the House of Commons and to point out that the legislation had passed by a vote of only 90 to 58 in a house of 235 members, he was reminded by the Speaker that according to Senate rules he was not supposed to refer to anything which had happened in the House of Commons. When Reid attempted to get around this ruling by stating that everyone could have read in the newspapers that 90 out of 235 was not even half the members "in another place," he was again called by the Speaker, who insisted that he could not allude to the House "in any way at all." Reid bowed to the Speaker's decision but insisted that he had a right to refer to what was in the newspapers. He continued, therefore, to analyse the vote of the 235 members in the House of Commons by pointing out that anyone could read "in the newspapers" that of those people "assembled" 178 were from between "Manitoba and Sydney, Cape Breton; yet out of that 178, where the majority of Presbyterians live 50 voted for and 53 against and 75 did not vote at all."

Again he was called by the Speaker for he was obviously continuing to analyse the vote in the Commons. Reid protested that Gideon Robertson in introducing the bill had referred "to what took place in the House of Commons" and no one had said to him "you must not refer to that." The government leader of the Senate, Raoul Dandurand, admitted that "there is no question that the rule is very often abused," but he continued, "when the chair draws attention to the necessity of respecting the rule I think we owe it to the chair to abide by his ruling." Reid continued to protest but eventually he accepted the ruling, and the next day he made an extensive apology to the Speaker.[50]

The point Reid had been making was important, and it is unfortunate that he was ruled out of order on a technicality, for it placed all the other opponents of the bill in a difficult position. As for Reid, there was little that he could do but complain about the way in which the bill was being "railroaded" through. The bill had come to the Senate seven days before Parliament was scheduled to prorogue. The Senate did not sit on Saturdays or Sundays, and no debates were held on the day of prorogation. Therefore, they had only four working days to deal with a bill which, in Reid's view, would wipe the Presbyterian Church out of existence. Besides, there were only nineteen Presbyterians in the Senate and seventy-seven of other denominations. This meant that the rights of the minority were in the hands of the members from other denominations. Were these members, he asked, prepared to deny the minority their rights, to take away their religious liberty, to cancel the charter of their church, and to take away its bequests? If they were, they ought to know that the minority would fight for justice.[51]

The other major opponent of the bill, the Hon. W.B. Ross, focused his attack on a narrow point. He objected to clause 10 of the bill, which provided for voting in the congregations between 10 December 1924 and 10 June 1925 in order to allow those who did not wish to enter the united church to vote themselves out. Ross did not object to the vote but rather to the fact that the vote was to be taken at a congregational meeting. He thought that some members, either through sickness or because of business, might not be able to be present. Therefore, he proposed in an amendment that a ballot be distributed two weeks before the meeting to all those who were eligible to vote. G.G. Foster in seconding this amendment cited the case of a ninety-one-year-old woman who had written to him saying that she had not been out of bed for six years and appealing to him not to let Parliament "legislate the Presbyterian Church out of existence without giving me a chance to vote for the church I love." He asked the Senate, therefore, to arrange the ballot so that it would be possible for this woman to vote at home.

Gideon Robertson initially refused to accept such an amendment on the grounds that Parliament would be dictating to the churches the form and manner in which they must conduct their business. Eventually, however, he was persuaded by his colleagues to accept an amendment which instructed that the voting had to be by ballot rather than by a show of hands. But he refused to accept any suggestions that would force a congregation to grant the ballot to those who were unable to attend the meeting.

Unfortunately, so much time was spent on this point that many of the broader issues concerning the legislation as a whole were passed over. This was partly owing to the narrow issues on which the opposition focused and the way they became embroiled in procedural wrangles. But they did get an important amendment through, and before the bill was passed, J.D. Reid managed to have the last word in which he reminded the Senate that "no Parliament can make a man change his religion." Although an attempt had been made in the legislation to wipe out the Presbyterian Church, he predicted, "Presbyterians will live, and they will build their churches, for no man, woman or child in this country can destroy the religion which Presbyterians were taught at their mother's knee, and which they have lived up to and believed in; and no Parliament will be able by passing an Act, to force them to desert their doctrines."[52]

On 19 July 1924 after the House of Commons had approved the Senate's amendment, the United Church of Canada Act received Royal Assent and became law. But following the passage of the bill, there were still a number of provincial legislatures to be heard from. Consequently, after the summer recess, attention shifted back once again to the provinces for the final stage of the legislative struggle.

In Prince Edward Island the legislation had to be reintroduced. After Lapointe had ruled that the lieutenant-governor had acted improperly in withholding his assent, the passage of the legislation was a foregone conclusion. The same was true in British Columbia: though there were several prominent dissidents there, such as W.L. Clay in Victoria and R.G. MacBeth in Vancouver, the majority in the legislature supported the bill in spite of the fact that attorney-general Manson opposed it. With a clear majority in favour, the bill was passed on 19 December 1924.

In Ontario, however, everyone expected that there would be some fireworks when the bill was again introduced into the legislature on 1 March 1925. Several days after the unionists reintroduced the church union bill, the dissidents countered with a bill of their own dealing with the issue of the continued use of the name and demanded that in the congregational voting a two-thirds majority should be substituted for a bare majority. Faced with two bills, the Ontario legislature barred the general public from the Private Bills Committee except for forty invitations issued to each side. Furthermore,

W.S. Haney and A.C. Lewis introduced a motion that the parties get together and settle their differences before coming to the committee in order to avoid "long and contentious discussion." In commenting on this motion, W.F. Nickle, the chairman of the Private Bills Committee said, "I think both sides are making an honest effort to get together, but I am rather inclined to the conclusion that they are going up and down rather than forward."[53] In the same wry vein Lewis said, when Haney explained the intent of his motion, "I nominate Mr. Haney as President of the Optimists Club."[54]

After some preliminary discussions which brought no agreement, the Private Bills Committee appointed a subcommittee consisting of nine members to meet with representatives of both sides in order to work out a compromise. This sub-committee met seven times between 24 March and 2 April and finally came up with a compromise which contained two major amendments to the church union bill. The first set up a congregational property commission consisting of one member from each side and the chief justice of Ontario as chairman. The second granted Knox College to the dissidents and the principal's residence to the unionists and gave both parties equal access to the Caven Library, which was to be run by a group of trustees representing both groups. Questions concerning the college's charter and endowment were left to the Dominion Property Commission. Losing Knox College was a major blow to the unionists, for most of the money to build it had been raised by Alfred Gandier, and it had been considered to be firmly in unionist hands since 1909 when Gandier became principal. Yet it was clear that without this major concession, the legislation was not likely to pass. Even with that larger interest in view, it was a blow. And it was not just a question of Knox College because Quebec had indicated that it would deal with the bill as Ontario did. Consequently, the decision to give Knox to the dissidents in Ontario meant that the Presbyterian College in Montreal would go to them as well. This compromise which was worked out in the subcommittee was endorsed by the Private Bills Committee as its recommendation to the legislature. In the debate on the second reading there were a number of objections to this compromise, but eventually it was passed and the legislative struggle came to an end.

Though many aspects of the dissidents' preparations for the legislative struggle had backfired and though they had not succeeded in preventing the passage of the legislation, nevertheless they came out of this phase of the struggle holding a stronger position than before. They were assured of two important colleges, of a Dominion Property Commission to oversee an equitable distribution of the church's assets, and most importantly the opportunity to vote themselves out of union between 10 December 1924 and 10 June 1925. Not all the coercive aspects of the legislation had been removed, for dissidents were still denied any claim to continuity with the Presbyterian Church in Canada and any right to use the name. But they at least had an opportunity to set up an alternative administrative system before the new church came into existence. It was this opportunity of a final vote, therefore, which set the stage for the next phase of the conflict.

11

The Final Vote

The United Church of Canada Act contained provisions for individual congregations to hold a vote to determine whether or not they wished to enter the United Church of Canada. For many years the opponents of union had requested a third vote to demonstrate that there was no desire for union in the Presbyterian church. But now the choice was between staying in the Presbyterian Church and leaving it to enter the United Church of Canada. Union was already an accomplished fact, and all that the dissidents could do was to try and prevent as many of the congregations as they could from leaving the Presbyterian Church. At this point, therefore, the dissident's organization was put to its final test.

The executive of the Presbyterian Church Association met in Toronto on 14 July 1924 and announced that it would be their policy to hold a vote in every Presbyterian congregation in the country. To accomplish this goal, they intended to hold convocations in as many synods and presbyteries as possible and wherever practicable to organize committees in every congregation to assure that a vote was held.[1] Furthermore, to make certain that everyone was aware of the issues, they planned to produce a wide range of literature and to provide speakers for every congregation that wished to make certain that both sides of the question were fully presented. With 8 synods, 79 presbyteries, and 1,809 self-sustaining congregations to cover, this goal was obviously ambitious.[2] How successful they would be in achieving it would be determined in large measure by their finances.

The amount of money which the association had spent on legal fees alone during the legislative struggle was considerable, and in July 1924 when the executive met in Toronto the legislative struggle was far from over. Explaining the financial situation to John McKeen, the treasurer of the Maritime branch of the association, J.W. MacNamara indicated that in 1923 the expenditures of the association for federal purposes had amounted to $7,573.98, the largest single item being $2,391.41 for legal expenses. But by the first quarter of 1924, from 1 January to 31 May, the federal expenses had risen to $16,876.81 with the two largest items being $7,000 for the Advertising Service Co. and $2,800 in legal expenses. Moreover, by 1 June 1924 there were outstanding accounts amounting to $23,690 with several accounts from legal counsel not yet rendered.[3]

The initial budget of expenses for 1924 had been set at $30,000 with Ontario to raise $14,000, Montreal and Ottawa to raise $8,500, the Maritimes, $2,500 and the West, $5,000. On 3 June 1924, however, the finance committee revised their budget by increasing the total to $70,000 with Ontario raising $35,000; Ottawa and Montreal, $25,000; the Maritimes, $7,500 and the West, $2,500. Up until 31 May 1924 the association had received $19,158 from Ontario; $9,637 from Montreal and Ottawa; $1,316 from the Maritimes, and $195 from the West.[4] Furthermore, by October 1924 they had unpaid legal expenses of $19,238.12, not including the accounts of Eugene Lafleur and George Campbell and a bank overdraft of $4,532.20.[5] These figures clearly indicated not only the limits of what they could hope to accomplish but also where it would be possible to concentrate their greatest amount of effort.

Raising money for the expenses of the Presbyterian Church Association, however, was not their only problem. They also had to be sure that sufficient funds would be available to carry on the work of the Presbyterian Church after 10 June 1925. Consequently, they created a Board of Trustees consisting of thirty ministers and laymen from across the country "to ask for and to receive funds for carrying on the work of the continuing church at home and abroad."[6] The necessity of carrying on two simultaneous financial campaigns limited even further the amount of money they had available to spend on literature, newspaper advertising, speakers and organizers for the third vote.

These financial constraints resulted in two types of literature: first, pamphlets produced at the local level by branches of the Presbyterian Church Association and paid for out of local funds; and second, pamphlets and newspaper advertising paid for by the national executive, which assumed responsibility for major statements of policy and rebuttals of the unionists' campaign propaganda. The local literature was so extensive that it is impossible to discuss all of it. But an example will provide some indication of its diversity. The local branch of the Presbyterian Church Association in Sault Ste. Marie produced one of the least sophisticated but nevertheless most interesting pamphlets. In this community the basic issue in the campaign on the third vote appears to have been modernism which, according to the pamphlet, denied the inspiration of the Scriptures; the divinity of Christ; the virgin birth; the miracles of Christ; the necessity of Christ's death for the salvation of men; and the presence of the Holy Spirit in Pentecost. It was not the definition of modernism that was unique but rather the suggestion that in Sault Ste. Marie it was only the Methodists who were tainted by this evil. The pamphlet continued:

These are the teachings of the *Christian Guardian*, the official organ of the Methodist Church, and of tracts issued by the Board of Evangelism and Social Service, under authority of the Methodist General Conference. Within the present month some of these doctrines have been proclaimed from a Methodist pulpit in our own city. Are you willing to accept or identify yourself with these teachings?[7]

Apparently the majority in St. Paul's Church were not prepared to accept such an identification, for they opposed union by a vote of 169 to 143. On the other hand, St. Andrew's Church in the same community went into the United Church by a vote of 399 to 329.[8]

While local committees of the Presbyterian Church Association and individual churches were issuing their own statements, the federal executive monitored the unionists' propaganda and counteracted its claims in pamphlets such as "Presbyterian Facts versus Unionist Statements."[9] In most of this literature there was little that was new, but when the unionists issued a pamphlet entitled "The Fate of Anti-Unionism," it became immediately clear that in their attempt to paint the blackest possible future for those who remained out of the United Church, the unionists had allowed their enthusiasm to get the better of their judgment to the point where they were guilty of a serious breach of ecumenical courtesy.[10]

"The Fate of Anti-Unionism" began with a question about what had happened to the opponents of the Presbyterian union of 1875. The answer it supplied was that most of the dissenting congregations came in sooner or later and that those which did not simply died or were disbanded. Not content with this Canadian analogy, the pamphlet then went on to state that the same fate had dogged the footsteps of the anti-unionists in Scotland known as the "Wee Frees." Next it proceeded to make a series of totally false statements about the failure of the "Wee Free Church" and to suggest that it had "no spiritual message for the people, no appeal to youth and is void of national significance or influence." If anti-unionism has failed in the past, the pamphlet concluded, what ground is there for the larger hope that it shall succeed in the future?

When this pamphlet appeared, W.D. Reid of Stanley Church, Montreal, who had spent the summer of 1924 in Scotland and had found the Wee Frees to be a growing, virile, evangelical church, wrote to Scotland to get some up-to-date statistics, for the authority the unionists were quoting was *The Life of Principal Rainy*, which had been published in 1909. On the basis of this source the unionists' pamphlet claimed that:

In 1905 the "Wee Frees" had 170 churches and manses; today 74 of these are derelict. Many once beautiful edifices are vacant and out of repair; the hinges of their closed doors are rusted stiff; splendid memorial windows are boarded up, and roofs let in the rain. Among the fruits of twenty years of anti-unionism in Scotland are 74 desolate churches—sans ministers, sans people!

When W.D. Reid received the current statistics on the Free Church of Scotland, however, it was apparent that since 1903 the Wee Frees had increased by 40 per cent, and this represented a rate of growth larger than that reported by the United Free Church.

This information formed the basis of the association's pamphlet "The Wee Free Story," which began by denying the validity of the unionists' analogy.[11] There was a basic difference between the opposition to a confessional union and a transconfessional union such as was being proposed in Canada. But, it concluded, that if the two cases could be considered parallel, the 40 per cent growth rate of the Wee Frees since 1903 could hardly support the prophecies of failure and speedy extinction and therefore need strike no terror in even the faintest heart. On grounds of pure fact, then, the unionists stood guilty of misrepresentation. Had this been the end of the matter, it could have been counted as simply a minor victory for the dissidents in the propaganda war leading up to the third vote. But the Wee Frees were gravely offended by the unionists' pamphlet, and they were not prepared to let the matter pass unnoticed.

The Free Church of Scotland addressed an official letter of complaint to George Pidgeon, the convenor of the Joint Committee on Church Union.[12] The letter gave a paragraph by paragraph refutation of the facts and figures contained in the unionists' pamphlet and stated that "the description you give of our Church to the People of Canada may serve your purpose in the controversy that is raging among you, but that does not, in the least, justify you in maligning (unintentionally, I hope) a sister Church among a community where she could not be instantly heard in her own defence." The sharpest cut in the letter, however, was directed against the unionists' suggestion that the Wee Frees were "void of national significance and influence." "If so," the letter asked, "why did your distinguished representative, Dr. C.W. Gordon, [Ralph Conner], ask permission to address our Assembly last May?...He said 'he felt he was coming to the truest home of his deepest heart' in coming among us, the despicable body you describe to Canadians. Does your Church speak with two voices?"[13]

The offence generated by this unionist pamphlet was not to be voiced simply through an official letter of complaint. The April 1925 issue of *The Monthly Record* of the Free Church of Scotland was almost entirely devoted to a series of condemnations of the unionists' tactics.[14] In these articles it was not only the pamphlet that was condemned but also an article by George Pidgeon, the convenor of the union committee, which had appeared in the *Presbyterian Witness* on 20 November 1924 and had made some disparaging references to the Free Church. Pidgeon had claimed that the attempt to remain independent would cut a congregation off from the greatest religious movement of the time and that "any minority staying out will be insignificant, because the Church is sure to follow the leaders which she herself has chosen." To this *The Monthly Record* replied, "The convenor now knows to his sorrow that the minority staying out will not be insignificant and that the Church, to a very formidable extent has refused 'to follow the leaders' in whom he made his boast." In warning his readers against the danger of casting in their lot with "a dying cause," Pidgeon had made specific reference to what he claimed to be the feebleness of the Free Church of Scotland, suggesting that this is the fate of ecclesiastical minorities. *The Monthly Record* countered by stating that the union movement in Canada appears to be "essentially a clerical movement" whose leaders had proceeded to accomplish their design without any mandate from their people; "it has no force of public opinion behind it: on the contrary, the high handed policy of the ecclesiastical leaders seems to be bitterly resented by a large proportion of the rank and file of the people."

Elsewhere in the same issue of *The Monthly Record*, A.M. Renwick of Dumbarton indicated that many letters from the Free Church of Scotland had been sent to Canadian newspapers and that Dr. J.R.P. Sclater had been entrusted with the task of replying to these letters. Renwick's complaint against Sclater was that he had failed to deal with the points at issue and though he had formerly professed to be a friend of the Free Church of Scotland, he had joined hands with the Canadian unionists to distort the facts concerning the Free Church's missionary work completely and had declared that the church was "doomed to destruction." In view of these charges and the continuing misrepresentation, the publications committee of the Free Church indicated that it was sending one thousand copies of the April issue of *The Monthly Record* to Canada in an effort to counteract these false and malicious statements. By itself, this episode in the propaganda war which preceded the third vote and continued while the voting was taking place was not too important, but it indicates how errors of judgment on the part of the unionists enabled their opponents to balance the scales and to gain a degree of advantage in spite of their limited funds. Unable to count on such tactical windfalls or on sizeable funds, the dissidents had to plan their organization meticulously and to use their resources where the greatest numbers could be significantly canvassed.

In 1924 the total membership of the Presbyterian Church in Canada was 374,951. Of these 55 per cent, or 206,330 members, resided in Ontario.[15] Even before the federal legislation was finally passed on 19 July 1924, therefore, it was clear that the major campaign for the third vote would take place in Ontario, for if the Presbyterian Church Association failed to make a showing in this province, the future of the church would be in jeopardy. As in previous phases of the struggle, the dissidents' main emphasis was on organization. The responsibility for this task was placed in the hands of a Committee on Organization chaired by A.J. MacGillivray and consisting of T. McMillan, D.T.L. McKerroll, J.D. Cunningham, James Wilson, Lt.-Col. J. Forbes Michie, and J.W. MacNamara, who acted as secretary.[16]

This committee was responsible for all aspects of the campaign. It hired the organizers, assigned their duties, received their reports, decided where and when convocations would be held and who would be the speakers. It also kept careful records of the provincial, synodical, presbyterial, and congregational organizations. The primary strategy was to form a committee in every congregation which would be responsible for petitioning the various sessions for a congregational vote, distributing literature, house-to-house canvassing, and providing transportation to convocations in neighbouring towns and villages. This aim proved too ambitious. The only part of the country in which they came even close to realizing their goal was Ontario. Elsewhere the organization was either much more haphazard or completely non-existent.

Outside of Ontario and Quebec, the committee's major organizer was W.F. McConnell who from August 1924 until May 1925 seemed to be constantly on the move across the country trying to strengthen the association's organization and in some areas proving to be its only effective voice. From 28 August until mid-October 1924 the focus of McConnell's attention was the Maritimes, and his reports reveal the problems which the dissidents' experienced in organizing the Maritime region.

When McConnell arrived in St. John, he met with several members of the New Brunswick provincial executive, and his report revealed that he was not too impressed with them. They did not have a list of committees in New Brunswick and had not formulated any campaign plans. Finlay McIntosh, the organizer in the Maritime Synod was supposed to have a list of the committee members, but he had not sent a copy either to McConnell or the head office in Toronto as promised.[17] When McConnell finally caught up with McIntosh in Prince Edward Island, he discovered that a number of excellent meetings had been held on the Island but that little had been done in the way of congregational organization and no arrangements had been made for McConnell's visit by the local committee.[18] He reported, therefore, that it was essential to set up a new organization in P.E.I. because "we simply cannot be satisfied with local leadership which I think has been 'weighed in the balance and found wanting.'"[19]

When McConnell arrived in Nova Scotia, he was more hopeful because he thought "the organization here is taking fine hold of things."[20] He was also able to report that arrangements were being made to release R. Johnston of New Glasgow and Dr. F.S. MacKenzie of Sydney Mines from their pulpits for two or three months so that they could assist Finlay McIntosh in organizational work in the Maritimes. McConnell added that he had been in touch with the women's groups to get "a few capable women to help in the work of congregational organization." On the basis of this brighter picture in Nova Scotia, McConnell thought that he would be ready to move to Quebec by the end of September. The Toronto committee, however, instructed McConnell to "remain in the Maritime provinces until he. . . was assured that the local organizations are completed to carry out the work of organization in every congregation in that territory."[21] In explaining this directive, MacNamara said, "the further we go with our work the more convinced we are that the names of workers and of organizations in every congregation should be secured and forwarded at the very earliest time both to the Federal Organization here, and to the Provincial Association concerned."[22]

To have fully realized this objective, McConnell would have had to spend the next nine months in the Maritime Synod, but because he was the eyes, ears, and often the voice of the Toronto committee, he was much too valuable to be left there indefinitely. In fact, as a result of his previous work in the West, requests for his assistance were continually reaching the federal committee, and towards the end of October 1924 the Toronto Committee pulled him out of the Maritimes so that they could get an assessment of the situation in the West.[23]

McConnell arrived in Edmonton for the Alberta Synod meeting on 27 October 1924. Passing through Winnipeg and Saskatoon on the way, he met with key committee members. He thought the committee in Winnipeg was very enthusiastic and "thoroughly representative of the churches in that city," but the organization in Saskatoon "as well as all over the province has been somewhat inactive." The meeting in Edmonton, which was held in conjunction with the Synod, "had good representations from all the churches and [we] sent each group back with the information necessary for the taking of the vote."[24]

At the synod meetings that were taking place across the country at this time, both the unionists and dissidents had to make arrangements for the continuance of the church's synodical structure after 10 June 1925. Dissidents like J.S. Shortt, the clerk of the Alberta Synod, who had done all the planning for the 1924 meetings, were replaced by unionists. To counter this action, the dissidents drew up a parallel synodical and presbyterial structure to make sure there would be no loss of continuity through overlooking those congregations which decided to remain out of the United Church. In Alberta, Dr. McQueen was elected moderator and F.D. Roxburgh was elected clerk of the new synod of the continuing Presbyterian church which would take over after 10 June.[25]

The dissidents' Committee on Organization was pleased with the situation in Alberta, but they were becoming alarmed by reports from British Columbia where it was essential not only to prepare for the third vote but also to appear before the Private Bills Committee of the B.C. legislature. A.E. Vert of New Westminster had written to MacNamara complaining that the provincial organization was not working, and H.W. Boak, a lawyer from Vancouver, had complained that while the unionists were flooding the churches with literature, there was nothing available from the Presbyterian Church Association. The problem, as MacNamara confided to McConnell, was R.G. MacBeth, who was president of the B.C. Branch of the association. MacBeth's idea of how to run a campaign was to flood the letters-to-the-editor columns of the local newspapers, and he was constantly involved in this task. But he was the sort of person who could not see the point of calling meetings or distributing literature. As MacNamara put it, "MacBeth writes me for technical information but. . .never a scratch of the pen to show the state of their own organization, the condition of affairs there or the plans they are making in connection with the legislature or for the carrying out of our campaign."[26] To determine what was going on in B.C., therefore, the Committee on Organization asked McConnell to go there as soon as possible and "put the organization on a sound working basis."

When McConnell arrived in B.C., he found things in a complete shambles. No plans had been made for his visit, and he was expected to make all his own arrangements.[27] Furthermore, it was apparent that they expected Ontario to send McConnell out to B.C. to do the work for them "at no cost whatever to themselves." "It makes me mad," said McConnell, "to think that they don't even attempt to billet me or pay hotel expenses and save our Executive that much."[28] When he arrived in Victoria, it was also clear that because the provincial executive was not functioning properly, the three local organizations in Victoria, Vancouver, and New Westminster were working at cross purposes and could not even agree on what amendments to the legislation they should present to the B.C. legislature. With the help of Leslie Clay, McConnell eventually managed to get this problem solved, but he reported that "it is most discouraging to find how little seems to have been done in B.C. where the field seemed to promise so much."[29]

Spending part of his time in Vancouver organizing and part in Victoria helping to prepare the dissidents' case, McConnell was eventually able to report that he had managed to convince MacBeth to accept A.E. Vert as the new provincial secretary of the B.C. organization and E.G. Thompson, the Home Mission convenor for B.C., as a vice-president of the Vancouver branch of the association. But he was not able to get Duncan Campbell of Chilliwack as an organizer. This was disappointing because, as he put it, "I am afraid that I may get them started and when I go things will come to more or less a standstill again."[30]

If McConnell's reports from the Maritimes and the West provided something less than an encouraging picture of the association's state of readiness for the third vote, the situation in Ontario and Quebec provided more cause for hope. The Committee on Organization had teams of organizers in both provinces led by J.H. Borland in Quebec, R.J.M. Glassford in Eastern Ontario, and H.R. Horne in Western Ontario. They had organized convocations in all parts of Ontario and Quebec and had set up local committees in the presbyteries and congregations. Indeed, such a thorough job had been done that the committee was confident they would make a good showing in Ontario, and in many communities they had a fairly clear idea of how the voting in the various congregations would go long before the votes were actually cast. In one of his many letters MacNamara described for McConnell what was happening in Ontario during the week of 19 November 1924.

> Our series of convocations have been going on in splendid shape, not a flat meeting yet, good results and securing organization through them. We are still going on with them although we will soon have to change to congregational work. This week there was one in Wingham on Monday, two meetings in Toronto last night, Windsor, Thursday, Glencoe, Friday, Orangeville, on the 28th, Paris and Kincardine on the 15th and no less than four meetings in Toronto that night, Milton on the 27th and so on.[31]

With this sort of activity taking place, it would have been difficult for anyone who was involved with the Presbyterian Church in Ontario to avoid the issue or to complain, as they were elsewhere in the country, that Presbyterians were not being properly informed about the issues.

The United Church of Canada Act instructed that the voting in the congregations was to take place between 10 December 1924 and 10 June 1925. This appeared straight-forward enough at the time but there were a number of complications. In the first place, not all the provincial legislation had been passed by 10 December, and in several cases provincial legislation had been passed which set different dates for the voting. In New Brunswick and Manitoba, for example, the legislation instructed that the vote had to be taken between 10 June and 10 December 1925. Insofar as the provincial legislation affected the congregational property, this raised a question as to whether the vote should be taken under both the federal and provincial acts or whether one vote would suffice. Secondly, the federal legislation did not say that a vote had to be taken. It simply said that a vote might be taken. In some provinces the provincial legislation made the vote mandatory, but this was not true everywhere. The federal legislation made it clear, however, that a vote had to be held if it was requested in writing and signed by the following number of members:

10 members in congregations of 100 members or less

> 25 members in congregations having over 100 and not more than 500
> members
> 50 members in congregations having over 500 and not more than 1000
> members
> 100 members in congregations having over 1000 or more

The initial meeting regarding the vote had to be held within thirty days of the receipt of such a requisition, and notice of the meeting specifying its object had to be presented before the congregation at each diet of worship on two successive Lord's Days on which public service was held.[32]

The emphasis that the P.C.A.'s Committee on Organization placed on congregational organization was designed to assure that in as many congregations as possible there would be a committee to gather sufficient names to assure that a congregational vote would be held. To make certain that both those requesting a vote and those voting were qualified, the legislation specified who was eligible. Only those persons who were in full membership on 19 July 1924 (the date when the federal legislation was passed) and whose names were on the roll of the church on that date would be entitled to vote. Some congregations, however, had their own constitutions which specified slightly different qualifications for voting on matters affecting the disposal of property. The legislation allowed for these differences providing no one was included who had not been qualified to vote on 19 July. In Manitoba and New Brunswick the provincial legislation specified 10 June 1925 as the date that would be used to determine membership. In these cases the provincial legislation took precedence over the federal because the voting affected the disposal of property.

Within these general guidelines, however, there was some room for congregations to determine when the vote would be held and how it would be administered. In St. Andrew's, King Street, Toronto, where the vote was 733 to 19 against union, it was agreed at a congregational meeting on 22 December 1924 that the voting would take place on alternate days in the afternoon and evening until 9 January 1925 when the poll would close at 3 P.M. A meeting of the congregation would then be held that night at which the results of the vote would be announced. At Knox Church, Toronto, where the vote was 788 to 20 against union, it was decided that the polls would be open every afternoon and evening during the week and on Saturday afternoons but that there would be no voting on Sundays, Christmas Day or New Years Day.[33]

In churches where there were more significant minorities, it was necessary to make more elaborate preparations. At Riverdale Presbyterian Church in Toronto, where the vote was 527 to 509 against union, a meeting was held on 11 December 1924 at which both sides of the issue were presented. Rev. J.G. Inkster of Knox Church spoke for the dissidents, and Rev. H.I. Pritchard of

North Broadview Church spoke for the unionists, and strict rules against applause, interruptions, and comments were enforced by the minister of Riverdale, Rev. L.J. Hunter, who chaired the meeting.[34] At Bloor Street, where the vote was 1055 to 311 in favour of union, both sides of the issue were presented when Dr. George Pidgeon preached at the morning service and Rev. J.S. Shortt spoke at the evening service.[35] At College Street, where the vote was 1055 to 311 in favour, the session had denied the dissidents the right to use the church for a meeting. This action allowed Banks Nelson to accuse the unionists of preventing "a proper vote" by denying members in good standing a Presbyterian auditorium for their meeting.[36] It was perhaps for this reason that in making preparations for taking the vote at College Street special care was taken to be scrupulously fair. Consequently, the committee in charge of the preparations for the vote consisted of three unionists and three dissidents and arrangements were made so that five unionists and five dissidents were appointed as scrutineers.[37]

The problems involved in taking the vote, however, were minor in comparison with the problems that arose as soon as the results were announced. In many cases congregations split down the middle. In Toronto, for example, Chalmers Church remained out of union on a vote of 458 to 454. St. Paul's also remained out on a vote of 496 to 406. In Hamilton the same thing happened. Central Church remained out on a vote of 398 to 381, Erskine on a vote of 460 to 416, and St. Andrew's on a vote of 480 to 441. The reverse was also true. St. Andrew's, Brantford, for example, went into union on a vote of 236 to 235; St. Andrew's, Peterborough on a vote of 211 to 191; and St. Andrew's, Markham, on a vote of 64 to 57. In Toronto, St. David's went into union on a vote of 444 to 334, and Eglinton, on a vote of 410 to 309.

In large urban centres with minorities of four or five hundred it was relatively easy for these groups to move out and survive on their own in rented accommodation, but in rural communities like Tait's Corners, Ontario, where the church went into union on a vote of 55 to 51, or at Knox Church, Fort Frances, which went into union on a vote of 73 to 71, it was much more difficult for minorities to carry on, and this was especially true of the dissident minorities who did not have the option of moving in with the Methodists.[38]

Even congregations where the vote was much more decisive experienced difficulties. In Paris, Ontario, for example, where the vote against union was 372 to 161, the question that arose was in effect, "what do we do now?" In reply to this question, J.W. MacNamara set out the official policy of the Presbyterian Church Association. He said:

Our opinion is that everything is to be gained by our people showing a spirit of patience, forbearance and courtesy at the present time....For instance, a message could be conveyed to the members of the congregation voting out that whilst the congregation has settled the question as to its future, yet all who have worshipped in the church and made it their church home are and will be welcome in the future.

Then, in regard to the minister, MacNamara continued:

> If he puts his resignation in the hands of the Presbytery at once, representatives could be appointed to appear before Presbytery in the interests of the congregation. They could say whatever kind words they desired regarding the ministry and the work of the pastor, pointing out that the verdict of the congregation made the resignation of the minister inevitable at some time, but that there would be no need for his resigning at once; providing he was willing to bow to the verdict of the people, and to carry on the work impartially without stirring up fresh trouble, it would be satisfactory for him to remain on for some time.[39]

This policy, as MacNamara made clear, was not entirely dictated by considerations of magnanimity. As the executive well knew, "if the minister leaves at once and tries to take a section of the congregation with him, he is more likely to do harm than if he is induced to stay on a while. When things calm down and people settle back into their places, there will be less likelihood of carrying a large section of the congregation out with him."[40]

All of this was fine advice, but unfortunately it did not work either at Paris or at most other places. As John Penman later explained, both the minister and the clerk of session were unionists who refused to hand over the church's books and records. Furthermore, they circulated a list among those who voted against union, attempting to bind them to a commitment to leave the church, and when individuals signed it, they issued them their membership certificates. In response to this information, MacNamara replied:

> I wish to state, most emphatically, that all books of the congregation, including Session Records, the Treasurer's Books, Baptismal Record; in other words, all books in the possession of the Session clerk or any other officer of the congregation, or any organization of the congregation, are the property of that congregation. The Session Clerk has no right to retain them, and if he does not hand them over at once, proper steps should be taken to secure possession of them. The congregation is entirely within its rights in insisting on no delay in this matter.[41]

Similar situations were apparently cropping up elsewhere for MacNamara concluded:

You can easily see that a number of unionist leaders are deliberately trying to frighten our people, and by assumptions that are entirely unfounded, are trying to retain certain authority to which they are not entitled.[42]

Initially the unionists had advocated that congregations should stay together as a unit and abide by the will of the majority in the congregation. But when it became apparent that many of the largest and wealthiest churches were voting themselves out of union, that policy was changed because the unionists could not afford to lose the financial support of the unionist minorities in these congregations.[43] By the end of 1923 the total indebtedness of the Presbyterian Church in Canada was $400,000, which consisted of $328,113 deficit on the Common Budget and $69,965 on five of the theological schools.[44] In spite of severe curtailment of the church's work, the money which had been budgeted for the church's work was not coming in, and by 30 November 1924 there was a $16,366 decrease in contributions as compared with the previous year.[45] By January 1925 the situation was so serious that editorials in the *Presbyterian Witness* were urging Presbyterians to meet their obligations. As one editorial put it, "Whatever their [the church members] views or decisions on the question of church union these are sacred obligations assumed at the last General Assembly from which there is no honorable discharge until June 10, 1925."[46] Many individuals and congregations had, of course, been withholding their contributions for they had no intention of supporting those who were going into union.

This financial situation, therefore, led to some very strange unionist arguments concerning minorities. In congregations which voted into union, they wanted the non-concurring minorities to stay until at least 10 June 1925. But in congregations which voted against union, minorities were urged to leave immediately. The reasoning behind this contradictory advice was that "the anti-unionist. . .is not called upon to give up a single principle. . . .On the contrary, in following his church into the United Church, he is remaining true to his vows, [and] loyal to the church to which he owes so much." On the other hand, "unionists conscientiously feel that to ally themselves with the dissidents in non-concurring congregations is disloyalty to their church and a violation of solemn vows. They are standing for a great principle, and they cannot trifle with their conscience."[47] Such self-serving semantics were hardly likely to persuade many dissidents either to remain with their congregations or to contribute to that part of the church which was entering union. Consequently, by the end of January 1925, the Presbyterian Church was faced with the difficult problem of congregations splitting up and ministers resigning. Trying to put a bright face on all this, the editors of the *Presbyterian Witness* hailed this as a "spontaneous movement." In an editorial entitled "Loyalty Manifested to a Great Ideal," the editors said, "without waiting for any suggestion from without, minorities are pledging themselves to enter the United Church the moment their congregations vote out. . . . It is creating a deep enthusiasm and assuming the proportions of a crusade."[48]

Not everyone, however, felt so cheerful. In November 1924, George Pidgeon had predicted that "any minority staying out will be insignificant."[49] But when his prediction proved to be wide of the mark, he commented sourly that "the revolt against the Presbyterian Church is largely confined to Ontario. The reactionary element is strong in certain sections of this province, but in so far as their influence goes they are setting their province against the rest of the Dominion."[50]

Others, however, saw the results as a total disaster. Most prominent among these individuals was Dr. D.W. Dyde, the principal of Queen's Theological College. Dyde was so upset over the situation that in a gesture of desperation he wrote to the attorney general of Ontario, W.F. Nickle, suggesting that he act as a mediator. He recommended that both parties be called together and that the unionists should say to the dissidents: "If we suspend (for a definite period of time) the operation of the bill, what will those opposing organic union concede? How far will they go towards intimate co-operation?" Nickle, however, refused to get involved. He said: "From me anything by way of a suggestion would, I fear, be construed as an impertinence, as there are those, not confined to any one group, who can only see the side of the shield that is towards them."[51] The wisdom of this remark was confirmed when J.G. Inkster of Knox Church, Toronto, said: "It is too late now," and Dr. Gandier of Knox College pointed out that this was the proposal of Dr. Drummond all over again.[52] The editors of the *Presbyterian Witness* were even more emphatic in their dismissal of Principal Dyde's proposal. They wrote:

> Dr. Dyde's proposal seems to us to be equivalent to an invitation to the church to hoist the white flag and capitulate to a minority who have all along flouted the authority of the church courts and who will accept nothing short of surrender of the vital principle embodied in the Basis upon which the uniting churches have agreed . . . . We believe . . . that Principal Dyde and others are taking far too seriously the defection among the Presbyterians of Ontario.[53]

To show that not all took these defections seriously, some unionist wags christened the non-concurring churches as "The Presbyterian Church in Ontario"[54] When the final returns were in, however, it was apparent that a major disruption of the Presbyterian Church in Canada had taken place. Indeed, in the urban centres of Eastern Canada, there had been a major rebellion against those leaders of the church who had forced the union issue in the face of mounting opposition.

Arriving at an accurate statistical picture of how the vote went over the entire country is extremely difficult because the two sides tended to present the results of the voting in different forms and to interpret the results in a manner that cast their side in the most favourable light. For example, the dissidents emphasized only the actual votes in the congregations, for on this basis the result was 122,966 to 114,298 in favour of union. There were, however, a number of congregations which instead of taking a vote, simply passed a resolution that they would enter the United Church of Canada. Naturally the unionists insisted on including this group in their statistics because the membership in these congregations raised the total in favour of union by 29,256. They also insisted on including the membership of those congregations which entered union by default (that is, without taking a vote or passing a resolution), for this added a further 26,318 to the number entering union. The unionists, therefore, claimed that the final figure was 178,630 to 114,298 in favour.[55]

The most favourable way of looking at the results from the unionists' point of view, however, was to present the figures in terms of congregations voting for or against union. On this basis 4,512 congregations were in favour of union and only 784 against. It became apparent later, however, that 2,316 of these unionist congregations were aid receiving (that is, dependent on mission funds for their survival).[56] But even taking this into consideration, the unionists had a clear majority of the self-sustaining congregations. Therefore, it is difficult to see why Principal Dyde of Queen's Theological College panicked when the results of the voting began to come in. Dyde's appeal to W.F. Nickle might have been unrealistic at that late stage in the proceedings but Dyde was no fool. Consequently, he must have seen something which does not appear in these aggregate figures.

One way of looking at the early returns which would have been enough to frighten any careful observer would be to look at the amount given to missions, to education and to other benevolences by the large urban churches that were voting themselves out of union. The combined 1923 total of givings for these purposes from two Toronto churches which voted against union, Knox and St. Andrew's, is $29,191.[57] This figure exceeds the combined givings of the Presbyteries of Yorkton, Kamsack, Kindersly, Assiniboia, Battleford, Prince Albert, and Arcola in the Synod of Saskatchewan. If three more Toronto churches which voted out of union, Chalmers, Rosedale, and St. John's are added to Knox and St. Andrew's, the combined givings of these five churches stands well in excess of ten of the fourteen presbyteries in the Synod of Saskatchewan. That the unionists were aware that some would look at the early returns of the voting in this way is apparent from an editorial in the *Presbyterian Witness* which observed that there is "a danger that undue importance should be attached to the number or the numerical and financial strength of the congregations which decline to follow their church into the United Church of Canada." To counteract this danger, the editorial went on to argue that "congregations which have been misled into revolt against the regularly constituted courts of their church will in the end, we are persuaded, be the great losers by the divisive course which they have chosen and the schism they are causing in the body of Christ."[58] While this represented the official unionist response to the losses and gains in the Presbyterian Church, it was hardly the sort of argument which would allay Dyde's sense of the impending catastrophe.

When the dust cleared by 1926, J.W. MacNamara was able to report that the continuing Presbyterian Church had 1,140 congregations and preaching stations and a total membership of 154,243. Ten per cent of these members were scattered thinly across the four western provinces. Slightly more than 10 per cent were in the Maritimes and the rest were located in Ontario and Quebec. The total amount of money raised for all purposes during the first year was $3,219,113.[59] Compared with the Presbyterian Church in Canada prior to 10 June 1925, the continuing church was a minority representing approximately one third of the church's membership. But it was still considerably larger than the church had been in 1875, and during its first year of operation it had succeeded in raising three times as much money as the church had raised in 1875. They were, therefore, hardly the negligible and insignificant minority the unionists had predicted they would be and their defection has to be seen as a major disruption of the Presbyterian Church in Canada.

How is this disruption to be explained? No single explanation is sufficient to cover such a complex phenomenon but there seem to have been at least three factors at work: a rural-urban split, a rift between theological liberals and conservatives, and an overlapping of other community conflicts, especially in Ontario. There were, as we shall see, congregations whose voting was influenced by unique circumstances, and therefore they do not follow the general pattern. Erskine Church, Montreal, provides a particularly dramatic example of how specific circumstances could alter the way a congregation voted. As a wealthy and prestigious urban congregation, Erskine should have voted against union. It was the congregation to which Dr. Ephraim Scott belonged, and the clerk of session, James Rodger, was one of the most prominent Montreal laymen in the resistance movement. Rodger had been an elder at Erskine since 1879 and had served as clerk of session since 1884. He was a very old-fashioned Presbyterian elder who believed that ministers were simply the teaching elders of the congregation while laymen were the ruling elders and overseers of the congregation. It was this view which brought him into conflict with the minister of Erskine, the Rev. George Hanson. Hanson was an Irishman from Belfast who had come to Erskine in 1912 after spending several years as minister of Marylebone Presbyterian Church in London, England. Hanson was committed to church union, and he did not hesitate to speak his mind on the subject. Consequently, he came into head-on conflict with James Rodger.

In 1923 Rodger, while absent from Montreal, addressed several letters to the session on the question of union. Hanson, as moderator, read these letters to the session as a matter of courtesy to Rodger rather than as an item of congregational business. But he did not read all of the correspondence, saying that it contained matters which were none of the session's business. When Rodger returned to Montreal, he was furious and gave notice of a motion which he believed would settle the matter. As the motion revealed, Dr. Hanson had invited, without knowledge of the kirk session, Rev. Principal Oliver of Saskatoon, a pronounced supporter of the proposed union, to occupy the pulpit of Erskine church on the morning of Sunday, 7 January 1923. Rodger, therefore, demanded that equal time be given to an opponent of union. This motion was unanimously supported by the session, and Dr. Hanson agreed that Dr. A.J. MacGillivray should be invited to preach on this subject. When MacGillivray arrived, however, Hanson conducted the preliminary part of the service and sat down refusing to introduce MacGillivray or welcome him as the guest preacher. Furthermore, Hanson chose to ignore the session's ruling that after both sides had been heard, the question would not be raised in Erskine church again without the consent and approval of the session.

Hanson's preaching on church union, therefore, made Rodger bring the matter before the session at which he extracted the following apology out of Hanson:

> I desire to express frankly and at once my great regret that in speaking at a recent diet of worship on the subject of church union, I inadvertently violated a resolution of the session which forbade any discussion of church union unless the consent of the majority of the resident members of the session. . .had been previously secured. . . . I offer my sincere apologies to the session for my unintentional discourtesy and apparent disregard of my brethren's recorded judgment. . . . Nothing was further from my intention than to say or do anything that might be interpreted as in any way derogatory to the dignity and authority of this court.[60]

Not satisfied with this humiliation, Rodger further demanded that Hanson read this apology to the session before the whole congregation at a service of worship, and the session unanimously concurred in this action.

By pressing the matter this far, Rodger had stepped over the line, for the "Blue Book" on *The Rules and Forms of Procedure* specifically stated that "the session cannot entertain a complaint against its moderator."[61] Only the presbytery was allowed to deal with such matters in order to protect ministers from personal vendettas that might arise within a congregation. But when no one raised this point, Hanson resigned. The difficulty in this case was that the session had acted unanimously, and therefore to take the matter to presbytery could have resulted in a formal reprimand of the session. Rather than expose the congregation to this sort of action, Guy Toombs, who had been a member of the board of management of Erskine since 1921, quietly approached all those members of the congregation who had been offended by this episode pointing out the unfairness of the tactics adopted by the dissidents within the congregation. When the vote on union was taken, Erskine went into the United Church by a majority of sixty-nine votes. It was a very expensive resolution of the conflict within the congregation, for James Rodger and 173 members left the congregation. But it was nevertheless an effective solution to the problem.[62]

There were perhaps other instances where the voting was influenced by similar circumstances. They are extremely difficult to document, however, because most congregational histories tend to pass discreetly over the details of such painful episodes. Nevertheless, it seems highly likely wherever congregations appear to have voted contrary to established patterns, their voting was influenced by special circumstances. The number of such instances were perhaps not small, but a major part of the division that took place in the Presbyterian Church in Canada can be accounted for by examining the broader social forces that were moulding the moral climate of the nation.

In the half century between 1875 and 1925, the most important social change affecting the Canadian churches was the rapid growth of cities. Urbanization increased the size of city congregations while rural depopulation decreased the size of country congregations. The major urban congregations were ten to twenty times larger than most rural ones. Consequently, they provided most of the financial support for the wider enterprises of the denomination. Along with size went status and independence. The large urban congregations necessarily became the first class congregations of the denomination, while the rural churches sank into second class status. In many cases they were shrinking to the point where they were no longer self-supporting. This dwindling of rural congregations was accompanied by a loss of status, but strangely enough it did not result in an equal loss of power in the church courts. The city churches which produced most of the money for missions did not have a final say in spending it, nor did they control the church courts. In fact, each city church had exactly the same representation as any rural congregation. The growth of the large urban congregations therefore distorted the representative character of the Presbyterian polity. The result was that rural congregations, many of whom were dependent on mission funds, could easily out-vote the city churches if they found themselves at cross purposes.

This possibility became a reality when the Presbyterians were faced with the church union question. Church union offered little to the large urban congregations, but to the rural churches it offered hope. By pooling the depleted resources of their communities behind a single church, they might be assured of at least one flourishing church. Consequently, when the final votes were counted, it was found that most of the rural churches were in the United Church of Canada, and many of the largest and wealthiest Presbyterian churches in the urban centres of eastern Canada remained out.

The disruptive effects of the shift from rural to urban dominance coincided with an intellectual change from a static to a developmental world view in western Christendom which caused further division within the Presbyterian Church in Canada by the end of the nineteenth century. From this new developmental perspective the Bible, as William MacLaren pointed out, became "not a revelation" but "a history of revelation," and instead of being "the sole rule of faith and practise," it became "only one of many useful but imperfect sources of information."[63] Moreover, the new theology which adopted this developmental perspective linked the immanence of God with the doctrine of evolution and tended to deny the transcendence of God to the point where it entirely eliminated the miraculous element from Scripture and went even further to emphasize the human element in its composition.[64] A similar attitude was displayed toward the historic creeds and confessions of Christendom. Instead of being eternally valid statements of Christian truth, they were seen simply as statements which were valid for a particular moment in history. Consequently, they were thought to be in need of continual updating and reformulation in the light of new circumstances and changed conditions.

This new developmental worldview proved to be very disturbing for Presbyterian conservatives, and they vigorously resisted it until well into the twentieth century. As a result, many conservatives found the suggestion of transconfessional organic union threatening because it involved an abandonment of the Westminster Confession and a departure from the Presbyterian system of church government which many believed was part of the *jus divinum*. Their opposition to union, therefore, was motivated by the fear that it involved a fatal compromise with the truth that would ultimately lead to some vague secular humanism and the loss of a precious heritage.

The third element in the making of this disruption was a conservative reaction, especially in Ontario, against the politics of uplift and moral extremism which many associated with the Progressive Party of Ontario during the years 1919-23 when E.C. Drury and the Farmer-Labour administration were in power. The belief that brought the Druryites to power was that rural depopulation and the beguiling attractions of city life were eroding dangerously the superior values of the agrarian way of life. The Druryites, therefore, conceived it to be their most urgent duty to cleanse the moral and social climate of Ontario. What this meant in practice was an attempt to put teeth in the Ontario Temperance Act, the Lord's Day Act, and other legislation directed against gambling and horse-racing. The man charged with this task was W.E. Raney, a Toronto lawyer who was appointed attorney general in the Drury administration. When he was appointed the Toronto *Evening Telegram* denounced Raney as "a moral reform bigot who will hasten to establish a reign of the saints."[65] This was exactly what he was, and he pursued his intention of cleaning up Ontario with such fanatical zeal that by 1923 it was with some relief that the Ontario voters turned to the Conservatives under Howard Ferguson's leadership.[66] The memory of Raney, a Presbyterian who favoured church union and the Social Gospel, was a factor in the reaction to church union in Ontario. Of course, some Presbyterians favoured his reform programme, and this probably accounts for urban congregations like Bloor St., St. James Square, and College St. entering union with large majorities, for ministers like George Pidgeon, D.N. Morden and R.B. Cochrane were well-known supporters of temperance and moral reform. For many Presbyterians, however, the legislation of righteousness was abhorrent, and they believed that there was no way in which they could be comfortable in a church dominated by uplifters and social gospellers. The reaction against the politics of moral extremism in Ontario, therefore, had a tendency to overlap with the church union question and to intensify that reaction. On the Prairies and in the Maritimes there was no similar overlapping of community and church issues in a negative way. As for the West, if there was any overlapping of these issues it worked in favour of church union. These three factors, namely, a rural urban split, the rift between theological liberals and conservatives, and the overlapping of other community conflicts, therefore, provide a basis for understanding some of the forces which were at work in producing the disruption of the Presbyterian Church in Canada.

12

The Parting of the Ways

The break up of the Presbyterian Church in Canada began as soon as the results of the voting in the congregations were announced, and it continued for a long time, even after the formal separation of the two parties at the General Assembly in Toronto on 9 June 1925. More was involved than the grand parting gestures of congregational minorities walking out en masse or the formal declarations of the unionists and dissidents at the General Assembly in 1925. These were largely symbolic gestures which were carefully planned and organized in advance, and as a result they provided few surprises. These dramatics, however, were followed by a long drawn-out period of haggling over property and seemingly endless court battles which brought out the worst in everyone and provided many surprises as well as disappointments for all concerned.

In 1925 the General Assembly was divided into two parts: the first took place in the College Street Church in Toronto from 3 to 9 June; the second part was held in St. Andrew's Church, Toronto from 11 to 16 June. The two-part assembly had two moderators. George C. Pidgeon presided over the first part and Ephraim Scott over the second. There were also two separate bodies of commissioners, only seventy-nine of whom were official participants in both parts of the assembly. The United Church has never acknowledged the legitimacy of the second part of the 1925 Assembly, but whenever the Presbyterian Church in Canada lists the moderators of the General Assembly since 1875, it always lists both George Pidgeon and Ephraim Scott as moderators in 1925. In this way the dissidents have stressed that, though part of the church left to enter the United Church, there was no break in the essential continuity of the Presbyterian Church in Canada.

Those who were in charge of the first part of the 1925 Assembly did everything in their power to assure that the identity and continuity of the Presbyterian Church in Canada went into the United Church of Canada. The three key events in the first part of the 1925 Assembly were the report of the union committee, the answer to the dissent of the minority, and Leslie Pidgeon's motion to adjourn the assembly until 24 June 1925 "unless in the meantime its rights, privileges, authorities and powers shall have ceased under the terms of Section 22(a) of the United Church of Canada Act. . . which Act gives effect to the union form[ed] by the free and independent action of the negotiating churches."[1] These three statements merit examination because they contain the essence of the unionists' case and clearly indicate what they were trying to accomplish at their final assembly as part of the Presbyterian Church in Canada.

In presenting the report of the union committee, George Pidgeon reviewed the events of the past year, commending the spirit, patience, fortitude, and unshakeable faith in the "Ideal of Union" evinced by the church's membership. Speaking on behalf of the union committee, he said, "We acknowledge our failures, we regret the sorrow that the long controversy has occasioned, but for all that has been achieved for the advancement of Christ's cause and for the unifying of His disciples—we give the praise and honour unto Him whose we are and whom we seek to serve." Then, he recommended that the assembly "reaffirm and authoritatively declare the historic claim. . .inspiring, directing and authorizing us to enter into union." This claim, which was affirmed by the first part of the assembly, read as follows:

> Our Church, acknowledging the sole Headship of Jesus Christ and looking only to Almighty God for guidance, possesses the inherent and inalienable right and freedom to unite with other branches of the Church of Christ which share with us the heritage of Christian faith and the purpose to serve continually the cause of Christ's Kingdom, and that in proceeding to union with the Methodist and Congregational Churches of Canada, the Presbyterian Church in Canada is exercising this liberty under a deep sense of imperative obligation to answer the call and fulfill the will of God, and is making full proof of its spiritual independence, "without loss of its identity" or of a single truth, principle or practice which has proved vital to its history, but on the contrary the Presbyterian Church in Canada does by its corporate and constitutional action enter into this Union as an organized and living body, taking with it its full spiritual heritage of noble traditions, divine ideals and holy purposes and dedicating all these to the further service of God and to the life of the great Church of which it is to form a part.[2]

Cast in the formal language and rhetoric of historic occasions, this claim does not, on first reading, appear like a radical document. But when it is recalled that the justices of the House of Lords had in 1904 rejected most of these arguments, the defiant character and radical thrust of some of its phrases begin to become clear.

The unionists claimed that the Presbyterian church possessed an "inherent and inalienable" right to unite with other branches of the Christian church. This "historic claim," they said, was based on the action of the Presbyterian Churches of Scotland and the churches of the same order in Canada. But, in fact, no Presbyterian church in Scotland or Canada had ever before entered into such a transconfessional union in which the doctrines and polities of the uniting churches were so radically different from the Standards of the Presbyterian Church. But if the unionists' historical precedents were weak, it did not matter, for as far as the unionists were concerned, their final justification in taking this step was "a deep sense of imperative obligation to answer the call and fulfill the will of God." It was on this basis, therefore, that they asserted their "liberty" to unite with other branches of the Christian church.

To speak of freedom, liberty, and spiritual independence assumed some form of restriction or hindrance against which the unionists were struggling. This hindrance was not the minority nor Parliament, which had granted them the legislation they had requested, but rather the dead hand of the past embodied in the common law definition of the church as a "trust." From this perspective the church was a body of people with a set of convictions, and those who contributed their means towards the support of the church had a right to be assured that their property would not be diverted to those who did not share those convictions. As Lord Eldon put it, "a church's property is held in trust for the principles of the church," and the principles of a church are its creed or doctrinal beliefs. The unionists thought it was absurd "to say that each denomination is permanently imprisoned within its creedal cage or that the separating bars can only be removed on peril of crippling mutilation."[3] They also believed it was intolerable to suggest that "the church has no liberty to modify her standards in any degree, no matter what new light may break forth from God's Word or from the progress of human knowledge."[4] Therefore, in asserting their liberty to unite with other branches of the Christian church "without loss of identity," they were stating that God's will, as they perceived it, was superior to the common law. To make such a statement had always meant in the past that church and state were on a collision course. In the case of the church union movement in Canada, it did not appear as if it would come to that because Parliament had already granted the unionists the legislation they had requested. But whether the courts would accept such a challenge remained to be seen.

On many previous occasions the dissidents had set forth the legal objections to the unionists' claims. Therefore, in their first dissent from the assembly's action in 1925 they focused on the unrepresentative character of the assembly. Pointing to the voting statistics from the provinces of Nova Scotia and Prince Edward Island, the dissent noted that though only 3,432 voted for union and as many as 7,755 voted against union, the 3,432 were represented by seventy-one commissioners while the 7,755 had only one commissioner to speak for them. The same was true of the representation from other areas. There was only one non-concurring commissioner from the Synod of British Columbia and none from the great metropolitan presbytery of Montreal. Furthermore, the dissent concluded, "out of 79 Presbyteries 49 have no commissioners to represent the non-concurring members within their bounds, and. . .no Assembly constituted in such a manner can give fair representation of the mind of the people who constitute the church."[5] In a sense it was too late to protest against the unrepresentative character of the assembly, but this had been a major complaint of the dissidents throughout the controversy, and it was a point they wished to emphasize as they were laying their plans to continue the 1925 assembly after the unionists left.

In their formal reply to this dissent, the unionists made an unfortunate choice in asking G.G.D. Kilpatrick to present the reply, for he was one of those ministers who had lost his pulpit at St. Andrew's Church in Ottawa. To select a lame-duck Presbyterian minister to make the reply emphasized the unrepresentative character of the first part of the assembly and increased the offence of the main contention to the reply which stated:

> when the church, speaking through its courts, reaches a decision and proceeds to act upon that decision, it is the church as such and as a whole that moves, nor can the dissent or refusal of any minority, however substantial, affect the validity of the claim that the church as an entity gives form and effect to the decision of the constituted courts. No minority can over-ride the purpose of the church or usurp the name and authority of the Presbyterian Church in Canada by the claim that the decision for union is not unanimous. We do not deny to the non-concurrents the liberty to withdraw from the church. We simply deny their claim to be the Presbyterian Church in Canada, as we deny their power to continue the Church which, by its own free decision, has resolved to enter the union.[6]

It was a bold declaration, but just how bold it was does not become apparent until it is seen in relation to the opinions of the judges in the Scottish Free Church case. Lord Low in the Scottish Court of Session had been the first to maintain that the powers of the assembly "were not unlimited." In his opinion it could not, for example, declare that the Westminster Confession was no longer accepted by the church and suggest that in future the church's government would be Episcopalian.[7] Later in the House of Lords this view was upheld by Lord Davey who denied that even under the Barrier Act the General Assembly had "plenary powers of legislation."[8] Similarly, Lord James of Hereford denied that the Barrier Act conferred legislative powers on the General Assembly. Its purpose, he said, was "the preventing of innovations." "Certainly," he continued, "nothing within it gives any power to alter the identity of the church."[9] Lord Robertson went even further when he declared that the Barrier Act was a power only "affecting the internal affairs of the church."[10] "It is not too lightly to be assumed," he continued, "that such unions are within the competency of any majority, however large, even if there existed no essential differences between the uniting bodies."[11] In view of these judicial opinions, the unionists' reply seems very bold indeed. The fact that Parliament had granted them their legislation, however, made them feel secure enough to deal high-handedly with the minority.

The decisiveness of the claims in the union committee's report and the reply to the dissent stood in stark contrast to the apparent indecisiveness of Leslie Pidgeon's motion to adjourn the assembly until 24 June. The reason for the peculiar form of this motion was that on the next day, 10 June, the United Church of Canada Act would come into effect, and with it the Presbyterian Church in Canada would become a part of the United Church of Canada. The intention of the motion for adjournment, therefore, was to let the act take the still-functioning church into union with all its "right, privileges, authorities and powers" intact. The motion to adjourn, however, allowed the seventy-nine non-concurrents who were present to protest the adjournment, and because their number was in excess of the Assembly's quorum of forty it also allowed them to reconvene the assembly after the unionists had left.

As the hour of adjournment approached at 6:00 p.m. on 9 June, the drama of the final separation began to unfold. Dr. Wardlaw Taylor stepped to the platform and said he wished to read to the assembly a protest signed by seventy-nine commissioners "protesting against the limitation of the powers they hold or of any interference with their duties."[12] Before he could go any further, however, Dr. Clarence MacKinnon rose to a point of order. "Such a protest is out of order, unconstitutional and unprecedented," he said. In ruling on this point, George Pidgeon said, "The Assembly has full power to direct when it shall adjourn. It cannot entertain a protest against a motion which has been regularly passed." This ruling was followed by a number of calls from the floor against receiving the protest to which Taylor replied, "I cannot now say the one word I had intended to say. . .of the hope of kindlier feeling between us." When Pidgeon heard this, he smiled and, turning to Taylor, urged him to go on. "Though we cannot accept this protest not knowing what it is," he said, "I think Dr. Taylor should be allowed to say any word that he cares to say about it." But Taylor would not continue. He left the typed protest behind him on the table where the moderator had laid it and walked down from the platform. As he made his way to his seat someone shouted, "The moderator had the protest in his hand." "But it was not received," countered Dr. Pringle. Dr. Henderson of Vancouver said that the "protest should be handed back where it belongs." Pidgeon paid no attention, but Dr. E.H. Brandt handed it back to the dissidents during the singing of the final hymn.[13]

As everyone rushed out after the benediction, the dissidents gathered in the northwest corner of the church to reconvene the assembly. To make this as difficult as possible, C.W. Gordon instructed the organist to play the Hallelujah Chorus at full blast to drown out all further discussion. Those reporters who were present said it was impossible to hear what was being said, but they saw Dr. D.G. McQueen, a former moderator, lead the group in prayer and then everyone put up their hand to indicate their agreement with a motion to adjourn to Knox Church at 11:45 p.m. standard time. Wardlaw Taylor later explained to the press that "the meeting at Knox Church was to keep the Presbyterian church alive over the midnight hour when according to the Church Union Act the union of the three denominations became effective. As the Act takes effect on standard time they fixed the time of the meeting accordingly."[14]

For two hours prior to 11:45, Dr. Inkster led those who had assembled at Knox Church in devotions. Then at 12:05, Dr. McQueen declared the court open for the transaction of business and said: "This, of course, is a continuance of the General Assembly which opened in College Street church on June 3 and at present only those who are commissioners to the General Assembly are entitled to transact business."[15] Of the several items of business which were dealt with at this evening session, the most important was the reading of the "Protest and Claim of Right" which had been declared out of order by George Pidgeon when Wardlaw Taylor had attempted to read it. This document contained the basis upon which the dissidents claimed the right to be able to carry on the assembly, and it was therefore appropriate that it should be read as they were reconstituting it in the small hours of the morning of 10 June.

After reviewing the standards of doctrine and worship and the forms of discipline and government which formed the basis of the covenant entered into by the Presbyterian churches in 1875, the protest declared:

It is in her faithful adherence to the aforesaid standards. . . adequately secured unto her by the said covenant of union in 1875, that the real historical and hereditary identity of the Presbyterian Church in Canada consists, as well as her continuity as lawful successor in this dominion of the Reformed churches of the motherland.

Then pointing out that the "Basis of Union" contained many features that were inconsistent with the standards of the church agreed to in 1875, the protest indicated that its signatories could not comply with the course pursued by the prevailing party or acquiesce in their decision to merge the Presbyterian Church in Canada into another church. This statement was then followed by their claim of right which stated:

> We do further protest that, notwithstanding the action of the Assembly in 1916 or any further action by the prevailing party in this Assembly, it shall be lawful for us, together with such other commissioners as may adhere to us, to continue in session in St. Andrew's Church, Toronto, on Thursday, June 11, 1925, as commissioners to the fifty-first General Assembly of the Presbyterian Church in Canada, and there, in humble dependence on God's grace and the aid of the Holy Spirit, and maintaining with us the confession of faith and standards of the church as hitherto understood, to adopt such measures as may be competent to us, for the continuance of the Presbyterian Church in Canada, to the advancement of God's glory, the extension of the gospel of our Lord and Saviour throughout the world, and the orderly administration of Christ's house according to His holy word.[16]

It was on the basis of this claim of right that, a few days later, the dissidents reaffirmed their intention, in spite of the United Church of Canada Act, to continue calling themselves the Presbyterian Church in Canada. Within the course of a week, therefore, Canadians witnessed the rather unusual spectacle of one group of Presbyterians making claims in defiance of the common law and another group making claims in defiance of an act of Parliament. As a result it was clear that the parting of the ways had resolved nothing. It had simply set the stage for continuing the conflict.

When the assembly reconvened on 11 June 1925 in St. Andrew's Church, no one was surprised when Ephraim Scott was elected moderator. At eighty, he was one of the few members of the older generation of ministers who had opposed union still alive, and in electing him to the moderatorship, the continuing Assembly honoured not only his own part in the struggle but also the contribution which others of his generation had made in the early years of the controversy. In spite of his age, however, Scott undoubtedly surprised many when he introduced a motion calling for the abandonment of "all highsounding titles such as Very Reverend, Right Reverend and Most Reverend" as these were applied to moderators. Dr. Bruce Muir of Sherbrooke, Nova Scotia, opposed this motion saying that it was "a case of democracy run riot." "Those are historic titles," he continued, "which have been worn by previous moderators, and I think we should go slowly before we allow democracy to rob church officials of the respect which is due them from the people." Banks Nelson also opposed the motion saying that perhaps Dr. Scott "has looked back at some other moderators who have worn such titles, who were not qualified for them and so he wished to strike at the past." But,

Nelson continued, if the church dropped all titles, representatives of the Presbyterian church might find themselves placed in inferior positions at official functions. Scott replied that he was not interested in getting the chief seat at the banquet or in being at the head of the procession. His only concern was that these titles had been borrowed from churches where they mean things which his church did not recognize. His motion, therefore, was simply a recognition of the parity of ministers and the fact that the Presbyterian Church is really the people.[17]

Another motion which caught many by surprise was that a Board of Administration be appointed, "not to exceed forty in number and to be composed of laymen experienced in business and finance whose duty it shall be to take the oversight of all business and financial affairs of the church." With Thomas McMillan as convenor, the membership of the new board included many familiar names: James Rodger of Montreal, C.S. McDonald of Brampton, John Penman of Paris, Dr. Murray McLaren of St. John, G. Tower Ferguson of Toronto and Judge H.A. Robson of Winnipeg. There were others, but these men were the ones who had originally established lay control of the resistance organization and had played a major role in financing its operations over the past ten years.

The establishment of such a board was opposed by Dr. Robert Johnston of Calgary, who said:

> There is considerable doubt as to the wisdom of such a change. It is too radical. We have always been proud of our church administration; and I think it has been administered in a much more economical manner than have business organizations with the same finances. You are suggesting something for which there is no parallel in the church of Jesus Christ. We do know of one case in a so-called Christian denomination where the method has been applied, and where the body has been deprived of the great spiritual power which it once exerted. It seems a departure so serious that we should see where it may lead us. We are placing ourselves under a form of government which may become a domination greater and far more serious than anything we have yet felt.[18]

Johnston was right in referring to this serious departure as radical; by altering the customary balance in the Presbyterian polity between lay and ministerial representation on such an important committee, the new church was endangering the very identity and continuity which it had fought to maintain. There was, however, so much resentment among the laity over the attempt of their ministerial leadership to destroy the church that they were determined never to let it happen again.

Speaking at a pre-Assembly meeting in Cooke's Church, Toronto, Dugald Darroch, a layman from Collingwood had given voice to this feeling when he had declared that "since all are agreed that clerical domination is responsible for the present conditions, we are of the opinion that the constitution of our church should be so amended that at least, an 80 or 85 per cent membership vote be required as a mandate from the pew before consummating any drastic changes like the present in our church."[19] He had also suggested that the General Assembly be more representative in the future and be composed not only of ministers and elders but also women, managers, and other officers in the church. It was against this sort of radical restructuring of the church that Johnston raised his voice.

Had it not been for Dr. A.S. Grant, who had been named to this committee, there might have been more opposition to the formation of this board. But Grant disarmed the opposition with his humour. "I have one exception to take to this report," he said, "the fact that I may not be able to preach is no reason why I should be classified as a layman." Otherwise, he did not think the new board was a very radical departure from custom. "We are faced at the present time," he said, "with a crisis, not only with the ordinary budget of the church but also in regard to helping those thrown out of their churches. I consider it a layman's job and inasmuch as it is only for one year I don't think we should hesitate for a moment."[20] Besides, he concluded, "if they make a mess of it we can get back at them next assembly." As it turned out, it was not until 1928 that the assembly finally acted in response to an overture from the Presbytery of London, Ontario, and insisted on appointing ministers to this board.[21]

But if the Board of Administration reflected the dissidents' resentment against clerical domination, the parting of the ways also provided a dramatic example of the unionists' resentment against the clerical leaders of the opposition to union. During the first part of the 1925 Assembly, the unionists made a point of removing Daniel J. Fraser and Thomas Eakin from their teaching positions at Presbyterian College, Montreal, and of appointing a new board of management under the chairmanship of Brigadier-General J.G. Ross. Before the second part of the 1925 Assembly could reinstate Fraser as principal and Eakin as professor of homiletics and pastoral training at the college, Brigadier-General Ross, who had been paymaster general of the Canadian Overseas Military Forces during World War I and was now the senior partner in P.S. Ross & Sons, Chartered Accountants, together with Principal elect R.E. Welch, Professor A.R. Gordon, and the Rev. Richard Roberts of the American Presbyterian Church, Montreal, took formal possession of the college buildings. They removed the seal, the registers and other official documents from the principal's office and placed private detectives at the door to prevent anyone from entering the building. Although this action was carried out with military efficiency and dispatch, it proved to be somewhat premature, for in 1926 the Quebec legislature gave possession of the college to the dissidents, and the unionists had to return the college and its seal on 1 June 1926.[22] It was this event in the parting of the ways which gave a foretaste of the struggles over property and assets which would take place before the provincial and dominion property commissions.

The task of the Dominion Property Commission was to make an equitable division of those properties and funds of the Presbyterian Church in Canada that were not directly related to specific congregations. These properties and funds included schools, hospitals, colleges, settlement houses, redemptive homes, community centres, and residences in the mission fields both at home and abroad as well as the Aged and Infirm Minister's Fund, the Widow's and Orphan's Fund, the Famine Fund, the Forward Movement Peace Thank Offering Fund, the royalties from The Book of Praise, and various church extension and memorial funds. In all they were evaluated at $10,500,000. Consequently, the way they were divided was of considerable interest to both parties, for the decision of this commission was final, subject to no kind of review either civil or ecclesiastical. Initially the dissidents objected to this proviso, calling it "compulsory arbitration with a vengeance."[23] But as it turned out, both the work and the rulings of this commission created fewer problems than the rulings of the provincial property commissions.

The commission consisted of nine members. The Rev. Thomas Eakin, Thomas McMillan and G. Tower Ferguson represented the dissidents. Dr. Walter C. Murray, Isaac Pitblado and Professor J.W. MacMillan represented the unionists. The Right Honourable Mr. Justice Duff, Dyce W. Saunders, K.C. and Thomas Percy Gault, K.C., were appointed as the three remaining commissioners. Both Galt and Saunders were Anglicans and Lyman P. Duff, the chairman of the commission, was the son of a Congregationalist minister.[24] When the commission held its first meeting in Ottawa on 28 June 1926 both sides were represented by legal counsel. W.N. Tilley, G.W. Mason and Ward Wright represented the United Church, and D.L. McCarthy and N.S. Macdonnell represented the dissidents. C.H.A. Armstrong acted both as counsel for the commission and as its secretary. The official reporters of the arguments of counsel before the commission were provided by Nelson R. Butcher and Company.[25]

At its thirteen sessions between 28 June 1926 and 22 January 1927 the commission functioned much like a court of law. It heard testimony from the legal counsel of both parties and then met in private to reach its rulings. These rulings were then announced to the legal counsel by the commission's chairman before they proceeded with the next round of testimony. The commissioners, therefore, acted much like a jury. During the presentations of counsel, the commission members rarely said anything. The chairman, on the other hand, was actively engaged during these presentations, searching for clarification, attempting to define exactly the areas of agreement and disagreement, and when he did not like a particular line of argument, pursuing counsel with very sharp and searching questions. Consequently, the majority of the seven hundred page stenographic report of the proceedings reads like a formal dialogue between the chairman and counsel for the two parties concerning the proper way to evaluate the various properties and the most reasonable method of dividing the assets.

At the outset of the proceedings the chairman let it be known that anything on which counsel could agree would be automatically accepted by the commission. What the commissioners wished to hear about, therefore, were only those issues on which no agreement could be found. The first of these issues was the United Church's refusal to allow the dissidents to examine the financial records of the Presbyterian Church prior to 31 December 1924, which was the date of the last audit accepted by the General Assembly prior to the formation of the United Church on 10 June 1925. There was no objection to allowing the dissidents to examine the books on all matters since 31 December 1924, but the unionists did not want the dissidents to go behind the audits accepted by the General Assembly on all previous years.

McCarthy argued that it was unreasonable to expect his clients to accept on faith alone the unionists' statement of the property and assets of the Presbyterian Church, and therefore it was essential to allow their accountant, Mr. Nash of Clarkson, Gordon, and Dillworth, free access to the books in order to verify the various lists of property and assets which had been drawn up for the unionists by P.S. Ross and Sons. The commission agreed with McCarthy that the dissidents' accountant should have free access to the church's financial records not for re-auditing but simply for purposes of verification.

Exactly what McCarthy was after did not become clear until much later. It transpired that the Forward Movement Peace Thank Offering Fund initiated in 1919 had collected between four and five million dollars, of which $1,730,000 went to the Church and Manse Board. Between June 1920 and 15 February 1925, this board spent $758,961 on loans; $205,974 on grants, and $765,065 on the purchase of real property for both congregational and non-congregational purposes. On the face of it these seemed justifiable expenditures, but when they were probed, it became apparent that while the number of self-sustaining congregations had declined between 1919 and 1923, the number of augmented congregations had doubled. Augmentation, as N.S. Macdonnell explained to the commissioners, was "a scheme by which charges which are not self-supporting receive aid. The minimum salary of a minister is $1,800. A congregation has a right to call its own minister. If the congregation can only pay $1,200, then augmentation makes up the $600 balance. If the congregation can only make up $900, then the congregation does not have the right to call its own minister, but the augmentation makes up the difference."[26] There was nothing new about augmentation for it had been established in the West when James Robertson was superintendent of Home Missions. What was new was the sudden increase in the number of augmented charges which was directly attributable to the Forward Movement Peace Thank Offering Fund. It was obvious, of course, that much of the money which was raised for this fund was given for purposes of augmentation and assistance to Home Missions. McCarthy, therefore, did not want to question its use, but rather its effects.

To illustrate these effects, he chose the Presbytery of Kamloops. Referring the commissioners to the appropriate statistics in *Acts and Proceedings* for 1924, he pointed out that while Zion Church in Armstrong had a membership of 157, some of the congregations in the presbytery had memberships as low as 2, 7, 11, and 25. In fact, there were only six self-sustaining congregations in the whole presbytery. The other fifty-one congregations were augmented as were the thirty-two preaching on the five mission fields in the presbytery. Furthermore, many of these congregations gave either nothing or not more than $5.00 to the schemes of the budget.[27] Then, comparing these churches to Bloor Street in Toronto with a membership of 1,694 which subscribed $18,695 to the schemes of the budget, McCarthy finally made his point:

> You can see how unfair it would be, where the contributions were augmented and the churches have not given even sufficient money to pay the stipend of the minister, and were unable to contribute to the general schemes of church, that they should have a vote as a congregation in determining how this money should be divided, or that the congregation should be used as the unit of such determination.[28]

It took McCarthy a long time to finally make his point, but when he did, it had a noticeable effect on the commissioners as they scrambled to follow him through the statistical reports. Moreover, it was also clear that there were many more augmented charges in Manitoba, Saskatchewan, and Alberta than there were in B.C.

According to the unionists' figures, 3,748 Presbyterian congregations went into union and 761 were non-concurring. If this had become the basis of the division between the two parties, the dissidents would have received only about one-fifth of the assets. It was essential, therefore, from the dissidents' perspective, that the division be made not on the basis of congregations, but on the number of individuals voting in or out. There was a difficulty here, however, for on the basis of individual votes 113,000 voted to enter union while 114,000 voted not to enter the union.[29] Therefore, if McCarthy had pressed these figures they would have been as obviously unfair as the unionists' method of calculating the results of the voting. Thus, it was necessary to come up with a compromise concerning the membership of all those congregations which did not take a vote or went into union by resolution. If these figures were to be included, however, it was necessary to eliminate the "deadwood" (that is, those who were literally dead and those who had long since moved away but whose names had never been removed from the congregation's membership roles) and to come up with some method of determining what percentage of these congregations ought to be considered as non-concurring. Needless to say, considerable time was spent arguing about such figures, and the only hint of irritation revealed by the chairman, Lyman Duff, was on this issue for he found it incomprehensible that there was no set of figures on the voting which was completely acceptable to both parties. As previously noted, the problem was that the figures had been used for polemical purposes and they had been collected in two entirely different ways. When the commission first met, all the unionists had was a list of congregations voting one way or the other. But when it became clear that the commission was sympathetic to McCarthy's argument, it became necessary for the United Church to collect all the voting statistics from the clerks of presbyteries across the country which had never been sent to Toronto. Furthermore, because the unionists had made certain that all the clerks of presbyteries and synods would be unionists back in 1924, many of the dissident congregations had not sent their results to the clerks of presbyteries but had forwarded them directly to the offices of the Presbyterian Church Association in Toronto. Consequently, two years after the vote it was impossible for the commission to come up with a set of results on which both parties could agree.[30]

It gradually became apparent that it would be impossible to find a single mathematical formula which could be applied to the division of all the property and assets. For example, when it came to Foreign Mission property, the counsel for both sides simply threw up their hands and suggested that the whole area was completely beyond them. There was no way to evaluate what these properties were worth except at exorbitant expense, and there was no obvious way of making an equitable division. Therefore, the whole matter was turned over to a subcommittee consisting of Dr. A.S. Grant for the Presbyterians and Dr. A.E. Armstrong for the United Church, who were able in a relatively short time to come to complete agreement on the division of these properties.[31] The same method of procedure was followed with Home Missions, and again Dr. A.S. Grant and Dr. J.H. Edmison were able to come to complete agreement over the division of these properties in a relatively short period of time.[32] Once these divisions of property were made, the only thing left for the commission to do on these two matters was to divide the various Home and Foreign Mission funds and to determine the amount which the dissidents would have to pay the United Church for the maintenance and operation of these missions between 10 June 1925 and the point when they were officially transferred to the dissidents in 1927.

Agreement was also quickly reached on the question of the division of the Aged and Infirm Ministers' Fund and the Widow's and Orphan's Fund.[33] The major disagreements, therefore, arose primarily over the question of the basis of division of the general funds of the church, the Women's Missionary Society property and funds, and the college property. The colleges were an especially knotty problem because while the provincial legislation in Ontario and Quebec had awarded Knox and Presbyterian College, Montreal, to the dissidents, it had left the question of endowments unanswered and in the case of Knox College the question of its charter had been left to the Dominion Property Commission. Because these two colleges were the most heavily endowed of all the church's colleges, no easy agreement between counsel could be reached. Thus, while many questions were settled by mutual agreement, there were still a number on which the commission had to make rulings which were bound to disappoint the contending parties.

When the commission's report was published, it became clear that out of assets of which the total value was calculated as $10,500,000, the dissidents had been awarded assets worth $3,261,000 or about 31 per cent of the whole. Because a larger number of Presbyterian ministers went into the United Church, the dissidents received only about 22.04 per cent of the pension funds. Furthermore, because the United Church had taken responsibility for a larger portion of the mission fields, the dissidents received only 23.3 per cent of the Home Mission Board's property and funds which had been evaluated at $2,814,599. In Foreign Missions the award to the dissidents was 25 per cent of the total property and funds which had been evaluated at $1,970.000. The area in which the dissidents received a much larger share than was anticipated was the colleges. They received the charters and endowments of both Knox and Presbyterian College, Montreal. The endowments of these colleges amounted to $550,000, and their property and buildings had been evaluated at approximately $1,650,000. As a result of this award, therefore, the dissidents received approximately 50 per cent of the total college assets of the Presbyterian Church in Canada.[34]

The dissidents accepted the commission's report without comment, publishing its entire findings in *Acts and Proceedings 1927* and passing unanimously a motion of appreciation to Lyman P. Duff for his services as chairman and for "the expedition with which under your wise guidance, it was brought to completion."[35] In sharp contrast, the executive officers of the United Church, George Pidgeon, T. Albert Moore, and Robert Laird, issued a statement which said:

The United Church of Canada will fail to find justification for the decision as it affected the theological colleges of the church, but it recognizes that owing to legislative action in Ontario and Quebec in regard to Knox and Montreal Colleges the Commission was not free to deal with the college question in its entirety. . . .The loss of two valuable college buildings and more than half a million dollars of endowment at the two important educational centres of Montreal and Toronto will be felt severely by the United Church.[36]

They had to admit, however, that "taking the situation as a whole, an earnest effort was made to deal justly with all interests concerned."[37] The subexecutive of the United Church's General Council thanked Lyman Duff for his "outstanding service" in an "exceedingly difficult situation," and when the General Council met in 1928, a more formal resolution of thanks to the chairman of the commission was unanimously passed.[38]

In 1927, then, the Presbyterian Church in Canada was content with the share of assets it was awarded. But second thoughts were to come. After the 1931 Census revealed that more Canadians still identified themselves as Presbyterians than was thought to be the case when the commission met, several overtures were sent to the General Assembly indicating that steps should be taken to get a larger share of the property and funds than had been awarded in 1927. For example, an overture from the Presbytery of London, stated:

> Whereas it is no surprise that the Dominion census established the fact that there are 872,482 Presbyterians in Canada, and that the number of Presbyterians who went into union should on any fair computation be less than 50 per cent instead of 64 per cent. And whereas the 1931 census was taken, only after careful and earnest instruction had been given to all Presbyterian people attending the United Church, to state that they belong to the United Church of Canada . . . .Therefore be it resolved, that we respectfully overture the General Assembly. . .to take steps to have. . . .the division of the property of our church re-considered and revised and made more equitable to the attitude of the people in the 1931 census.[39]

While such overtures indicated the frustration many Presbyterians continued to feel concerning their ambiguous legal status, when they were referred to the Board of Administration of the Presbyterian Church, they were simply ignored, for the commission's decisions were based not on census figures but membership figures. Besides, there was no way of taking any action against the final decision of the commission. In fact, it was the far-reaching powers of the Dominion Property Commission and the finality of its decisions that made it so effective. Such was not the case with the provincial property commissions. In all the provincial legislation, except Prince Edward Island, the powers of the provincial property commissions were so restricted that they created as many problems as they solved.

The only provinces which did not create commissions to deal with property disputes arising out of the controversy over church union were Nova Scotia, New Brunswick, and Manitoba. All of the others established commissions which met with varying degrees of success. The most successful was the commission in Prince Edward Island. Its decisions were subject to review by the Court of Appeal in Equity which was empowered to confirm or amend the commissions findings. The least successful was the Ontario commission, which was granted very limited powers, and as a result Ontario encountered the greatest amount of difficulty in resolving property disputes. Had the provincial property commissions been given the mandatory powers of the Dominion Property Commission, many of the problems that arose at the local level might have been solved with less bitterness. But it was thought that it would be possible to work out the problems which arose in many communities through a process of reasonable negotiation. Unfortunately, that assumption was false, and many of the problems arising out of the parting of the ways, especially in small communities, continued to fester long after 1925.

In Prince Edward Island the property commission heard thirty applications, seven of which were made by United Church minorities. The commission delivered its awards in December 1926, and in March 1927, the Court of Appeal in Equity sat in Charlottetown to hear arguments on the awards of the commission. In three cases, namely, West Coveland, Murray Harbour, and Breadalbane, the three commissioners had different findings, and the court therefore held that there was no award for the court to consider. In these places the property was retained by the United Church. When the court delivered its final judgment in April 1927, however, the United Church majorities in Westpoint, North Tryon, Marshfield and Kensington were deprived of their property.[40]

In British Columbia, the legislature appointed in December 1925 a property commission "to make an equitable adjustment of congregational properties." It consisted of ten members, five representing the United Church and five representing the Presbyterian Church, and it considered thirty applications for relief. When it presented its findings to the legislature in the spring of 1927, it was able to report that a private settlement had been arranged between the parties in seventeen of these cases. The findings of the commission in the remaining thirteen cases were adopted by the legislature, and the United Church Act was amended accordingly.[14] With the power of enforcement provided either by the legislature as in B.C. or by the courts as in Prince Edward Island, the work of the commissions was very effective and produced little local bitterness or resentment.

In Alberta and Saskatchewan, however, the legislatures refused to give the commissions mandatory powers and did not enforce their findings either with court or legislative action. The result was that it was only in those situations where the contending parties voluntarily accepted the recommendations of the commission that a satisfactory resolution of local conflicts was possible. There are no known cases of dissident majorities questioning the commission's awards. But there were instances of United Church majorities flatly refusing to accept the commission's recommendations. In such cases the dissidents were denied any relief of the hardship which they claimed existed. If such conflicts could arise in provinces such as these where the numbers involved were small, one may appreciate how bitter the contention was in Ontario where there were 150 such cases. There the refusal of United Church majorities to comply with the recommendations of the commission reached proportions which caused problems not only for the dissidents but also for the government and the United Church itself.

The Ontario commission held weekly sittings from September 1925 until March 1926 at twenty-six different centres.[42] It considered 149 applications, 137 of which were made by the dissidents and 12 by unionist minorities.[43] When the commission submitted its final report in March 1926, C.S. McDonald and J.W. MacNamara summarized the results of the commission's work as follows:

Places where recommendations were made	45
Places where the vote invalid	9
Places where an order given	14
Places where [applications were] withdrawn	25
Places re Manse property	25
Places where no recommendation was made	31
	149

In recommending these results, they said: "Considerable dissatisfaction developed regarding the work of the commission. Applicants expected relief that was not granted." Furthermore, while the work of the commission laid heavy expenditures upon the church "for legal fees, salary and the expense of the commission, it did not produce the results which many had expected of it, for there remain many minority groups still in a position of extreme hardship for whom no relief has been obtained and among these are to be found some outstanding instances of great injustice."[44] They believed there were two reasons for the commission's failure: first, the very limited powers granted to the commission by the Ontario legislature, and second, "in a number of cases the recommendations of the commission were ignored by the United Church concerned."[45]

As a result of their dissatisfaction with the commission's work, in 1926 the dissidents sought through Major A.C. Lewis, the Conservative member for North East Toronto, an amendment of the Ontario legislation which would grant the property commission "absolute power, and without any right of appeal therefrom, to make any order they see fit for the benefit of minorities."[46] The amendment also sought to secure a second vote in all congregations in which the first vote had been declared invalid by the commission.[47] The reaction of the unionists to this amendment verged on hysteria. R.J. Wilson, the head of the United Church's publicity office, declared that the amendment would pave the way to "intolerable acts of injustice."[48] Later when the amendment came before the Private Bills Committee, its chairman, Attorney-General Nickle, was deluged by United Church resolutions opposing the amendment. One from Avenue Road United Church in Toronto declared its opposition to the amendment because "it provides for the taking of church property from a congregation in rightful possession thereof, and giving it to a people of another faith, and this we consider absolutely unjust."[49] Another from Elgin county suggested that "stirring up religious war as you are doing is devilish."[50] And one from Dr. T. Albert Moore, to which many members of the Private Bills Committee took exception, stated that "the United Church has 75 per cent of the Presbyterian property and we do not propose to take one stick of Methodist property for use of Presbyterian congregations."[51] In response Major Lewis accused Moore of "endeavoring to mislead Methodists into the belief that the legislature contemplated taking Methodist church property away from its original owners," and he was applauded by members of the committee when he deprecated "the action of intemperate clergymen on both sides who have been stirring up strife."[52]

After hearing evidence presented by both sides and considering several motions, the Private Bills Committee eventually accepted a motion by W. Finlayson, the Conservative member from East Simcoe, which called for peace parleys between the unionists and dissidents with the attorney-general acting as adjudicator. It was clear that the members of the committee did not want any more votes taken, and they did not want to give the property commission mandatory powers. They wanted the two sides to settle their differences by negotiation, and they were convinced that the attorney-general could assist.

In the first session with Nickle what was thought to be a settlement was worked out in the Beaverton case. Buoyed by this initial success, Nickle said to MacGregor Young as they were leaving, "the least you and McCarthy can do for me now is to see that I am canonized." "In which church—the United or the nonconcurring?" queried Young. "It had better be both," Nickle replied.[53] But even though Nickle had spent a lot of time on the church union question in 1924, 1925, and now again in 1926, it was a bit early to be thinking of canonization, for what he sincerely believed to be settlements dissolved shortly after they were made. Some progress, however, was made in these negotiations, and when they were concluded the attorney-general announced that there would be a new vote in the six churches of Dalhousie Mills, South Lancaster, Conn, Richmond Hill, Burlington, and Maple Valley. The voter's list in each of these cases was to be determined by Mr. Justice Orde, who was appointed for this purpose by the attorney-general. Furthermore, any questioning of the validity or effect of any vote after 31 March 1926 was prohibited. Disputes at Beamsville, Grimsby, and Tillsonburg were declared resolved, and it was decided that the disputes at Owen Sound, Allanbank, St. George, Guthrie, Kintore, Mansfield, Laurel, Embro, and Waterloo could be resolved without legislation. Three cheers were proposed for the attorney-general, and A.W. Gray led several members of the legislature in the singing of the Doxology, for everyone thought that the problems created by church union had been solved.[54]

Unfortunately, the issues were far from settled. In Beamsville, for example, the minority claimed there had been an irregular vote, and the Ontario property commission recommended that the Morrow Fund of $8,000 (an estate left by Mr. Morrow to the Presbyterian Church in Beamsville) be given to the dissidents. The United Church in Beamsville, however, refused to accept the commission's recommendation. Therefore, in 1926 under the threat of possible legislation, Gershom Mason on behalf of the unionists in Beamsville worked out a compromise with D.L. McCarthy whereby the dissidents would receive $5,000 and the unionists at Beamsville would keep $3,000 of the Morrow Fund. On the basis of this compromise, Nickle announced that the problems in Beamsville were settled. A month later, however, when the dissidents had not received payment, they hired N.S. Macdonnell, a Hamilton lawyer, to inform G.W. Mason that legal action would be taken if there was any further delay.[55] In an effort to get the congregation to act, Mason wrote to the minister at Beamsville, F.C. Overend, indicating that if a compromise had not been made the congregation would have lost the whole of the Morrow Fund. He recommended, therefore, that they act immediately to honour the arrangement which had been made on their behalf.[56] Overend, who was obviously part of the problem at Beamsville, replied that nothing would be done until a copy of the amendment to the legislation was received. But, as R.B. Whitehead explained, the arrangement had not been part of the 1926 amendment, it was an off-the-record agreement between Mason and McCarthy made in the presence of W.F. Nickle. The response of the Beamsville congregation to this explanation was the hiring of C.V. Langs, another Hamilton lawyer, to enquire on what authority Mason had entered into an agreement that was binding on the Beamsville congregation. As a result, almost a year after the so-called 1926 settlement had been made, the dissidents had not received their money because the unionists were still arguing about who was entitled to the interest and how they could be assured that the dissidents would spend the $5,000 on a church building and not on something else.

If this had been an isolated case, it might not have been too serious, but there were so many of them that it was impossible to prevent local Conservative politicians from being deluged by dissident complaints. Therefore, when several applications for legislation were received in 1927, the Private Bills Committee refused to listen to the unionists' objections, and passed legislation which ordered a new vote in Wickes and gave the dissidents what they had requested in Martintown and Beaverton. But as the Beaverton case was to reveal, it was difficult to settle some of these cases even with legislation.

The Beaverton case was so complex that the Ontario Property Commission had made no recommendation concerning the minority's appeal even though there were two technical irregularities in their vote. The problem was rooted in the history of the congregation. In 1914, the Presbyterian congregations of St. Andrew's and Knox in Beaverton had united, and then in 1918 the Methodists had affiliated with the Presbyterians to form a union congregation. Having sold their property and become an integral part of the union congregation, the Methodists participated in the 1925 vote. The dissidents claimed the Methodists had no right to vote, and the Ontario property commission agreed that it was irregular, but it took no action because even without the Methodists a majority of the Presbyterians in Beaverton had voted for union. Nonetheless, R.S. Cassels, the dissidents' representative on the Ontario Property Commission accepted the minority's claim of hardship and pointed out that the vote could also be considered irregular because a signed ballot had been used.

In an effort to settle the dispute, the unionists offered to give the dissidents Knox church if they would buy the Knox church manse for $5,000 and undertake to pay $3,000 toward the liquidation of a floating loan on the Knox church property.[57] The dissidents initially accepted this offer in 1926 but later decided that the manse was not worth $5,000 and backed out of the arrangement. When they did so, Knox church was sold to a local builder who demolished it. There was, however, a third Presbyterian church in Beaverton known as the Old Stone Church, which had been the original Presbyterian church in the community and the site of a cemetery which was still in use. In 1927, therefore, the minority applied for legislation which would give them the Old Stone Church, the Knox Church manse, half of the furnishings, and half of the organ fund. The Private Bills Committee complied with their request, and legislation was passed to this effect. But when the parties could not agree on the division of the assets, James Ernest Thompson, a County Court Judge of Ontario, was appointed to make the division. He divided the organ fund, the pew cushions, the choir gowns, the furnaces, the electrical fans and fixtures, and because the church bell could not be divided, he ordered it sold and the proceeds divided equally.[58] Even the judge's order, however, did not settle the matter, for the unionists had already spent the organ fund, and they argued that the choir gowns were really not church property because they had been purchased by the Ladies' Aid group rather than with church funds. Furthermore, the trustees of the cemetery had accumulated a considerable fund for the perpetual care of the graves in the cemetery, and the unionists were afraid that if the money was turned over to the dissidents, they would use it for some other purpose. When these difficulties were raised with Judge Thompson, he became furious, refused to change any part of his judgment, and ordered the sheriff to carry out his decision immediately. While Gershom Mason managed to postpone immediate action by the sheriff, it became obvious that it would cost more to appeal the judge's decision than it was worth. Moreover, such non-compliance with legislation and court orders made it even more likely that the dissidents would receive a favourable hearing for legislation in other cases.

That further cases would be forthcoming became clear to the United Church when a special legal committee appointed under the chairmanship of Banks Nelson by the 1927 General Assembly requested a meeting with United Church officials. The Presbyterian legal committee prepared a long list of properties concerning which they believed negotiations might be profitable. But in the three sessions which were held it became apparent that the United Church was only prepared to discuss eight cases and even with regard to these they made it clear "that their good offices must be confined to the exercise of their influence upon local trustees, and beyond that they could not go."[59] In some cases it proved possible to work out an arrangement whereby property was transferred to the Presbyterians on the payment of a sum which was agreed to by local committees. In those cases where local agreements could not be arranged, however, the Presbyterians once again appealed to the Ontario legislature for relief. All in all, in 1928 the Ontario legislature received nine more applications for legislation.

To deal with these appeals the Private Bills Committee appointed a subcommittee of five members chaired by Finlay Macdiarmid. Under Macdiarmid's direction a further set of negotiations were conducted which issued unanimous recommendations for settlement in the cases of Owen Sound, Rutherford, Markham, Dorchester, and Wardsville. The Wyevale, Melbourne, and Auburn bills were withdrawn because satisfactory settlements had already been made, and no action was taken in the Grafton case because there was action pending in the courts. The Private Bills Committee approved the work of its subcommittee and recommended that these bills not be reported to the house. In the legislature Premier Ferguson congratulated the committee on its work but made it clear that he had heard enough about the church union controversy. He said:

It is now two years since legislation was passed in this House and a tribunal appointed to hear the disputes. That should be enough time to settle them. Neither the committee nor the House should be asked to sit as a court of review on these disputes. I hope the public will take cognizance of the fact, and that we will not hear of any controversies again and that any differences will be satisfactorily adjusted among the contending parties themselves.[60]

While the premier's statement effectively closed the legislature to any further appeals for legislation, it did not of course bring the disputes to an end, and the difficulties which ensued raised problems not only for the dissidents but also for the United Church.

The situation in Owen Sound, for example, continued to create problems for the United Church long after the question was supposedly settled in 1928. In 1925 the Division Street and Knox Presbyterian churches in Owen Sound recorded a two-thirds vote for union. The dissenting one third in each congregation joined together to form St. Andrew's Presbyterian Church and sought redress from the legislature because the United Church congregations had ignored the recommendations of the Ontario property commission. In 1928 Macdiarmid's subcommittee recommended that the United Church settle this case by paying the Presbyterians $7,500. Sir Joseph Flavelle guaranteed the money, but the Owen Sound congregations refused to accept any responsibility for this arrangement. Consequently, it was necessary for the United Church to seek contributions from prominent laymen throughout the country to pay back this amount. Unfortunately, they were unable to raise the whole amount, and Flavelle, a former Methodist, was left paying $2,000.[61]

No one had expected that the parting of the ways would be easy, but few had apprehended that it would provide an occasion for the public display of some of the most ornery and fractious aspects of human nature. It came as little surprise to the dissidents, who had not abandoned their Calvinistic outlook and were convinced that the law was the only means of keeping man's lower nature within bounds. But it was extremely depressing for many United Church leaders, who had seen union as an appeal to man's higher nature and broader sympathies. It was also disconcerting to outside observers like Sir Henry Lunn, the English ecumenical journalist and editor of *The Review of the Churches,* who visited Canada in 1926. The atmosphere was so intense that several of his speaking engagements were cancelled because it was thought unwise to mention church union on public platforms in the major eastern Canadian cities. Lunn's long career in the ecumenical movement had not prepared him for this shock, and he returned to England convinced that whatever Christian unity might mean, it could hardly be what he had observed in Canada.[62]

13

The Continuing Battle

While the struggle over property was taking place, other battles were being fought which ultimately proved to be of more significance. These campaigns took place in international denominational organizations such as the Alliance of Reformed Churches, the international Protestant press, and the Canadian courts. Between 1925 and 1930 the United Church won the majority of these encounters, but when the central issues of identity and continuity reached the Supreme Court of Canada, the tide of battle turned in the dissidents favour, and the United Church experienced some severe setbacks in its efforts to sustain its claim that the Presbyterian Church in Canada had entered the United Church. Throughout the controversy the unionists had never seriously considered any compromise on their basic principles, but when the Canadian courts refused to sustain their claim, compromise became a necessity.

Recognizing the importance of world opinion in establishing their claim, George Pidgeon forwarded copies of the "Basis of Union" and the proposed union legislation to the secretary of the Western Section of the Alliance of Reformed Churches in 1923 and asked "if in their judgment the United Church of Canada would be eligible for membership."[1] This question was referred to a meeting of the Western Section of the Alliance in Newport News, Virginia, in February 1924. After carefully considering the documents, they arrived at the following conclusion:

In the event of the United Church of Canada seeking admission to membership in the Alliance of Reformed Churches holding the Presbyterian System, the Western Section, having examined carefully the Basis of Union of the United Church of Canada adopted by the Presbyterian Church in Canada, the Methodist Church and the Congregational Churches of Canada, is of the opinion that the said Basis of Union satisfies the conditions of membership laid down in the constitution of the Alliance, viz:—in regard to the authority of the Scriptures and the doctrine and policy of the Reformed Churches and would recommend the admission of the United Church of Canada.[2]

The committee on union was so pleased by this response that they dispatched Clarence Mackinnon and C.W. Gordon to present their case to the April meetings of the Eastern Section of the Alliance. Again after careful consideration, they stated:

> that while the proposed United Church of Canada in the "Basis of Union" presents some departures from recognized practises of the older Presbyterian Churches of the English-speaking world, Presbyterian Principles are sufficiently preserved in its constitution to justify the Alliance in admitting the church to its membership, should an application be made.[3]

While this statement was more cautious than that of the Alliance's Western Section, it nevertheless made it clear, even before there was a United Church of Canada, that it would be accepted as a member of the Alliance of Reformed Churches.

Acceptance by the Alliance was important for two reasons. First, it enabled Pidgeon to argue that if the world body of Presbyterian churches was prepared to recognize the United Church as a Presbyterian church, there could be no authority by which the Canadian dissidents might deny the unionists' claim. Second, because their membership in the Alliance was already approved, the unionists were in a position to protest when the dissidents applied for membership as the Presbyterian Church in Canada. This placed the dissidents in an extremely awkward position for it meant that although they had struggled to preserve and maintain the witness of the Presbyterian Church, they could not be accepted for membership in the Alliance under this name, and it would take many years before this problem could be finally sorted out.

For several years Stuart Parker, the convener of the Presbyterian Committee on Correspondence with other Churches, counselled "patience and self-restraint until the difficulties in the way of ourselves and the Alliance can be removed."[4] But in 1929 the General Assembly insisted that a protest, prepared by Ephraim Scott, "against the wrongful designation of the church as 'The Presbyterian Church of Canada' be sent to the secretariat of the Alliance." This protest led to a meeting during the Boston Council of the Alliance in 1929 at which representatives of the Presbyterian Church and the United Church were given the opportunity to state their respective cases. The outcome was a resolution which stated:

The special Committee further recommends that until an authoritative decision has been reached and made effective, the Council shall designate this church as "The Presbyterian Church in Canada," and shall protect its own records by a footnote to the effect that "This designation is in dispute and is here used without prejudice, implying neither approval or disapproval on the part of the Council."[5]

This footnote was a clear indication that the Canadian Presbyterians were not yet accepted without qualification by the Alliance as "The Presbyterian Church in Canada." But insofar as it was closer to their goal than any of the previous designations which had been used, they accepted it as the best that was possible for the time being.

The reason why the General Assembly of 1929 could not be restrained from sending an official protest to the Alliance concerning its status was that in 1928 they were dealt a grievous blow in the battle for recognition. The incident began on 5 January 1927 when Charles Clayton Morrison published a letter in the *Christian Century* from R.G. Stewart of Belleville, Ontario, under the heading "The Point Well-Taken."[6] In this letter Stewart argued that in spite of the union legislation which stated that the Presbyterian Church in Canada had entered the United Church, the right of the non-concurring congregations to use the name had been recognized in three separate actions: first, by giving the moderator of the Presbyterian Church the place he had always occupied in all state functions; second, by giving this church the charter of Knox College; and third, by the United Church accepting and endorsing a cheque issued by the Presbyterian Church in Canada as part of the settlement made by the Dominion Property Commission. In a private letter to Morrison, R.J. Wilson of the United Church's Bureau of Literature and Information made a vigorous rebuttal with six pages of documentation, challenged the correctness of these assertions, and suggested that the heading "The Point Well-Taken" was totally inappropriate.[7]

Wilson's letter placed Morrison in an awkward position because he was not close enough to the Canadian situation to be able to evaluate Wilson's rebuttal which, by implication, charged Morrison with hasty judgment. As a journalist he could not have been unaware that the controversy between the unionists and the dissidents was far from over. Thus his publication of Stewart's letter lent it a certain acceptability, which was resented by the unionists. His counterpart in Britain, John H. Hutton, the editor of *The British Weekly*, was also under attack from United Churchmen in Canada for publishing letters and articles by the dissidents. Indeed, the situation had become so tense that George Pidgeon had suggested to Wilson that a public declaration ought to be made "that *The British Weekly* has been unfair to the United Church of Canada."[8] Accordingly, it was impossible for anyone like Morrison who read the international Protestant press reports not to be aware of how this controversy was intruding itself into such gatherings as the Assembly of the Southern Presbyterian Church, the Assembly of the Church of Scotland, and the meetings of the Alliance of Reformed Churches.[9] It was with an awareness of the international dimensions of the continuing conflict, therefore, that Morrison decided to come to Canada for three weeks to do research for a series of articles on church union, one of which was devoted to "Canada's Non-Concurring Presbyterians."[10]

Admitting that he could not make head nor tail of the story of dissension and rupture, Morrison decided that the most appropriate way to approach this subject was to ask, "What does Christ think about it?" Feeling on relatively safe and familiar ground with this question, he said: "Christ looks upon the anti-union Presbyterians with the same eyes through which he looked on Simon Peter when the cock crew, and he has every reason for thinking the same thoughts which he thought then. For if there is any such thing as denying Christ, this non-concurring Presbyterian Church has surely denied him." He conceded that all churches were guilty of the sin of sectarianism. He was convinced, however, that:

> the defectionist group in Canada is peculiarly guilty because its eyes were smitten with the heavenly vision of a united church and it proved disobedient to it. This group made the great refusal. It set up standards that are not Christian standards, and closed its heart to the most elementary Christian appeal. It willfully, and proudly, and selfishly thrust itself in the path of fulfillment of the most Christian movement which has found expression in the ecclesiastical life of the church since the Protestant Reformation. It lowered the Christian banner and caused it to be sullied with shame. For itself it carries a different banner; it is not a Christian banner, but the banner of anti-Christ.[11]

Those Canadians who were closer to the situation never went quite so far as Morrison in their condemnation of the Presbyterian opponents of union. They were aware that there had been excesses on both sides, and many regretted the resulting bitterness. This awareness, however, did not prevent W.B. Creighton, the editor of the United Church's *New Outlook*, from publicly thanking Morrison "for seeing in our union movement what we have seen in it."[12] Nor did it prevent R.J. Wilson from privately thanking Morrison and saying that although the article on the non-concurrents was severe, he could "scarcely suggest the change of a comma."[13]

Understandably, the Presbyterians were shocked by Morrison's indictment, but what offended them even more was the reprinting of this offensive article in several of Canada's leading daily newspapers. Only one United Church minister, R.E. Knowles, a novelist and feature writer for the Toronto *Daily Star*, publicly dissociated himself from Morrison's "deplorable deliverance" and regretted that no "outstanding voice" from the United Church had disavowed all responsibility for Morrison's "unfortunate opinions."[14] Consequently, with no one else to speak up for them, W.M. Rochester, Scott's successor as the editor of the *Presbyterian Record*, mounted a counter attack in the newspapers suggesting that Morrison "for ignorance, prejudice and presumption" was like his fellow citizen "Big Bill Thompson," the mayor of Chicago, who had recently poured out his wrath upon all persons, books, and things British. The only difference was that Thompson spoke for himself, while Morrison presumed to speak for God in delivering his "unqualified, unrelieved, unmitigated and final judgement." For those outside Toronto, where most of this debate was carried on in the newspapers, Rochester later gathered these materials together and published them in a pamphlet entitled "A Prophet from Chicago and His Canadian Sponsors."[15] Unfortunately, Rochester's pamphlet did not have the same international circulation as the *Christian Century,* and as a result few outside of Ontario were aware of his rebuttal of Morrison's attack.

It was perhaps for this reason that Ephraim Scott published his book on *"Church Union" and the Presbyterian Church in Canada* in 1928.[16] Scott was eighty-three when this book appeared and not surprisingly it was largely a summary of the arguments he had used in many of the articles and pamphlets he had written on the subject over the past eighteen years. As a polemicist Scott was noted for the acerbity of his style, and this book did little to dispel that impression. Scott's effort to place the story of the resistance to union within the wider framework of the struggle for religious liberty, therefore, was largely lost in the rhetoric of acrimony, and rather than being a public relations victory for the dissidents, it was generally dismissed as a cranky book. It did serve, however, to make the unionists aware of the necessity of telling the "true" story of union, and it prompted two major unionist participants in the controversy to publish books on the subject.

S.D. Chown's *The Story of Church Union in Canada,* which was published in 1930, looked at union from the perspective of a major Methodist participant in the union struggle. Knowing the movement from the "inside," Chown indicated that the purpose was to create "a better understanding of the real inwardness of the movement" and to do so "before wrong impressions became embalmed in the memory."[17] Despite its claims to be "a careful and truthful history," however, its polemical character was clearly revealed in its suggestion that the opposition to union was significant only for providing "much interesting material for a psychological study of the contagion of prejudice."[18] Like many theological liberals elsewhere, Chown utilized the psychology of religion to establish a perspective for viewing the opponents of union as misfits.[19] This ploy involved as much character assassination as Scott ever devised, but when it was cast in a rhetoric which seemed to suggest that it was based on the insights of William James, George Albert

Coe, and other psychologists of religion, it somehow seemed more acceptable, and this perspective has characterized the unionists' interpretation of the dissidents ever since.[20]

E.H. Oliver's *The Winning of the Frontier,* which also appeared in 1930, was a more ambitious religious history of Canada that saw union as a response to the needs of the frontier and as an essential step in Christendom's continuing struggle to illuminate the dark barbarism beyond its frontiers with the light of Christian civilization.[21] This perspective reduced the opposition to insignificance, and church union became a major factor not only for understanding God's design but also for understanding the pattern of Canadian religious development. Church union was seen as one of the unique characteristics of religion in Canada that distinguished its history from both that of Europe and of the United States. All of the subsequent interpretations of Canadian religious history have accorded church union this significant position. Thus, these two books by major participants in the controversy constituted significant public relations victories for the unionists and were seen by them as important perceptions of the true meaning of church union in Canada.

Having accomplished so much, the executive of the General Council was therefore a bit hesitant when in 1930 they received a letter from Galen M. Fisher of the Institute for Social and Religious Research in New York seeking permission to do a study of the United Church of Canada.[22] At its meeting on 7 March 1930 the subexecutive recommended that a copy of this correspondence be sent to all its members with the instruction that it be given "careful examination in preparation for thorough consideration at a subsequent meeting."[23] Then on 17 March Dr. Fisher, the executive secretary of the Institute, was invited to Toronto "to discuss with a number of members of the executive the various phases of the proposed survey."[24] When it was revealed that C.E. Silcox would be the director of the study for the Institute, it was difficult for the United Church to turn them down because Silcox was a Canadian whose family roots lay deep within Canadian Congregationalism. He was the great-grandson of the first Congregational minister in Upper Canada, and his father, the Rev. E.D. Silcox, had been editor of the *Canadian Congregationalist* and a member of the joint committee on union. On 4 July, therefore, the subexecutive gave general approval to the project. But after some second thoughts a committee was set up on 26 November "to represent the United Church in matters that come under consideration in the conduct of the survey of church union in Canada now being made by the Institute of Social and Religious Research."[25] The committee consisted of T. Albert Moore, Robert Laird, George A. Little, Sir Robert Falconer, George C. Pidgeon, J.J. Coulter, N.W. Rowell, A.W. Barker, and R.P. Stouffer.

What Silcox and the Institute thought of this committee is not known, but it ought to have been clear to them that the United Church, in appointing a committee which consisted of the president of the University of Toronto, the first moderator of the United Church, the secretary, treasurer, and deputy treasurer of the General Council, and the chairman of the church's law and legislation committee, was not about to give either Silcox or the Institute complete freedom to arrive at whatever conclusions they saw fit. If this was not apparent at the beginning, it quickly became so as soon as the study was completed. The committee was not pleased with the manuscript, and it instructed Robert Laird to point out to Fisher and the Institute the weaknesses which it perceived in the study before it was published.[26]

Among the "serious inadequacies" which the committee noted were the author's "very limited apprehension of the deeper causes and forces behind and within the union movement," his failure to do justice to "the glow and spiritual enthusiasm of those who experienced the union," his "slight treatment" of Home Missions, Foreign Missions, and "the virility and scholarship of their educational institutions," his lack of awareness "of the spirit of intellectual enquiry and deepening spiritual passion which was animating younger ministers and many of the laymen of the churches in the two decades prior to union," and finally, the unhappy and cumulative colouration which his use of such words as "aftermath" and "debacle" gave to the study as well as his "pronounced tendency to view church union as a tragedy rather then an triumph."[27] To underline the seriousness of these inadequacies, the moderator of the United Church of Canada, Dr. T. Albert Moore, who had recently published his own version of the story, went to New York in February 1933 to discuss them with Fisher and other officials of the Institute of Social and Religious Research.[28] As a result of this meeting, the Institute gently suggested that if the United Church felt so strongly about the matter, they should publish a statement similar to the one drafted by Laird along with Silcox's survey of church union. Although Moore assured the Institute that this suggestion would be considered at once by the United Church, nothing came of it and the book was published without comment from the committee.[29]

After such a series of public relations victories, it seems strange that such a prestigious United Church committee should have been so sensitive to even the mildest criticism. It is stranger still that the moderator of the United Church should have considered the inadequacies of this study serious enough to warrant a trip to New York. For as everyone, except the members of this committee, could see, Silcox's book was a very substantial pro-union study that quickly established itself, especially in academic circles, as the standard work on the subject. Why this committee should have felt so embattled and sensitive eight years after the consummation of union, therefore, seems inexplicable until their reaction is seen against the background of the battle over the identity and continuity of the Presbyterian Church in Canada which had been going on since 1925.

The first inkling the United Church had of the difficulties they would experience in maintaining their claim that the Presbyterian Church in Canada had gone into union came when Dr. T. Albert Moore wrote to the Honourable A.S. Copp, the secretary of state, who was in charge of corporate nomenclature, objecting to the minority's continued use of the name "The Presbyterian Church in Canada" and asking that the government prevent any religious body or association from using the names of the churches that went into union.[30] The secretary of state replied that if any application for incorporation was made under any of the names in question, the United Church would be given the opportunity to oppose the grant of a name.[31] The rub here was that the Presbyterian church would never apply for incorporation. Therefore, it was unlikely that the government would ever have to deny the dissidents the right to the use of the name.

In order to hold property, the Presbyterian Church had incorporated numerous boards of trustees. But unlike the Methodist church, it had never sought incorporation as a church. As the assembly in 1926 put it:

> The Presbyterian Church in Canada is not a civil corporation. Its name is not a corporate name, which some power outside itself, gave or can take away. The church is a free voluntary fellowship of Christians holding the Presbyterian System of Doctrine and Polity, and who have the free, sovereign right to choose their own name.[32]

In other words, it was their contention that whatever the state had not created, it could not dismantle or merge into another corporation, and they defied the United Church or anyone else to prove otherwise.

Another irritating aspect of this question from the United Church's point of view was that at state functions in Ottawa, the moderator of the Presbyterian Church was still being addressed as the moderator of the "Presbyterian Church in Canada," and he was given precedence over the moderator of the United Church. George Pidgeon wrote to Prime Minister King, who had remained a Presbyterian, objecting to the fact that the non-concurrents were "recognized under a name which the law of the land provides they must not take."[33] King, however, refused to take any responsibility for the matter and referred Pidgeon's letter to the governor general, "who was, he said, responsible for what had been done."[34] Arthur F. Sladen, the governor general's secretary, in turn referred the question to W. Stuart Edwards, the deputy minister of justice, who suggested, in response to another letter on this matter from N.W. Rowell, that the legal questions raised by Rowell could not be determined by the governor general or the minister of justice. They were matters upon which the courts would have to rule. In the meantime, he thought it was appropriate to point out that when the governor general "extends an invitation to the head of the Presbyterian Church he cannot do other than invite him under the name which he uses and which is doubtless the only name under which he would feel free to accept the invitation."[35] With his two-sentence reply, Sladen sent a copy of Edwards' opinion, indicating that he was in entire agreement with Edwards on this matter.[36] This response left the United Church in the awkward position of having continually to protest their mistreatment by Ottawa. Not wishing to attack the governor general directly, however, these protests were usually directed to Mackenzie King. In 1929, for example, W.T. Gunn wrote to King, "I am sure that you will quite understand that the United Church of Canada, cannot, without protest, be officially represented at functions at which use is made of a title distinctly forbidden by the Act of Parliament incorporating the United Church."[37] But, somehow, as long as King was prime minister no one in Ottawa seemed to be able to resolve the question in a manner satisfactory to the United Church.

To determine whether the United Church could bring a civil action against the Presbyterian Church, the law and legislation committee hired R.L. Kellock to prepare a memorandum on the possibilities of restraining the Presbyterians from using the name "The Presbyterian Church in Canada." In reviewing the precedents for such an action, Kellock left no stone unturned. He even unearthed such unlikely cases as the Society of the War of 1812 v the Society of the War of 1812 in the state of New York and the Loyal Order of the Moose v the Improved Benevolent and Protective Order of Moose in the state of New Jersey. In spite of going to these lengths, it was difficult to establish a clear case. If the United Church was not using the name and there was no threat to property, Kellock concluded, it was unlikely the courts would take action to restrain the Presbyterians from using the name.[38] In a subsequent brief, McGregor Young, professor of international law, constitutional law and history at the University of Toronto and one of the drafters of the legislation, made a stronger case, but it was not strong enough to tempt N.W. Rowell, the chairman of the law and legislation committee, into taking action.[39]

This hesitation by the committee prompted Pidgeon to write a letter to Rowell pointing out that the continued use of the name the Presbyterian Church in Canada by the non-concurring Presbyterians was confusing people in the United Church. "They ask," he said, "Did our church really enter union after all? Unionists in the old country ask almost in despair:—'What did happen in Canada—You say that the Churches united, and yet 'The Presbyterian Church in Canada' continues apart from union." The problem, as Pidgeon pointed out, was of concern to not only United Churchmen but also to unionists everywhere. They were asking: "Is it possible for a Presbyterian Church to unite with another church and to make the changes in its doctrinal statements and its policy necessary for such a union 'without loss of its identity'? Does the church as a church go into the union, or does the uniting group leave their own church and merely enter another?" In view of the importance of the matter, therefore, Pidgeon suggested that a commission consisting of representatives of the Scottish and American Presbyterian Churches should be appointed to resolve this question. He had to admit, however, that there might be some difficulties in getting either the churches or the Alliance of Reformed Churches to make a ruling on this question.[40]

Under this sort of pressure, the executive of the United Church's General Council passed a long resolution in 1927 on the identity of the uniting churches which read, in part, as follows:

> Whereas the central principle underlying the union of the Presbyterian Church in Canada, the Methodist Church and the Congregational Churches of Canada, to form the United Church of Canada is that they entered the union as organized bodies by their free and independent action through their governing bodies in accordance with identity. . .
> And whereas the non-concurring congregations . . . deny that the Presbyterian Church in Canada entered the said union and insist that they constitute the Presbyterian Church in Canada as organized prior to the said union and in the records and proceedings of their Assemblies for the years 1925, 1926 and 1927 have declared that such Assemblies are respectively the fifty-first, fifty-second and fifty-third General Assemblies of the Presbyterian Church in Canada, and in their literature and publications and in their relations with other churches have held themselves out as being the Presbyterian Church in Canada as it existed prior to the said union. . . . Therefore resolved that correspondence be entered into with the Moderator of the General Assembly of the non-concurring congregations of the Presbyterian Church in Canada, with a request for a conference. . .or for the submission of the said claim to the courts in a friendly action to declare and determine the rights of the parties.[41]

The constraining influence behind this resolution was that in June 1927 the Church of Scotland and the United Free Church of Scotland, which had been considering the question of their relationship to the Presbyterian Church in Canada for a year, decided to maintain the same relations as had existed prior to 1925.[42] This recognition of the non-concurrents by the Presbyterian churches of Scotland constituted such a threat to the United Church that it became necessary for them to restate once again their understanding of the fundamental principle of their union. It also prompted the moderator of the United Church, James Endicott, to discuss this question at a meeting in Victoria with a group of United Church ministers and laymen. Endicott declared categorically that "there is no Presbyterian Church as such apart from the existing United Church of Canada," and he suggested that the United Church "should maintain a position of protest against an illegal use of the name, The Presbyterian Church in Canada."[43]

In a sharply worded reply to Endicott, Banks Nelson, convenor of the assembly's Legal Committee, made it plain that the Presbyterian Church "By action of the General Assembly had reaffirmed its right and its wish to the continued and unbroken use of this name 'Presbyterian Church in Canada' and. . . we would not hazard our freedom and right in this matter in any lawsuit, because we would regard such action as the unlawful use of the law."[44] That this was more than Nelson's personal opinion became clear when a telegram, sent to the moderator of the Presbyterian Church in June 1928, was not acknowledged.[45] Therefore, in 1929 the executive of the United Church's General Council asked its secretary, Dr. T. Albert Moore, to send a letter of protest to the General Assembly. This letter stated:

Our position is that the Presbyterian Church in Canada, by its free and independent action and in accordance with its constitution, joined with The Methodist Church and the Congregational Churches of Canada to form The United Church of Canada, that it is now a part of the United Church and cannot and does not exist apart therefrom.[46]

To this statement the Presbyterian Church replied:

The Board of Administration cannot accept the position that The United Church of Canada is entitled to restrain in any way those who have remained Presbyterians from continuing to use the designation which has been in use by them and their predecessors in faith and doctrine for fifty-five years. Essentially and primarily the question is one of ecclesiastical continuity and no secular power had or has any jurisdiction to deal with and arbitrarily decide that question. That there is ecclesiastical continuity does not in the view of the Board admit of contradiction and the Presbyterians who continue to adhere to the doctrines and forms of government of the Presbyterian Church as they existed on and prior to the 10th of June 1925, are necessarily still Presbyterians, and as necessarily are still entitled to the use of the name, The Presbyterian Church in Canada.[47]

This exchange of letters showed that the controversy was far from being resolved and would need very little provocation to break out again into open hostility.

The necessary provocation occurred at the meetings of the General Assembly of the Presbyterian Church in 1932. Dr. Endicott, a former Methodist and moderator of the United Church, had been appointed as a fraternal delegate to bring greetings to the Presbyterian Church. But when it was announced that he would address the assembly, Dr. Wardlaw Taylor, who as clerk of the Assembly had just received Dr. Moore's annual letter denying the church's claim to continuity and identity as the Presbyterian Church in Canada, protested against Endicott being allowed to address the assembly. During the furore which followed, Endicott was informed of the protest, and he quickly returned to Toronto. The newspapers, however, had a field day with this event. The Toronto *Telegram* commented that "church leaders do not hesitate to assume that they are capable of solving the weighty problems which confront the nation. It is too bad that they have been unable to adjust the trifling differences which exist between themselves."[48] In an editorial ironically entitled "The Hands of Fellowship," the *Hamilton Review* blasted the United Church, stating:

> Church union was to have been a great and forward step to extend the frontiers of Canadian christendom. It was to have given the word of the Master a tremendous stimulus in this country. It was to have strengthened the ranks of Christian soldiers and consolidated the ramparts of the church militant. Such was the cry. Such was the promise. But instead . . . the crowning prosecution of this crushing hierocracy has been to stamp underfoot this weaker vessel, obliterate it, by seeking to strip it even of its name. In the high councils of this Temporal Mightiness has been framed a new negative for the decalogue—"Thou Shalt Not Call Thyselves the Presbyterian Church in Canada."[49]

The Lindsay *Daily Post* took the position that now that the United Church was established, "it is neither useful nor becoming for it to prolong the bitterness of past controversies by academic insistence on a copyright monopoly in the name Presbyterian." On the other hand, it thought that the assembly "would have been in a stronger position if, instead of refusing to hear the United Church delegates, it had received them and accepted their visit as an acknowledgment of the Assembly's legal status and identity which Dr. Moore's letter denied."[50]

The advice and ridicule of newspaper editors across the country, however, did not prevent Moore from continuing to send these annual letters of protest to the General Assembly until he retired in 1936. What finally brought them to an end was a series of legal decisions which began to erode the United Church's claims concerning the issues of identity and continuity. While it was possible for United Church leaders to ignore public opinion, they could not afford to ignore the court's.

The case which set the pattern for a series of decisions during the 1930's was the ruling of the Supreme Court of Canada in an appeal from the judgment of the Supreme Court of Nova Scotia concerning the Patriquin estate.[51] In her will dated 5 January 1924 Eliza Patriquin left one hundred dollars to the trustees of the Tatamagouche Presbyterian Church. When a vote was taken in this congregation on 12 January 1925, a majority of the congregation voted for union and entered the United Church. The dissidents from this congregation formed the Sedgwick Memorial Presbyterian Church in Tatamagouche, and Eliza Patriquin transferred her membership to this church some months before she died on 22 May 1926. When the case first came before Judge Chisholm, he held that the bequest belonged to the United Church in Tatamagouche.[52] This decision, however, was unanimously reversed by the Supreme Court of Nova Scotia,[53] and when the case came before the Supreme Court of Canada, Justice Smith in giving his opinion said:

> I think that the Supreme Court *in banco* has correctly held that the present congregation of the United Church of Canada at Tatamagouche is not the same entity as "The Tatamagouche Presbyterian Church" to which the testatrix made this bequest and therefore cannot take it. We have incorporated by the Act an entirely new and distinct legal entity, and what we have to consider is whether or not that entity is the same organization as that which she had in contemplation as her beneficiary.[54]

Justice Smith believed they were not, and therefore he dismissed the appeal.

Commenting on this case in a memorandum prepared for the Presbyterian Church, R.S. Cassels observed:

> The salient principle is that, in the opinion at least of those two courts, [the Supreme Court of Nova Scotia and the Supreme Court of Canada] a United Churchman is not a Presbyterian, but something different and apart, and that a Presbyterian congregation which goes into the United Church has a new and independent status as a part of that body, and has ceased to be a Presbyterian congregation.[55]

As a result Cassels believed that the decision involved "a complete negation of the specious metaphysical doctrine of merger without loss of identity." It left open, however, the question of the status of the Presbyterian Church in Canada as it existed after 10 June 1925. That question would eventually have to be answered, but Cassels was not sure that the decision in the Patriquin case would be helpful in answering it, because what it appeared to say was that the Presbyterian Church in Canada had ceased to exist. If this was so, then the church which Cassels represented was a new denomination. The court, however, had not ruled on the status of the continuing Presbyterian church, it had only ruled against the United Church's claim to be the Presbyterian Church in Canada. This ruling set the pattern for its next major decision in the case of the Jessie Gray estate.

On 7 July 1921 Jessie Gray of Hopewell, Nova Scotia, made out her will leaving five hundred dollars to the Home Mission Fund of the Presbyterian Church in Canada and five hundred dollars to the Foreign Mission Fund of the Presbyterian Church in Canada. As in Tatamagouche, the St. Columba Presbyterian Church in Hopewell voted to enter the United Church, and Jessie Gray remained a member of this congregation until her death in 1931. On 31 December 1931 the executors of her estate took out an originating summons calling upon the United Church, the Presbyterian Church, and a number of other beneficiaries to appear in order to determine whether the bequests should be paid to the United Church, the Presbyterian Church, or, if to neither, how otherwise. In 1932 the matter came before the Nova Scotia Supreme Court, and Judge Graham ruled that the bequests should be paid to the Presbyterian Church.[56] On appeal to the Supreme Court of Nova Scotia,[57] the court affirmed the decision of Judge Graham, and the United Church appealed this decision to the Supreme Court of Canada.[58] Here both Justice Lamont and Justice Crockett agreed, referring to the Patriquin case, that the United Church was not entitled to receive the bequests. Noting the slight difference in the two cases, in that the bequests in the Patriquin case were to a congregation and in the Gray case to the "funds" of the church, Justice Lamont nevertheless stressed that the testatrix intended to augment the funds controlled and administered by the Presbyterian Church. The fact that later she had become a member of the United Church of Canada for six years apparently did not matter, for she had not changed her will. Therefore, the Presbyterian Church received her bequest. Justice Lamont carefully pointed out, however, that the fact that the United Church had no claim to the money did not establish that the continuing Presbyterian Church was the same entity as the Presbyterian Church in Canada prior to union. "On that question," he said, "I express no opinion." All he was clear about was that the United Church had no claim whatever to the money.

Justice Crockett was much more specific on this question. He said that the only way the United Church could claim any interest in these bequests was on the grounds that the Presbyterian Church in Canada was now a constituent part of the United Church of Canada "without loss of identity." He argued, however, that this claim would only be valid if each of the negotiating churches had "continued to exist within the new church corporation as a distinct and separate body. . .(each retaining) the right to control its own internal affairs within the United Church without reference to the others, which was clearly never intended by the incorporating Act." In conclusion, he said that in the Patriquin case "the clear ground of decision was that the

United Church of Canada did not answer the description of the Presbyterian Church in Canada as the latter church existed before the United Church of Canada Act came into effect."[59] He therefore dismissed the appeal.

The major difficulty which these cases presented to the United Church was that the precedents which they set went well beyond their contention with the Presbyterian Church. Indeed, they had begun to affect decisions on bequests to both the Methodist and Congregationl Churches. For example, in Re Thorne a will made in 1917 bequeathed legacies to the Methodist churches in Sandy Cove, Centreville, and Port Wade. When these legacies were vested in 1932, however, it was held, on the basis of the Patriquin case that the three Methodist Churches referred to in the will had ceased to exist after the coming into force of the United Church of Canada Act of 1924.[60] Again, in Re Kelley the annual income of a $20,000 trust fund was bequeathed "for the benefit of the Congregational Church at Cheboque." If certain conditions were not fulfilled by the minister and the church, or if the church ceased to exist or changed its adherence, then the income from the trust fund was to revert to the Halifax School for the Blind. After Mr. Kelley died, the Congregational Church at Cheboque became part of the United Church, and as a result, the Supreme Court of Nova Scotia, referring to the Patriquin decision, ruled that the church had ceased to exist and therefore the income of the trust fund was awarded to the Halifax School for the Blind.[61] In view of these cases, it was becoming clear that the United Church's once proud claim that its constitutent churches were free to enter into union "without loss of identity" was becoming unravelled not only in relation to the Presbyterian Church but also in relation to the Methodist and Congregational Churches as well.

In spite of these decisions, however, the courts were not in a position to resolve the conflict between the United and Presbyterian churches, for they were dealing with specific cases, and their task was not to rule on the legitimacy of the church union legislation as a whole but rather to determine where funds from particular estates ought to go. Therefore they could not force the United Church to recognize the Presbyterians' claims to identity and continuity, nor could they bring an end to the litigation. As a result, by 1938 Judge Fisher of the Ontario Court of Appeals became so frustrated by this continued legal bickering that in the course of giving his judgment in the case of Laird v. MacKay, he said:

> Having considered this appeal on its legal merits I cannot part with it without expressing regret that it was found necessary for a great Christian organization to engage this estate in litigation. . . .If this litigation is to continue thousands of dollars will be expended which would otherwise be spared to missions as desired by this generous and

well meaning testator. It is to be hoped that instead of these Christian
bodies frittering away the income from this fund in litigation that the
testators intentions will be given more serious consideration.[62]

While such statements undoubtedly brought pressure to bear on both parties,
the courts were not in a position to initiate negotiations for a compromise.
This had to be done by the churches themselves. Fortunately, by 1938 steps
were already being taken.

14

The Resolution of the Controversy

In societies with a close relationship between church and state, the resolution of ecclesiastical conflicts was relatively simple. Decapitation, impalement, and burning at the stake were common means of resolving religious conflicts throughout Christendom until relatively recent times. But with the growth of religious toleration and the separation of church and state these means of settling religious differences became obsolete. In deconfessionalized states all religious groups are equal before the law, and the state will not interfere in their affairs providing their controversies do not involve physical violence, property damage, or other violations of the law. With no external means of control, therefore, the only way religious controversies can be resolved in modern democratic societies is by the churches themselves.

In these circumstances the most effective limitation on a conflict is the recognition by one party or the other that there is more to be lost than gained by its continuation. Yet, because both sides in a religious controversy tend to identify their position with the will of God, it often takes a long time before the participants are prepared to accept the fact that they cannot win and must compromise. In the case of the church union controversy in Canada, it took the United Church a very long time to arrive at this conclusion and even longer before it could place an individual of imagination and insight in a position of authority from which it was possible to work out an acceptable compromise.

In some respects it is curious that it should have taken fourteen years to resolve the conflict, because in spite of the battles over recognition and property and the bitterness which this created in certain quarters, there was at the same time a considerable amount of goodwill on both sides and a genuine desire to establish better relations. In 1927, for example, the Manitoba and London Conferences of the United Church of Canada sent fraternal greetings to the General Assembly at its meetings in Stratford, Ontario.[1] Again in 1932, the year in which there was an explosion over Dr. Endicott's attempt to convey the United Church's greetings to the General Assembly, the Manitoba Conference sent "cordial greetings" to the General Assembly.[2] These greetings were accepted, and it was agreed that the moderator should send a suitable reply in the name of the assembly.[3] Thus the assembly found itself in the rather peculiar position of rejecting the greetings of the United Church's General Council while at the same time accepting the greetings of one of the United Church's lower courts. Moreover, despite the widespread publicity given to the Assembly's refusal to hear Endicott, the following year when the assembly met in Peterborough, the United Church's Bay of Quinte Conference, by a unanimous resolution, sent greetings "praying that in all your work you may be greatly prospered, and that the Catholic Church may be strengthened by your endeavours."[4] All of these greetings and expressions of goodwill from the lower courts of the United Church represented a form of *de facto* recognition and they also reflected a certain impatience on the part of large segments within the United Church with the legal details which were prolonging the controversy.

But still the controversy continued. Part of the problem was George Pidgeon's uncompromising insistence that the Presbyterian Church in Canada had gone into union. But a far more important figure in the continuation of the conflict was Dr. T. Albert Moore, the former secretary of the Methodist General Conference and the first secretary of the General Council of the United Church of Canada. Moore had been a member of the Methodist union committee from the beginning of the negotiations, and during that time he had served first as the secretary of the Methodist committee and then from 1914 to 1925 as the secretary of the joint committee on union.[5] His experience in the union negotiations, therefore, was greater than that of Presbyterian leaders, such as George Pidgeon, who came into prominence only in the later stages of the controversy.

Throughout the twenty years of negotiations, the dissidents were not hesitant in making insulting remarks about the Methodists. But Moore, unlike S.D. Chown, the general superintendent of the Methodist Church who lashed out against these indignities on several occasions, remained in the background and ignored these jibes. It was not until the six months prior to 10 June 1925 that the dissidents finally goaded Moore to anger, and when it happened, something snapped in Moore which henceforth would turn him into an implacable foe of the dissidents. In two almost identical private letters written on 4 February 1925 to Principal Dyde of Queen's Theological College and to Dr. D.R. Drummond of Hamilton, Moore revealed what had finally pushed him over the edge.

Moore's purpose in writing to Dyde was to explain why it was impossible for Methodists to have anything to do with Dyde's appeal to the attorney general of Ontario asking him to mediate in the dispute over union within the Presbyterian Church. He said:

Six months ago the situation was simple. Then the issue was whether two or three Christian societies, reciprocally recognizing each other as such would unite. Now the proposal put forth by you is that we should meet with a body which has publicly proclaimed us as non-Christian and "an apostate church," and which has supported this by a studied and calculated fabrication of falsehoods.

Moore was referring to the local pamphlets produced by the Kew Beach and Sault Ste. Marie branches of the Presbyterian Church Association and to the pamphlet "An open letter to the Members and Adherents of the Presbyterian Church" which was signed by elders from Cooke's Church, Dale Church, Rhodes Avenue, College Street, and Kew Beach churches. This pamphlet specifically accused the officials of the Methodist Church of being "apostate." Moore had examined all of these pamphlets and he declared them to be "deliberate and malicious lying," which, he said, clearly indicated that "the inspiration of the opposition is plain antipathy to Methodism, whether voiced as hatred, contempt or mere distrust."

The question he directed to Dyde, therefore, was "How can we meet men whom we know to be liars, and how can they meet us knowing us to be apostates?" "To send one or two men to meet these who are deliberate liars, whose attitude to us is one of utmost bitterness — can you not see the position in which you ask us to place ourselves?" Furthermore, as Moore went on to point out, the problem had implications which went beyond Dyde's proposal. As a result of this campaign of hatred towards Methodism, we will be "forced to face a generation in which we are confronted with a body organized in fierce antipathy to us, animated by hatred and misled by falsehood." When at some time in the future this new church seeks co-operation with us in the various activities of the church, "Do you imagine that one of us would sit at the table with these men? If so, you credit us with a magnanimity which even I would hesitate to claim for my church."[6]

In writing to Drummond, Moore's purpose was to ask him to take steps "to elicit or to utter a definite repudiation of the assaults on the Methodist Church which have made and must make any intercourse impossible until the views there expressed are emphatically repudiated." He indicated that he could accept Drummond's position. "I take it for granted," he said, "that you and some others were at heart and in principle in favour of church union but the actual state of opinion in your church made you resist consummation. That is a fair position and one which is entitled to respect. So also can one respect those who did not think church union a wise policy but who nevertheless respected the Methodist Church as a real Christian society." But what was totally unacceptable in Moore's eyes was the malicious antipathy to Methodism and the slanderous charges that the Methodist church was "apostate" and "unfit to have spiritual charge of any souls or be regarded as a Christian body." Until these "studied, deliberate and malicious" lies were publicly retracted, Moore declared, "absolute nonintercourse in any field of activity" would be the result.[7]

Unfortunately, Moore was apparently unaware that he was writing to the wrong persons if he expected any action in his appeal for a public retraction. Dyde was never affiliated with the dissidents, and Drummond had made his decision to oppose the consummation of union much too late for him to have any influence with those who were at the centre of the resistance movement. If Moore, for example, had written the same sort of letter to John Penman, his appeal undoubtedly would have received a sympathetic hearing because Penman had reacted negatively to the Kew Beach pamphlet when he first read it. Moreover, what Moore failed to realize was that these charges did not emanate from any of the literature published by the national executive of the Presbyterian Church Association. They were contained in pamphlet literature published and paid for by branches of the Presbyterian Church Association in local congregations. It is true that the national executive never took any steps to repudiate these charges, but it is conceivable that they would have if Moore's letter had been directed to them through MacNamara and if they had considered seriously the implications of the phrase "absolute non-intercourse in any field of activity."

The United Church, on the other hand, had no idea of what the appointment of Moore to the position of secretary of the General Council might mean in terms of their future relations with the continuing Presbyterian Church because he had not publicly expressed his feelings. There is no evidence that such knowledge would have made any difference, for at the time many felt the same way about the dissidents, and few expected that the controversy would continue for another fourteen years. It is also unlikely that many realized when they created the position of secretary of the General Council that this would become the most powerful administrative position in the church. Moderators would come and go but the secretary of General Council seemed to go on forever; the appointment was without term, and at that time there was no mandatory retirement age. On a day-to-day basis, therefore, few others in the church were in a position to exercise the same influence on the church's decisions. His power and authority, of course, was not so extensive that it could block expressions of goodwill from the conferences of the United Church. But in the national offices of the church, there was virtually no way around him. Therefore, in spite of any willingness to recognize the Presbyterian Church at the local level, there was very little that the national church could do until Dr. Moore decided to retire in 1936 at the age of seventy-six.

Similar pressures for a resolution of the controversy were felt by the Board of Administration of the Presbyterian Church in Canada throughout this same period. From the beginning there was pressure to bring the question of the church's status before the civil courts in order to remove uncertainty and doubt about its position. In 1926, for example, the Presbytery of Lanark and Renfrew overtured the assembly asking for immediate action on this matter.[8] The following year the assembly received overtures on the same subject from the Presbytery of North Bay and Temiskaming and the Presbytery of Winnipeg.[9] On both occasions these overtures were referred to the legal committee of the Board of Administration, and nothing further was heard of them. But in 1928 when the Committee on Correspondence with Other Churches recommended that a committee be appointed to investigate this matter, the board finally decided to take action.[10]

The course of action which the Board of Administration decided upon was to ask R.S. Cassels to formulate a series of questions on the United Church of Canada Act and to send them to Eugene Lafleur for his opinion. The first question Cassels asked was "Has the United Church Act any validity or effect insofar as it assumes to carry, *eo nomine,* the Presbyterian Church in Canada, a voluntary unincorporated association of individuals into the new corporate body?" Lafleur replied, "Yes, it is within the powers of the Dominion parliament to incorporate a voluntary association and as an incident of that power to deal with the name of the new corporate body." Cassels second question was, "Has the United Church Act any validity or effect insofar as it assumes to change the status of individual members of the Presbyterian Church into that of members of the United Church unless the individual registers his dissent within the time limited by the Act?" Lafleur replied, "No, parliament has no power to change the status of individual members of the Presbyterian Church. This would be an interference with religious liberty. . . .Insofar as failure to dissent would affect property rights within the provinces, the legislation would be unconstitutional." To the third question which concerned the use of the name, Lafleur said that in his opinion "the United Church of Canada Act is valid insofar as it prohibits the use of the name—The Presbyterian Church in Canada—and the United Church could enforce it." In reply to the fourth and fifth questions, Lafleur said that "the United Church of Canada Act is *ultra vires* insofar as it assumes to incorporate boards, congregations and other corporations which were incorporated by special acts of provincial legislatures."[11]

Lafleur's replies to questions one and three were the sort of answers which the Presbyterians did not want to hear, but having consulted one of the top lawyers in the country, they could not ignore his advice. The Board of Administration, therefore, became very cautious and determined not to be pressured into any precipitous litigation to clarify the church's status. However, when Cassels indicated that he disagreed with Lafleur, they were prepared to listen to him.

In a letter to MacNamara in March 1929, Cassels wrote:

In spite of Mr. Lafleur's opinion to the contrary, I think there is very grave doubt whether the legislation purporting to carry the Presbyterian Church in Canada, by that name, into the United Church of Canada had really any effect; because of want of jurisdiction but not because legally speaking there was no such entity as the Presbyterian Church in Canada and therefore nothing to which legislation using that name could attach. There is no doubt that Parliament had jurisdiction to incorporate the United Church of Canada and there is no doubt that individuals had the right to join that church but it seems clear that the legislation does not really go any further than this as far as the religious status of the Presbyterians is concerned.[12]

Cassels conceded that the position was quite different with regard to property. The combined effect of both the federal and provincial legislation was to vest the property in the United Church of Canada, and "there is nothing now open to objection in that respect."

Concerning the name, however, Cassels thought that this provision in the act was of doubtful validity even though it had been adopted and affirmed in the legislation passed by all of the provinces except Ontario. Cassels was sure that "in Ontario it might be contended successfully that the right to use the name still exists even on the strict legal basis."[13] This possibility was sufficiently intriguing for the Board of Administration to authorize Cassels, as the convenor of the Board of Trustees, to make a recommendation to the 1929 General Assembly concerning the incorporation of a Board of Trustees in the Province of Ontario. In his report to the assembly Cassels said:

The appropriate and most satisfactory procedure from the legal point of view would be the incorporation of a board by special Act of the Dominion Parliament, with supplementary confirmatory and enabling legislation in each province. But from 1900 to 1925 there were in existence a number of separate boards incorporated by provincial legislation and no board incorporated by Dominion legislation, and no special difficulty developed during that time in dealing with the assets of the church. To obtain legislation at Ottawa and in each Province would be an expensive and possibly a somewhat troublesome matter and probably a board incorporated by special Act of the Legislature of Ontario will have sufficient powers and status.

In concluding his report, which was dated 16 May 1929, Cassels indicated that an act had been drafted for presentation to the Ontario legislature, and subject to the approval of the assembly an application for the passing of this act would be made under the direction of the Board of Administration.[14]

The 1929 Assembly gave its approval and named the trustees who would serve on this board when it was incorporated.[15] The Board of Administration also recommended that when the Board of Trustees was incorporated all the funds and property held by those named under the order of the Dominion Property Commission should be transferred to the new board.[16] Yet, with all these preparatory steps taken, when it came to applying for legislation, the Board of Administration hesitated to act because of Lafleur's advice.

By 1931 this hesitation precipitated a lengthy overture from the Presbytery of Saskatoon pointing out that the failure to clarify the church's status was seriously interfering with the work of the church in such matters as dealing with bequests, the holding of lands, charters, and trusts, and the proper tabulation of Presbyterians in the national census. It therefore requested the appointment of a committee to review the whole question and to bring in such a report "as might guide the Assembly as to the best method to proceed in the prosecution of this matter to a final conclusion."[17] Insofar as the Board of Administration had been given authority to deal with the question of incorporation in 1929, this overture was a reminder that many could not understand the board's reasons for not acting. Thus when another year passed with no action, another overture was received from the Presbytery of Montreal pointing out the difficulties the congregations were experiencing in such matters as wills, deeds, mortgages, and litigation as a result of the lack of clarification in the church's status. Reacting to this, the General Assembly decided it was time once again to review the situation. After hearing recommendations of a special committee, however, the assembly decided that no application for incorporation should be made to any legislative assembly or the Parliament of Canada.[18] But while this action took the pressure off the Board of Administration, the issue would not go away. Therefore, in 1933 it was necessary for the assembly to appoint yet another committee to investigate this matter. But, as before, it arrived at the conclusion that the time was not opportune to apply for incorporation.[19]

Unfortunately, neither the Board of Administration nor the various special committees set up by the assembly to review the question ever gave a full public explanation of why the time for action was not opportune. To have given such an explanation, of course, would have informed not only the members of the Presbyterian Church but also the United Church of the plans and strategies of the Board of Administration. Consequently, the congregations and lower courts of the church continued to voice their bewilderment at the church's failure to act. In 1934, the Presbytery of Toronto pointed out the extreme difficulty it had experienced in effecting the sale of the Forest Hill Church and property in Toronto. Because of the lack of a recognized incorporated body to carry out the sale, they said, the costs on this transaction amounted to $405.85 on a property that sold for

$7,500. Therefore, they asked the assembly to give effect to Mr. Cassels proposed Act to Incorporate the Presbyterian Trustee Board.[20]

No one, of course was more aware than N.W. Rowell, the chairman of the United Church's Law and Legislation Committee, of how hard it would be for the Presbyterian Church to carry on without some form of incorporation. In refusing to take action on behalf of the United Church to clarify the issues of continuity and identity in the courts, therefore, it is more than likely that he expected the Presbyterians to crack under the pressures which lack of incorporation would create. In this waiting game, Rowell might have won had it not been for the fact that this was one point that the Presbyterians could not yield without nullifying their whole struggle. The Presbyterians were in a better position than the United Church to withstand both the internal and external pressures because they had more to lose. Moreover, with the legal decisions going against them, the United Church by 1936 felt obliged to take the initiative. Fortunately, the possibilities for such action arose with the appointment of Gordon A. Sisco to succeed Dr. Moore as the secretary of the General Council of the United Church of Canada.

Like Dr. Moore, Sisco was a former Methodist, but he had not played a major part in the union negotiations, and the controversy had not shaped his understanding of the issues. Indeed, his background and training had provided him with a perspective on the relation of the Canadian churches which proved invaluable to him in giving the type of leadership necessary to resolve the controversy. Moreover, when he assumed his new duties as secretary of the General Council on 1 January 1937, the time was ripe for a resolution of the controversy, for it had become much more damaging to the United Church's image and integrity than anything that could be gained from continuing it.

In his first address to the United Church, Sisco apologized for his lack of experience and asked for the forebearance and assistance of his brethren.[21] But this very lack of involvement in the church's bureaucracy and its national committees left him free to approach the problems facing the church in new ways. Not having been ordained until 1916, when the controversy was already well advanced, he had never participated in any of the major decisions leading up to union. As a young minister he had assisted in effecting the union of Trinity Methodist Church and St. Andrew's Presbyterian Church in Renfrew, Ontario, but this experience had given him quite a different view of union from those who had carried on the struggle at the national level in the churches, Parliament, and the courts. There the issues were highly technical and abstract, whereas at the local congregational level they were mainly practical. The emphasis here was more on resolving group tensions than on contending for the principles embodied in a piece of legislation. Consequently, the fact that Sisco was not a veteran of the union negotiations or of the "period of mechanics" following union when the structures of the new church were hammered out meant that he could develop fresh solutions to the problems that had emerged during this period.

Sisco's family had migrated from Vermont to the Eastern townships of Quebec in the late nineteenth century at a time when that part of the country was beginning to change from a predominantly English to a French-speaking area. As a Yankee Methodist from Quebec, therefore, Sisco grew up as a member of a minority, and in this he differed from most Methodists in Ontario. Moreover, when he began his training for the ministry at Wesleyan Theological College in Montreal, the theological college there had already begun a programme of co-operative education in anticipation of the coming union. Consequently, the teacher who had the greatest influence on Sisco was John Scrimger, the principal of Presbyterian Theological College, Montreal, who taught Sisco systematic theology. Scrimger was an ardent unionist and an able exponent of the new theological liberalism which had become dominant in Canadian Presbyterian theological colleges since the turn of the century.

Unlike the Presbyterians who normally completed their training in arts prior to studying theology, many Methodists, like Sisco, took their theological training first and then after ordination and some pastoral experience returned to university to take an arts degree. By returning to Queen's University to complete his education, Sisco was once again exposed to Presbyterian liberalism and especially to the philosophical idealism of John Watson, which still dominated Queen's when Sisco received his degree in Arts in 1925. The ecumenical nature of his education gave him a viewpoint that was extremely important for the resolution of the controversy. At Queen's he had been exposed to some of the finest traditions of Auld Kirk Presbyterianism, and in Scrimger he had encountered the power and evangelical zeal of Free Kirk Presbyterianism. Thus, his thinking had been shaped in a Presbyterian academic atmosphere far from the power struggles taking place over union. Something of the continuing personal importance of this part of his background can be seen in the fact that at the time of his appointment as secretary, he was president of the Queen's Theological Alumni Association.

Sisco made the transition from Danforth United Church in Toronto to the General Council offices, just as relations between the Presbyterian Church and the United Church became extremely critical. Thus it became one of the first items on his agenda. The manner in which he handled this problem revealed many of the qualities which later made him one of Canada's most outstanding ecumenical statesmen.[22] As early as 1927, Lord Sands pointed out to the United Church's fraternal delegates to the Scottish Assemblies that a minority as well as a majority had a right to claim continuity with the Presbyterian Church in Canada.[23] Furthermore, many of the leading Scottish ministers who did not question the United Church's claim to continuity nevertheless stressed that no Presbyterian Church in Scotland had ever denied a minority the right to the use of a name. They advised therefore that the United Church should give over the use of the name, the Presbyterian Church in Canada, to the non-concurring body "even as they gave over the name 'The United Free Presbyterian Church of Scotland' to the minority who failed to enter [their] recent union."[24] These were the two suggestions that Sisco picked up when he tackled this problem. Then he asked, if these two points were conceded, what would be necessary to secure the Presbyterian properties and assets that came into the United Church and what could be done to stop these churches taking one another to court? The answer, which was being worked on by a joint committee of the two churches within four months after Sisco assumed office, was an amendment to the United Church of Canada Act and a solemn declaration of intention by both churches to work out their differences through mutual consultation instead of continual litigation.

By October of 1937 drafts of this agreement and the proposed amendment to the United Church of Canada Act were being circulated by Sisco for consideration by members of the United Church's Law and Legislation Committee. Some members of the committee, like J.K. Sparling of Winnipeg, were hesitant when Sisco's letter arrived. "Like all lawyers," Sparling said, "I am fearful of making admissions. We cannot foresee what event will happen in the future to which the draft report and amendment will be applicable. In other words, I'm afraid that the concessions suggested may prejudice our position in some unforeseen future event, and yet I realize the necessity of establishing harmony between the two churches."[25] However, Sisco maintained that the United Church's position would be best protected if harmony with the Presbyterians was established, and therefore he overrode the fears and hesitation of the lawyers on the Law and Legislation Committee.

By 9 November 1937, the joint committee of the two churches had unanimously agreed on the wording of an amendment to the United Church of Canada Act, the acknowledgement of each other's claim to continuity, and a statement regarding their intention to "seek to dwell together in mutual understanding composing their differences. . .by consultation. . . without recourse to the civil courts, seeking fellowship in all good works for the Kingdom of God; thus afresh commending the Gospel of Jesus Christ."[26] On 27 December 1937, the Law and Legislation Committee of the United Church of Canada met and, with a few minor revisions, gave its approval to the document. Thus within a year of assuming office Sisco had finally worked out the compromise necessary to bring the controversy to an end. The executive of the General Council, however, did not possess the authority to complete such an agreement without the approval of the General Council.[27] It was agreed therefore that it would be presented to the meetings of the

General Council in September 1938 before any steps were taken to seek legislative action.

When the agreement was presented to the General Council, it was adopted by a standing vote with only two commissioners dissenting, one of whom, the Rev. E.H. Gray, M.D., a former Presbyterian, insisted that his dissent be recorded. While these dissents marred the desired unanimity on the issue, the General Council nevertheless marked the occasion with a prayer led by Dr. George C. Pidgeon and the singing of the Doxology.[28] Following the meetings, Sisco explained this agreement to the church in an article published in the *New Outlook*. He began by stating that the representatives of both churches believed that all matters of serious difference "should be removed for the sake of the Kingdom of God and the contribution of Protestantism to the unity and well-being of Canada." After explaining why past negotiations with the Presbyterians had failed, he indicated that the new agreement had been possible because the United Church representatives had approached the problem from a new angle. In the past the United Church had been willing to grant the use of the name only if the Presbyterians would concede that "The Presbyterian Church in Canada" had gone into union. The Presbyterians naturally could not make such a concession. The new negotiations had been successful because there was a mutual acknowledgment of each church's claim to continuity. As Sisco put it: "We still maintain that 'The Presbyterian Church in Canada' is in union, but we do not ask the Presbyterians to endorse that claim. We grant them the right to the use of the name, but in granting that right we still make our claim to continuity."[29] The balance between what was being conceded and what was being maintained was so subtle that it is no wonder that no one else in the church dared to try explaining it. Explanation, however, was less important than the fact that the agreement permitted concrete action in the form of an amendment to the United Church of Canada Act. And, as Sisco pointed out, for the first time since 1925, it made possible the exchange of fraternal greetings between the two churches when Dr. Stuart Parker of St. Andrew's Presbyterian Church Toronto addressed the General Council and was cordially received.

After the General Council meetings, the next step was to get the amendment through Parliament without any alteration in the wording of the agreement and as little discussion as possible. To this end Prime Minister Mackenzie King, Arthur Meighen, J.S. Woodsworth, W.R. Motherwell, Senator William Duff, and Senator Lorne C. Webster among others were carefully briefed on the issue by Dr. J.W. Woodside and Dr. Robert Johnston. Letters of explanation from both churches were also sent to all members of parliament to make sure the amendment went through smoothly. When the amendment was first presented in the Senate by Mr. Meighen and then in the House of Commons by W.R. Motherwell, there seemed to be such a sense of relief at the settlement that no one was prepared to interfere with its immediate passage.

Consequently, on 5 April 1939 the amendment to the United Church of Canada Act received its third reading and passed into law without incident, thereby ending a controversy which had lasted for thirty-five years.[30]

Amending the United Church of Canada Act was primarily a United Church undertaking, but in the negotiations leading up to the amendment the Presbyterians had two major concerns which had to be met: the removal of the asterisk and note against their name in the records of the Alliance of Reformed Churches and the incorporation of their Board of Trustees. Once an agreement had been reached on the wording of the amendment in December 1937, it was possible for the United Church delegates to the General Council of the Alliance of Reformed Churches which met in Montreal on 23 June 1938 to co-operate with Dr. W.M. Rochester and Dr. A.J. MacGillivray in having the asterisk and note against the Presbyterian Church's name removed from the Alliance's records.[31] Furthermore, once the General Council of the United Church had accepted the agreement in September 1938, it was possible to approach Parliament not only with an amendment to the United Church of Canada Act but also with an Act to Incorporate the Board of Trustees of the Presbyterian Church in Canada. These two pieces of legislation were presented to Parliament at the same time, and both received approval on 5 April 1939. While it took until after World War II to get this legislation through all of the provincial legislatures, once the act incorporating the trustees had been passed in Parliament, it was possible for the Presbyterian General Assembly meeting at Midland, Ontario, in June 1939 to welcome fraternal delegates from the United Church of Canada.

As previously noted, the greetings exchanged between two churches are usually nothing more than formal courtesy calls. But the controversy over church union began and ended with the exchange of such greetings. When Banks Nelson stood up to introduce J.R.P. Sclater, who was representing the moderator of the United Church, and Gordon Sisco to the 1939 General Assembly, it was obvious to everyone that the controversy was truly at an end. Banks Nelson and Stuart Parker, the moderator of the General Assembly who welcomed the United Church delegates, had both been highly visible opponents of union in the years immediately prior to 1925 and Sclater's ridicule of the dissidents' position both in Canada and in Scotland had deeply wounded many. Sisco's role in the negotiations leading up to the final compromise was, of course, appreciated by everyone, and the assurances he gave to the General Assembly of the United Church's good wishes were accepted as an augury of better relations in the future.

The outbreak of World War II three months later hampered the solution of many outstanding issues. But the agreements reached during the negotiations for the compromise provided a framework for resolving these questions after the war. The most important of these was the difficulty created by the

Ontario legislation which granted Knox College to the Presbyterian Church but placed the college library under the control of the United Church. This arrangement continued until 1948 when the United Church finally gave up any interest in the Caven Library in return for the records of the Presbyterian Church prior to 1925.

In 1939 neither side received all it had initially wanted, but both received what was necessary for them to function freely, to establish normal relations, and to move on to new concerns. It was not the sort of solution that would enable either side to claim a victory, and perhaps this is the reason that this end to the fighting has never been celebrated. The controversy ended, however, because justice was perceived to have been done, and it proved to be a happy solution to a difficult problem, a solution that has enabled these institutions to live together without mutual hostility ever since.

Conclusion

Looking back over this struggle, it is evident that the primary objective of the opponents of union from beginning to end was the preservation of the Presbyterian Church in Canada. It is also clear that their realization of this goal was important for the future of both the Presbyterian and the United Churches. But the wider significance of this conflict is less obvious because it is difficult to see how it might be relevant to other religious groups and to those interested in the relationship between religion and society in twentieth-century Canada. Before leaving the resistance to church union, therefore, it is necessary to conclude by attempting to place this controversy into a broader historical context.

All studies of church union in Canada have placed the formation of the United Church in an evolutionary framework which has emphasized national expansion and the search for a Canadian identity. But in highlighting this dimension of the story, they have overlooked the fact that a debate over the value of denominationalism is an argument over the effects of the separation of church and state. Undoubtedly, this oversight has occurred because disestablishment, which took place in Canada during the 1850's, was never an issue in the conflict.[1] Both sides took it for granted that the Canadian state should be deconfessionalized and that no religious group should have special privileges or financial support from the state. Both sides also believed in the "neutrality of the state" and the principle of its non-interference in church affairs, especially in matters of faith and doctrine. But while both parties affirmed the separation of church and state, they were nevertheless deeply divided over three of its major effects: denominational competition, religious pluralism, and secularization.

Putting an end to state-supported religious monopolies transformed all religious groups in Canada into denominations by making them equal before the law and forcing them to compete with one another for the loyalty and financial support of their respective constituencies. This competition took three basic forms: (1) evangelistic campaigns to rekindle the waning religious commitments of their constituents; (2) Christian education programmes to indoctrinate the younger generation; and (3) home mission projects to establish a group's presence in new areas of settlement. In all cases this competition was expensive and the confessional unions of the nineteenth century can be seen as attempts to provide a broader financial base for these endeavours. But, while confessional and transconfessional unions could rationalize competition, they could not eliminate it. Under the system of voluntary support created by disestablishment, denominations must either compete or die.

The opponents of union accepted this aspect of the denominational system because they were confident that Presbyterianism could hold its own in competition with other Protestant groups and because they were only interested in providing religious services to their own constituency. As Robert Campbell put it, "the duty of the denominations throughout the Dominion is to try and provide the means of grace to people of their own faith. This is the first call upon the organization as a whole; and so far as the other denominations are concerned they may well leave the responsibility of caring for them to the large community to which they profess adherence."[2] From the dissidents' perspective it was both unreasonable and pretentious to assume that the other denominations would not make every effort to look after the religious needs of their own adherents. Consequently, they believed that Presbyterians should direct their efforts primarily toward their own constituents.

The unionists, on the other hand, desired a Canadian church which would have the resources to evangelize the large influx of new immigrants from Eastern and Southern Europe and to introduce them to the standards and values of Anglo-Saxon Protestantism. They also wanted a united Protestant church which would be large enough to make its influence felt in Parliament and the provincial legislatures when they were seeking legislation on such issues as Sunday observance, temperance, gambling, salacious literature, and prostitution. Therefore, they rejected denominational divisions and competition, apparently without recognizing that they were rejecting one of the major effects of disestablishment.

The failure of the dissidents to respond to the call for a national crusade to "Canadianize the immigrants by Christianizing them" was attributed by some to their "clannish bigotry." It was, however, primarily an affirmation of the second major effect of distablishment: religious pluralism.[3] The end of state-supported religious monopolies in Canada meant not only that all religious groups were equal before the law but also that they had to proceed on the basis of persuasion rather than coercion. The opponents of union saw this as a guarantee of religious liberty for it meant that everyone was free to belong or not to belong to any religious group and they could not be penalized for this decision.

Furthermore, they were aware that all the new immigrants had their own religions, and even though some of these like Judaism and Buddhism were not Christian, the vast majority owed allegiance to various types of Eastern Christianity. Granted these new groups would broaden the base of religious pluralism in Canada, but if one took religious pluralism seriously as a guarantee of religious liberty, then the same rights and privileges had to be granted to the new immigrants as were enjoyed by Roman Catholics and Anglo-Saxon Protestants.

Not all the opponents of union accepted this viewpoint or saw its full implications. But the logic of their position was clear. If they wished to preserve one denomination, they had to defend the denominational system and accept all of its implications. If they were opposed to religious uniformity and cultural homogeneity, then they had to support the religious pluralism and cultural diversity which this conception of Canadian society implied.

The unionists, on the other hand, were genuinely alarmed by the influx of so many new religious groups not only from Europe and Asia but also from the United States. Were Mormons, for example, to be granted the same rights and privileges to propagate their views in Canada as the more established Anglo-Saxon Protestant denominations? If so, what would happen to the institutions of Canadian society which, in their view, embodied Anglo-Saxon Protestant standards and values? If there were to be no limits to religious pluralism and cultural diversity, Canadians would surely end up creating a kaleidoscope of religions, races, and cultures, and the nation would disintegrate for lack of a solid moral and religious consensus. The unionists were hopeful, therefore, that their movement would result in a church which might eventually include the vast majority of Canadian Protestants and provide the basis for a moral and religious consensus that would help to hold the nation together.

Although there was no mention of a reversal in the relations of church and state, the idea of creating a national church for Canadians which would be similar to the Church of Scotland in its impact on Canadian life was clearly present in the minds of many. Indeed, this was so important that the preamble to the Basis of Union describes the United Church as "a national church with a national mission." What no one bothered to mention, however, was that all the national churches of Europe were established churches. Moreover, no one apparently thought of asking whether it was possible to have such a church in a religiously pluralistic country. With no one clarifying these issues, therefore, it was possible for some confusions to arise in the unionist's thinking about the new church they were trying to create, and these confusions compromised their initial reactions toward those Presbyterians who refused to join them.

The third major effect of disestablishment was the secularization of Canadian society which occurred because the worldview of no single religious group had the support and force of the state behind it. Both sides in the church union controversy were aware of the secularization that had overtaken Canadian society since the middle of the nineteenth century. They could not agree, however, on either its causes or on the measures needed to counteract it.

Many opponents of union believed that secularization was caused by the undermining of biblical authority by the higher critics and the watering down of doctrine by the modernists. In order to stem the tide of secularization, therefore, they insisted on adhering to the Westminster Confession and demanded that their ministers subscribe to it. Subscription, however, had only been an effective weapon against secularization when it was backed by the coercive power of the state. When, as in England and Scotland prior to the nineteenth century, it was impossible to sit in Parliament, to have a government position or a teaching job or even access to a university without subscribing either to the Thirty-nine Articles or the Westminster Confession, subscription acted as a curb, if not a complete barrier to secularizing tendencies. But without the policing powers of the state behind it, subscription had virtually no effect in stemming the tide of secularization as Presbyterian experience in Canada had shown prior to 1925.

The unionists, on the other hand, saw the roots of secularization in religious pluralism and in the spectacle of denominational competition. With so many groups presenting the particulars of their creeds and polities as the only road to salvation, the great unifying truths which all Protestant groups shared seemed to get lost. Indeed, even the moral principles which many believed were essential for the well-being of a Christian society failed to command the respect and support which they deserved because of Protestant divisions. With such a divided witness, how would it be possible to protect these standards and values against the different attitudes towards Sunday observance and the use of alcoholic beverages which the immigrants were bringing with them? Surely this could only lead to further secularization, especially when the upper classes also appeared to be adopting European and "Americanizing" attitudes towards these issues with consequent losses in church attendance. Furthermore, they were convinced that secularization was rooted in compromises which churches made with the world by organizing themselves on the basis of class, race, and region rather than on the clear imperatives of the gospel that Christ's followers should transcend these barriers and manifest the same unity which existed between God and Jesus Christ.

While all these effects of the separation of church and state were at the centre of the debate from the beginning, it was not until the opponents of union were confronted with the legislation that they realized the unionists were not only attempting to reverse the effects of disestablishment, but also proposing to to act like an established church by using an instrument of the state (the United Church of Canada Act) to deny them the right to remain in the church of their fathers.

If the issue had not been clear previously, it now became apparent that the act contained serious violations of religious liberty, and cries against coercion, confiscation and religious tyranny were widely raised. Ephraim Scott emphasized this point by characterizing the twenty-year conflict over church union as a struggle for religious liberty.[4] It was difficult, however, for other denominations to see how their positions might be affected because Scott related the Canadian conflict to the struggle of the Covenanters in Scotland without any reference to the foundations of denominationalism and religious pluralism in Canada. Consequently, no Canadian denomination spoke up on behalf of the Presbyterian minority.

When the legislation was presented to Parliament, the effects of disestablishment were again ignored, and the only aspect of the question which was emphasized was the "neutrality" of the state. A one-sided emphasis on this aspect of disestablishment, however, led to difficulties because while the unionists, on the one hand, were asking Parliament for the incorporation of a merger which would deny a sizeable minority the right to remain in the church of their fathers, they demanded, on the other hand, that their request, as Eugene Lafleur put it, be rubber-stamped without alteration because of the "great principle of non-interference of Parliament in religious matters." Lafleur contended that this was a self-serving interpretation of the "neutrality" of the state and that when a group applied to the state for incorporation and the right to take property which belonged to others, the state had a duty to do what was just and fair.[5] Parliament sought to be just and fair by removing the most coercive aspects of the legislation, but it remained so narrowly focused on the "neutrality" of the state that it backed away from altering the central principle of the legislation.

This principle, that a church has "a right to unite with any other church without loss of identity," was taken directly from the 1921 Church of Scotland Act. In using this precedent, however, the unionists neglected to mention that the Church of Scotland was an established national church and, therefore, of necessity it had to go to Parliament for authority to unite with other churches. In Canada, however, the churches seeking union were free churches and had been ever since disestablishment. Consequently, as Dr. Murray MacLaren pointed out, the British legislation which applied specifically to an established church was not relevant to the Canadian case.[6]

John Dougall, the Methodist editor and owner of the Montreal *Witness,* made a similar point when he said that "the present bill looks as though it had been drawn up by some one who had not got rid of the old world notion of a state church."[7] Picking up this idea William Duff went even further and suggested that those who drafted the legislation were not only thinking of a state church but also of a church which would come to Parliament year after year telling it what to do. Therefore he was confident that the Presbyterians who were fighting to preserve their church were "fighting the battle of religious liberty for all the churches in Canada." For, if Parliament blotted out the Presbyterian Church this year, "then next year Parliament might do the same to any other church." Thus, there would be "no safety for any church and no assured religious liberty for any member of any church."[8] In spite of these warnings, however, Parliament passed the legislation, thereby giving the United Church a legal basis for denying the Presbyterian minority any right or claim to identity and continuity with the Presbyterian Church in Canada.

Once the church union legislation was passed there was little or nothing the state could do to remedy the situation. The courts helped to clarify the issue by undermining the validity of the unionist's basic claim that the Presbyterian Church in Canada went into union. But again because of the separation of church and state, they could not resolve the conflict. Only the churches themselves could resolve it.

When the resistance to church union is placed in this context it becomes apparent that it was more than just a struggle to preserve the Presbyterian Church in Canada. It was also an affirmation of the denominational pattern of Canadian religious life and a defence of religious pluralism in Canadian society. This struggle, therefore, is important for all Canadians because without it the structures of denominationalism, religious pluralism, and religious liberty would have been seriously weakened. Moreover, the levels of tolerance and civility which exist between religious groups and between these groups and Canadian society as a whole would have rested on even more fragile foundations than they do today.

Notes

NOTES TO THE INTRODUCTION

1. Stephen C. Neill, "Plans of Union and Reunion, 1910-1948," in *A History of the Ecumenical Movement 1517-1948,* eds. Ruth Rouse and Stephen Charles Neill, 2d ed. (Philadelphia: Westminster Press, 1968), p. 495.
2. Samuel P. Huntingdon, "Conservatism as an Ideology," *American Political Science Review* 51 (1957); 454-73.
3. Ibid.
4. Prior to ordination ruling elders were asked five questions. Question 2 enquired whether they were prepared to adhere faithfully to the Westminster Confession, and Question 5 asked if they were prepared to perform their duties as "overseers." See *Rules and Forms of Procedure in the Church Courts of the Presbyterian Church in Canada* (Montreal: William Drysdale, 1899), pp. 76-77.
5. John MacDougall, *Rural Life in Canada* (1913), reissued with an introduction by R. Craig Brown (Toronto: University of Toronto Press, 1973).
6. C.E. Silcox, *Church Union in Canada: Its Causes and Consequences* (New York: Institute of Social and Religious Research, 1933).
7. H. Richard Niebuhr, *The Social Sources of Denominationalism* (New York: Holt, 1929). See also Alan W. Eister, "H. Richard Niebuhr and the Paradox of Religious Organization: A Radical Critique," in *Beyond The Classics? Essays in the Scientific Study of Religion,* eds. C.Y. Glock and P.E. Hammond (New York: Harper and Row, 1973), pp. 355-408; and Jon Diefenthaler, "H. Richard Niebuhr: A Fresh Look at His Early Years," *Church History* 52 (1983): 172-85.
8. Sidney E. Mead, "Denominationalism: The Shape of Protestantism in America," *Church History* 24 (1954): 291-320.
9. Many of the most important essays in this reassessment of denominationalism have been conveniently gathered together in *Denominationalism,* ed. Russell E. Richey (Nashville: Abingdon, 1977).
10. H.H. Walsh, "A Canadian Christian Tradition," in *The Churches and the Canadian Experience,* ed. John Webster Grant, (Toronto, Ryerson, 1963), pp. 157-58. See also John W. Grant, "'At least you knew where you stood with them': Reflections on Religious Pluralism in Canada and the United States," *Studies in Religion* 2:4 (1973): 341-42.
11. Bryan Wilson, *Religion in Secular Society* (1966), reissued (Harmondsworth: Penguin Books, 1969).
12. Peter Berger, "A Market Model for the Analysis of Ecumenicity," *Social Research* (1963): 77-93.
13. Peter L. Berger and Thomas Luckmann, "Secularization and Pluralism," *International Yearbook for the Sociology of Religion* 2 (1966): 73-84.
14. Bryan S. Turner, "The Sociological Explanation of Ecumenicalism," *The Expository Times* 82 (1970-71): 356-61.
15. William T. Gunn, "Uniting Three United Churches" (Toronto: Bureau of Literature and Information of the Joint Committee on Church Union, 1923).
16. These volumes were as follows: (i) Jane Porter, *The Christian's Wedding Ring, Containing Five Letters written by a Lady, with the Sincere Desire of Sowing Seeds of Union in the Christian Church* (Montreal: Lovell, 1974); (ii) James Carmichael, *Organic Union of the Canadian Churches* (Montreal: Dawson, 1887); (iii) Herbert Symonds, *Lectures on Christian Unity* (Toronto: W. Briggs, 1899); (iv) John Langtry, *Come Home: An Appeal on Behalf of Reunion* (Toronto: Church of England Publishing Co., 1900).
17. R. Millman, "The Conference on Christian Union, Toronto 1889," *Canadian Journal of Theology* 3 (1957): 165-74. See also Richard Ruggle, "Herbert Symonds and Christian Unity," *Journal of the Canadian*

Church Historical Society 18 (June-Sept. 1976): 53-84.

18. R.G. MacBeth, *The Burning Bush and Canada* (Toronto: Westminster Press, n.d.), 204-5. [While no date of publication is indicated on the front matter, the final sentence of the book indicates that it was written in 1926].

19. Ibid.; E. Scott, *"Church Union" and the Presbyterian Church in Canada* (Montreal: John Lovel, 1928), pp. 48-51; and M.D.M.

Blakely, "A Breach of Faith in Chruch Union Proceedings," [pamphlet] (Pembroke, Ontario: n.p. 1922). This pamphlet is probably the best and fullest statement of the argument and it does not confuse this argument with the quesiton of origins.

20. Robert Haddow, "No Breach of Faith," *The Presbyterian and Westminster* (19 April 1917), p. 451.

21. Ibid.

NOTES TO CHAPTER ONE

1. *Christian Guardian* (17 September 1902), p. 600.
2. Robert Campbell, "The People's Rights Usurped," *Presbyterian Advocate* 2 (1915), p. 13.
3. *Presbyterian* (21 June 1907), p. 781.
4. Ephraim Scott, "The Presbyterian Church in Canada: Its Preservation and Continuance" (Montreal: Lovell, 1914). This pamphlet was the manuscript of Dr. Ephraim Scott's address at the Woodstock General Assembly in 1914. It was circulated by the Executive Committee of the Organization for the Preservation and Continuance of the Presbyterian Church.
5. *St. John Daily Sun* (7 June 1904), p. 1.
6. William Patrick, "The Case for Church Union," *Presbyterian* (12 March 1910), pp. 583-84.
7. *St. John Daily Sun* (7 June 1904), p. 5.
8. *Presbyterian* (21 June 1906), p. 775.
9. Ibid. p. 782.
10. William MacLaren, "The Unity of the Church and the Church Unions" (Toronto: Presbyterian News Co., 1890).
11. *Presbyterian* (21 June 1906), p. 784.
12. Ibid. (17 June 1909), p. 747.
13. *Manitoba Free Press* (29 September 1911), p. 1.
14. Ibid. (29 September 1911), p. 11.
15. Ibid. (18 April 1900), p. 6.
16. *Westminster* (September 1904), p. 190-94.
17. William Patrick, "Some Reasons for Church Union," *Presbyterian Record* (October, 1906): 327-29.
18. *Presbyterian* (26 May 1910), p. 653.
19. Ibid. (17 June 1909), p. 744.
20. Ibid. (21 June 1905), p. 780.
21. *Presbyterian Record* (1906), pp. 427-29.
22. *Presbyterian* (17 June 1909), p. 744.
23. Ibid. (26 May 1910), p. 653.
24. Ibid., p. 653.

25. R.L. Orr, *The Free Church of Scotland Appeal Case* (Edinburgh, 1904), p. 529.
26. Ibid., p. 223.
27. Alfred Gandier, "Predestination and the Historical Decision," *Presbyterian* (26 November 1904), pp. 642-44, and (3 December 1904), pp. 676-77.
28. *Presbyterian* (18 June 1908), p. 779.
29. *Westminster* (17 February 1900), pp. 188-89.
30. The interconnections between these men can be traced through the following biographies and autobiographies: John Dow, *Alfred Gandier* (Toronto: Ryerson, 1951); Clarence McKinnon, *Reminiscences* (Toronto: Ryerson, 1936); C.W. Gordon, *Postscript to Adventure* (New York: Farrar and Rinehard, 1938); James S. Thomson, "Walter Charles Murray (1866-1945)," *Royal Society of Canada Proceedings* (1945), pp. 103-8; James S. Thomson, "Sir Robert A. Falconer," *Dalhousie Review* 30 (1951): 361-68.
31. Alfred Gandier, "Church Union," *The Theologue* (March 1899): 109-16.
32. For a discussion of this incident, cf. Margaret Prang, *N.W. Rowell: Ontario Nationalist* (Toronto: University of Toronto Press, 1975), pp. 70-88.
33. *Westminster* (November 1902), p. 314.
34. Cf. Sir Thomas W. Taylor, *Public Statutes Relating to the Presbyterian Church in Canada* (Toronto: Willing and Williamson, 1879; second revised edition, 1897).
35. R.P. MacKay to William Patrick, 10 March 1911, U.C.A., Presbyterian Church in Canada, Box 7, file 156.
36. William Patrick to R.P. MacKay, 11 March 1911, U.C.A., Presbyterian Church in Canada, Box 7, file 156.
37. *Westminster* (17 February 1900), pp. 188-89.
38. *Manitoba Free Press* (29 September 1911), pp. 1 and 11. See also James Denney's

tribute to Patrick in the *British Weekly* 51 (5 October 1911), p. 3, and his comment to W.R. Nicholl that Patrick "was well-known in our church, but owing to superficial peculiarities never valued as he should have been," in W.R. Nicholl, ed., *Letters of Principal James Denney to W. Robertson Nicholl 1893-1917*, (London: Hodder and Stoughton, 1920), pp. 184-85.

39. T.B. Kilpatrick, "William Patrick: 1852-1911, An Appreciation," *Presbyterian* (5 October 1911), pp. 359-60. All the Canadian evidence suggests that Patrick suf-

fered from some kind of stomach ailment. Dr. W.Y. Blakely, however, gives his cause of death as "successive cerebral haemorrhages [over a period of] three years." See Patrick's Death Certificate, Parish of Kirkintilloch, County of Dumbarton, 28 September 1911, General Register Office, New Register House, Edinburgh, Scotland.

40. *Manitoba Free Press* (29 September 1911), pp. 1 and 11.

41. Austin L. Budge, "Manuscript Articles on Church Union" P.C.A., Knox college, Toronto, articles 4 and 9.

NOTES TO CHAPTER TWO

1. For biographical information on Robert Campbell (1835-1921), see H.J. Morgan, *Canadian Men and Women of the Time* (1912); G. Colborne Heine, "A Brief Sketch of the Life and Work of the Rev. Robert Campbell, D.D." (Montreal, 1922); Robert Campbell, *A History of the Scotch Presbyterian Church, St. Gabriel Street, Montreal* (Montreal: Drysdale, 1887), pp. 612-18; Hew Scott, *Fasti Ecclesiae Scoticone*, vol. 3 (Edinburgh: Oliver and Boyd, 1928), p. 629; and N.K. Clifford, "Robert Campbell, the Defender of Presbyterianism," in *Called to Witness*, ed. W. Stanford Reid (Toronto: Presbyterian Publications, 1975), pp. 53-66.

2. *Presbyterian* (18 June 1904), p. 790.

3. *Toronto Globe* (23 December 1905), pp. 1, 5.

4. *Montreal Gazette* (1 January 1906), p. 9. See also the *Toronto Globe* (1 January 1906), p. 9, and (25 January 1906), p. 11.

5. Robert Campbell, "Union or Co-operation — Which?" (Montreal: Foster Brown, n.d.). This pamphlet is given two different dates, 1904 and 1906, in the *Catalogue of Pamphlets in the Public Archives of Canada*, ed. M. Casey (1931). Rejean W. Heroux of the Public Archives has confirmed that the *Catalogue* is in error by giving the same pamphlet two different dates. Internal evidence on pages 1, 2, 13, 36, and 41 points to a publication date at some time during the first five months of 1906.

6. *Acts and Proceedings 1904*, p. 297.

7. *Acts and Proceedings 1906*, p. 36.

8. *Presbyterian* (28 June 1906), p. 807.

9. *Acts and Proceedings 1907*, p. 336.

10. *Presbyterian* (21 June 1906), p. 782, and *Presbyterian* (18 June 1908), p. 781.

11. *Acts and Proceedings 1910*, pp. 44-45.

12. Robert Campbell, "Church Union" (Montreal, 10 July 1910).

13. *Presbyterian* (1 December 1910), p. 626.

14. Ibid., (15 December 1910), pp. 700-701.

15. Ibid., (22 December 1910), p. 735.

16. *Acts and Proceedings 1910*, p. 45, and *The Presbyterian Record* (July 1910), pp. 291-95. For biographical information on Ephraim Scott (1845-1931), see Morgan, *Canadian Men and Women*, p. 1002, and B.A. MacNab, "Rev. Ephraim Scott, D.D., First Moderator of the Continuing Presbyterian Church," *Saturday Night* (23 May 1925), and DeCourcy H. Rayner, "Ephraim Scott: Editor Extraordinary," in *Called to Witness*, ed. W. Stanford Reid (Toronto: Presbyterian Publications, 1975), pp. 203-12.

17. *Presbyterian* (28 July 1910), p. 75.

18. Ibid. (22 September 1910), pp. 296-97. For biographical information on John Forrest (1842-1920) see Morgan, *Canadian Men and Women*, p. 411; *Acts and Proceedings 1921*, p. 560; and J.A. MacGlashen, "John Forrest," *Presbyterian Witness* (15 January 1925), p. 5.

19. Ibid. (23 September 1910), p. 296.

20. Ibid. (6 October 1910), p. 359.

21. Ibid. (22 June 1911), pp. 775-76.

22. *Acts and Proceedings 1911*, pp. 23-24, and *Acts and Proceedings 1912*, pp. 31, 330-33.

23. Robert Campbell, *The Relations of the Christian Churches to One another and the Problems Growing Out of Them, Especially in Canada* (Toronto: William Briggs, 1913).

24. Ibid., p. 6.

25. See Timothy L. Smith, "Religious Denominations as Ethnic Communities: A Regional Case Study," *Church History* 35 (1966):

207-26, and "Religion and Ethnicity in America," *American Historical Review* 83 (1978): 1155-85. Also Andrew M. Greely, *Ethnicity in the United States: A Preliminary Reconnaissance* (1974), and *the Denominational Society: A Sociological Approach to Religion in America* (1972). For the remark that Campbell was a "religious snob," see the *Toronto Daily Star* (13 June 1906), p. 2.

26. Robert Campbell, "Another View of Church Union," *Presbyterian* (23 January 1907), pp. 147-48.

27. *Presbyterian* (14 February 1907), pp. 211-12.

28. Robert Campbell, "Dr. Campbell on Church Union," *Presbyterian* (7 March 1907), pp. 306-8.

29. A.S. Morton, "Methodists and Presbyterian Scotland," *University Magazine* 11 (April 1912): 327-47.

30. Robert Campbell, "On the Union of Presbyterians in Canada" (Montreal: F.E. Grafton, 1871).

31. The Natural History Society of Montreal was founded in 1827, and after 1855 it came increasingly under the influence of Sir William Dawson, the principal of McGill University. Shortly after his arrival in Montreal in 1866, Campbell became associated with the society, and for many years he served as one of its vice-presidents. In 1895 he was elected president, and in 1916 he was made honourary president of the society. Between 1890 and 1916 Campbell published seventeen essays on botanical and scientific subjects in the society's journal, *The Canadian Record of Science*, of which he was editor for many years. Campbell died at the age of eighty-six as a result of an accident on a Montreal streetcar while on his way to a meeting of the Natural History Society. For general background on religion and science in this period, see Theodore Dwight Bozeman, *Protestants in an Age of Science* (Chapel Hill, 1977), and Herbert Hovenkamp, *Science and Religion in America 1800-1860* (Philadelphia, 1978). See also Carl Berger, *Science, God, and Nature in Victorian Canada* (Toronto, 1983).

32. J.A. Macdonald, "The Christianization of Our Civilization," in *Canada's Missionary Congress* (Toronto: Canadian Council of the Layman's Missionary Movement, 1909): 115-21.

33. Arthur S. Morton, *The Way to Union* (Toronto: William Briggs, 1912). For reviews of Morton's book, see Alfred Gandier, "The Way to Union," *Presbyterian* (5 December 1912), pp. 635-36; Clarence MacKinnon, "The Way to Union," *the Presbyterian Witness* (28 December 1912), p. 5; and Frank Baird, "Mr. Morton's Book on Union," *Presbyterian* (16 January 1913), pp. 87-90. For Morton's reply to Baird's attack see A.S. Morton, "The Way to Union," *Presbyterian* (20 February 1913), pp. 232-34.

34. Adolf Harnack, "The Relation between Ecclesiastical and General History," trans. Thomas Bailey Saunders, *Contemporary Review* 86 (1904): 848-59.

35. For a decade or more after the rediscovery of Mendel's work in 1900, many like Campbell did not see the significance of his work for the theory of evolution. See Garland E. Allen, "Thomas Hunt Morgan and the Problem of Natural Selection," *Journal of the History of Biology* 1 (1968): 113-39.

36. William D. Tait, "Democracy and Mental Hygiene," *Canadian Journal of Hygiene* 3 (July 1921): 31-36.

37. Unfortunately, there have been no Canadian studies of hereditarianism such as Nicholas Pastore, *The Nature-Nurture Controversy* (New York: King's Crown Press, 1949), and Mark H. Haller, *Eugenics: Hereditarian Attitudes in American Thought* (New Brunswick, NJ: Rutgers University Press, 1963). Some dimensions of the Canadian debate, however, have been discussed in Neil Sutherland's *Children in English-Canadian Society* (Toronto: University of Toronto Press, 1976), pp. 71-78. See also Terry L. Chapman, "Early Eugenics Movement in Western Canada," *Alberta History* 25 (Autumn 1977): 9-17. Following the lead of Donald K. Pickens in his *Eugenics and the Progressives* (Nashville: Vanderbilt University Press, 1968), but ignoring the serious reservations expressed by J.C. Burnham concerning his work (*Journal of American History* 56 [1969]: 409), Ms. Chapman suggests that eugenics was an aspect of the reform mentality of Canadian Progressives and Social Gospellers. To avoid confusion in establishing such a connection, however, it is necessary to make careful distinctions between Mendelian and Lamarckian eugenics as Lorne R. Graham has shown in his essay "Science and Values: The Eugenics Movement in Germany and Russia in the 1920's," *Amer-*

ican Historical Review 82 (1977): 1133-64.

38. James A. Sedgewick to Robert Campbell, 25 November, U.C.A., Presbyterian Non-Concurrence, Box 1, file 13.

39. Thomas T. Smellie to Robert Campbell, 9 October, U.C.A., Presbyterian Non-Concurrence, Box 1, file 13.

40. Ernest R. Sandeen, *The Roots of Fundamentalism: British and American Millenarianism 1800-1930* (Chicago: University of Chicago Press, 1970). Sandeen mentions both of these men but does not note that Kellogg succeeded John Mark King as the minister of St. James Square Church in Toronto in 1883.

41. See Sandeen cited above, and Lefferts A. Loetscher, *The Broadening Church* (Philadelphia: University of Pennsylvania Press, 1957).

42. Robert Campbell, "The Pretensions Exposed of Messrs. Lang, Burnet & Co." (Montreal: W. Drysdale, 1878).

43. On Dawson, Grant, and Watson, see Charles F. O'Brien, *Sir William Dawson: A Life in Science and Religion* (Philadelphia: American Philosophical Society, 1971); A.B. McKillop, *A Disciplined Intelligence: Critical Inquiry and Canadian Thought in the Victorian Era* (Montreal: McGill-Queen's University Press, 1979) and a suggestive essay by James Angrave, "William Dawson, George Grant and the Legacy of Scottish Higher Education," *Queen's Quarterly* 82 (Spring 1975): 77-91.

44. *Vancouver Daily World* (9 June 1903). See also Robert Campbell, "The Future of Queen's," *Queen's University Journal* (16 October 1903), pp. 21-24, and Robert Campbell, "Statement Regarding the Present Position of Queen's University" (Montreal, 1910).

45. Alexander R. Gordon, "The Religious Value of the Narratives in Genesis," *The Hibbert Journal* 4 (1905-1906): 163-79. See also an account of this episode in the *Montreal Daily Herald* (11 June 1907), p. 3.

46. Sandeen, *Roots of Fundamentalism,* and George M. Marsden, *Fundamentalism and American Culture: The Shaping of Twentieth Century Evangelicalism 1870-1925* (New York: Oxford University Press, 1980). p. 118.

47. In 1909-10 the Toronto Branch of the Bible League of North America published a series of pamphlets by J.S. Ross, S.H. Blake, and Albert Carman. The list of officers of the Toronto branch of the League is printed on the back of these pamphlets (U.C.A.).

48. J.F. McCurdy, ed., *Life and Work of D.J. Macdonnell* (Toronto: William Briggs, 1897). Note that Robert Campbell wrote the chapter on the heresy trial for this book. See also Joseph C. McLelland, "The Macdonnell Heresy Trial," *Canadian Journal of Theology* 4 (1958): 273-84.

49. William MacLaren, "The Unity of the Church and Church Unions" (Toronto: Presbyterian News Co., 1890). For biographical information on MacLaren, see G.M. Rose, *A Cyclopedia of Canadian Biography* (Toronto, 1886), pp. 225-26. For information on MacLaren's family, who played a major role in the development of the lumber industry in the Ottawa Valley, see Charles G.D. Roberts, *A Standard Dictionary of Canadian Biography,* vol. 1 (Toronto: Trans Canada Press, 1934), pp. 317-19.

50. Andrew Thompson, *The Life and Letters of Rev. R.P. MacKay D.D.* (Toronto: Ryerson, 1932), p. 123.

51. *Toronto Daily Star* (12 June 1906), p. 1.

52. "Principal MacLaren and the Liberties of the Church," *Presbyterian* (4 December 1913), pp. 645-46.

53. Ephraim Scott, "Letters to an Inquirer" (Montreal, 1917), p. 14. See also Daniel Walker Howe, "The Decline of Calvinism: An Approach to its Study," *Comparative Studies in Society and History* 14 (1972): 306-27.

54. *Presbyterian Witness* (24 March 1921), pp. 8-9.

NOTES TO CHAPTER THREE

1. For biographical material on John Mackay (1870-1938) see Morgan, *Canadian Men and Women,* his obituary in the *Toronto Globe* (17 May 1938); and D. Kyle and W.M. Gardner, *Knox Crescent Church, 1878-1938* (Montreal, 1938).

2. Lefferts A. Loetscher, *The Broadening Church* pp. 95-97; and John T. Ames, "Cumberland Liberals and the Union of 1906," *Journal of Presbyterian History* 52 (1974): 3-18.

3. *Presbyterian* (2 December 1909), p. 617.

4. *Acts and Proceedings 1906,* p. 36.
5. *Presbyterian* (21 June 1906), p. 764 and the Toronto *Daily Star* (13 June 1906), p. 2.
6. John Mackay, "The Case against Church Union," *Presbyterian* (18 November 1909), pp. 533-54; (25 November 1909), pp. 584-85; (2 December 1909), pp. 616-17; (9 December 1909), pp. 650-652; (16 December 1909), pp. 682-83; (23 December 1909), pp. 716-17.
7. On the Ruthenian experiment see A.J. Hunter, *A Friendly Adventure* (Toronto: Ryerson, 1929), and Michael Zuk, "The Ukrainian Protestant Missions in Canada," M.A. thesis, McGill University, 1957.
8. *Presbyterian* (25 November 1909), p. 595.
9. *Presbyterian* (9 December 1909), pp. 663-65.
10. *Presbyterian* (16 December 1909), pp. 692-93.
11. *Presbyterian* (16 June 1910), pp. 747-49.
12. "The Church Union Question" (Paris, Ontario: The Review Print, n.d.). A copy of this pamphlet is in the University of Toronto Library. The probable date of publication is early September 1910. The fact that it was printed in Paris, Ontario, indicates that R.G. MacBeth, the secretary of the Church Federation Association, had something to do with the printing and circulation of the pamphlet. It is also possible that John Penman put up the money for its publication. There are some similarities between the contents of this pamphlet and Mackay's six articles on "The Case against Church Union." Mackay, however, was not the sort to emphasize a "conspiracy theory." Consequently, it is possible that MacBeth was part author.
13. *Presbyterian* (22 September 1910), pp. 309-10.
14. *Presbyterian* (15 December 1910), p. 676. See also E.K.H. Jordan, *Free Church Unity: History of the Free Church Council Movement 1896-1941* (London: Lutterworth Press, 1956).
15. *Presbyterian* (15 December 1910), p. 680.
16. For Patrick's criticism of federation, see the *Presbyterian* (17 June 1909), p. 747. For biographical materials on W.G. Brown (1875-1940), see the *Presbyterian Record* (May 1940), and J.M. Pitsula, "W.G. Brown: 'Righteousness Exalteth a Nation,'" *Saskatchewan History* 33 (Spring 1980): 56-70.
17. *Presbyterian* (2 February 1911), pp. 139-40.
18. Ibid., pp. 158-59.
19. *Presbyterian Witness* (4 March 1911), and (11 March 1911), also the *Presbyterian* (2 March 1911), pp. 260-73.
20. *Presbyterian Witness* (4 March 1911).
21. The six Toronto ministers and their congregations were: Rev. T. Crawford Brown, St. Andrew's; Rev. Andrew Robertson, St. James Square; Rev. Daniel Strachan, Rosedale; Rev. J.W. Stephen, Avenue Road; Rev. A. Logan Geggie, Parkdale; and Rev. D.T.L. McKerroll, Victoria, West Toronto.
22. *Presbyterian Witness* (11 March 1911), and the *Presbyterian* (2 March 1911), p. 260.
23. *Presbyterian* (9 March 1911).
24. *Acts and Proceedings 1911,* pp. 23-24.
25. *Presbyterian* (9 March 1911).
26. For MacBeth's statement, see the *Presbyterian* (23 March 1911), pp. 361-61, and for Mackay's statement see the *Presbyterian* (30 March 1911), p. 402.
27. *Presbyterian* (2 March 1911), p. 286.
28. *Presbyterian* (30 March 1911), p. 402.
29. Ibid.
30. *Presbyterian* (6 April 1911).
31. For biographical materials on James Ballantyne (1857-1921), see Morgan, *Canadian Men and Women,* and *In Memory of Rev. James Ballantyne, B.A., D.D. (1857-1921),* compiled by his family (Toronto: Ryerson, 1922).
32. *Acts and Proceedings 1911,* pp. 25, 31.
33. Ibid., p. 61, and the *Presbyterian* (22 June 1911), pp. 779-88.
34. *Presbyterian* (23 November 1911), pp. 583-84.
35. *Presbyterian* (30 November 1911), p. 617, and (7 December 1911), p. 647.
36. *Presbyterian* (23 November 1911), pp. 579-80.
37. *Presbyterian* (16 November 1911), pp. 490-96.
38. W.J. Clark, "In Support of Church Union," *Presbyterian Record* (January 1912), pp. 22-26.
39. *Acts and Proceedings 1912,* pp. 330-33, and 340-42.
40. Ibid.
41. Wilhelmina Gordon, *Daniel M. Gordon, His Life* (Toronto: Ryerson, 1941), pp. 252-55.
42. *Acts and Proceedings 1912,* pp. 31-32, 45-47.
43. John Mackay, *The Corpus Christi Crusade* (Winnipeg 1923). See also John Mackay, "The Church and the Churches: An Essay Towards Reunion," *Canadian Journal of Religious Thought* 2 (July-August 1925): 273-83.

NOTES TO CHAPTER FOUR

1. *Presbyterian* (20 June 1912), p. 774.
2. Ibid., p. 779.
3. Ibid. (2 May 1912), pp. 554-55.
4. W.G. Brown, "Why I Remained with the Presbyterian Church in Canada," *Sermons in Answer to Questions* (Saskatoon: Saskatoon Printers, 1937).
5. *Acts and Proceedings 1913*, pp. 306-14.
6. Ibid., pp. 315.
7. *Acts and Proceedings 1914*, p. 336.
8. Ibid., p. 352.
9. Ibid., p. 353.
10. Ibid., p. 393.
11. Ibid., p. 360.
12. Ibid., pp. 392-93.
13. *Presbyterian* (18 June 1914), p. 779. See also Ephraim Scott, "The Presbyterian Church in Canada. Its Preservation and Continuance," (Montreal: Lovell, 1914). On page 14, Scott says that the dissidents asked to have a part in the survey, but their request was refused.
14. *Presbyterian* (5 September 1912), p. 247.
15. J.P. Gerrie, "Church Union in the Prairie Provinces," *The Westminster* (June 1913), pp. 589-90.
16. *Presbyterian* (7 January 1915), pp. 30-31.
17. Ibid., (23 April 1914), pp. 541-42.
18. Ibid., (28 May 1914), pp. 693-96.
19. *Acts and Proceedings 1913*, p. 305.
20. *Presbyterian* (17 July 1913), p. 69.
21. Ibid. (18 September 1913), pp. 302-3.
22. Ibid. (23 October 1913), p. 438.
23. Ibid. (6 November 1913), p. 526.
24. *The Presbyterian Record* (December 1913).
25. *Acts and Proceedings 1914*, p. 337.
26. *Canadian Textile Journal* (22 October 1931).
27. *Acts and Proceedings 1914*, p. 629, and "The Numerical Distribution of Population by Religious Denominations, 1871-1961," *1961 Census of Canada*.
28. *Acts and Proceedings 1914*, pp. 343-44.
29. Frank Baird, "Mr. Morton's Book on Union," *Presbyterian* (16 January 1913), pp. 87-90.
30. *Acts and Proceedings 1914*, pp. 41-42.
31. *Presbyterian* (18 June 1914), p. 775.
32. *Acts and Proceedings 1914*, pp. 50-51.
33. *Presbyterian* (3 December 1914), p. 552.
34. Scott, "The Presbyterian Church in Canada."
35. *Presbyterian* (3 December 1914), p. 552.
36. For the full text of this letter, see *Presbyterian* (5 August 1915), pp. 139-40, and also *The Presbyterian Advocate* 1 (October 1915): 7.
37. *Presbyterian* 16 August 1915), pp. 208-9.
38. Ibid. (10 June 1915), p. 617.
39. *Acts and Proceedings 1915*, pp. 42-43.
40. *Presbyterian* (10 June 1915), p. 617.
41. Ibid. (17 June 1915), p. 644.
42. Ibid., p. 645.
43. Ibid., p. 646.
44. *Acts and Proceedings 1915*, pp. 320-21.
45. *Presbyterian* (17 June 1915), p. 645.

NOTES TO CHAPTER FIVE

1. *Acts and Proceedings 1915*, pp. 320-21.
2. Cf. P.C.A. Papers, Case 4, files 9 and 43, for all the correspondence concerning this arrangement. Penman in a letter to Farquharson, 21 September 1915, for example, specifically asked that he reply to Haddow's editorial of 16 September 1915 on "Make it Unanimous." It is not entirely clear how long this arrangement was in effect, but once Farquharson received a call to Quebec City later in 1916, he does not appear to have been in the employ of the committee, but was still in correspondence with them later. In 1925, however, he went into the United Church of Canada.
3. *Presbyterian* (16 September 1915).
4. *Presbyterian* (30 September 1915), p. 335.
5. D.D. McLeod, "The Present Duty to Preserve The Presbyterian Church: A Brief Reply to the Nine Advocates of the desertion of our Church for a New Denomination" (Barrie, Ontario, July 1915). A copy is available in the U.C.A., Presbyterian Non-Concurrence, Box 1, file 45.
6. "Church Union: An Opportunity and a Duty"; this pamphlet is undated but was probably published immediately prior to the 1915 Assembly (that is, in April or May 1915). It consists of eight articles with an introduction by D.M. Ramsay. This pamphlet should not be confused with a later one entitled "The Need of Church Union" by a group of Presbyterians. That too is undated, and there is a

certain amount of overlap between the materials in both pamphlets. The latter one, however, consists of twelve articles. Both are available in the United Church Archives.

7. T.B. Kilpatrick was born and trained in Scotland. Like John Watson of Queen's, he was a pupil and disciple of Edward Caird. He came to Canada in 1899 as professor of systematic theology at Manitoba College, where he remained until he accepted an appointment at Knox College in 1905. See C.G.D. Roberts and A.L. Tunnell eds., *A Standard Dictionary of Canadian Biography* (Toronto: Trans-Canada Press, 1938), p. 219.

8. McLeod interpreted Kilpatrick as saying that refusal to realize "outward uniformity" was a sin. Kilpatrick denied this in a letter cf. *Presbyterian* [28 October 1915, pp. 410-11]), but insofar as Kilpatrick's object was to emphasize that Christians ought "to repent of our sinful state of disunion" and to declare that "the reunion of the sister churches in Canada is a duty," it would appear that McLeod interpreted him correctly even though he misquoted him.

9. *The Presbyterian Advocate* 1, p. 1.

10. A.H. MacGillivray to J. Penman and C.S. McDonald, 22 September 1915, P.C.A. Papers, Case 4, file 13.

11. A.H. MacGillivray to J. Penman and C.S. McDonald, 22 September 1915, P.C.A. Papers, Case 4, file 13.

12. The second number of the *Presbyterian Advocate* also contained a letter from one member of the Methodist Union Committee who was opposed to union, Rev. D.M. McCamus of London, Ontario.

13. Cf. the statement of Judge Finlayson and R. McVicar, LL.B., on behalf of the local committee in Sydney, Nova Scotia, *Presbyterian Advocate* 2.

14. Frank Baird to R.G. MacBeth, 28 July 1915, P.C.A. Papers, Case 4, file 34.

15. R.G. MacBeth to C.S. McDonald, 14 July 1915, P.C.A. Papers, Case 4, file 34.

16. *Acts and Proceedings 1915*, p. 43.

17. *Presbyterian* (16 September 1915).

18. Ibid. (14 October 1915), pp. 382-83.

19. Ibid. (8 October 1915).

20. Ibid. (23 December 1915), p. 525. These figures differ markedly from those of C.E. Silcox, *Church Union*, p. 173. Unfortunately, Silcox gives no source for his figures.

21. *Presbyterian* (30 December 1915), p. 637.

22. Ibid. (3 February 1916), p. 119.

23. Ibid. (6 January 1915), p. 5.

24. Ibid. (27 January 1916), p. 77.

25. Ibid. (24 February 1916), pp. 173-74.

26. Ibid. (16 March 1916), pp. 259-60.

27. Ibid. (16 March 1916).

28. Ibid. (16 April 1916), p. 327.

29. Ibid. (25 May 1916), pp. 491-92: also *Acts and Proceedings 1916*, pp. 282-85.

30. Ibid. (18 May 1916), pp. 476-78.

31. Ibid. (1 June 1916), pp. 432-533.

32. Ibid. (1 June 1916), pp. 432-533.

33. Ibid. (15 June 1916), p. 568.

34. *Acts and Proceedings 1916*, p. 37.

35. *Presbyterian* (22 June 1916), p. 594.

36. Ibid. (22 June 1916), p. 596.

37. W.G. Brown, "Why I Remained with the Presbyterian Church Canada," Sermon 15 (Saskatoon: Saskatoon Printers, 1937).

38. C.S. McDonald to R.G. MacBeth, 13 July 1916, P.C.A. Papers, Case 4, file 34.

39. Ibid. (22 June 1916), p. 596.

40. *Acts and Proceedings 1916*, p. 58.

NOTES TO CHAPTER SIX

1. *Presbyterian* (1 June 1911), p. 693.

2. *Toronto Globe*, (24 June 1916).

3. Ibid. (30 June 1916).

4. C.S. McDonald to J.W.W. Darling, 31 July 1916, P.C.A. Papers, case 4, file 4. For biographical material on J.W. MacNamara (1864-1948) see *Acts and Proceedings, 1948*, p. 357 and *The Centennial of Presbyterianism: 1856-1956 Knox Church Ripley, Ontario*, p. 35.

5. C.S. McDonald to R.G. MacBeth, 13 July 1916, P.C.A. Papers, Case 4, file 34.

6. C.S. McDonald to J. Penman, 27 July 1916, P.C.A. Papers, Case 4, file 49.

7. R.G. MacBeth to J.W. MacNamara 24 August 1916, P.C.A. Papers, Case 4, file 34.

8. Cf. "Committed to Union," *The Outlook*, (28 June 1916) pp. 447-48 and J. Kier Fraser's letter on "Church Union in Canada," *The Outlook*, (19 July 1916), p. 679.

9. J. Kier Fraser to J. Penman, 14 August 1916, P.C.A. Papers, Case 4, file 9. The final programme carefully featured representatives of both the old guard and the new. Dr. D.D. McLeod, Robert Campbell,

Ephraim Scott, and W.G. Brown all made major addresses together with a number of newcomers such as Rev. Robert Johnson of Halifax, J.D. Cunningham of Welland, Logan Geggie of Toronto and T.F. Fullerton of Charlottetown. The programme also featured a number of prominent laymen such as the Hon. J.C. Brown of New Westminster, F.W. Monteith of Edmonton, John MacKay of Toronto, the Hon. R.M. MacGregor of New Glasgow, N.S., Sir W. Mortimer Clark of Toronto and John Penman (cf., "Programme of the Presbyterian Convocation 17 to 19 October 1916," U.C.A. Presbyterian Non-Concurrence, Box 2, file 68.

10. Kingston adherent to J.W. MacNamara, 21 August 1916. P.C.A. Papers, Case 4, file 4.

11. Undated newspaper clipping from the *Victoria Daily Times*, P.C.A. Papers, Case 4, file 34.

12. R. Campbell to J.W. MacNamara 13 October 1916, P.C.A. Papers, Case 4, file 31.

13. Cf. *Montreal Star,* 13 October 1916.

14. E. Scott to R. Falconer, 11 October 1916, U.C.A. Church Union Collection, P.C.C., Box 7, file 176.

15. R. Falconer to E. Scott, 21 November 1916, U.C.A. Church Union Collection, P.C.C., Box 7, file 176.

16. *The Presbyterian,* (19 October 1916).

17. Cf. Loetscher, *The Broadening Church,* pp. 94, 117 for a discussion of parellel developments in American Presbyterianism.

18. *The Montreal Gazette,* (21 August 1916).

19. *The Montreal Gazette,* (25 September 1916).

20. *The Mail and Empire* (20 October 1916).

21. *The Presbyterian* (26 October 1916) pp. 351-52.

22. Ibid.

23. Cf. Frank Baird, Newspaper Clippings on the Church Union Movement 1915-1925, p. 31, Frank Baird Papers.

24. These remarks had been attributed to W.G. Brown in a speech at Saskatoon prior to the convocation, cf. a typescript entitled, "Denies Theft of Mission Money" by Andrew Baird, U.C.A. Church Union Collection, P.C.C., Box 7, file 176.

25. For confusion on this matter even in the unionist ranks, cf. *The Presbyterian* (2 November 1916) p. 376, where the amount quoted is $27,519.43. Whether this was a misprint is not known, but it added to the confusion.

26. Cf. Frank Baird Newspaper Clippings, p. 31. Frank Baird Papers, P.C.A.

27. *The Presbyterian,* (2 November 1916) pp. 371-72.

28. Ibid. (9 November 1916) pp. 395-96.

29. Ibid. (16 November 1916) pp. 438-39.

30. Ibid. (30 November 1916) p. 486 and cf., U.C.A., Church Union Collection, P.C.C., Box 7, file 177.

31. *The Message* (1 February 1917) p. 2.

32. Cf. U.C.A., *The Minutes of the Presbytery of Toronto* 7 November 1916) pp. 79-80.

33. D.M. Gordon to Andrew Robertson, 18 December 1916, P.C.A. Papers, Case 4, file 7.

34. A. Robertson to D.J. Fraser, 21 December 1916, P.C.A. Papers, Case 4, file 10.

35. A. Robertson to D.M. Gordon, 23 December 1916, P.C.A. Papers, Case 4, file 7.

36. R.G. MacBeth to A. Robertson, 20 December 1916, P.C.A. Papers, Case 4, file 34.

37. A. Robertson to R.G. MacBeth, 26 December 1916, P.C.A. Papers, Case 4, file 34.

38. *The Presbyterian* (4 June 1917) pp. 6-7.

39. *The Message* (1 February 1917) p. 4.

40. *The Toronto Globe* (8 January 1917).

41. Ibid. (18 January 1917).

42. Cf. Daniel J. Fraser "Recent Church Union Movements in Canada," *Harvard Theological Review* 8 (1915): 363-78.

43. *The Message* (1 February 1917) pp. 5-6.

NOTES TO CHAPTER SEVEN

1. *Presbyterian and Westminster* (19 April 1917), pp. 451-52.

2. Ibid. (24 May 1917).

3. Ibid. (24 May 1917), p. 604. On W.R. Motherwell's early career in Saskatchewan, see Allan R. Turner, "W.R. Motherwell: The Emergence of a Farm Leader," in *Historical Essays on the Prairie Provinces,* ed. D. Swainson (Toronto: McClelland and Stewart, 1970), pp. 166-78, and David E. Smith, *Prairie Liberalism: The Liberal Party in Saskatchewan 1905-71,* (Toronto: University of Toronto Press, 1975).

4. *The Message,* (May 1917), p. 11.

5. Ibid. (April 1917), p. 6.
6. Ibid. (March 1917), p. 8.
7. *Presbyterian and Westminster* (24 May 1917).
8. Scott, "Letters To An Inquirer."
9. *Montreal Star* (6 June 1917).
10. *Montreal Gazette* (6 June 1917).
11. Ibid.
12. *Montreal Star* (6 June 1917).
13. *Presbyterian and Westminster* (14 June 1917), p. 695.
14. *Acts and Proceedings 1917*, (14 June 1917), p. 695.
15. Ibid., pp. 44-46.
16. *Presbyterian and Westminster* (21 June 1917), p. 724.
17. *The Record* (July 1917), pp. 193-94.
18. A. Robertson to Prof. D.A. Murray, 14 February 1918, P.C.A. Papers, Case 4, file 36.
19. Circular letter, 6 September 1917, P.C.A. Papers, Case 2, file 32.
20. *Presbyterian and Westminster* (22 November 1917).
21. George Pidgeon, "Memorabilia" (undated, handwritten notes on the history of church union). George Pidgeon Papers, U.C.A. See also George Pidgeon, *The United Church of Canada: The Story of the Union* (Toronto: Ryerson, 1950), p. 56.
22. Ibid.
23. A. Robertson to D.J. Fraser (1 March 1918), P.C.A. Papers, Case 4, file 1.
24. A. Robertson to D.A. Murray, (14 February 1918), P.C.A. Papers, Case 4, file 36.
25. James Rodger to C.S. McDonald (1 May 1918), P.C.A. Papers, Case 4, file 42.
26. A. Robertson to G. Colborne Heine, 4 February 1918, P.C.A. Papers, Case 4, file 32.
27. A. Robertson to H.M. Mowatt, 12 January 1918, P.C.A. Papers, Case 4, file 33.
28. A. Robertson to Robert McMillan, 13 June 1918, P.C.A. Papers, Case 4, file 20.
29. A. Robertson to C.S. McDonald, 15 February 1918, P.C.A. Papers, Case 4, file 21.
30. A. Robertson to A.H. MacGillivray, 4 June 1918, P.C.A. Papers, Case 4, file 20. For biographical information on Andrew Robertson (1856-1920), see Morgan, *Canadian Men and Women,* p. 949 and J.M. Cameron and S.D. Macdougall, eds., *One*

Hundred and Fifty Years in the Life of First Presbyterian Church, New Glasgow, N.S., (Toronto: Presbyterian Publications, 1939), pp. 135-213. See also the *Minutes of the Presbytery of Toronto* (28 May 1918), pp. 58-59. In 1918 Robertson accepted a call to the Broadway Presbyterian in Nashville, Tennessee. He died while on holiday in Toronto on 1 July 1920 and was buried in Mount Pleasant Cemetery.
31. R.A. Falconer, "The Present Position of the Churches in Canada," *Constructive Quarterly* 1 (June 1913): 269-81. For biographical information on Sir Robert Alexander Falconer (1867-1943) see Morgan, *Canadian Men and Women,* and James S. Thompson, "Sir Robert A. Falconer," *Dalhousie Review* 30 (1951): 361-68.
32. Daniel James Fraser, "Present Church Union Movements in Canada," *Harvard Theological Review* 8 (July 1915): 363-78.
33. Herbert Kelly, "The United Church of Canada," *Constructive Quarterly* 5 (Septmber 1917): 435-52. For biographical information on Herbert Hamilton Kelly (1860-1915), see George Every "Memoir of Father Kelly," in H. Kelly, *The Gospel of God* (London: S.C.M. Press, 1959). See also George Every "The Ecumenical Theology of Father Kelly," *Ecumenical Review* 3 (1950-51): 372-78.
34. T.B. Kilpatrick, "A Response to Father Kelly," *Constructive Quarterly* 5 (December 1917): 617-33. For biographical information on Thomas Buchanan Kilpatrick (1857-1930), see Morgan, *Canadian Men and Women,* p. 611, and George Pidgeon in the Foreword to T.B. Kilpatrick and K.H. Cousland, *Our Common Faith* (Toronto: Ryerson, 1928).
35. Herbert H. Kelly, *The Church and Religious Unity* (London: Longmans Green, 1912).
36. Ernest Thomas, "Church Union in Canada," *American Journal of Theology* 23 (July 1919): 257-73.
37. Edward J. Bidwell, "The Church of England in Canada and Reunion," *Hibbert Journal* 18 (1920): 729-36.
38. See J.W. Grant, *George Pidgeon: A Biography* (Toronto: Ryerson, 1962), pp. 81-83.

NOTES TO CHAPTER EIGHT

1. *Acts and Proceedings 1920*, p. 58.
2. *Acts and Proceedings 1921*, pp. 542-45.
3. Ibid., pp. 29-31.
4. *Presbyterian Witness* (23 June 1921), p. 12.
5. Ibid., p. 12 (italics mine).
6. *Acts and Proceedings 1921* pp. 50-51.
7. Ibid., p. 51.
8. Ibid., pp. 51-52.
9. Ibid., p. 102.
10. Cf. *Church Union Committee Minutes,* Vol. 2, 19 October 1921, U.C.A.
11. Ibid.
12. *Acts and Proceedings 1922*, p. 31.
13. Ibid.
14. *Christian Guardian* (28 June 1922), pp. 12-13.
15. *Presbyterian Witness* (10 August 1922), pp. 21-22.
16. Ibid. (28 June 1922), p. 22.
17. Ibid. (21 September 1922), p. 24.
18. Ibid. (28 September 1922), pp. 19-20.
19. Ibid. (21 September 1922), p. 24, also the *Toronto Globe,* (26 August 1922) and the *Mail and Empire* (28 August 1922).
20. McQuesten to MacNamara (13 and 17 July 1922), P.C.A. Papers, Case 5, file 13.
21. MacNamara to McQuesten, 21 August 1922, P.C.A. Papers, Case 5, file 13.
22. Penman to MacNamara, 26 August 1922, P.C.A. Papers, Case 5, file 4.
23. Penman to MacNamara, 26 August 1922, P.C.A. Papers, Case 5, file 4.
24. *Mail and Empire* (28 August 1922).
25. *Toronto Daily Star* (22 September 1922).
26. Ibid. (21 September 1922).
27. Scrapbook of undated and unidentified newspaper clippings, P.C.A. papers, Case 2, file 37.
28. *Toronto Daily Star* (23 September 1922).
29. Ibid. (25 September 1922).
30. Scrapbook of undated and unidentified newspaper clippings P.C.A. Papers, Case 2, file 37.
31. Ibid.
32. *Toronto Mail and Empire* (13 October 1922).
33. *Toronto Daily Star* (19 October 1922).
34. Ibid. (19 October 1922).
35. *Toronto Globe* (14 October 1922).
36. Ibid. (9 November 1922), p. 20.

NOTES TO CHAPTER NINE

1. Penman to MacNamara (7 December 1922) P.C.A. Papers, Case 5, file 4.
2. Ibid.
3. D.A. Murray to MacNamara (25 November 1922) P.C.A. Papers, Case 3, file 44.
4. Frank Baird, Newspaper Clippings, p. 51, Frank Baird Papers, P.C.A.
5. *Acts and Proceedings 1923,* pp. 614-15.
6. *Presbyterian Witness* (1 February 1923), p. 19.
7. Ibid., (22 February 1923), p. 17.
8. MacNamara to T.B. McQuesten, 13 February 1923, P.C.A. Papers, Case 5, file 3.
9. *Acts and Proceedings 1938,* pp. 304-5. For further biographical information on Alexander James MacGillivray (1867-1938) see Morgan, *Canadian Men and Women,* p. 690.
10. A.J. MacGillivray to J.K. MacGillivray, 23 March 1923, P.C.A. Papers, Case 3, file 34.
11. *Minutes of the Federal Executive,* P.C.A. Papers, Case 3, file 15.
12. For a history of the Women's Missionary Society W.D., of the Presbyterian Church in Canada, see Murial J. Gray, ed., *The Royal Road* (Toronto, 1927). See also Priscilla Lee Reid, "The Role of Presbyterian Women in Canadian Development," in *Enkindled by the Word: Essays in Presbyterianism in Canada,* ed. Neil G. Smith (Toronto: Presbyterian Publications, 1966), and John T. McNeill, *The Presbyterian Church in Canda 1875-1925* (Toronto, 1925), especially Ch. 8 on "The Contribution of Women." For a more modern approach to this subject, see Wendy Mitchinson, "Canadian Women and Church Missonary Societies in the Nineteenth Century: A Step Toward Independence," *Atlantis* 2 (Spring 1977): 57-75.
13. McQuesten to MacNamara, 7 July 1923, P.C.A. Papers, Case 5, file 3.
14. MacNamara to McQuesten, 9 July 1923 P.C.A. Papers, Case 5, file 3.
15. Frances Dickey Cunliffe of Fort Kent, Maine, married John James McCaskill in 1909, see Morgan, *Canadian Men and*

Women, p. 750. In 1927 J.J. McCaskill accepted a call to the Presbyterian Church in Fort Kent.

16. McCaskill to MacNamara, 12 May 1923, P.C.A. Papers, Case 5, file 10.
17. McCaskill to MacNamara (from the Empress Hotel in Peterborough, undated), ibid.
18. McCaskill to MacNamara, 25 May 1923, ibid.
19. McCaskill to MacNamara, 3 June 1923, ibid.
20. *Presbyterian Witness* (22 March 1923), pp. 6-7.
21. Ibid. (5 April 1923), pp. 6-10.
22. Penman to MacNamara, 27 March 1923, P.C.A. Papers, Case 5, file 4.
23. S. Banks Nelson and T.B. McQuesten, "An Indigenous Church," *Presbyterian Witness* (12 April 1923), ibid.
24. D.R. Drummond, "Is There Not a Way Out?" (Hamilton: Ontario, The Federal Church Committee, 1923). See also D.R. Drummond, "Is There Not a Way Out?" *Presbyterian Witness* (26 April 1923), pp. 7-9; J.H. Turnbull, "Dr. Drummond's Way Out," ibid., 10-11; and Dr. Drummond Replies" [to J.H. Turnbull] *Presbyterian Witness* (10 May 1923), pp. 16-17.
25. Ibid.
26. Ibid.
27. Ibid.
28. Ibid. See also Daniel M. Gordon, "The Present Crisis in Church Union Negotiat-

ions," *Presbyterian Witness* (24 May 1923), pp. 17-18.

29. E.D. McLaren, "The Church Union Situation" (Vancouver, 1923). The text of this pamphlet was a sermon preached at Knox Church, on 28 October 1923 which was published "by some of those who heard and were deeply impressed by said statement." See also E.D. McLaren, "Church Union," *Presbyterian Witness* (19 April 1923), pp. 18-19.
30. *Toronto Globe* (April 1923). See also the unionist pamphlet, "Has Dr. Drummond Found The Way?" (Toronto: The Presbyterian Church Union Movement Committee, 1923), U.C.A.
31. *Toronto Star* (9 April 1923).
32. *Acts and Proceedings 1923,* pp. 67-68.
33. Typescript Report of the Union Debate, Port Arthur Assembly 1923, U.C.A. Although the Presbyterian unionists seriously misjudged the extent of women's grievances, after union the United Church had less difficulty with the ordination of women than the Presbyterians because the Methodists, prior to union, had moved further on the women's question than the Presbyterians. See Mary E. Hallett, "Nellie McClung and the Fight for the Ordination of Women in the United Church of Canada," *Atlantis* 4 (Spring 1979): 2-19.
34. *Acts and Proceedings 1923,* p. 107.

NOTES TO CHAPTER TEN

1. MacNamara to Penman, 6 July 1923, P.C.A. Papers, Case 2, file 22. For biographical materials on William Fishbourne McConnell, see *Acts and Proceedings 1940,* pp. 312-313 and the *Toronto Mail* (6 August 1923).
2. The three most important organizers for Ontario were Rev. H.R. Horne, Rev. J.H. Borland, and Rev. W.M. MacKay. There were, however, many others who worked for the Committee on Organization from August 1923 until May 1925 for brief periods of time. See the Minute Book of the Committee on Organization, P.C.A. Papers, Case 2, file 38.
3. *The Toronto Star* (3 December 1923), p. 6, published a letter under the heading "Our Problems Are New to Them" by "Presbyterian" which referred to Parker and McConnell as "foreigners." Comment-

ing on this charge an editorial, in *Saturday Night* (15 December 1923), p. 1, asked: "Has Canada reached such a pitch of civilization where she can afford to dismiss intellectual leaders from the motherland as 'undesireable aliens'?"

4. "A Statement of the Case of the Presbyterian Church Association" (Toronto 1923), P.C.A.
5. *The Presbyterian Standard* (Toronto: The Presbyterian Church Association), vol. 1, no. 1 (July 1923), and vol. 1, no. 2 (October 1923).
6. McConnell to MacNamara, 25 August 1923, P.C.A. Papers, Case 3, file 39.
7. E. Lloyd Morrow, *Church Union in Canada: Its History, Motives, Doctrine and Government* (Toronto: Thomas Allen, 1923).
8. *The Expository Times* (February 1924).

See also an unsigned review which was not too critical in the *Presbyterian Witness* 9, (7 June 1923).

9. John T. McNeill, "Church Union in Canada: An Estimate of Dr. Morrow's Book" (Toronto: Bureau of Literature and Information of the Joint Committee on Union, 1924). For biographical information on McNeil, see Holley M. Shepherd, *A Bio-Bibliography of John Thomas McNeil* (Cambridge, MA: Andover-Harvard Theological Library, 1960).

10. Morrow to MacNamara, 6 March 1924, P.C.A. Papers, Case 2, file 15.

11. For biographical information on Lafleur, see Morgan, *Canadian Men and Women,* p. 626 and Sir Lyman Duff, "Eugene Lafleur," *Canadian Bar Review* 7 (September 1934): 417-21. For George Archibald Campbell, see the Canadian newspaper Service, *Reference Book 1929-1930* (Montreal: Canadian Newspaper Service, 1930), pp. 61-62.

12. George F. Macdonnell to Daniel Fraser, 17 May 1923, and G.F. Macdonnell to J.W. MacNamara, 14 September 1923, P.C.A. Papers, Case 3, file 37.

13. Pelton to Fraser, 9 August 1923, P.C.A. Papers, Case 2, file 6.

14. For biographical information on Francis Henry Chrysler, see Morgan, *Canadian Men and Women,* pp. 231-32, and H. Charlesworth, ed., *A Cyclopedia of Canadian Biography* (Toronto: Hunter-Rose, 1919), pp. 80-81.

15. George Campbell to Chrysler, 8 October 1923, P.C.A. Papers, Case 2, file 6.

16. George G. Pidgeon to D.J. Fraser, 1 October 1923, P.C.A. Papers, Case 2, file 6.

17. Chrysler to Campbell, 6 October 1923, P.C.A. Papers, Case 2, file 6.

18. *Writ,* Supreme Court of Ontario (25 January 1924), U.C.A.

19. "The Gospel of Anti-Unionism" (Toronto: Bureau of Literature and Information of the Joint Committee on Union, 1924), P.C.A. Papers, Case 3, file 10.

20. J.R.P. Slater, "An Address on Church Union" (Toronto, 18 November 1924), U.C.A.

21. McCarthy to Chrysler, 26 February 1924, P.C.A. Papers, Case 3, file 56.

22. C.C. Robinson to Chrysler, 26 February 1924, P.C.A. Papers, Case 3, file 56.

23. *Commons Debates* (26 June 1924), p. 3754.

24. H.A. Robson to T. McMillan, 27 December 1923, P.C.A. Papers, Case 2, file 25.

For biographical information on Hugh Amos Robson, see the Canadian Newspaper Service, *Reference Book 1929-1930,* p. 374.

25. *Manitoba Free Press* (1 February 1924), pp. 3, 5, 7. For further information on John Queen, see A.B. McKillop, "Citizen and Socialist: The Ethos of Political Winnipeg, 1919-1935," M.A. thesis, University of Manitoba, 1970, and A.B. McKillop, "The Socialist as Citizen: John Queen and the Mayoralty of Winnipeg," Historical and Scientific Society of Manitoba, *Transactions* 3 (1973-74): 61-77.

26. *Manitoba Free Press* (14 February 1924), p. 6.

27. *Manitoba Free Press* (16 February 1924), p. 7.

28. *Manitoba Free Press* (23 February 1924), p. 6. For the possible connection between H.A. Robson and John Queen, it should be noted that Queen was jailed for his part in the 1919 Winnipeg General Strike, and Robson was the commissioner appointed by the Manitoba government to investigate the causes of the strike. Writing about Robson's report, W.L. Morton has said, that "the Commissioner, to his honour, submitted a moderate and sympathetic report which laid proper stress on the legitimate grievances from which the strike had originated." It is conceivable, therefore, that Queen, in arguing the dissident's case before the Manitoba legislature, was paying a personal debt of appreciation to Robson for his fairness to the strikers. See W.L. Morton, *Manitoba: A History* (Toronto: University of Toronto Press, 1957), p. 371.

29. *Manitoba Free Press* (15 February 1924), p. 4.

30. McConnell to MacNamara, 13, 14, 17, 24 February 1924, P.C.A. Papers, Case 3, file 39. On especially important events like this, McConnell reported to MacNamara almost every other day. These reports often offer very colourful commentary on these events.

31. For biographical information on William Melville Martin see Morgan, *Canadian Men and Women,* p. 736, and Smith, *Prairie Liberalism.*

32. *Regina Morning Leader* (28 February 1924), p. 11.

33. Ibid. (12 March 1924), p. 2.

34. Ibid. (13 March 1924), p. 1.

35. Ibid. (26 February 1924), p. 1.

36. *Manitoba Free Press* (1 March 1924), p. 10.
37. *Edmonton Journal* (6 March 1924), pp. 1, 5.
38. Ibid. (7 March 1924), p. 8.
39. Ibid. (13 March 1924), p. 18.
40. Gershom W. Mason, *The Legislative Struggle for Church Union* (Toronto: Ryerson, 1956), pp. 48-49.
41. For a discussion of this case, see Eugene A. Forsey, "Disallowance of Provincial Acts, Reservation of Provincial Bills, and Refusal of Assent by Lieutenant-Governors Since 1867," *CJEPS* 4 (February 1938): 47-59; Frank Mackinnon, "The Royal Assent in Prince Edward Island: Disallowance of Provincial Acts, Reservation of Provincial Bills, and the Giving and Withholding of Assent by Lieutenant-Governors," *CJEPS* 15 (May 1949): 216-20; and Frank Mackinnon, *The Government of Prince Edward Island* (Toronto: University of Toronto Press, 1951): 154-55.
42. The Minute Book of the Private Bills Committee, Ontario Legislative Assembly, 1922-26 (P.A.O.), pp. 177-95. For biographical information on William Folger Nickle, see H. Charlesworth, ed., *A Cyclopedia of Canadian Biography* (Toronto: Hunter-Rose, 1919), pp. 107-8.
43. Ibid., pp. 195-201.
44. George Pidgeon to Leslie Pidgeon, 10 April 1924, George Pidgeon Papers, U.C.A.
45. Thomas Bengough, "Stenographic Report of the Proceedings before the Private Bills Committee of the House of Commons, concerning the United Church of Canada Act," 2 vols. Lafleur's address was also printed in pamphlet form and circulated by the dissidents. See U.C.A., Presbyterian. Non-concurrence, Box 1, file 41.
46. Margaret Prang, *N.W. Rowell: Ontario Nationalist*, (Toronto: University of Toronto Press, 1975), p. 402ff.
47. Mason, *Legislative Struggle for Church Union*. p. 100.
48. *House of Commons Debates* (21 June 1924), pp. 3562-3571.
49. *Senate Debates* (9 July 1924), p. 656.
50. Ibid., pp. 653-61.
51. Ibid., p. 743.
52. *Toronto Globe* (11 March 1925).
53. Ibid.

NOTES TO CHAPTER ELEVEN

1. Hector Charlesworth, "Churches and Social Problems," *Canadian Annual Review 1924-1925*, p. 515.
2. *Acts and Proceedings 1924*, p. 472.
3. MacNamara to John Keen, 8 July 1924, P.C.A. Papers, Case 3, file 31.
4. MacNamara to McConnell, 8 July 1924, P.C.A. Papers, Case 3, file 39.
5. T. MacMillan to Col. John F. Michie, 18 October 1924, P.C.A. Papers, Case 3, file 31.
6. "Statement of the Presbyterian Church Association" (1 August 1924).
7. Sault St Marie Branch of the Presbyterian Church Association, Pamphlet (no title).
8. These figures are taken from the papers filed by the Presbyterian Church Association in 1925 with the attorney-general of Ontario, W.F. Nickle, P.A.O.
9. "Presbyterian Facts versus Unionist Statements" (Toronto: Presbyterian Church Association, 1924).
10. "The Fate of Anti-Unionism" (Toronto: The Bureau of Literature and Information of the Joint Committee on Church Union, 1924) U.C.A., Presbyterian Church Committee on Church Union, Box 6, file 145.
11. "The Wee Free Story" (Toronto: Presbyterian Church Association, 1924).
12. D. MacLean to George Pidgeon, 16 December 1924, George Pidgeon Papers, U.C.A.
13. Ibid.
14. *The Monthly Record* of the Free Church of Scotland (April 1925), pp. 56-62.
15. *Acts and Proceedings 1924*, p. 471, and the Presbyterian Church Association, *Summary of Ontario Ballot vote*, p. 8.
16. Committee on Organization, Minute Book, P.C.A. Papers.
17. McConnell to MacNamara, 28 August 1924 and 4 September 1924, P.C.A. Papers, Case 3, file 39.
18. McConnell to MacNamara, 10 September 1924, P.C.A. Papers, Case 3, file 39.
19. McConnell to MacNamara, 15 September 1924, ibid.
20. Ibid.
21. MacNamara to McConnell, 24 September 1924, P.C.A. Papers, Case 3, file 39.
22. Ibid.
23. MacNamara to McConnell, 26 Septem-

ber 1924, ibid.

24. McConnell to MacNamara, 30 October 1924, ibid.
25. Ibid.
26. MacNamara to McConnell, 5 November 1924, ibid.
27. McConnell to MacNamara, 21 November 1924, ibid.
28. McConnell to MacNamara, 17 November 1924, ibid.
29. Ibid.
30. Ibid.
31. MacNamara to McConnell, 19 November 1924, ibid.
32. Joint Committee on Union, "Method of taking the vote on Church Union under the Federal Act in the Province of Ontario," U.C.A., Church Union Collection, Committee on Law and Legislation, Box 5, file 82.
33. Toronto *Globe* (23 December 1924).
34. *Toronto Mail* (12 December 1924).
35. Ibid. (15 December 1924).
36. *Toronto Globe* (26 November 1924).
37. Ibid. (23 December 1924).
38. All figures on the congregational voting in Ontario are taken from the P.C.A.'s *Summary of the Vote*, presented to the Private Bills Committee of the Ontario legislature on 14 March 1925, P.A.O., RG8, 1-7H, #18, 1925.
39. MacNamara to Penman, 2 February 1925, P.C.A. Papers, Case 2, file 22.
40. Ibid.
41. MacNamara to Penman, 20 June 1925, P.C.A. Papers, Case 3, file 50.
42. Ibid.
43. John W. Grant, *George Pidgeon: A Biography* (Toronto: Ryerson, 1962), p. 100.
44. *Presbyterian Witness* (6 November 1924), p. 4.

45. Ibid. (18 December 1924), p. 3.
46. Ibid. (15 January 1925), p. 2.
47. Ibid. (29 January 1925), p. 2.
48. Ibid. (26 February 1925), p. 2.
49. Ibid. (20 November 1924).
50. Ibid. (5 February 1925), p. 19, and also the Toronto *Mail* (30 January 1925).
51. *Toronto Star* (4 February 1925), p. 3.
52. Ibid.
53. *Presbyterian Witness* (19 February 1925), p. 2.
54. *Toronto Star* (3 February 1925), p. 1.
55. Silcox, *Church Union*, p. 281.
56. Ibid., p. 282.
57. *Acts and Proceedings 1924*, pp. 332-33.
58. *Presbyterian Witness* (22 January 1925), p. 2.
59. *Acts and Proceedings 1926*, pp. 122-23.
60. Session Minutes, Erskine Church Montreal (14 May 1923), pp. 204ff., McGill Archives, Montreal.
61. *The Rules and Forms of Procedure of the Presbyterian Church in Canada* (Toronto: Presbyterian Publications, 193), p. 19.
62. For biographical information on James Rodger (1853-1932) see *Acts and Proceedings 1933*, p. 279, and for Guy Toombs see Canadian Newspaper Service, *Reference Book 1929-1930*, pp. 430-31. See also Guy Toombs et al., *100 Years of Erskine Church Montreal 1853-1933* (Montreal, 1933), McGill Archives, Montreal.
63. William McLaren, "The New Theology and Its Sources," *Canadian Presbyterian* (13 October 1886), pp. 661-63.
64. Ibid.
65. *Toronto Telegram* (13 December 1919).
66. See Peter Oliver, *Public and Private Persons: The Ontario Political Culture, 1914-1934* (Toronto: Clarke, Irwin, 1975) for excellent background on these issues.

NOTES TO CHAPTER TWELVE

1. *Acts and Proceedings 1925*, p. 84.
2. Ibid., pp. 34-35.
3. Robert Haddow, "An Intolerable View of the Church," *Presbyterian* (2 October 1913), pp. 340-41.
4. Ibid.
5. *Acts and Proceedings 1925*, p. 37.
6. Ibid., pp. 82-83.
7. A.M. Neil, *The Free Church Case* (Edinburgh: W. Hodge and Co., 1904), pp. 113ff.
8. Ibid., pp. 175-76.
9. Ibid., p. 187.

10. Ibid., p. 201.
11. Ibid., p. 189.
12. *Toronto Star* (10 June 1925), p. 5.
13. Ibid., p. 5.
14. Ibid., p. 5.
15. Ibid., p. 7.
16. *Toronto Star* (11 June 1925), p. 29.
17. Ibid. (16 June 1925), p. 5.
18. Ibid., p. 5.
19. Ibid. (10 June 1925), p. 7.
20. Ibid. (16 June 1925), p. 5.
21. *Acts and Proceedings 1928*, pp. 145, 190.

22. *Acts and Proceedings 1926*, pp. 29-31.
23. Daniel Gordon to Arthur Meighen, 12 March 1924, Daniel Gordon Papers, Box 2, file 37, Queen's University Archives.
24. All of the commissioners except Thomas McMillan were prominent enough by 1912 to be included in Morgan's *Canadian Men and Women*.
25. *Proceedings of the Dominion Property Commission* stenographic report, vol. 1, pp. 1-2, P.C.A.
26. Ibid., vol. 4, p. 195.
27. *Acts and Proceedings 1924*, pp. 458-61, and for Bloor Street, pp. 330-31.
28. *Proceedings of the Dominion Property Commission*, p. 199.
29. Ibid., p. 90.
30. See the exhibits filed with the commission relating to the voting results, and especially exhibit 7, "Memo Re- Vote," filed by D.L. McCarthy, Box 11, file 185; also exhibits 11 and 12, filed by W. Tilley, Box 11, file 186, Committee on Law and Legislation, U.C.A.
31. See exhibit 16, file 188, ibid.
32. See exhibit 20, Box 11, file 191, ibid.
33. See exhibit 22, Box 11, file 193, ibid.
34. *Toronto Star* (20 April 1927), p. 32.
35. *Acts and Proceedings 1927*, p. 43 and Appendices 1-35.
36. *New Outlook* (27 April 1927), p. 13.
37. Ibid.
38. *U.C. Year Book 1927*, p. 28, and the *Record of Proceedings 1928*, p. 140.

39. *Acts and Proceedings 1933*, p. 132. See also the overture from the Synod of Montreal and Ottawa, p. 129 and the overture from the Presbytery of Regina, p. 135.
40. *U.C. Year Book 197*, p. 46.
41. Ibid., p. 44.
42. *U.C. Year Book 1926*, p. 190.
43. Silcox, *Church Union*, p. 360.
44. *Acts and Proceedings 1926*, pp. 57-62.
45. Ibid.
46. *Toronto Star* (11 March 1926), p. 1.
47. *U.C. Year Book 1926*, p. 189.
48. *Toronto Star* (29 March 196), p. 19.
49. *Toronto Star* (30 March 1926), p. 2.
51. Ibid., p. 1.
52. Ibid., p. 2.
53. *Toronto Star* ((31 March 1926), p. 5.
54. *Toronto Star* (31 April 1926), p. 3.
55. N.S. Macdonnell to G.W. Mason, 12 May 1926, Committee on Law and Legislation, Ontario Church Property Commission, Box 1, file 28, and Box 34, file 173, U.C.A.
56. Mason to Overend, 12 May 1926, ibid.
57. Ibid., Box 1, file 30, and Box 34, files 175-76.
58. See Silcox, *Church Union*, pp. 356-57.
59. *Acts and Proceedings 1928*, pp. 185-86.
60. *Toronto Globe* (28 March 1928), pp. 13-14.
61. Committee on Law and Legislation, Ontario Church Property Commission, Box 31, file 116, and Box 34, file 189.
62. Sir Henry Lunn, "Church Union and Prohibition in America," *Review of the Churches*, n.s. 3 (July 1926): 304-10.

NOTES TO CHAPTER THIRTEEN

1. *Acts and Proceedings 1924*, p. 38.
2. Ibid.
3. Ibid.
4. *Acts and Proceedings 1927*, p. 151.
5. *Acts and Proceedings 1930*, p. 310.
6. R.G. Stewart, "The Point Well-Taken," *Christian Century* (5 January 1927).
7. Wilson to Morrison (6 January 1927), Church Union Collection, Bureau of Literature and Information, Box 3, file 61, U.C.A.
8. Wilson to John A. Dow, 16 November 1928, ibid., U.C.A.
9. *The Scots Observer* (11 June 1927) and J.R. Fleming to Wilson, 5 July 1926, ibid., Box 3, file 52, U.C.A.
10. C.C. Morrison, "Canada's Non-Concurring Presbyterians," *Christian Century* (3 May 1928), pp. 568-71. For Morrison's earlier

assessments, see the following: "Sectarianism's Perfect Work," *Christian Century* (2 July 1925), pp. 852-54; "Canada's Continuing Presbyterians," ibid., pp. 869-70; and "Canada's Churches outside the Union," ibid. (6 August 1925), p. 993.
11. Ibid.
12. *New Outlook* (16 May 1928).
13. Wilson to Morrison, 18 May 1928, Church Union Collection, Bureau of Literature and Information, Box 3, file 61, U.C.A.
14. *Toronto Star* (5 October 1928).
15. W.M. Rochester, "A Prophet from Chicago and His Canadian Sponsors," P.C.A.
16. Ephraim Scott, *"Church Union" and the Presbyterian Church in Canada* (Montreal: Lovell, 1928).
17. S.D. Chown, *The Story of Church Union in Canada* (Toronto: Ryerson, 1930), pp.

xii-xiv.
18. Ibid., p. 80.
19. See John Jentz, "Liberal Evangelicals and Psychology during the Progressive Era," *Journal of Religious Thought* 33 (Autumn-Winter 1976): 65-73.
20. See N.K. Clifford, "The Interpreters of the United Church of Canada," *Church History* 46 (June 1977): 203-14.
21. E.H. Oliver, *The Winning of the Frontier* (Toronto: Ryerson, 1930).
22. *Record of Proceedings*, p. 152.
23. Ibid., p. 154.
24. Ibid.
25. Ibid., p. 171, and the *Record of Proceedings*, p. 138.
26. Laird to Pidgeon, 5 January 1932, George Pidgeon Papers, Box 21, file 354, U.C.A. (Note that this letter should have been dated 5 January 1933).
27. Pidgeon Papers, ibid.
28. T.A. Moore, "The United Church of Canada," in *The Reunion of Christendom*, ed. Sir James Marchant (London, Cassell, 1929), pp. 233-48.
29. Laird to Pidgeon, 20 February 1933, Pidgeon Papers, Box 21, file 354, U.C.A.
30. *Record of Proceedings 1925*, pp. 224-26.
31. T.A. Moore to the Honourable Arthur Bliss Copp, 18 June 1925, and reply from the under-secretary of state, 22 June 1925.
32. *Acts and Proceedings*, p. 50.
33. George Pidgeon to N.W. Rowell, 7 May 1926.
34. Ibid.
35. Edwards to Sladen, 8 June 1926, Committee on Law and Legislation, Box 2a, files 37, 41, U.C.A.
36. Sladen to Rowell, 9 June 1926, ibid.
37. Gunn to King, 1 April 1929, ibid.
38. R.L. Kellock, "Memorandum," prepared for G.W. Mason, typescript, U.C.A.

39. McGregor Young, "Draft Memorandum with respect to the Rights of the United Church of Canada," Law and Legislation Committee, Box 2A, file 41.
40. Pidgeon to Rowell, 25 July 1927.
41. *Record of Proceedings 1928*, pp. 141-42.
42. *Acts and Proceedings 1927*, pp. 51, 150-51.
43. *The Western Recorder* (December 1927), p. 6.
44. *Acts and Proceedings 1927*, p. 186.
45. *U.C. Year Book 1929*, p. 92.
46. *Record of Proceedings 1930*, p. 138.
47. Ibid., p. 139.
48. Quoted in the *Lindsay Daily Post* (7 June 1932). See also the *Presbyterian Record* 57 (July 1932), pp. 198-99.
49. *Hamilton Review* (10 June 1932).
50. *Lindsay Daily Post* (7 June 1932).
51. Re Patriquin. McLellan v Fraser [1930] 3 D.L.R., 241-45.
52. [1928] 2 D.L.R., 791.
53. [1929] 2 D.L.R., 197.
54. [1930] 3 D.L.R., 241-45.
55. *Acts and Proceedings 1930*, Appendices, 2-3.
56. [1932] 3 D.L.R., 250. See also the *Presbyterian Record* (June 1932), pp. 163-64.
57. [1933] 2 D.L.R., 400.
58. Re Gray, United Church of Canada v Presbyterian Church of Canada [1935] 1 D.L.R., 1-7.
59. Ibid. For an analysis of these cases which is sympathetic towards the United Church's position see Benson A. Rogers, "Canadian Church Union Cases and the Law of Wills," *Canadian Bar Review*, 17 (1939): 399-415.
60. [1935] 4 D.L.R., 778.
61. [1933] 4 D.L.R., 416 and [1934] 3 D.L.R., 379.
62. Laird v MacKay [1938] 3 D.L.R., 474-86. See also the *Presbyterian Record* (July 1938), pp. 214-20.

NOTES TO CHAPTER FOURTEEN

1. *Acts and Proceedings 1927*, pp. 34-35.
2. *Acts and Proceedings 1932*, p. 31.
3. Ibid., p. 32.
4. *Acts and Proceedings 1933*, p. 63.
5. For biographical information on Thomas Albert Moore (1860-1940), see the *New Outlook* (30 December 1936), p. 1217, and the *Toronto Globe* (1 April 1940) and Morgan, *Canadian Men and Women*, pp. 819-20.

6. Moore to Dyde, 4 February 195, Methodist Church, General Conference Office, General Correspondence 1925, file 200, U.C.A.
7. Moore to Drummond, 4 February 1925, Methodist Church, ibid.
8. *Acts and Proceedings 1927*, p. 76.
9. *Acts and Proceedings 198*, pp. 130, 135.
10. *Acts and Proceedings, 1928*, pp. 174-75.
11. Eugene Lafleur to George Campbell, "Re-

The United Church Act" (undated), R.S. Cassels Papers, Box 4, file 2097, ibid.
12. Cassels to MacNamara, 1 March 1929, ibid.
13. Ibid.
14. *Acts and Proceedings 1929*, p. 168.
15. Ibid., 173. The list of trustees contained the names of many who had played a significant role in the controversy: C.S. McDonald; J.A. Milne; G. Tower Fergusson; Judge A.G. Farrell; Col. James Chisholm; R.S. Cassels; and James Rodger. It should be noted that James A. Milne, G. Tower Fergusson, and R.S. Cassels had all been members of Bloor Street Church, Toronto, prior to union. See W.G. Wallace, *These Forty Years—And After being The Story, 1887-1927 of Bloor Street United Church Toronto*, (Toronto: Rous and Mann, 1927), pp. 83-84, 86.
16. *Acts and Proceedings 1929*, p. 175.
17. *Acts and Proceedings 1931*, pp. 151-52.
18. *Acts and Proceedings 1932*, pp. 77, 154-55.
19. *Acts and Proceedings 1934*, p. 42.
20. Ibid., p. 132.
21. *New Outlook* (15 January 1937), p. 38.
22. For biographical information on Gordon

A. Sisco (1891-1953), see the Toronto Star (30 January 1936); the *United Church Observer* (1 January 1954), p. 4; and ibid. (15 January 1954), p. 5.
23. George Pidgeon to N.W. Rowell, 25 July 1927, U.C.A.
24. Sisco to G.W. Mason, 22 December 1937, U.C.A.
25. J.K. Sparling to G.W. Mason, 22 December 1937, U.C.A.
26. Draft Report of the Joint Committee (9 November 1937), U.C.A.
27. Minutes of the Law and Legislation Committee (27 December 1937), U.C.A.
28. *Record of Proceedings 1938*, p. 59.
29. Gordon A. Sisco, "Praise God From Whom All Blessings Flow!" *New Outlook* (7 October, 1938), p. 943. See also W.M. Rochester, "A Happy Issue," *Presbyterian Record* 63 (November 1938), pp. 323-24.
30. *Statutes of Canada 1939*, 3 George VI Parts I-II C. 65, and the Debates of the Canadian Senate 1939: 1 (9 March 1939), p. 63; (14 March 1939), p. 106; (28 March 1939), pp. 127-28; and (5 April 1939), p. 139.
31. *Acts and Proceedings 1938*, p. 110.

NOTES TO THE CONCLUSION

1. As E.R. Norman has pointed out the state churches in Canada "were not actually disestablished. They evaporated as establishments when their privileges and properties were withdrawn by government action." See *The Conscience of the State in North America* (Cambridge: Cambridge University Press, 1968), p. 68.
2. R. Campbell, *the Relations of the Christian Churches*, pp. 296-97.
3. E.R. Norman sees "religious pluralism" as a cause rather than an effect of disestablishment. Prior to the disestablishment, however, religious pluralism had no recognized status. Therefore, I have chosen to follow Peter Berger and Thomas Luckmann in seeing religious pluralism as an

effect rather than a cause of disestablishment. See "Secularization and Religious Pluralism," *International Yearbook for the Sociology of Religion*, 2 (1966): pp. 73-84.
4. Ephraim Scott, *"Church Union" and the Presbyterian Church in Canada* (Montreal: John Lovell, 1928), p. 8.
5. Eugene Lafleur, "Address on Bill 47 An Act Incorporating the United Church of Canada before the Private Bills Committee House of Commons," [pamphlet] (7 May 1924), pp. 26-27, *P.C.A. Papers*, Box 1, file 41.
6. *Commons Debates* (24 June 1924), p. 3585.
7. Ibid., p. 3570.
8. Ibid., p. 3570-71.

Selected Bibliography

There is no adequate bibliography of either the church union movement or the controversy over church union in Canada. Kenneth H. Cousland's *A Bibliography of Church Union in Canada* (American Theological Library Association Summary of Proceedings, Thirteenth Annual Conference, Toronto, 1959), pp. 89-101, made no pretense about being comprehensive, and it is now out of date. There are also no published guides to manuscript collections in the various denominational archives in Canada, but *The Bulletin* of the United Church's Archives Committee has periodically published brief articles on its holdings, and its finding aids to the various collections are extremely helpful. In locating pamphlets M. Casey, ed, *Catalogue of Pamphlets in the Public Archives of Canada* (1931) is of some value, but it must be used with extreme caution. The best sources for contemporary works are the bibliographies published in the *Canadian Historical Review, Canadiana,* and the *Study Sessions* of the Canadian Catholic Historical Association. *The Register of Post-Graduate Dissertations in History and Related Subjects* is useful for locating theses, but it does not include dissertations from the Canadian Theological Colleges.

Primary Sources

ARCHIVAL COLLECTIONS

The Presbyterian Church Archives, Knox College, Toronto.

    For the study of the controversy over church union, the most important collection in this archives is the Presbyterian Church Association papers. They contain the correspondence, minute books, and financial records of the association from 1916 to 1925. They also contain a few items from the Organization for the Preservation and Continuance of the Presbyterian Church in Canada for the years 1913 to 1916. The A.S. Morton Papers, Frank Baird Papers, and the Banks Nelson Papers are minor collections which contain some material on the controversy. More important for the legal questions arising after 1925 are the R.S. Cassels Papers, but they are not open to the general public and special permission is required to use them.

The United Church Archives, Victoria University, Toronto.

The Church Union Collection in this archive is, apart from the papers of the Presbyterian Church Association, the most extensive collection on this subject. It contains the papers of the Joint Committee on Union, the Presbyterian Church, Presbyterian Non-Concurrence, Co-operation and Local Union, The Bureau of Literature and Information, and the Law and Legislation Committee. There are also smaller collections of the Robert Campbell Papers, Andrew Baird papers, Walter C. Murray Papers, and a large collection of the George Pidgeon papers.

The Queen's University Archives, Kingston, Ontario.

The Daniel Gordon and S.W. Dyde papers in this archive are important for the study of the controversy. Daniel Gordon supported union from the beginning, but when it was pressed to the point of a disruption of the Presbyterian Church, he found that he could not enter the United Church. S.W. Dyde played a lesser role, but his reaction to the disruption is also important.

McGill University Archives, Montreal, Quebec.

D.A. Murray was the secretary of the Montreal Branch of the Presbyterian Church Association from 1916 to 1925. His diaries and papers which have recently become available in this archive are therefore an important supplement to the P.C.A. Papers. J.A. Ewing, K.C., was the United Church's lawyer for the province of Quebec. His papers together with the Erskine Church papers are important for understanding the controversy in Montreal and the province of Quebec.

Public Archives of Ontario, Toronto.

For the study of the controversy the most important collection in this archive is the papers of the Private Bills Committee of the Ontario Legislature. They contain the minutes of the committee and correspondence on this issue addressed to the Hon. W.F. Nickle, the chairman of the committee.

GOVERNMENT AND CHURCH DOCUMENTS

The Acts and Proceedings of the General Assembly of the Presbyterian Church in Canada. Toronto, 1900-1939.

The United Church of Canada Record of Proceedings of the General Council. Toronto, 1925-1939.

The United Church of Canada Year Book. Toronto, 1925-1939.

House of Commons Debates. 1924 and 1939.

Senate Debates. 1924 and 1939.

Statutes of Canada 1924. 14-15 George V c. 100.

Statutes of Canada 1939. 3 George VI, Parts I and II c. 63 and c. 64.

PAMPHLETS

There was a seemingly endless stream of pamphlets published by both individuals and groups throughout the controversy. In this study only those pamphlets which sparked some identifiable response or were a response to an identifiable event have been singled out for comment.

Campbell, Robert. "Union or Co-operation — Which?" Montreal: Forster Brown and Co. Ltd., n.d.

_____. "Church Union." Montreal, 10 July 1910.

"The Church Union Question." Paris, Ont.: The Review Print, n.d.

Scott, Ephraim. "The Presbyterian Church in Canada. Its Preservation and Continuance." Montreal: Lovell, 1914.

McLeod, D.D. "The Present Duty to Preserve The Presbyterian Church: A Brief Reply to the Nine Advocates of the Desertation of our Church for a New Denomination." Barrie, Ont., July 1915.

Church Union: An Opportunity and a Duty."

"The Need of Church Union."

Drummond, D.R. "Is There Not a Way out?" Hamilton: The Federal Church Committee, 1923.

"Has Dr. Drummond Found The Way?" Toronto: The Presbyterian Church Union Movement Committee, 1923.

"A Statement of the Case of the Presbyterian Church Association." Toronto, 1923.

McNeill, John T. "Church Union in Canada: An Estimate of Dr. Morrow's Book." Toronto: Bureau of Literature and Information of the Joint Committee on Union, 1924.

The Gospel of Anti-Unionism." Toronto: Bureau of Literature and Information, 1924.

The Fate of Anti-Unionism." Toronto: Bureau of Literature and Information, 1924.

"Presbyterian Facts versus Unionist Statements." Toronto: Presbyterian Church Association, 1924.

"The Wee Free Story." Toronto: Presbyterian Church Association, 1924.

Rochester, W.M. "A Prophet from Chicago and His Canadian Sponsors." Toronto, 1928.

BOOKS AND ARTICLES BY PARTICIPANTS AND OBSERVERS

Campbell, Robert. *The Relations of the Christian Churches to One Another and the Problems Growing out of Them, Especially in Canada.* Toronto, 1913.

Chown, S.D. *The Story of Church Union in Canada.* Toronto, 1939.

_____. "Some Ideals and Responsibilities of the United Church of Canada." *The Christian Union Quarterly* 15 (January 1926): 259-61.

Dyde, S.W. "Church Union in Canada — From a Presbyterian Standpoint." *The Journal of Religion* (2 March 1922): 147-58.

Falconer, Robert A. "The Present Position of the Churches in Canada." *Constructive Quarterly* 1 (June 1913): 269-81.

Fraser, Daniel J. "Recent Church Union Movements in Canada." *Harvard Theological Review* 8 (July 1915): 363-78.

_____. "The Church Union Situation." *Presbyterian Witness* (22 March 1923), pp. 6-7.

Gandier, Alfred. "The Doctrinal Basis of Union and the Historic Creeds." Ryerson Essay No. 34, Toronto: Ryerson, 1926.

_____. "The Church Union Bill." *Presbyterian Witness* (14 December 1922).

_____. "Church Union." *The Theologue* (March 1899): 109-16.

_____. "Predestination and the Historical Decision." *Presbyterian* (26 November

1904), and (3 December 1904).

Gordon, Daniel M. "The Present Crisis in the Church Union Negotiations." *Presbyterian Witness* (24 May 1923), 17-18.

Graham, W.C. "On 'Getting Together.'" *University Magazine* 17 (April 1918): 284-28.

Keenleyside, Hugh L. "Church Union in Canada." *The Christian Union Quarterly* 15 (July 1925): 40-45.

Kelly, Herbert. "The United Church of Canada." *Constructive Quarterly* 5 (September 1917): 435-52.

Kilpatrick, T.B. *Our Common Faith.* Toronto, 1928.

———. "A Response to Father Kelly." *Constructive Quarterly* 5 (December 1917): 617-33.

Lund, Sir Henry. "Church Union and Prohibition in America." *Review of the Churches,* n.s. 3 (July 1926): 304-10.

MacBeth, R.G. *The Burning Bush and Canada.* Toronto, n.d.

MacKay, John. "Spiritual Conditions in Canada: A Reply." *Hibbert Journal* 21 (1922-23): 773-27.

———. "The Church and the Churches: An Essay Towards Reunion." *Canadian Journal of Religious Thought* 2 (1925): 273-93.

MacKay, R.P. "Church Union in Canada." *The Christian Union Quarterly* 14 (October 1924): 143-53.

Macmillan, Cyrus. "The Medievalism of Church Union." *Presbyterian Witness.* (5 April 1923), pp. 6-10.

McNab, John. "Why I Remained a Presbyterian in Canada." *Christendom* 1 (1935-36): 674-86.

McNeil, John T. *The Presbyterian Church in Canada 1875-1925.* Toronto, 1925.

———. "The Contribution of the Presbyterians to the United Church." *New Outlook* (10 June 1925).

McQuesten, T.B. "An Indigenous Church." *Presbyterian Witness* (12 April 1923), p. 8.

Mason, Gershom. *The Legislative Struggle for Church Union.* Toronto, 1956.

Miller, James M. "The Union of Protestant Churches in Canada." *Current History* 25 (1927): 513-16.

Moore, T.A. "The United Church of Canada." In *The Reunion of Christendom,* ed by Sir James Marchant. London, 1929.

Morrison, Charles Clayton. "Sectarianism's Perfect Work." *Christian Century* (2 July 1925), pp. 852-54.

———. "Canada's Continuing Presbyterians." ibid. (2 July 1925), pp. 869-70.

———. "Canada's Churches Outside the Union, ibid. (6 August 1925), p. 993.

———. "Canada's Non-Concurring Presbyterians." ibid. (3 May 1928), pp. 568-71.

Morrow, E. Lloyd. *Church Union in Canada: Its History, Motives, Doctrine and Government.* Toronto, 1923.

Morton, A.S. *The Way to Union.* Toronto, 1912.

———. "Methodists and Presbyterian Scotland." *University Magazine* 11 (April 1912): 327-47.

Murray, Walter C. "Early Plans and Negotiations Looking Toward Union." *New Outlook* (10 June 1925).

Nelson, Banks. "An Indigenous Church." *Presbyterian Witness* (12 April 1923), p. 8.

Oliver, E.H. *The Winning of the Frontier.* Toronto, 1930.

———. "The Place and Work of the United Church in the Life of Canada." *New Outlook* (10 June 1925).

Parker, Stuart C. *The Book of St. Andrew's.* Toronto, 1939.

Patrick, W. "Some Reasons for Church Union." *Presbyterian Record* (October 1916).

———. "The Case for Church Union." *Presbyterian* (12 March 1910).

Pedley, Hugh. *Looking Forward: The Strange Experience of the Rev. Fergus Mc-Cheyne.* Toronto, 1913.

Pidgeon, George C. *The United Church of Canada: The Story of Union.* Toronto, 1950.

Roberts, Richard. "The United Church of Canada." *Review of the Churches* M.S. 2 (April 1925): 287-97.

———. "Getting Together in Canada." *Federal Council Bulletin,* vols. 8-9 (1925-26), pp. 14-15.

Scott, Ephraim. *"Church Union" and the Presbyterian Church in Canada,* Montreal, 1928.

Silcox, C.E. *Church Union in Canada: its Causes and Consequences.* New York, 1933.

———. "Ten Years of Church Union in Canada." *Christendom* 1 (1935-36): 80-91, 350-61.

Sisco, Gordon. "Praise God from Whom All Blessings Flow!" *New Outlook* (7 October 1938), p. 943.

Stanley, Carleton W. "Spiritual Conditions in Canada." *Hibbert Journal* 21 (1922-23): 276-86, 773-27.

Taylor, Sir Thomas W. *Public Statutes Relating to the Presbyterian Church in Canada.* Toronto, 1979. 2d. ed. Winnipeg, 1897.

Taylor, T. Wardlaw. "Church Union and the Law." *Presbyterian Witness* (29 March 1923), pp. 10-11.

Thomas, Ernest. "Church Union in Canada." *American Journal of Theology* 23 (July 1919): 251-73.

Wilson, R.J. "The Ecumenical Mind." *Social Welfare* 17 (June 1938): 103-5

———. *Church Union in Canada after Three Years.* Toronto, 1929.

Secondary Sources

BOOKS

Allen, R. *The Social Passion: Religion and Social Reform in Canada 1914-1928.* Toronto, 1971.

Armour, L. and Trott, E. *The Faces of Reason: An Essay in Philosophy and Culture in English Canada 1850-1950.* Waterloo: 1981.

Berger, Carl. *Science, God, and Nature in Victorian Canada.* Toronto, 1983.

Bozeman, Theodore D. *Protestants in an Age of Science.* Chapel Hill, 1977.

Brown, R.C. and Cook, R. *Canada 1896-1921: A Nation Transformed.* Toronto, 1974.

Drummond, A.L. and Bulloch, J. *The Church in Late Victorian Scotland 1874-1900.* Edinburgh, 1978.

Flemming, J.R. *A History of the Church of Scotland 1875-1929.* Edinburgh, 1939.

Gibson, Dale and Lee. *Substantial Justice: Law and Lawyers in Manitoba 1670-1970.* Winnipeg, 1972.

Grant, J.W. *The Canadian Experience of Church Union.* Richmond, VA. 1967.

––––––. *George Pidgeon: A Biography.* Toronto, 1962.

Henderson, H.F. *The Religious Controversies of Scotland.* Edinburgh, 1905.

Hoeveler, J.D., Jr. *James McCosh and the Scottish Intellectual Tradition: From Glasgow to Princeton.* Princeton, 1961.

Hovenkamp. H. *Science and Religion in America 1800-1860.* Philadelphia, 1978.

Hutchison, W.R. *The Modernist Impulse in American Protestantism.* Cambridge, MA, 1976.

Loetscher, Lefferts A. *The Broadening Church: A Study of Theological Issues in the Presbyterian Church Since 1869.* Philadelphia, 1957.

Marsden, George M. *Fundamentalism and American Culture: The Shaping of Twentieth Century Evangelism 1870-1925.* New York, 1980.

McCurdy, F.F. ed. *Life and Work of D.J. Macdonnell.* Toronto, 1897.

McKillop, A.B. *A Disciplined Intelligence: Critical Inquiry and Canadian Thought in the Victoria Era.* Montreal, 1979.

Moir, John S. *Enduring Witness: A History of the Presbyterian Church in Canada.* Toronto, 1974.

Moore, James B. *The Post-Darwinian Controversies: A Study of the Protestant Struggle to Come to Terms with Darwin in Great Britain and America 1870-1900.* Cambridge, 1979.

Morton, W.L. *The Progressive Party in Canada.* Toronto, 1950.

Neil, A.M. *The Free Church Case.* Edinburgh, 1904.

O'Brien, Charles F. *Sir William Dawson: A Life in Science and Religion.* Philadelphia, 1971.

Oliver, Peter. *Public and Private Persons: The Ontario Political Culture 1914-1934.* Toronto, 1975.

Orr, R.L. *The Free Church of Scotland Appeal Case.* Edinburgh, 1904.

Prang, Margaret. *N.W. Rowell: Ontario Nationalist.* Toronto, 1971.

Russell, C. Allyn. *Voices of American Fundamentalism.* Philadelphia, 1976.

Sandeen, Ernest R. *The Roots of Fundamentalism: British and American Millenarianism 1800-1930.* Chicago, 1979.

Shortt, S.E.D. *The Search For An Ideal: Six Canadian Intellectuals and their Convictions in an Age of Transition 1890-1930.* Toronto, 1976.

Sölinder, Rolf. *Presbyterian Union in Scotland 1907-1921.* Edinburgh, 1962.

Smith, David E. *Prairie Liberalism: The Liberal Party in Saskatchewan 1905-1971.* Toronto, 1975.

Williams, David R. *Duff: A Life in the Law.* Vancouver, 1984.

ARTICLES

Ames, John T. "Cumberland Liberals and the Union of 1906." *Journal of Presbyterian History* 52 (1974): 3-18.

Angrave, James. "William Dawson, George Grant and the Legacy of Scottish Higher Education." *Queen's Quarterly* 82 (Spring 1975): 77-91.

Clifford, N.K. "The Interpreters of the United Church of Canada." *Church History* 46 (June 1977): 203-14.

Corbett, D.J.M. "The Legal Problems of the Canadian Church Union of 1925." The Canadian Society of Presbyterian History, *Papers 1979,* 53-67.

Farris, Allan L. "The Fathers of 1925." In *Enkindled by the Word: Essays on Presbyterianism in Canada.* Ed. N.G. Smith. Toronto, 1967.

Forsey, Eugene A. "Disallowance of Provincial Acts, Reservation of Provincial Bills, and Refusal of Assent by Lieutenant-Governors Since 1867," *CJEPS* 4 (February 1938): 47-59.

Hallett, Mary E. "Nellie McClung and the Fight for the Ordination of Women in the United Church of Canada." *Atlantis* 4 (Spring 1979): 2-19.

Howe, Daniel Walker. "The Decline of Calvinism: An Approach to its Study." *Comparative Studies in Society and History* 14 (1972): 306-27.

Huntingdon, Samuel P. "Conservatism as an Ideology." *American Political Science Review* 5 (June 1957): 454-73.

Jentz, John. "Liberal Evangelicals and Psychology during the Progressive Era." *Journal of Religious Thought* 33 (1976): 65-73.

Kiesekamp, Burkhard. "Presbyterian and Methodist Divines: Their Case for a National Church in Canada, 1875-1900." *Studies in Religion* 2 (1973): 280-302.

Laski, Harold. "Notes on the Strict Interpretation of Ecclesiastical Trusts." *Canadian Law Times* 36 (1916): 190-206.

Mackinnon, Frank. "The Royal Assent in Prince Edward Island: Disallowance of Provincial Acts, Reservation of Provincial Bills and the Giving and Withholding of Assent by Lieutenant-Governors." *CJEPS* 15 (1949): 216-20.

Mann, W.E. "The Canadian Church Union 1925." In *Institutionalism and Church Unity.* Ed. N. Ehrenstrom and W.G. Muelder. New York, 1963, pp. 171-94.

Masters, D.C. "The Rise of Liberalism in the Canadian Protestant Churches." Canadian Catholic Historical Association. *Study Sessions 1969,* pp. 27-39.

McLelland, Joseph C. "The Macdonnell Heresy Trial." *Canadian Journal of Theology* 4 (1958): 273-84.

Millman, Thomas R. "The Conference on Christian Union, Toronto 1889." *Canadian Journal of Theology* 3 (1957): 165-74.

Pitsula, J.M. "W.G. Brown: 'Righteousness Exalteth a Nation'." *Saskatchewan History* 33 (Spring 1980): 56-70.

Robertson, James. "The Dangers of Promiscuous Immigration." In *Vital Questions: The Discussions of the General Christian Conference.* Sponsored by the Montreal Branch of the Evangelical Alliance 22-25 October 1888. Montreal, William Drysdale, 1889, pp. 104-11.

Rogers, Benson A. "Canadian Church Union Cases and the Law of Wills." *Canadian Bar Review* 17 (1939): 399-415.

Smith, Neil G. "1925 and After." In *A Short History of the Presbyterian Church in Canada.* Ed. N.G. Smith. Toronto, 1967.

Turner, Bryan S. "The Sociological Explanation of Ecumenicalism." *Expository Times* 82 (1970-71): 356-61.

Vipond, Mary. "Canadian National Consciousness and the Formation of the United Church of Canada." The United Church Archives Committee. *Bulletin* 24 (1975): 5-27.

THESES

Barnhart, G.L. "E.H. Oliver: A Study in Religious, Intellectual and Social Progressivism in Saskatchewan 1909-1932." M.A. thesis, Regina, 1978.

Buck, John M. "The Community Church and Church Union." M.A. thesis, McGill University, 1961.

Corbett, D.J.M. "The Canadian Church Union of 1925 and the Law." B.D. thesis, Knox College, Toronto, 1957.

File, Edgar F. "A Sociological Analysis of Church Union in Canada." Ph.D. thesis, Boston University, 1962.

Fraser, Brian. "The Emergence of Social Christianity among Canadian Presbyterians 1875-1907." Ph.D. thesis, York University, 1982.

Gunn-Walberg, Kenneth W. "The Church Union Movement in Manitoba 1902-1925: A Study in the Doctrine of Denominationalism within the Protestant Ascendency." Ph.D. thesis, University of Guelph, 1972.

Kiesekamp, B. "Community and Faith: The Intellectual and Ideological Bases of the Church Union Movement in Victorian Canada." Ph.D. thesis, University of Toronto, 1974.

Morrison, George. "The United Church of Canada, Ecumenical or Economical Necessity." B.D. thesis, Emmanuel College, Toronto, 1956.

Ross, John A. "Regionalism, Nationalism and Social Gospel Support in the Ecumenical Movement of Canadian Presbyterianism." Ph.D. thesis, McMaster University, 1973.

Thompson, J.A. "The Great Paper War of Canadian Church History." B.D. thesis, Knox College, Toronto, 1960.

Index

Alberta Plan for Co-operation in the Home Mission Fields, 50
Alliance of Reformed Churches, 1, 207, 208, 216
American Journal of Theology, 114
Anglican Church of Canada, 9, 27, 31, 39, 63, 88, 113, 114, 115, 127, 142, 156, 194
Armstrong, A.E., 197
Armstrong, C.H.A., 194
Armstrong, W.D., 23

Bachynsky, N.V., 149
Baird, Andrew, 41
Baird, Francis (Frank), 27, 68, 76, 77, 103, 105
Ballantyne, Adam W., 140
Ballantyne, James, 41, 54, 55, 56, 57, 96, 97, 99, 100, 109
Baptist Church, 27, 31, 142
Barclay, James, 14
Barker, A.W., 212
Barrier Act, 15, 28, 29, 47, 49, 52, 54, 79, 84, 118, 188
Basis of Union, 28, 40, 44, 46, 56, 60, 61, 63, 72, 79, 80, 97, 113, 118, 190
Bayley, W.D., 149
Beckstedt, A.J.N., 78
Bennett, R.B., 154
Berger, Peter, 7, 8
Bible League of North America, 39
Bible Student and Teacher, 39
Bidwell, Edward J., 115
Bird, T.W., 158
Birks, W.M., 99
Black, F.M., 149
Black, James H., 150
Blake, S.H., 39
Blanchard, Percy, 140
Bland, Salem, 125
Boak, H.W., 172
Borland, J.H., 122
Boyle, J.R., 153
Bracken, John, 149
Brandt, E.H., 190
Brown, John C., 87
Brown, T. Crawford, 51, 127
Brown, W.G., 27, 50, 51, 61, 68, 85, 93, 131, 132, 152, 153
Bryce, George, 23, 80
Bryden, Walter, 4
Budge, Austin L., 24, 137
Burning Bush and Canada, The (MacBeth), 10

Burwash, N., 40
Butcher, Nelson R., 194

Calvinism, 36, 40, 147
Cameron, D.A., 154
Cameron, Donald, 153
Campbell, Duncan, 172
Campbell, George A., 106, 166
Campbell, Robert, 10, 14, 23, 26, 27, 28, 29, 30, 31, 34, 33, 34, 35, 36, 37, 38, 39, 40, 41, 45, 50, 52, 53, 54, 55, 68, 75, 77, 84, 85, 87, 89, 90, 91, 92, 93, 110, 116, 118, 134, 136, 145, 146, 238
Canadian Record of Science, 33
Carman, Albert, 13, 21, 39
Cassels, Richard S., 119, 204, 219, 227, 228
Caven Library, 163, 235
Caven, William, 16, 22, 39, 54
Chown, S.D., 64, 120, 121, 122, 123, 124, 125, 211, 224
Christian Guardian, 167
Chrysler, Z.H., 145, 146, 147
Church and Religious Unity, The (Kelly), 114
Church Federation Association, 43, 51, 54
Church of Scotland, 16, 19, 21, 44, 84, 159, 168, 239, 241
Church Union in Canada (Morrow), 144
Church Union in Canada (Silcox), 5, 9
"Church Union" and the Presbyterian Church in Canada (Scott), 211
Clark, W.J., 30, 47, 48, 51, 60, 61, 65, 68, 70, 74, 84, 90, 117, 119, 126, 141
Clay, W. Leslie, 55, 56, 76, 84, 90, 105, 106, 162, 172
Cochrane, R.B., 118, 184
Coe, George A., 212
Congregational Church of Canada, 1, 2, 9, 26, 27, 28, 31, 35, 39, 40, 46, 55, 61, 62, 64, 68, 79, 91, 92, 142, 155, 186, 194
Conspiracy theory, 49
Constructive Quarterly, 113
Convocation, 87, 88, 89, 90, 91, 92, 93, 94, 95, 96, 97, 98, 99, 103, 104, 107, 123, 126, 127, 128, 129, 165, 170, 173
Copp, A.S., 214
Corpus Christi Movement, 59
Coulter, J.J., 212
Craig, James, 127
Craig, R.W., 149
Creighton, W.B., 210
Crocket, Mr. Justice O.S., 220
Cumberland Presbyterian Church, 44

Cunningham, J.D., 170

Dalhousie University, 23, 29, 203
Dandurand, Raoul, 161
Darroch, Dugald, 193
Darwin, Charles, 34
Davey, Lord, 188
Dawson, Sir William, 37
Denominationalism, 6, 7, 9, 27, 31, 32, 44, 45,
    46, 50, 58, 60, 68, 115, 156, 161, 190, 236,
    237, 238, 239, 241
Dickie, R.W., 104, 105, 139
Disestablishment, 236, 237, 238, 239, 241
Dissidents, 8, 11, 13, 15, 23, 28, 30, 36, 37, 40,
    41, 43, 44, 45, 48, 49, 52, 53, 54, 55, 56, 57,
    58, 59, 60, 61, 63, 65, 68, 69, 70, 71, 72, 74,
    75, 76, 77, 80, 81, 82, 83, 85, 87, 88, 89, 91,
    92, 93, 94, 95, 96, 97, 98, 99, 100, 101, 103,
    104, 108, 109, 115, 117, 118, 119, 120, 123,
    124, 129, 130, 131, 134, 135, 137, 139, 140,
    141, 142, 143, 144, 145, 146, 147, 148, 149,
    151, 152, 154, 155, 157, 158, 159, 162, 163,
    165, 168, 169, 170, 171, 172, 175, 177, 178,
    179, 182, 185, 187, 188, 190, 191, 193, 194,
    195, 196, 198, 201, 202, 203, 204, 205, 206,
    238
Dominion Property Commission, 163, 194, 199,
    200, 229,
Dougall, John, 240
Downes, J.K., 149, 150
Drummond, D.R., 106, 137, 138, 139, 140, 178,
    224, 225
Drummond, Henry, 35
Drury, E.C., 183, 184
Duff, Mr. Justice Lyman P., 194, 197, 198, 199
Duff, William, 158, 159, 233, 240
Dunning, C.A., 152
DuVal, F.B., 22, 32, 91, 92
Dyde, D.W., 178, 179, 224, 226

Eakin, Thomas, 102, 193, 194
Ecumenism, 4, 5, 6, 7, 8, 9, 10
    confessional union, 2, 10, 168, 237
    co-operation, 70
    federalism, 52
    federation, 50, 51
    transconfessional union, 2
Edmison, J.H., 197
Edwards, W. Stuart, 214
Eldon, Lord, 187
Endicott, James, 216, 217, 223, 224
English Free Church Council, 49
Environmentalism, 17, 33, 35, 83
Evening Telegram, 184

Falconer, Sir Robert A., 17, 21, 22, 71, 84, 90,
    98, 104, 106, 108, 112, 116, 138, 212

Farquharson, William, 40, 75, 76, 80, 81, 82
Farrell, A.G., 72, 105, 151, 152
Ferguson, G. Tower, 194
Ferguson, Howard, 184, 206
Fisher, Galen M., 212
Flavelle, Sir Joseph, 206
Fleming, John, 104
Forrest, John, 23, 29
Forward Movement Peace Thank Offering
    Fund, 196
Foster, G.G., 161
Fotheringham, J.T., 126
Fraser, Daniel J., 97, 99, 106, 109, 117, 119,
    123, 124, 127, 128, 130, 135, 141
Fraser, J. Kier, 89
Fraser, J.B., 30, 122
Fraser, Thurlow, 106
Fullerton, T.F., 106

Galoway, J.J., 152
Gandier, Alfred, 17, 20, 21, 54, 61, 80, 82, 83,
    88, 98, 138, 139, 150, 163, 178
Garside, Robert, 64
Gault, Thomas Percy, 194
Geggie, H. Logan, 51
George, James, 37
Gibbon, J.M., 99
Glassford, R.J.M., 173
Globe, 15, 21, 95, 98
Gordon, Alexander R., 38, 193
Gordon, C.W., 16, 17, 24, 118, 120, 124, 138,
    139, 149, 168, 190, 208
Gordon, Daniel M., 23, 38, 58, 134, 137, 155
Gordon, Minnie, 134
Grant, A.S., 193, 197
Grant, George M., 16, 38
Gray, A.W., 203
Gray, E.H., 233
Gray, Jessie, 220
Greenfield, H.H., 152
Gregg, William, 54
Gunn, W.T., 9, 64, 215
Gzowski, C.S., 39

Haddow, Robert, 17, 21, 27, 29, 49, 53, 65, 75,
    78, 79, 91, 96, 97, 98, 102, 108
Haig, J.T., 150
Haldane, Lord, 19
Halsbury, Lord, 19
Haney, W.S., 163
Hanson, George, 180, 181, 182
Harnack, Adolph, 34
Harris, Elmore, 39
Harvard Theological Review, 112
Heine, G. Colborne, 72
Henderson, J.S., 190
Henderson, Joseph, 110

Herridge, W.T., 2, 72, 120
Hendrie, William, 111
Hope, George, 111
Horne, R.H., 173
House of Lords, 19, 156, 186, 188
Howson, Mrs. E.H., 134
Hunter, L.J., 175
Hutton, John H., 209

Inkster, John Gibson, 53, 54, 122, 174, 178, 190
Irwin, H.E., 66
Ivens, William, 149

Jackson, George, 21, 112
James, Lord (of Hereford), 189
James, T.C., 68
James, William, 211
Johnston, Robert, 117, 192, 233
Joint Committee on Church Union, 5, 10, 168
Jordan, W.G., 83

Kellock, R.L., 215
Kellog, Samuel H., 37
Kelly, Herbert H., 113, 114
Kilpatrick, G.G.D., 188
Kilpatrick, T.B., 24, 76, 113, 114
King, John M , 16
King, Mackenzie, 37, 48, 62, 78, 125, 126, 134, 136, 158, 160, 174, 186, 215, 233
Knowles, R.E., 210
Knox College, 4, 15, 39, 54, 76, 80, 82, 88, 113, 123, 139, 144, 163, 178, 198
Knox, John, 57

Lafleur, Eugene, 94, 145, 146, 157, 166, 227, 228, 240
Laird, Robert, 141, 198, 212, 213
Laird, V. MacKay, 221
Lamont, Mr. Justice J.H., 220
Langs, C.V., 203
Langtry, John, 39
Lapointe, Ernest, 154, 162
Lennox, John, 120
Lewis, A.C., 163, 202
Life of Principal Rainy, The (Simpson), 167
Little, George A., 212
Lord's Day Act, 184
Love, A.T., 68
Low, Lord, 188
Luckman, Thomas, 7
Lunn, Sir Henry, 206
Lyle, Samuel, 22, 61

MacBeth, R.G., 10, 11, 27, 51, 53, 55, 65, 66, 67, 68, 72, 75, 77, 78, 88, 89, 90, 97, 127, 131, 162, 172

Macdiarmid, Finlay, 205, 206
MacDonald, J.A., 15, 24, 33
Macdonnell, Daniel J., 37, 39, 127
Macdonnell, G.M., 38, 106
Macdonnell, George F., 127, 145
Macdonnell, Margaret, 34
Macdonnell, N.S., 194, 195, 203
MacDougall, John, 3
MacGillivray, A.H. (Alex), 51, 77, 104, 112
MacGillivray, A.J., 122, 128, 131, 143, 170, 181, 234
MacGillivray, M., 22
MacGregor, R.M., 103, 118
MacKay, R.P., 39
Mackay, John, 27, 43, 44, 51, 53, 110, 119
Mackenzie, F.S., 170
MacKinnon, Murdoch, 84
MacKinnon, Clarence, 17, 21, 137, 189, 208
MacLaren, Murray, 127, 240
MacLaren, William, 15, 16, 28, 39, 183
Macmillan, Cyrus, 135, 136, 137
MacMillan, J.W., 194
MacMurchy, Angus, 123
MacNamara, J.W., 88, 89, 90, 122, 123, 126, 128, 130, 131, 132, 133, 134, 136, 143, 145, 165, 170, 171, 172, 173, 175, 176, 180, 201
MacVicar, D.H., 16
Manitoba College, 13, 17, 23, 80, 149
Martin, W.A.J., 10
Martin, W.M., 151, 152, 204
Mason, Gershom W., 194, 203, 205
Matheson, D.M., 117
Matheson, Hugh, 50
Matheson, S.P., 115
McCarthy, D.L., 148, 149, 194, 195, 196, 197, 202, 203
McCaskill, Mrs. Frances, 133, 134
McCaskill, J.J., 133
McConnell, W.F., 131, 143, 144, 152, 153, 170, 171, 172, 173
McDonald, C.S., 66, 67, 68, 73, 85, 88, 89, 92, 106, 111, 122, 123, 126, 128, 143, 192, 201
McGill University, 37, 112, 135, 143
McGregor, A.M., 150
McIntosh, Finlay, 170, 171
McKeen, John, 165
McKeen, M.C., 153
McKerroll, D.T.L., 51, 137, 170
McKnight, Mrs. Louise, 64
McLaren, E.D., 23, 61, 137, 138, 183, 192
McLeod, A., 150
McLeod, D.D., 51, 55, 56, 65, 71, 75, 76, 90, 134
McMillan, Thomas, 122, 126, 128, 139, 140, 143, 149, 170, 192, 194
McMullen, W.T., 29, 54
McNab, A.P., 152

McNeill, John T., 144, 145
McPherson, O.L., 153
McQueen, D.G., 76, 152, 171, 190
McQuesten, T.B., 133, 136
Mead, Sidney, 6
Meighen, Arthur, 148, 160, 233
Mendel, Gregor, 34
Message, 94, 99, 102, 107
Methodism, 1, 2, 9, 10, 13, 14, 21, 22, 26, 27, 28, 31, 32, 35, 39, 46, 50, 51, 55, 60, 61, 62, 63, 64, 68, 69, 70, 79, 112, 114, 120, 121, 123, 124, 125, 126, 129, 135, 142, 149, 156, 159, 166, 167, 175, 186, 202, 204, 206, 241
Michie, John, 110, 170
Millar, D.D., 72
Monteith, F.W., 93
Monthly Record, 168, 169
Montreal Star, 103
Moore, T. Albert, 198, 202, 212, 213, 214, 217, 218, 224, 225, 226
Moral and Social Reform Council of Canada, 18
Morden, D.N., 184
Morrice, David, 66
Morrison, C.C., 209, 210, 211
Morrow, E. Lloyd, 144, 145
Morton, A.S., 33, 68
Motherwell, W.R., 84, 101, 159, 233
Muir, Bruce, 191
Mulligan, William O., 105
Munroe, T.A., 64
Murray, D.A., 110, 111, 130
Murray, Walter C., 60, 64, 84, 119, 127, 138, 141, 194

Natural History Society of Montreal, 33
Niebuhr, Richard, 57
Neil, John, 41
Neill, Stephen C., 2
Nelson, S. Banks, 118, 119, 120, 127, 136, 143, 145, 205, 217, 234
Nickle, W.F., 155, 156, 163, 178, 179, 202, 203

Oliver, E.H., 151, 156, 181, 212
O'Meara, T.R., 39
Ontario Temperance Act, 156, 184
Orde, Mr. Justice, 203
Outlook, 89
Overend, F.C., 203
Overtoun, Lord, 17

Parker, Stuart, 143, 145, 208, 233
Parsons, Henry M., 37
Patrick, William, 10, 13, 20, 28, 30, 38, 44, 120
Patriquin, Eliza, 219
Paul, Walter, 68
Pelton, J.S., 146

Penman, John, 66, 67, 68, 73, 75, 76, 88, 89, 92, 107, 111, 123, 128, 129, 130, 133, 136, 176, 192
Pidgeon, E. Leslie, 153, 156, 157, 186, 189
Pidgeon, George C., 30, 109, 115, 119, 120, 124, 128, 134, 135, 138, 140, 141, 149, 156, 168, 169, 175, 178, 184, 185, 186, 198, 207, 212, 214, 215, 224, 233
Pitblado, Isaac, 194
Porter, Gus, 158
Presbyterian, 27, 45, 65
Presbyterian Advocate, 76, 77, 89
Presbyterian Church Association, 129, 153, 174
Presbyterian Church in Canada,
    Adherents, 57, 64, 71, 78, 102, 238
    General Assembly, 10, 11, 13, 14, 15, 16, 17, 22, 23, 25, 26, 27, 28, 29, 30, 41, 43, 44, 48, 49, 51, 55, 56, 58, 70, 78, 79, 80, 82, 87, 88, 95, 96, 98, 99, 100, 103, 104, 115, 119, 120, 123, 124, 125, 131, 132, 133, 134, 135, 137, 139, 141, 146, 147, 148, 149, 150, 152, 153, 155, 158, 159, 160, 185, 189, 190, 191, 193, 195, 199, 205
    members, 3, 4, 8, 10, 11, 13, 26, 28, 43, 47, 49, 51, 56, 57, 58, 60, 62, 64, 67, 69, 70, 72, 76, 77, 78, 79, 81, 85, 91, 92, 93, 95, 96, 97, 98, 99, 102, 104, 110, 118, 119, 125, 126, 129, 131, 132, 133, 134, 140, 141, 142, 144, 146, 149, 150, 151, 153, 154, 155, 158, 159, 160, 161, 163, 169, 170, 171, 173, 174, 175, 176, 177, 179, 180, 181, 182, 186, 188, 191, 192, 193, 194, 195, 196, 197, 199, 200, 202, 203, 205
    Presbyteries, 11, 14, 15, 28, 29, 30, 47, 48, 49, 52, 53, 54, 62, 69, 70, 72, 78, 79, 80, 84, 98, 99, 104, 116, 131, 140, 165, 173, 179, 180, 188, 197
    sessions, 14, 15, 30, 36, 47, 48, 53, 55, 69, 72, 79, 90, 96, 104, 121, 170, 194, 205
    Synods, 80, 81, 99, 104, 116, 117, 140, 165, 197
Presbyterian College, Montreal, 38, 92, 99, 143, 193, 198
Presbyterian Friends of Union, 74
Presbyterian Record, 30, 56, 65, 90, 94, 104, 211
Presbyterian Standard, 134, 144
Presbyterian Union Committee, 70
Presbyterian Witness, 118, 131, 134, 168, 177, 179
Presbyterian Women's League, 132, 134, 136, 137, 139, 141
Pringle, John, 72, 189
Pritchard, H.I., 174

Queen, John, 149, 150, 151
Queen's University, 23, 37, 38, 58, 83, 97, 105, 134, 138, 150, 151, 155, 178, 179

Rainy, Robert, 17
Ramsey, D.M., 29, 70
Raney, W.E., 67, 184
Reid, J.D., 160, 162
Reid, W.D., 55, 160, 161, 167, 188
Relations of the Christian Churches, The (Campbell), 30, 40
Religion in Secular Society (Wilson), 6
Religious pluralism, 8, 237, 238, 239, 240, 241, 242
Renwick, A.M., 169
Resistance, 1, 2, 3, 4, 5, 10, 11, 13, 19, 21, 22, 25, 26, 28, 35, 36, 37, 38, 40, 41, 43, 47, 48, 49, 54, 58, 60, 62, 66, 67, 68, 69, 70, 72, 74, 79, 80, 81, 83, 84, 85, 87, 88, 89, 91, 92, 94, 96, 97, 98, 101, 102, 103, 105, 112, 117, 120, 125, 126, 127, 128, 131, 132, 133, 134, 137, 138, 139, 141, 142, 143, 144, 145, 149, 150, 151, 152, 153, 156, 162, 168, 179, 180, 183, 192, 193, 202, 237, 242
Re Kelley, 221
Re Thorne, 221
Review of the Churches, 206
Roberts, Richard, 193
Robertson, Andrew, 16, 51, 88, 92, 95, 96, 97, 98, 99, 102, 106, 107, 108, 109, 110, 111, 129, 160
Robertson, Gideon, 160, 161, 162
Robertson, James, 16, 23, 132, 196
Robertson, Lord, 189
Robinson, C.C., 148
Robson, A. Ritchie, 63
Robson, H.A., 149, 192
Rochester, W.M., 211, 234
Rodger, James, 68, 92, 106, 111, 141, 180, 181, 182, 192
Rollins, James, 53
Roman Catholic Church, 16, 24, 31, 45, 61, 92 113, 114, 142, 239
Ross, J.G., 193
Ross, P.S., 193, 195
Ross, W.B., 161, 193
Ross, W.D., 111
Ross, W.G., 152
Rowell, N.W., 123, 125, 127, 158, 212, 215
Roxburgh, F.D., 152, 153, 171
Rural Life in Canada (MacDougall), 3
Rules and Forms of Procedure, The, 182
Ruthenian experiment, 45, 46

Sandwell, B.K., 99
Saunders, Dyce, W., 194
Sclater, J.R.P., 147, 169, 234

Scott, Ephraim, 10, 14, 16, 17, 19, 20, 21, 24, 29, 30, 33, 37, 39, 44, 56, 57, 63, 65, 68, 69, 70, 72, 75, 76, 77, 84, 89, 90, 92, 99, 102, 103, 104, 106, 110, 118, 119, 120, 121, 122, 123, 124, 125, 134, 140, 156, 157, 180, 185, 188, 191, 192, 208, 240
Scott, James, 122
Scottish Common Sense Realism, 37, 39
Scrimger, John, 23, 39, 231
Secularization, 7, 8, 23, 34, 38, 62, 183, 237, 239, 240
Sedgwick, James A., 36
Sedgwick, Thomas, 16, 23, 38, 39, 68
Shannon, R.W., 152
Shortt, J.S., 152, 153, 171, 175
Silcox, C.E., 5, 9, 212, 213
Sinclair, Angus, 110
Sinclair, J.H., 126
Sisco, Gordon A., 230, 231, 232
Sladen, Arthur F., 214
Smellie, T., 36
Smith, Mr. Justice Robert, 219
Smith, Timothy, 6
Smith, W.H., 116
Smyth, James, 125
Social Sources of Denominationalism, The (Niebuhr), 5
Somerville, John, 23, 55, 56, 95, 132
Sparling, J.K., 232
St. Andrew's College, Saskatoon, 151
Stephen, J.W., 51
Stewart, R.G., 209
Story of Church Union in Canada, The (Chown), 211
Strachan, Daniel, 51
Subscription, 28, 40, 47, 102, 129, 130, 240
Supreme Court of Canada, 8, 146, 158
Survey of church conditions, 60, 61, 62

Tait, William D., 35
Taylor, R. Bruce, 99
Taylor, T. Wardlaw, 27, 88, 118, 189, 190, 218
Taylor, Sir Thomas W., 60
Thomas, Ernest (Edward Trelawney), 60, 114
Thompson, E.G., 172
Tilley, W.N., 119, 194
Toombs, Guy, 182
Tractarians, 16
Truce, 71, 72, 103, 106, 108, 109, 111, 112, 115, 116, 117, 119
Turnbull, James, 92, 111, 122
Turner, Brian, 8

Unionists, 2, 4, 5, 8, 9, 11, 14, 15, 16, 18, 19, 20, 21, 22, 23, 26, 28, 29, 30, 31, 32, 33, 36, 37, 39, 40, 41, 43, 47, 48, 49, 51, 52, 53, 54, 55, 56, 57, 60, 61, 62, 63, 65, 67, 68, 69, 70, 71,

72, 74, 75, 76, 79, 80, 81, 82, 83, 84, 85, 87,
90, 91, 92, 93, 95, 96, 97, 98, 99, 100, 101,
102, 103, 104, 108, 109, 111, 112, 113, 114,
115, 117, 118, 119, 120, 126, 127, 129, 135,
137, 138, 139, 140, 141, 143, 144, 146, 147,
148, 149, 150, 151, 152, 153, 154, 155, 156,
157, 158, 159, 160, 162, 163, 166, 167, 168,
169, 171, 712, 175, 176, 177, 178, 179, 180,
185, 186, 187, 188, 189, 193, 194, 195, 196,
197, 201, 202, 203, 204, 205, 238, 239, 240,
241, 242
United Church of Canada, 1, 5, 8, 9, 23, 79, 82,
83, 93, 101, 114, 116, 121, 122, 124, 129,
131, 133, 140, 141, 146, 154, 155, 158, 165,
167, 171, 179, 180, 182, 183, 185, 189, 191,
194, 195, 197, 198, 199, 200, 201, 202, 203,
205, 206, 237, 239, 242
United Church of Canada Act, 1, 8, 11, 162,
165, 173, 186, 189, 240
United Free Church of Scotland, 168
Universalism, 40
University Magazine, 33
Urbanization, 112, 179

Van Dyke, Henry, 39, 40
Vancouver Daily World, 38
Vert, A.E., 172

Walsh, H.H., 6
Warden, R.H., 16, 22, 23
Watson, John, 37, 231
Way to Union, The (Morton), 33
Webster, Lorne C., 233
"Wee Frees," 167-169
Welch, R.E., 193
Wesley, John, 33, 124
Westminster, 21
Westminster Confession, 2, 20, 36, 91, 239
Whitefield, George, 33
Whitehead, R.B., 203
Whyte, Alexander, 17
Willison, C.H., 66
Wilson, Bryan, 6
Wilson, F.B., 72
Wilson, G.B., 16
Wilson, James, 122, 170
Wilson, R.J., 202, 209
Winning of the Frontier, The, 212
Woodside, J.W., 233
Woodsworth, J.S., 157, 233
World Council of Churches, 4, 7
Workman, George C., 112
Wright, Ward, 194
Writ, 147, 148, 149, 150

Young, George A., 150
Young, MacGregor, 202, 215

45, 134